Technological Democracy

TECHNOLOGICAL DEMOCRACY

A Humanistic Philosophy of the Future Society

Reza Rezazadeh

VANTAGE PRESS
New York • Los Angeles

To those aspiring to a just society

FIRST EDITION

All rights reserved, including the right of
reproduction in whole or in part in any form.

Copyright © 1990 by Reza Rezazadeh

Published by Vantage Press, Inc.
516 West 34th Street, New York, New York 10001

Manufactured in the United States of America
ISBN: 0-533-08362-1

Library of Congress Catalog Card No.: 88-90501

Contents

Preface ix
Introduction: The Tragic End of Two Hundred Years xi
Notes xvii

PART ONE—THE TECHNOLOGICAL SOCIETY
   One: The Technological System 3
      Power and Technology 5
      Technology and the Theory of Human Liberties 8
      Toward Liberation from Technological Autonomy 12
      Notes 17
   Two: Information-Communication Technology 21
      Operational Problems 24
      Development of Electronic Information Technology 28
      Microcomputers and Supplementary Technology 31
      Data Display 32
      Information Telecommunication 33
      Information-Communications System 34
      Organizational Structures in Production of Goods and Services 36
      Production and Marketing 37
      Education 37
      Libraries and Information Delivery Systems 38
      Thinking Computers 39
      Compact Discs 40
      The Video Revolution 41
      Information-Delivery System 42
      Necessity for Democratization of Information-Communications Systems 44
      Necessity for Democratization of Information 47
      Notes 47
   Three: Uses of Information and Its Societal Impacts 51
      On-Line Data-Base Service 51
      Data Bases In Europe 55

Electronic Publishing and Information Distribution	57
Technological Literacy	59
Computer-Based Education	62
The Societal Effect of Information Availability	65
Economic and Social Uses and Benefits	69
Prospects and Possibilities During the Next Decade	75
A Concluding Overview	79
Notes	83
Four: Technology and Democracy	**87**
The New Technological Elite	97
Toward Democratization of Information System	98
Democratization of Information and the Issue of Privacy	101
Electronic Information and Privacy	102
Drive Toward Legal Restrictions	105
International Aspects of Electronic Information System	110
Privacy	112
Technical Issues	113
Political and Economic Issues	115
Technological Democracy and Privacy	117
Toward Technological Democracy	123
Transition to an Information-Based Society	124
Notes	129
PART TWO—TECHNOLOGICAL DEMOCRACY	
Five: The Future Use and Control of Technology	**133**
Toward a Democratic Information System	133
The National Information System: The Technodem	138
Information Upflow	143
Information Downflow	144
Services Available Through Technodem	146
The Technodem and the Pay System	166
Music, Fine Arts, Sports, and the Pay System	170
Notes	173

Six:	**Essential Principles of Technological Democracy**	**175**
	Introduction	175
	The Democratic Organism and Its Components	178
	Toward Technological Democracy	183
	Prevailing Power System	184
	Democracy as a System: An Introduction to Technological Democracy	185
	Democracy	187
	Equality of Opportunity	188
	Capital and Capital Accumulation	192
	The Working Class Under Technological Democracy	194
	Shared Opportunity and Employment Right	198
	The Wage System	200
	Characteristics of the Pay System	202
	The Work System	205
	Mobility	207
	Salary Range and Compensation	207
	Retirement	209
	Notes	214
Seven:	**The Structure and Function of Technological Democracy**	**217**
	Substantive and Procedural Democracy	220
	Economic Equality of Opportunity: Economic Democracy	227
	Technological Equality of Opportunity	238
	State and Its Role	245
	Electronic Technology and the Third World	254
	Judicial Council	258
	The Executive Branch	259
	Regional Governments	266
	The State Legislative and Coordinating Assembly	268
	The Governor	269
	Local Government	269

The Private Sector	272
Operation of the Private Sector	274
The Moral Standards of Technological Democracy	280
Notes	283

Eight: Technological Democracy: Some Analyses and Conclusions — 285

Democracy and Equality of Opportunity	285
Technological Democracy and Application of Equality of Opportunity	288
Social Democracy: Health Care and Education	290
Economic Democracy and Equality of Opportunity	297
Transfer of Wealth	298
Equitable Private Ownership of the Means of Production	299
Technological Decentralization	300
Shared Opportunity	301
The Essence and Meaning of Equality of Opportunity	302
Democracy and the Meaning of Life	315
Democracy and the Conduct of Life	317
The Essence of Democratic Economy	321
Some Characteristics of the Democratic System	328
Individualism	331
Religion	332
Conclusion	333
Notes	335

Glossary of Terms and Abbreviations	337
Bibliography	345
Index	363

Contents

Preface ix
Introduction: The Tragic End of Two Hundred Years xi
Notes xvii

PART ONE—THE TECHNOLOGICAL SOCIETY
- One: **The Technological System** 3
  - Power and Technology 5
  - Technology and the Theory of Human Liberties 8
  - Toward Liberation from Technological Autonomy 12
  - Notes 17
- Two: **Information-Communication Technology** 21
  - Operational Problems 24
  - Development of Electronic Information Technology 28
  - Microcomputers and Supplementary Technology 31
  - Data Display 32
  - Information Telecommunication 33
  - Information-Communications System 34
  - Organizational Structures in Production of Goods and Services 36
  - Production and Marketing 37
  - Education 37
  - Libraries and Information Delivery Systems 38
  - Thinking Computers 39
  - Compact Discs 40
  - The Video Revolution 41
  - Information-Delivery System 42
  - Necessity for Democratization of Information-Communications Systems 44
  - Necessity for Democratization of Information 47
  - Notes 47
- Three: **Uses of Information and Its Societal Impacts** 51
  - On-Line Data-Base Service 51
  - Data Bases In Europe 55

Electronic Publishing and Information Distribution	57
Technological Literacy	59
Computer-Based Education	62
The Societal Effect of Information Availability	65
Economic and Social Uses and Benefits	69
Prospects and Possibilities During the Next Decade	75
A Concluding Overview	79
Notes	83
Four: Technology and Democracy	**87**
The New Technological Elite	97
Toward Democratization of Information System	98
Democratization of Information and the Issue of Privacy	101
Electronic Information and Privacy	102
Drive Toward Legal Restrictions	105
International Aspects of Electronic Information System	110
Privacy	112
Technical Issues	113
Political and Economic Issues	115
Technological Democracy and Privacy	117
Toward Technological Democracy	123
Transition to an Information-Based Society	124
Notes	129
PART TWO—TECHNOLOGICAL DEMOCRACY	
Five: The Future Use and Control of Technology	**133**
Toward a Democratic Information System	133
The National Information System: The Technodem	138
Information Upflow	143
Information Downflow	144
Services Available Through Technodem	146
The Technodem and the Pay System	166
Music, Fine Arts, Sports, and the Pay System	170
Notes	173

Preface

The greatest threat to our future is not from atomic weapons or guided missiles; it is from our own ignorance of the real threat and lack of care. Nineteen of twenty-one civilizations have died from within and not by foreign conquest. Each decayed slowly from within until it fell apart. Our society shows many symptoms of such decay. But, as in those fallen societies, we do not see and feel the threat. We need understanding and action before it is too late. And the time is running short. This book is an attempt to awaken our people and those of other nations by illustrating the dangerous situation and by presenting the way to save our society and of course the future of humanity.

I have devoted all my adult life to development of a concept that would provide ground for better living conditions, opportunities, and freedom not only for my fellow countrymen but for all human beings regardless of place, race, sex, or origin. Toward this end I have tried to present a socioeconomic way of life that is the foundation for a truly democratic society. Political democracy, which has been erroneously presented as the main requirement for a democratic society, in my analysis, takes the backseat. Not that it is not important, but it is the least important. Economic democracy is the backbone of democratic society. With this understanding I have devoted much of my thinking and efforts toward realization of such a system. The heart of my theory is its economic system. With reference to human nature and individual expectations from life, I think I have discovered the appropriate economic system, which is not utopian like that of Marx, but practical, rational, and reasonable.

As a strong devotee of peace, all my life I have had great attention, not to the causes of conflict alone, but to the grounds for peace. Current approaches toward achieving peace have been, first, a piecemeal type and, second, through force and strength. This has been an utterly erroneous approach. Being obliged to keep peace through the presence of force means that there is a disequilibrium among the nations and thus force is necessary to sustain that disequilibrium. This is not actually a peaceful condition. Nations are being forced to accept the existing conditions regardless of injustices and suppressions these conditions create.

For a true and permanent peace there will be no need for any force to sustain it. It is automatically sustained when nations of the world enjoy equality of opportunity in existence along one another. Peace, on a prolonged and permanent basis, can be possible only when the grounds for conflict have been removed. Toward this phenomenal task I think I have taken a giant step. Under my theory, not only will we provide ground for prosperity and well-being of all the human race with equal opportunity, but also for the first time in human history we will provide conditions for permanent peace, without requirement of international agreements or treaties, but by the very nature of a technological democratic society and respect of the principle of equality of opportunity applied to the relations of the nations with one another.

Toward understanding this grand purpose in human history, one needs indulgence, patience, seriousness, and impartiality in reading, analyzing, and attempting to comprehend not only the content but the essence and implications of materials presented here. It is our life, our happiness, and our future that are at stake. Please join me and others who believe in true democracy, first, toward its understanding and then toward its realization.

Introduction: The Tragic End of Two Hundred Years

I am a United States citizen by choice. I did not make this choice on the grounds of the availability of better economic opportunities in the United States and the expectation of making lots of money, although I knew, based upon my educational background, that I would make a comfortable living here. Such a standard of living was not to be very different from the socioeconomic status I had held in my native country, Iran. At the time of my immigration I was a high-ranking officer within the privileged class of the armed forces and among the intelligentsia as well, since I was a graduate of military technical college, held a law degree, and spoke four languages. I chose the United States as my country because I found here a fertile ground for democracy with deeply rooted values relating to liberty, justice, and equality. I found Americans endowed with some of the greatest human values: honesty, integrity, and individualism.

I had one main objective in my new life in my new country: to seek knowledge leading toward the understanding of an advanced society from the social, economic, cultural, and political viewpoints and toward acquiring competence in making rationally sustainable projections about its future.

I chose the study of law as the most appropriate field to help me toward my aim. When I received my first law degree from the Indiana University Law School, I was not satisfied and continued my education in the areas of international law, economics, political science, and finally comparative law. All together I spent eighteen years as a university student, attempting to gain a comprehensive knowledge of an advanced society like the United States as well as the Third World.

As I was sitting back then and evaluating myself, one thing stood out in my mind: the more I sought knowledge, the more I found how little I knew. Consequently, striving for more knowledge, I concluded that the best way to satisfy my aim would be by sustaining my attachment to the academic community. Thus I accepted a teaching position in political science and rejected offers extended to me from some law firms and industries. After eighteen years as a university student, I change my official status to university professor, but in fact I remained, as always, a student. I will remain so until my last breath.

All these years I have looked upon the United States through the eye of an outsider, devoid of prejudices imposed upon native-born Americans by their socioeconomic values and their lack of intellectual contact with and understanding of other cultures.

The more one looks into the history of the American Revolution and the formation of its constitutional government, the more one becomes astonished about the depth of knowledge, dedication, and sincerity of a few men who led this nation from colonialism to independence. The Federalist Papers alone are indicative of the tremendous wealth of knowledge, wisdom, and intelligence of those who laid down, so carefully and so wisely, such a radically liberal foundation for the political system of this country. It is further astonishing how, after nearly two hundred years of advancement, leaders with the caliber and philosophical influence of the founding fathers have disappeared from our society and narrow-minded specialists and uncivilized, ignorant business executives have taken their place. Those individual rights and liberties for which the founders so persistently preached and violently fought have been overshadowed today by economic values and capitalistic monopolies or oligopolies. However, there is a consolation. What the revolutionaries did fight for has not been banished, only suppressed. It is at the foundation of American society, at the grass roots, that one finds honesty and integrity still strong. It has been molested but not destroyed. Erosion and corruption have moved in and firmly established themselves in the upper echelon of our society, fostered by norms established by what is variously known as the corporate state, military-industrial complex, or, as one writer labels it, the legal Mafia. Our representatives and leading bureaucrats are mostly a part of or heavily influenced by this cooperative power of industry and the military. None of these dominating factors existed in the early years of our independence, nor were they imaginable to this extraordinarily dominant extent until after World War II.

President Eisenhower was the first president to warn the American people, in his farewell address, of the dangers of a military-industrial complex to our democracy.

The result has been the suppression of individual rights and freedoms and, particularly since 1969, extraordinary privileges to big business and effective control of our socioeconomic and political system by a privileged group consisting of only .4 percent of American households.[1] Of all the investment assets, 1 percent are owned by the $5,000 to $9,999 income group, 7 percent by the $10,000 to $24,999 group, 11 percent by the $25,000 to $49,999 group, and 15 percent by the $50,000 to $99,999, or 34 percent in all. A small elite controls the remaining 66 percent.[2]

With the exception of this very small number of beneficiaries of American wealth and those who are ignorant of the facts, probably no one needs to be told today that there is much that is wrong in America. The events of the past three decades have demonstrated to every American the enormity and variety of the problems that plague this society and its economy. These problems take different forms for different people, and some people suffer much more than others. However, no one remains unaffected, since a society is an organic whole that is shaped by all its component parts, including every individual.

Corruption, hypocrisy, suppression, poverty, alienation, racism, crime, destruction of the environment, and waste and exploitation of our natural resources are just a few of our major problems. They are the result of our neglect and lack of interest in developing our social and political system, in contrast to our zeal and drive in developing our economic system. Thus we have created an imbalanced society—highly developed scientifically and economically, quite backward and outmoded socially and politically.[3] The combined effect has been not only to oppress a great many people at home and abroad, but to generate a widespread sense of anxiety among those who do not perceive themselves to be oppressed.

The big business or so-called legal Mafia controls our system openly. It influences and dominates our legislative bodies; it forces legislation that protects its dominance and authority in order to exploit the public through its control of the means of production, distribution, and prices. It loots billions of dollars each year in the form of tax benefits and subsidies from the public treasury and through price fixing and excess profits. It controls our educational programs, seeing to it that our youth are educated to become economically productive but less and less aware of democratic sociopolitical values and procedures. In this way, young people are programmed to avoid causing disturbances to the operation of the big business. In fact, they join it and contribute to its operation and growth. The elite has the law on its side, the military as its ally, friend, and partner, and the bureaucracy and police to support and protect its interests and operation.

To illustrate the operation of the legal Mafia let us take a look at one aspect of its exploitation of the public through our Internal Revenue Code. The following facts are extracted from Philip M. Stern's superbly documented book *The Rape of the Taxpayer,* published in 1973.[4]

According to Stern, we are victims in more ways than we know. In a single year:

- We paid most of Gulf Oil's taxes—because Gulf used the loopholes to pay a tax of only 2.3. percent on a billion dollars' worth of profits.
- Congress handed IBM a half-billion-dollar tax "gift" at our expense.
- An elderly member of the DuPont family saved $16 million in taxes with a deathbed gift of $36 million.
- ITT paid $139 million in taxes to foreign governments, but just $5 million to our own government.
- Auto heiress Mrs. Horace Dodge could have an income of $5 million and not even have to file a tax return.

An oil and gas operator sold at least 50 million dollars' worth of oil over a twelve-year period, at times had an annual income of more than $5,500,000, and yet paid no income tax for the entire twelve years.

America's three thousand upper families get an average of $720,000 each in "tax welfare" payments that we pay for.

Loopholes, inserted in the law by the economic elite, cost American taxpayers $77 billion each year or $367 for every man, woman, and child in the United States.

Tax rates could be cut nearly in half by getting rid of the loopholes.

The elite family, while it consists of only .4 percent of American households, controls the economy, government, media, and education. This nuclear family extends to embrace the top one-fifth of the population as its supporters and beneficiaries.

Accordingly, the richest fifth of the population owns about 77 percent of all personally held wealth and 97 percent of the personally owned corporate stock. This means that the richest one-fifth has three times as much wealth as the remaining 80 percent of the population.

Another area of the elite's ripoff of the American public is in the form of government subsidies. Gaylord Shaw of the Associated Press pointed out recently that private enterprise in the United States collects roughly $30 billion a year in government subsidies and subsidylike aid, much of it hidden or disguised. A governmentwide study undertaken by the Associated Press disclosed evidence that the total is at least $28 billion a year and may run as high as $38 billion.[5]

Federal aid for private enterprise is more than twice the government's expenditures for all its welfare programs, ten times that spent for pollution control, and fifteen times that spent to fight crime.

Assistance ranges from massive to miniscule, but big business gets the big bite: a $100 million loan guarantee to Penn Central Railroad, $4.4 million in subsidy checks for a single California farm, $450 million a year to maritime industry, and custody and use for commercial purposes by defense contractors of 14.6 billion dollars' worth of taxpayer-owned property are just a few examples.

The government's outstanding loans to private business—direct, guaranteed, and insured—came to about $250 billion in 1973, six times the outstanding credit advanced to business by all commercial banks. Yet the greatest portion of the ripoff by the big business is through commercial profits. In a span of just two years, the profits of the sugar industry climbed as high as 1200 percent, some oil companies profits hit the 400 percent mark, and those of the steel industry reached over 200 percent.

The marriage between the elite and the military should frighten every American. The alliance between the industry and the military becomes more evident if we take a look at the monopolistic nature of the military contracts and the cost overrun, frequently amounting to several times the cost in the original contract. The cost overrun was $4 billion for *Minuteman II*, $2.3 billion for the CSA cargo plane, both of the air force, and $1.3 billion for the army's main battle tank 70.[6]

Exploitive profits of the big business amount to about $380 billion or more—an annual ripoff of $1,700 from every man, woman, and child in the United States. If any of its members goes beyond the established legal limits, there is no effective punishment or remedy in the laws. In fact, such a person is often made privileged before the judiciary. Several big corporations that made illegal contributions to the 1972 Nixon election campaign were convicted by the courts and sentenced to pay a fine of only $5000. Of these executives who were convicted of committing a major crime, none received a prison sentence although the law prescribed a jail sentence of up to three years.

Examining these problems and other aspects of our society in a comprehensive way is not the purpose of this study. The aim here is to study the characteristics of capitalism versus democracy in a postindustrialized technological society, of which the United States is an example. This work is the result of twenty years of research and study attempting to discover the causes of our sociopolitical backwardness. For the lack of appropriate education for democracy, representative democracy, as practiced in our country, has become an outdated, undemocratic political system that sustains and protects the existing unjust economic system and its ruling elites; and the capitalistic economy as practiced in the United States has become an antiquated and suppressive system caused and sustained by an utterly defective capitalistic-oriented educational system. As a result, our social institutions have become very much backward and incapable of accommodating the demands and needs of a modern technological democratic society.

The study first attempts an overview of the current state of technology in technological societies, the United States in particular. Special attention is given to the information-communication system because of its utmost importance for democracy. The study shows a steady move toward monopolization of this area by a few big corporations.

The study then attempts to describe democracy as a system in technological society and examines the socioeconomic and political goals and procedures that are the necessary components of such a democratic system. A clear outcome of this concept is that capitalism and democracy are incompatible and cannot coexist. The same is true with socialism and democracy. Finally, efforts are made to illustrate this future democratic system, its principles, processes, and socioeconomic and political structure.

The study demonstrates that the advanced societies will tend toward a socioeconomic system quite dissimilar to what we know today as capitalism, socialism, or communism. This new theory of the future society is labeled technological democracy.

Because of capitalistic or socialistic control of the media and instruments of instruction, education toward comprehending the essentials of technological democracy becomes the responsibility of each individual. It can be achieved only through self-education and then educating the family and then spreading it outward to encompass the community and ultimately the whole society. The transformation to technological democracy then takes place.

Technological democratic society is a classless society. In its ultimate form it is also nearly a stateless society. The supervision of society is gradually transformed from political institutions into social organizations. In its developing stage, political institutions in technological democracy are substantially different from those currently existing. The scope of powers is minimal, the popular control is dominant, and there are no bases for the establishment of an accumulated or sustained political power. With these characteristics, political institutions operate very much like social organizations.

NOTES

1. Richard C. Edwards et al., *The Capitalistic System: A Radical Analysis of American Society* (Englewood Cliffs, New Jersey: Prentice-Hall, 1972), page 173.

2. *Ibid.*, p. 174.

3. Erwin Knoll and Judith N. McFadden, *American Militarism 1970* (New York: Viking Press, 1969), p. 2.

4. Philip M. Stern, *The Rape of the Taxpayer* (New York: Random House, 1973), pp. 5–33.

5. United Press International, "Tax Breaks Cost Treasury $44 Billion," *Wisconsin State Journal*, June 5, 1971, sec. 1, p. 3.

6. Friends Committee on National Legislation, *Washington Newsletter*, July 1969.

Part I

THE TECHNOLOGICAL SOCIETY

Chapter One

The Technological System

The twentieth century is marked with rapid development of technology. It has had, particularly since World War II, two spectacular effects upon society. First, it has enormously multiplied the processes of production and distribution and has introduced innumerable new products and processes. The result has been the multiplication of profits for the capitalists and a spectacular accumulation of wealth in their hands. Furthermore, since new technology has mainly been employed and used by big corporations, it has caused the monopolization of production in major sectors of the economy and centralization of power.

Second, advanced technology has entered every home and has gradually caused nearly total individual dependence on it in the process of daily life. Our homes are lighted by electricity, and the machine has become an indispensable part of our daily life: refrigerators, ovens, ranges, central heating and cooling systems, vacuum cleaners, toasters, microwave ovens, televisions, radios, stereo sound systems, automobiles, lawn mowers, personal computer systems, and many other technological devices, most of which have become necessary parts of our daily life.

Technology therefore dominates our private life, the operation of corporations, and the process of production as well as the state. It is the extent of this domination that has caused a philosopher like Ellul to see the technological order as a new environment in which an individual and all his institutions exist. From Ellul's viewpoint, this environment is artificial and independent of values, ideas, and even the state. The technical environment, as Ellul sees it, grows according to its own processes and rules, rather than in response to human ideas, values, or ends. Individuals adjust their lives to the rule of technology, rather than compelling technical processes to respond to patterns most suitable for human needs. Ellul sees even governmental and political processes being changed to conform to technical possibilities, though these changes make governments less responsive to the needs and aspirations of people.

Ellul concludes that man ultimately accepts a condition of slavery and pays for his technological happiness with his freedom. It is only by making men conscious to what degree they have become slaves in becoming "happy" that there is any hope of regaining liberty by asserting themselves, perhaps at the cost of much sacrifice, over the technological order that has come to dominate them.[1]

Another scientist, B. F. Skinner, asserts that the concepts of freedom and dignity are outmoded notions in technological society. What is needed is a technology of behavior in which a scientifically sound and workable system of controls is designed and applied to make people behave in ways most consistent with human survival and progress. He further claims that we are at the brink of the development and use of such a technology of behavior, but our outmoded concern for freedom and dignity is delaying the new age.[2]

It is clear that Skinner and Ellul differ on their fundamental views of human nature and thus on their meaning and purpose of society. A society accepting Skinner's theories as the basis for its concepts of human nature would develop social institutions very different from that of Ellul. Clearly there is not in existence or under development a science of behavior capable of producing a technological utopia. The negative aspects of technology have been so enormous that it makes us worry about the future of life on our planet. Our core cities are still full of rats and not livable; instead of hard homemade bread, the technology is giving us bread that is mass produced in presliced and prewrapped loaves of chemically treated "stay-fresh," tasteless and spongy to the touch.

There is an essential tackiness to much of modern technology that tends to keep men dissatisfied with the fruits of technology. Then there is pollution of air, water, and soil, toxic and radioactive wastes, and depletion of our limited natural resources in order to feed the production of enormous volumes of functionally unnecessary products, all being the consequences of technological development and for the purpose of maximizing profit for those institutions that employ it.

Technology has thus fallen mainly into the hands of capitalists and has been used for the purpose of maximizing profits without regard to resulting harm caused to human health, safety, or the environment as a whole.[3]

Each production and service institution uses technology at will, to the extent it desires and in manners it chooses. It is a haphazard and sporadic use of an enormous force that can be extremely dangerous and destructive if improperly used and highly beneficial to mankind and environment if properly employed.

There has been no systematic structure for technology to regulate its use. There is not a technological system by which the use of technology could be institutionalized and monitored. There is a collection of technologies without established relation to one another and not infrequently contrary to each other. It results in producing bad effects, and then it must be used in a different manner to eliminate or eradicate these effects. The former is done with desire, since it creates profits; the latter is not done because it requires spending without expectation of profits.

POWER AND TECHNOLOGY

In every society as far back as we know, power has been a desirable element to attain. In the tribal period, power was attained by establishing control over other men. While this source of power remained eminent in raising armed forces, the advance of agriculture brought into play the elements of ownership of land and men to operate it. With the advent of capitalism the source of power shifted from land to capital and control of the marketplace. Advance of nationalism in the twentieth century caused the capitalist systems to grant political independence to their colonial territories while keeping the economic ties aimed at controlling the markets.

In all these eras technology has played a dominant role in

the individual, institutional, and national drive for power. Yet except for the past 150 years, the advance of technology had been slow keeping pace with traditional societies. Since the middle of the last century, technology has developed with an accelerating pace, along with capitalism, so the capitalist has been the prime beneficiary of technological advancement. The phenomenal advance in technology since World War II has supplied the capitalists with extraordinary production and management means and has caused monopoly corporations to attain world prominence, each with spectacular bureaucratic and financial structures, rivaling those of many governments in the world.

Since corporations do not have enforcement power outside their hierarchies, they rely upon the coercive power of the state. For this reason the capitalist elite supports strengthening of the state's military and other enforcement means in order to maintain stability for its operation at home and abroad. For this purpose, while maintaining control over technological means it equips the state with high technological devices wherever necessary; the state, at the same time, through tax revenues supports research and further development of technology for corporate benefits.

Thus technology facilitates the control of men and nature.[4] Technology strongly affects the authoritative allocation of values and resources. It tends to condition the power relationship among those who employ it and between these and those subject to its use or receivers of its consequences, positive as well as negative.

Technologies once created, developed, and used have logic and consequences, foreseen and unforeseen, directly related to their nature. As technologies continue to be used and new ones are created and added, these consequences accumulate and interact, developing a core of historical background. For proper understanding of the impact of technology upon society one must pay close attention to this historical development.

Attention to this development reveals that despite the extreme importance of technology in modern society, it has been kept, apparently intentionally by capitalists who have been its primary beneficiaries, from becoming institutionalized and regulated for the good of technology itself and the good of human society as a whole.

For example, it is amazing to notice how disinterested political and social philosophers have been in taking into consideration the tremendous force of technology and its unavoidable substantial effect on every aspect of societal relationships. This lack of interest is specifically notable when one examines the currents of the past three decades, during which technology has experienced a spectacular advance.[5]

While recognizing that technology can and does play an important role in the concentration of power and wealth in the hands of industrial corporations, scholars do not focus on it as a problem in itself but only as an instrument of power and seek to eliminate it either by the use of public instrumentalities or by establishing industrial democracy.[6] Perhaps with the exception of John Kenneth Galbraith, liberal thinkers did not become centrally concerned with technology or think of it as an important variable in modern societal structure.[7] They looked upon technology mainly as a neutral constant. Galbraith, while recognizing the importance of technoeconomics and ensuing power relationships, looked for a solution to the problems of freedom through bringing about changes in attitudes among the ruling elite, which would tend to provide for a balance between societal organizational structure and technology. He did not attempt to deal directly with technology and its technostructural dominance.[8]

Friedrich Hayek, the leading social and economic theorist, does not pay special attention to technology,[9] nor does the Nobel Prize winner, a leading conservative economist Milton Friedman.[10] Robert Nozick, a leading contemporary libertarian, bases his theory of state on interpersonal relationships without paying attention to technology.[11] Others, while considering technology related to economic progress, do not believe in its effect on power relationships.[12]

Most scholars have failed to visualize that technology has been and is an essential element in development of modern society. They have not faced up to the implications of technology. The very few who consider technology important do not visualize it as the subject of prime concern in their study of human activities.[13]

Socialist thinkers in the United States and elsewhere have not done any better. They associate the operation of technology in capitalistic society with exploitation, alienation, and environmental degradation. They suggest that these are not the result of technology per se but the manner in which it has been used. From their viewpoint, technology is extremely important, but it has been misused under capitalism, causing grave consequences.[14]

Yet in a socialist society like the Soviet Union the application of socialism has not removed the problems. Soviet thinkers have recognized the problems generated by recent technological developments under socialism and accept the necessity for special attention to their solution.

However, a group of less orthodox Marxists has been active in developing a sophisticated critical study of technology and has concluded, with proper reasoning, that some particular technologies have politically decentralizing effects and thus are conducive to greater individual freedom.[15]

The New Left Marxists, including Herbert Marcuse, attempt to distinguish between technology and its effect and what is good or bad technology in their discussion of participatory democracy.[16] The New Left achievement has been, at least, a heightening awareness of technology as a political problem and generates further discussions and arguments.

TECHNOLOGY AND THE THEORY OF HUMAN LIBERTIES

In general, the history of political theory is an outcome of the response of thinkers to the existing or emerging social-economic problems of the time. Accordingly, the current interest in and ensuing controversies over the role of the state in dealing with technology arise primarily from the social impact of new technologies such as nuclear energy and weapons, advanced automation or robotization, environmental pollution, wasteful use of finite and exhaustible natural resources, and contamination of foodstuff through use of harmful chemicals and fertilizers.[17]

There is plenty of ground to inspire political thinkers regarding the role of technology in the societal process. On the one hand, there is the question of increasing dominance over society as well as nature through the use of new technologies; on the other, there is the question of environmental deterioration and scarcity of natural resources, both eminently endangering the continuation of industrial civilization. Of course, these are not separate questions but interwined, since the latter is also mainly affected by the use of technology.

On the pessimistic end, there are the "limits-to-growth" theorists, particularly including those associated with the Club of Rome, who associate the crises of technological society with unavoidable environmental deterioration, rapid exhaustion of natural resources, and widespread use of nuclear power for social controls. Donald H. Meadows and others who prepared *The Limits to Growth* conclude that the basic behavior mode of the world system is exponential growth of population and capital, followed by collapse. From their viewpoint, man can still choose his limits and stop when he chooses by weakening some of the strong pressures that cause population and capital growth or by instituting counter pressures. But these will certainly require profound changes in the well-established social and economic structures.[18] Short of such drastic actions, it would be a matter of time before the price of technology would exceed the capability of society to pay for it and the side effects of technology would suppress growth; finally, advancing technology will cause problems with no technical solutions. At any of these points we will lose our choice of limits and growth will be stopped by forces that are beyond our choice.

Technology often can relieve the symptoms of a problem without affecting the underlying causes. However, faith in technology as the ultimate solution to all problems can divert our attention from the most fundamental situation, which is the problem of growth in a finite society. We may then be prevented from taking effective action to resolve this fundamental problem. The population and capital, driven by exponential growth, reach their limits and then shoot beyond them before the rest of the system, with its inherent delays, reacts to stop growth. The system is continually forced into new policies and actions long before the results of old policies and actions are properly assessed.[19]

Others argue that the whole liberal democratic rule upon which the American political tradition has been based must be abandoned, giving way to a strong centralized government that would regiment its citizens to cope with problems of scarcity, pollution, and dangers of nuclear power.[20]

Another group consists of still pessimistic thinkers. These are thinkers who consider technology, particularly large-scale technology, genuinely harmful to human well-being. They do not believe that the harmful effects of technology or the manner of its use can be controlled or restrained. They regard technology as the all-pervasive force in life that is autonomous and irresponsible, making socioeconomic choices impossible and hopeless.

The major proponent of this concept is the French philosopher Jacques Ellul, who maintains that all-embracing technology is the consciousness of the modern world. It enters into every area of life, including the human.[21] With the use of technology, man accepts the specificity and autonomy of its ends and the totality of its rules. Man's desires and aspirations change nothing. The basic effect of state action on technology is to coordinate the whole complex.[22]

According to Ellul, technology has created an inhuman atmosphere with such factors as the concentration in our great cities, the slums, the lack of space, air, and time, the gloomy streets, the sallow lights that confuse night and day, our dehumanized factories, our unsatisfied senses, our working women, our estrangement from nature, our public transportation in which man is less important than a parcel, and our hospitals, in which a man is only a number. When technology enters into every area of life, including the human, it ceases to be external to man and becomes his very substance; it integrates with him and progressively absorbs him. This transformation is the result of the fact that technology is autonomous.

Ellul furthur argues that true technology will know how to maintain the illusion of liberty, choice, and individuality; but these will be carefully calculated so that they will be integrated into mathematical reality merely as appearances. Because of the deep infiltration of technology the individual will no longer be able, materially or spiritually, to disengage himself from society, and because of the autonomy of technology modern man cannot choose his means any more than his ends. If he makes use of technology, he must accept the specificity and autonomy of its ends and the totality of its rules; one's own desires and aspirations can change nothing. The reality is that man no longer has any means with which to subjugate technology, which is neither an intellectual nor a spiritual phenomenon.[23]

There is only one means to solve the problem, a worldwide totalitarian dictatorship that will allow technology its full scope and at the same time resolve the concomitant difficulties.[24]

Jacques Ellul's views have had substantial impact on American thought in relation to technology and have produced several distinguished followers.[25] According to Langdon Winner, one of Ellul's top exponents, technologies are virtually limitless in their power and often seem to resist guidance by preconceived goals or standards. Far from being neutral, technologies "provide a positive content to the area of life in which they are applied, enhancing certain ends, denying or even destroying others."[26]

Most important, technologies sometimes tend toward self-perpetuation or self-generation. Human beings, while having a nominal presence in the network, lose their roles as active, directing agents and "tend to obey uncritically the norms and requirements of the systems which they allegedly govern."[27] All together Winner states that the process and disposition create what we may call technological dynamism, a forceful movement in history, affecting every aspect of life, which continues largely without conscious human guidance.[28]

Winner concludes that "modern people" have filled the world with the most remarkable array of contrivances and innovations. If it now happens that these works cannot be fundamentally reconsidered and reconstructed, humankind faces a woefully permanent bondage to the power of its own inventions. But if it is still thinkable to dismantle, learn, and start again, there is a prospect of liberation. Perhaps means can be found to rid the human world of our self-made afflictions.[29]

In general, proponents of Ellul's theory without differentiating among different categories of technology feel that technology as a whole is not and cannot be subject to political control. Thus they consider making distinction among particular technologies immaterial. Some argue that the process of technology assessment for the purpose of differentiation itself necessarily requires use of technological methods of reasoning and action, thus making the problem inherently insoluble.[30]

"In summary," as Langdon Winner puts it, "the loss of mastery manifests itself in a decline of our ability to know, to judge, or to control our technical means. It is in this general waning of intellectual, moral, and political command that ideas of autonomous technology find their basis."[31]

It is sustained that once under way, technological reconstruction tends to continue. On a large scale, it requires that virtually everything in reach be transformed to suit the special needs of the technical ensemble. For whatever reason, anything that cannot be adapted is eliminated.[32]

A third group consists of more optimistic thinkers who propose that we must accept the new technologies of the postindustrial era, along with the older technologies associated with the industrial era, as they are, and attempt to create a properly planned and administered society capable of dealing in a pragmatic manner with technological problems. For this purpose they think that we don't need to modify or substantially alter the technostructure of society; problems ensuing from technology, such as scarcity of resources, pollution, and degradation of nature, can be managed properly within the existing technostructure. From their viewpoint the dangers to social stability stem from two directions: first, from the romantic intellectuals who attack the rational postulates of the technological system; second, through undue intrusion of the masses in the operation of technology by employing political means.[33]

Some more liberal thinkers in this category maintain that by encouraging technological change it will be possible to attain an era of abundance in which, more likely, the problems of self-realization and freedom will automatically be resolved.[34] A parallel to this thought is also found in the writings of the scientific technological-revolution scholars in the Soviet Union.

TOWARD LIBERATION FROM TECHNOLOGICAL AUTONOMY

All the above stated approaches to the problems of modern technological society essentially accept certain degrees of technological autonomy while making differing conclusions.

There is, however, another growing school of thought that refuses to accept the autonomous character of technology. It holds that human beings can, through their concrete and concerted actions, subject technology to human control and regulation. People are able to separate harmful aspects of technologies from beneficial ones and repress the formers while sustaining the latters. Through environmental protection and technology assessment for the appropriate use of technology people can control the context and consequences of the introduction and use of technologies.[35]

Leopold Kohr, for example, suggests that "there seems only one cause behind all forms of social misery: bigness.... Whereever something is wrong, something is too big."[36] Thus the only solution, he proposes, "must lie in the cutting down of the substances and organisms which have outgrown their natural limits."[37]

E. F. Schumacher, whose ideas received much of their inspiration from the writings of Kohr, feels that bigness is the nemesis of anarchism, whether it is that of public or private organizations, because from bigness comes impersonality, insensitivity, and a lust to concentrate abstract power. Small, more likely, is free, efficient, creative, enjoyable, and enduring.[38] In the excitement over the unfolding of his scientific and technical powers, states Schumacher, modern man has built a system of production that ravishes nature and a type of society that mutilates man.[39] The guidance we need to resolve the problem "cannot be found in science or technology, the value of which utterly depends on the ends they serve; but it can still be found in the traditional wisdom of mankind."[40]

Thinking along this line of thought are many of the energy activists such as Amory Lovins and Barry Commoner. According to Lovins, we have no choice but to change some of our basic ways of living. This change either has to be made on our own initiative in a planned and rational manner or will be forced on us with chaos and suffering by the intolerable laws of nature. Energy is but an end to social ends. Control of its use will open the door for the solution of our technological and other problems.[41] Energy—pervasive, symbolic, strategically central to our way of life—"offers perhaps the best integration principle for the wider shifts of policy and perception that we are groping toward. If we get our energy policy right, many other kinds of policy will tend to fall into place too."[42]

Commoner believes that the technological society of the United States has been confronted by a series of ominous, seemingly intractable crises of environment, energy and economy. These produce a tangled knot of problems that is poorly understood even by the specialists. It involves complex interactions among the *ecosystem,* the *production system,* and the *economic system.* These three basic systems, along with the social or political order, govern all human activity.[43]

The environmental crisis reveals that "the ecosystem has been disastrously affected by the design of the modern production system, which has been developed with almost no regard for compatibility with the environment or for the efficient use of energy."[44] This faulty design of the production system has been the result of a faulty economic system, which invests in productions that promise increased profits rather than environmental compatability or efficient use of resources.[45]

Thus the relations among the three basic systems on which society depends are upside down. The governing influence should flow from the ecosystem through the production system to the economic system. The actual situation has been the other way around.

Marxist inspirations have also made their contribution to this school of thought. One of the most notable among these is William Leiss, according to whom modern society "represents the first large-scale attempt to found stability and authority not upon the earlier patterns of inherited privilege or traditional associations, but rather directly on the achievements of economic production and the satisfaction of needs."[46] The primary social bond is the identification of self-interest of the individual, intent upon maximizing the satisfaction of his needs, along with the identical interest of society as a whole, which is to maximize total productive output. Not everyone benefits equally from this process; some may be ruined utterly in the endeavor. The social injustice represented by entailing disparities in wealth and control of resources are enormous.[47]

The continually rising level of consumption requires an adequate supply of energy and material resources. But we cannot estimate with much certainty the magnitude of possible shortages in natural resources. The main principle of legitimacy for technological society is the rationale for the acceptance of the prevailing distribution of rewards and power that consists in a permanently rising level of consumption. Thus a principal concern is to ensure that a sufficient quantity of energy and material resources is available for this purpose.

Leiss suggests certain ways of reconsidering the needs that might assist in overcoming the potentially dangerous tendencies of the current practices and in breaking out of the vicious circle of expanding productivity and expanding wants.[48] He concludes that the "abundance we have created is deceptive, in that we cannot perceive the depth of our dissatisfaction with the social forms through which we produce and consume it."[49] The only thing needed is to begin changing those social forms in order to release the immense potentialities for individual self-fulfillment. Satisfactions drawn from different forms of productive activities and proper attention to the relationship to nonhuman nature, which are presently so deeply suppressed, can minister to human needs far more effectively than can any assortment of goods.[50]

Along this line of "soft technology" thought are those labeled as "deep ecologists," distinguished from "reformist environmentalists." Reformist environmentalists favor incremental changes in laws and policies without questioning the premises of the dominant social paradigm, such as capitalism.[51] On the other hand,

> ...deep ecologists are pro-environmentalists who believe that human beings are not separate from or even above the rest of nature. The ultimate values of any society must be built within the context of these values. Societal interactions—political, economic, or else—must involve the rights of the whole nature and its various components including human beings.
>
> What are we witnessing in the world today [states one of the proponents of this school] is unparalleled waterfall of destruction of a diversity of human cultures; plant species; animal species; of the richness of the biosphere and the

15

millions of years of organic evolution that have gone into it."[52]

Referring to the future advance in humanistic aspects of life and its richness, he states that the poems "will leap out past the automobiles and television sets of today into the vastness of the Milky Way (visible only when the electricity is turned down), to richen and humanize the scientific cosmologies. These poesies to come will help us learn to be people of knowledge in this universe in the community with the other people—non-human included—brothers and sisters."[53]

Within this school of thought are also those who go beyond the effect of technology on human beings and extend it to sentient beings, plants, and other components of nature.[54] As one puts it, one finds it as odd to think that plants have value only for the happiness of the dusky-footed wood rats as to think that the dusky-footed wood rats have value only for the happiness of humans.[55] They argue that the massive suffering inflicted upon nonhuman animals is both unnecessary and uncompensated by the relatively trivial benefits to humankind.[56] That wildlife has its own intrinsic right to life, to exist in the world, to pursue its own destiny, and to follow the path of its own evolution.[57] Some go even further to extend these intrinsic rights to the whole of nature and "natural objects."[58]

Illustrating the harmful effects of dangerous large technologies, some members of this school envision the eventual public consciousness and upraisal and the formation of drastically new and different societal systems[59] based on citizens' demands for healthy conditions of life such as contaminant-free food, water, and air, freedom from threats of nuclear plants among others, and a decentralized, self-governing political system.[60]

If we are concerned just with values and the importance of individual integrity and identity in modern technological society, we should then, by necessity, devote particular attention to the status of technology as an independent variable and at least a strong conditioner if not direct determinant of ends as well as means in our societal life. The future relevance of American socioeconomic and political thought increasingly and more definitely depends on how we deal with the intellectual problems posed by technology and how we go about systematizing its development, use, and operation for the benefit of society and its members as a whole.

NOTES

1. Jacques Ellul, *The Technological Society,* trans. John Wilkinson (New York: Knopf, 1964).
2. B. F. Skinner, *Beyond Freedom and Dignity* (New York: Bantam, 1972), pp. 42–43, 101–104, 125–26, and 171–77. See also Lionel H. Frankel, *Law, Power and Personal Freedom* (St. Paul, Minnesota: West Publishing Co., 1975), pp. 14–25.
3. For a pessimistic view of the future technological society see Victor Ferkiss, "The Pessimistic View of the Future," in *Handbook of Future Research,* ed. Jib Fowles (Westport, Connecticut: Greenwood Press, 1978), pp. 479–96.
4. William Leiss, *The Dominion of Nature* (New York: George Braziller, Inc., 1972).
5. See, for example, the following two of the most important recent works in political philosophy: John Ravels, *A Theory of Justice,* 1971, and Robert Nozick, *Anarchy, State and Utopia* (New York: Basic Books, Inc., 1974).
6. See for, example, Henry Kariel, *The Decline of American Pluralism* (Stanford, California: Stanford University Press, 1961), and *The Promise of Politics* (Englewood Cliffs, New Jersey: Prentice-Hall, 1966).
7. See, for example, Arthur Schlesinger, *The Vital Center* (Boston: Houghton/Mifflin Co., 1949); Arnold Kaufman, *The Radical Liberal* (New York: Simon and Schuster, 1970); and John Rawls, *A Theory of Justice* (Cambridge, Massachusetts: Harvard University Press, 1971).
8. John Kenneth Galbraith, *New Industrial State* (Boston: Houghton/Mifflin, 1972).
9. Anthony de Crespigmy and Kenneth Minogue, eds., *Contemporary Political Philosophers* (New York: Harper and Row, 1975); and Friedrich Hayek, *Continuation of Liberty* (Chicago: University of Chicago Press, 1960).
10. Milton Friedman, *Capitalism and Freedom* (Chicago: University of Chicago Press, 1962).
11. Robert Nozick, *Anarchy, State and Utopia* (New York: Basic Books, Inc., 1974).
12. For example, Ayn Rand, *The New Left: The Anti-Industrial Revolution* (New York: New American Library, 1971).
13. For example, see Hannah Arendt, *The Human Condition* (Chicago: University of Chicago Press, 1970).
14. For example, see Paul A. Aran and Paul M. Sweezy, *Monopoly Capital: An Essay on the American Economic and Social Order* (New York: Monthly Review Press, 1966); Harry Magdoff and Paul M. Sweezy, *The Deepening Crisis of U.S. Capitalism* (New York: Monthly Review Press, 1981); Michael Herrington, *The Twilight of Capitalism* (New York: Simon and Schuster, 1977); also *Socialism* (New York: Dutton, 1972); and Mathilde Noel, "The Phenomenon

of Technology: Liberation or Alienation of Man," in *Socialist Humanism*, ed. E. Fromm (Garden City, New York: Doubleday, 1966), pp. 334–46.

15. See, for example, Murray Bookchin, *Post Scarcity Anarchism* (Berkley: Ramparts, 1980); Karl Hess, *Community Technology* (New York: Harper and Row, 1979).

16. See, for example, Hubert Marcuse, *One Dimensional Man* (Boston: Beacon Press, 1964); Erich Fromm, *Revolution of Hope: Toward a Humanized Technology* (New York: Harper and Row, 1974); and Arthur Lothstein, ed., *The Philosophy of the New Left* (New York: Putnam, 1975).

17. See Charles A. Thrall and Jerold M. Stokes, eds., *Technology, Power and Social Change* (Lexington, Massachusetts: Southern Illinois University Press, 1974).

18. Donald H. Meadows et al., "Technology and the Limits to Growth," in *The Limits to Growth: A Report for the Club of Rome's Project on the Predicament of Mankind*, by Donald H. Meadows and others (New York: Universe Books, 1972).

19. Ibid.

20. See, for example, William Ophuls, *Ecology Politics of Scarcity: Prolegomena to a Political Theory of the Steady State* (San Francisco: W. H. Freeman, 1977); Robert Heilbroner, *An Inquiry into the Human Prospect* (New York: Norton, 1974); and "The Human Prospect: Second Thoughts," *Futures* (1975), pp. 31–40; Rufus E. Miles, Jr., *Awakening from the American Dream: The Social and Political Limits to Growth* (New York: Universe Books, 1977); and Walt Anderson, *A Place of Power: The American Episode in Human Evolution* (Santa Monica, California: Goodyear, 1976).

21. Jacques Ellul, "The Technological Society," in *Technology and Man's Future*, Albert H. Teich, ed. (New York: St. Martin's Press, 1981), 3d ed., 43. For the entire work see Jacques Ellul, *The Technological Society*, trans. G. E. M. Anscombe (New York: Macmillan, 1958).

22. Teich, *Technology and Man's Future*, p. 54.

23. Ibid., p. 46.

24. Ibid., p. 59.

25. For example, Langdon Winner, *Autonomous Technology: Technics-Out-of-Control as a Theme in Political Thought* (Cambridge, Massachusetts: MIT Press, 1977); see also "The Political Philosophy of Alternative Technology," *Technology and Society* 1, no. 1, (1979), pp. 75–86; see also Carl F. Stover, ed., *The Technological Order* (Detroit: Wayne State University Press, 1963); Phillip E. Slater, *The Pursuit of Loneliness* (Boston: Beacon Press, 1970); R. J.Farber, *The Conquest of Nature: Technology and Its Consequences* (New York: New America Library, 1968).

26. Winner, *Autonomous Technology*, p. 29.

27. Ibid.

28. Ibid., p. 105.

29. Ibid., p. 335.

30. Winner, *Autonomous Technology*, pp. 89–92.

31. Ibid., p. 30.

32. Ibid., p. 208.

33. A sample of thinkers in this category includes Daniel Bell, *The Cultural Contradictions of Capitalism*, 2d ed. (Exeter, New Hampshire: Heinman Educational Books, 1979).

34. See, for example, Herman Khan, *The Coming Boom: Economic, Political, and Social* (New York: Simon and Schuster, 1982); Herman Khan and Anthony J. Wiener, *The Year 2000: A Framework for Speculation on the Next Thirty-three Years* (New York: Macmillan, 1967).

35. See, for example, E. F. Schumacher, *Small is Beautiful: Economics—As If People Mattered* (New York: Harper and Row, 1973); *A Guide to the Perplexed* (New York: Harper and Row, 1977); and Leopold Kohr, *The Breakdown of Nations* (London: Routlege and Keegan Paul, 1957).

36. Kohr, *The Breakdown of Nations*, p. ix.

37. Ibid., p. x.

38. Schumancher, *Small is Beautiful*, pp. 4–5.

39. Ibid., p. 277.

40. Ibid., p. 281.

41. Amory Lovins, *Soft Energy Paths: Toward a Durable Peace* (Cambridge, Massachusetts: Ballinger Publishing Company, 1977), pp. 3–7.

42. Ibid., p. 6.

43. Barry Commoner, *The Poverty of Powers: Energy and the Economic Crisis* (New York: Alfred A. Knopf, 1976), pp. 1–2.

44. Ibid., p. 2–3.

45. Ibid.

46. William Leiss, *The Limits of Satisfaction: An Essay on the Problem of Needs and Commodities* (Toronto: University of Toronto Press, 1976), p. 4. In this category see also his *The Domination of Nature* (New York: George Braziller, 1972); and Mark Satin, *New Age Politics* (New York: Dell Publishing Company, 1978).

47. Leiss, "The Limits of Satisfaction," pp. 4–5.

48. Ibid., p. 10.

49. Ibid., p. 130.

50. Ibid.

51. See William B. Devall, "Reformist Environmentalism," *Humboldt Journal of Social Relations* 6 (1979), pp. 129–58.

52. Gary Snyder *The Old Ways* (San Francisco: City Lights Books, 1977), p. 17.

53. Ibid., pp. 42–43.

54. See, for example, John Rodman, "The Liberation of Nature," *Inquiry* 20 (1977), pp. 83–131; Christopher Stone, *Should Trees Have Standing?: Toward Legal Rights for Natural Objects* (New York: Avon Books, 1975); Peter Singer, *Rights for Natural Objects* (New York: Avon Books, 1975); Peter Singer, *Animal Liberation: A New Ethics for Our Treatment of Animals* (New York: Random House, 1975); John C. Lilly, *Lilly on Dolphins* (New York: Doubleday, 1975); Tom Regan, "The Moral Basis of Vegetarianism," *Canadian Journal of Philosophy* 5:2 (October 1975); Joel Feinberg, "The Rights of Animals and Unborn Generations," in *Philosophy and Environmental Crisis*, ed. William Blackstone (Athens, Georgia: University of Georgia Press, 1974); and Tom Regan and Peter Singer, eds., *Animal Rights and Human Obligations* (Englewood Cliffs, New Jersey: Prentice-Hall, 1976).

55. Rodman, "The Liberation of Nature," p. 84.

56. Singer, *Animal Liberation*, see preface, chs. 1 and 6.

57. Garrett DeBell, ed., *The Voter's Guide to Environmental Politics* (New York: Ballantine, 1970), pp. 76 and 84.

58. Stone, *Should Trees Have Standing?*, pp. 27, 76–86.
59. See, for example, Earnest Callenback, *Ecotopia Emerging* (Berkeley, California: Banyan Tree Books, 1977).
60. Ibid., pp. 264–65.

Chapter Two

Information-Communication Technology

The future centralized and democratized information system, the Technodem, is the backbone of a future democratic society and an indispensable component of the technological democratic system. Proper understanding of its structure and operation requires certain preliminary knowledge relating to information as well as communication technologies. The purpose of the proceeding chapters is to provide for such a preliminary background. Though the structure and operation of the Technodem is quite simple and within the capability of current technological know-how, its understanding as well as implementation may encounter some complexities. For this reason, some explanations in the proceeding chapters may appear repitious, but they actually are brought in to connect a specific explanation in the reader's mind to the preceding materials.

The information technology is in a state of flux and highly dynamic. Whether it is called the "information revolution"[1] or "the postindustrial society",[2] the hemisphere is on the threshold of a phenomenal change, and information technology with its new methods of storage, transfer, and retrieval is playing an indisputably major role in bringing about this transformation.

High-tech society is basically an information society. The socioeconomic and political operation of such a society is highly dependent on various kinds of information technology, such as data collection, data processing, record keeping, market research, situation analysis, and information transmission. The creation, storage, use, and transmission of energy will be a prerequisite for the maintenance and continuation of information systems.

While new sources of energy will be discovered and developed, its per unit use will substantially decrease as a result of technological advancements. Based on recent developments, it appears that by 1995 the information industry will constitute the most important sector of the U.S. economy. By no means will this technological transformation be an American phenomenon. Western Europe and Japan are moving along with the United States and some other countries in the Middle East; Latin America and the Far East are expected to join the high-tech information caravan.[3]

Information is the source of knowledge of different kinds and degrees. For centuries information has been used as a commodity in the marketplace. The most important traditional marketplace for information has been the educational institutions where teachers have sold information and students have paid for receiving it. In modern times, when the cost has not been affordable to many who desire to receive knowledge, the public, for the benefit of society, has been subsidizing the price by a variety of means, including financial aid to students.

In high-tech society, education will move out of the borders of educational institutions. It will become universal and continuous. The modern information system will play the principal role. To sustain the public benefits the economic and political systems will be obliged to subsidize the price. The tendency will be to provide equal opportunity to receive information necessary for convenient life, liberty, and pursuit of happiness, with the latter having a quite different meaning in a technological democratic society of the future.

Some thinkers are reluctant to accept the commodity nature of information.[4] But historically speaking, information has been bought and sold for centuries. Even during the feudal period, informing was a business and informers were paid the price depending on the importance of information to the receiver. It has been suggested that information is a commodity that can be understood in terms of economic principles. While at times it may be a cognitive process, in some instances it is undoubtedly a marketable product.[5]

In technological democratic society, however, one may argue that for the maintenance of a democratic system, socioeconomic, political, and otherwise, certain sectors of information must be provided, accessible to all citizens, free of charge. This does not suggest by any means that the information thus supplied is not a commodity in the market. It certainly is a commodity, at least to the extent of its cost of production, storage, and transmission. The difference is that for the public good and benefit the cost is absorbed and paid by the system through certain kinds of public funding as embodied in the financial operation of a technological democratic society.

Technological societies, the United States in particular, are facing an information explosion. According to one source, the increase has been so exponential that more printed information has been generated in the past ten years than during the whole history of mankind.[6]

Under this information situation, along with the increasing complexity of socioeconomic and political institutions, it has become impossible for individuals to depend on personal perceptions and experiences in the decision-making process. Individuals are becoming almost totally dependent on external sources for necessary and often vital information. Currently in most cases so much potentially relevant information relating a question is available through the information system network that one hardly can reach and examine all that is necessary. Consequently, one has to make somehow uninformed or, at best, underinformed decisions. For this reason the situation has been referred to as ignorance explosion or information overload.[7] The situation clearly calls for appropriate technological means to search and screen information and make it conveniently accessible to the user.[8]

While the advance in information technology has been the cause of the information explosion, by facilitating collection, storage, and classification of information it has also provided means for electronic search, analysis, and retrieval of information sought by the ultimate users. High-tech methods make information available with incredible speed never imagined before. Currently one industrial technique or decision-making process discovered in one part of the country can be received and used in another part in a matter of hours. Despite the existing technophobia relating to the use of electronic information technology, continuous exposure to the system, and the necessity of use, are continually increasing the number of users as well as their sophistication. As a result, the information centers, including libraries, have been obliged to respond to demand and thus reform and transform their operations into electronic systems. However, such transformations have not been and are not easy and simple. Besides technical and organizational roadblocks and serious problems of adjustment there have been substantial financial constraints. This has been more true in the case of libraries, which are the conventional source of information for the ordinary user. This situation raises the serious question of financing these information centers. Should it be through a user's fee, public funding, or a mixture of both? The facts are that the continual and rapid advances in information technology, particularly the advent of on-line retrieval services, development of computer-based interlibrary networks, and increasing sophistication of the information users, all impose unavoidable pressures upon information centers to move into electronic information systems and transform and retransform themselves as the newly developing technologies overshadow the old ones.

OPERATIONAL PROBLEMS

Several problems are facing the user and provider of electronic information. First, most of the users are constantly faced with the nightmare of receiving the right information from a variety of potential sources. This has necessarily forced the experts in attempting to resolve the problem. It is quite obvious that any user's decision to employ an information system ultimately depends on how effectively, efficiently, and thoroughly the information system leads the user in tracking, processing, and retrieving the desired information. Second, a dilemma is facing the publicly supported institutions. That is whether to impose fees for the use of information acquired from other database vendors. This problem becomes crucial as a result of the progressively shrinking level of public financial support. The problem of decreasing public funding of publicly supported institutions becomes further critical by considering the increasing demand for on-line information services.

Third, users seeking information often require instant solutions and expect the vendors being able to provide instant answers. The problem here is that of pricing information products and services. These products and services are by their nature intangible and thus create problems of appropriate pricing. Was the price levied fair? Was the user being ripped off? For these reasons various pricing mechanisms have been developed. Relevant to this matter is the problem facing vendors or intermediaries who sell information that they receive free of charge or in a subsidized form from governmental or publicly funded institutions. For some commercial institutions it is highly desirable and profitable to utilize data bases available through governmental agencies and other publicly supported institutions in feeding in their own on-line data bases, and sell the information at high or higher prices on the open market. The problem becomes acute when the public agencies charge for the information, but with preferential rates for certain institutions, one rate for the commercial market, and a subsidized rate for educational and other publicly supported institutions.

Fourth, there is the problem of management of continually developing new information technologies such as teleconferencing, office automation, library technology, and word processing. These and other new technologies continue to add new dimensions to the operation of the various information systems. They necessitate a continuous, though periodic, restructuring of the operation and management systems. The need for this updating has necessitated the development of a new area of expertise knowledge labeled as information resource management.

The final problem relates to the cross-national data transfer. The flow of information across the border, particularly among industrialized countries, is being developed rapidly because of its importance in the area such as business, finance, economy, education, and research. It is being achieved through the use of modern communication systems combined with the electronic information centers. Many countries, including some less developed ones, are in the process of developing this kind of network. The problem is the manner of using and benefiting from such transferred information. The problem mainly relates to the question of privacy and national sovereignty. Both have been a hindrance to the free flow of cross-border information.

In the United States, according to a governmental study, the information sector has been growing faster than other sectors of economy[9] and accounts for 46 percent of the Gross National Product.[10] The first implication of this rapid growth is that the information institutions have to work much harder to keep up with the new technological development in information industries. The inroad of the modern electronic information technology has been rapidly, and sometimes painfully, changing the forms and processes of operation as well as management.

The changes further expand to embrace the intellectual dimension. Continually new areas of knowledge closely associated with the use of electronic information systems are being developed. Among these are artificial intelligence, decision science, library science, operation research, linguistics, systems analysis and methods, telecommunications, et cetera.[11] One great development in this regard has been the fantastic expansion of intellectual knowledge through the interdisciplinary nature of information science.

Along with these developments is the continued sophistication of information processing. One outcome has been the increasing reduction in the production and transmission of paper-based communication. Likely the society will not move toward a paperless communication system but the electronic processing will dominate the system. The Federal Paperwork Reduction Act of 1980 is an indication of such development.[12] It requires governmental agencies to reduce redundant paperwork by using electronic processing systems. The sharply reduced electronic processing costs along with development of systems that are more convenient and simpler to operate have been inducements toward accelerating the change.[13]

Developments in the electronic processing system are causing printed materials to gradually be replaced by electronic devices. Today, as a result, a large university library can have all its paper printed holdings stored on relatively few magnetic disks or tapes. The same applies to the personnel, financial, and other records of large business, industrial, or financial firms. Besides the sharply reduced space to keep the records, the facility by which the records are stored, processed, analyzed, or retrieved is the prime incentive to move in the direction of electronic communication-information systems.

All these factors have caused rapid development in the information services sector.[14] Today a great variety of information is easily accessible through these electronic service systems. Of course the phenomenal increase in the use of personal computers has facilitated this growth.[15]

Finally, transborder data flow is increasingly becoming a necessity in dealing with international business, finance, research, and many other areas. The importance of the international data transfer has been repeatedly expressed by differently related professional organizations. For example, at the 1981 Annual National Conference and Exposition (NICE V), which was held in Chicago, the issue was repeatedly brought up. It was ultimately stated that "speaker after speaker, addressing management problems, pointed to the fact that the world is getting smaller and smaller, more complex and interdependent. . . . We are becoming a global village."[16]

Crossborder data transfer causes problems requiring international solutions. Among these are violation of privacy when transmitting personal data across national borders, national sovereignty if data to be transferred relate to national security, often inflated fees for services rendered, and competition among developers and vendors of electronic on-line services.

Different efforts are being made to alleviate some of these problems. For example, the White House Conference on Library and Information Services, which convened in November 1979, recommended that the U.S. government take action to:

1. Eliminate international barriers to the exchange of library materials and information to encourage international data flow under appropriate guidelines.
2. Provide support for the development and adoption of national and international standards.
3. Convene an international conference on library and information services. Similar recommendations or steps should be taken by any country interested in participating in transborder data flow.[17]

Another example is the intergovernmental conferences and international meetings on data processing held at different times by the UN Educatonal, Scientific and Cultural Organization (UNESCO). The importance of international data flow was stressed by the director-general of UNESCO to the fact that "Informatics . . . has suddenly broadened our horizons . . . people are constantly accustomed to living in permanent contact with worlds other than their own."[18]

Perhaps the most significant problem in technological society is that of accessibility of information to the general public. Will the ordinary citizen who is the bona fide seeker of information obtain it with ease and convenience? In a technological democratic society the principle of equality of opportunity prescribes that through technological sophistication the use and accessibility must be simplified to the comprehension of the very ordinary citizen. Currently there are substantial problems involved concerning the question of accessibility. Many systems are quite sophisticated to be understood and used by ordinary people. There is the question of financing the operation, including collection, storage, processing, and retrieval. There is the problem of security of personnel and sensitive data, requirements for substantial national and international actions toward solving these and other relevant problems, and streamlining of the total operation and process toward coherence yet simplicity.

DEVELOPMENT OF ELECTRONIC INFORMATION TECHNOLOGY

For a better understanding of the rest of the materials presented here relating to electronic information technology, a brief review of the technology and its development appears appropriate.

Compared to all other technological developments it can be quite assuredly stated that the developments in electronic information technology during the last three decades has been incredible. The developments are continuing to be so dynamic that it is impossible to make safe categorized predictions about the future of the industry. Many related developments had been unpredictable yet materialized.

For a better understanding of the discussion of technological democracy the decisive role of information in the developments of electronic information technology during the last three decades appears to be useful, even necessary. The review is particularly useful in understanding of the current status of the industry and some of the terminology commonly used in dealing with and describing of the technology. The review also helps the understanding of modern data processing and enhances attempts to explain a variety of developmental processes, issues, and questions.

The span of human experience with the computer has been very short. The first stored program computer was put in operation in England in 1949, and in 1953 it was first commercialized in the United States.[19]

Generally speaking, a computer is a conglomeration of a very large number of electronic circuits put together in a logical form to perform certain specified functions. While the electronic engineers are busy with the minutia of circuit design and intricated combining of them, others such as computer and information scientists, librarians, et cetera, are keenly concerned with the operation and specific functions of various components of the machine. The main interest is centered around collection, storage, processing, retrieving, and analyzing of information and the contributions that the component parts can make to achieve these goals rapidly, effectively, and efficiently.

The first generation of computers appeared on the market in the 1950s. The ENIAC (Electronic Numerical Integrator and Calculator) of the University of Pennsylvania[20] and the EDSAC (Electronic Delay Storage Automatic Calculator) of Cambridge University were examples of the early computers.[21]

In the United States, IBM was in the forefront.[22] The key electronic component at the time was the electronic vacuum tube, used as the main calculating device. These computers were able to execute about one thousand instructions per second and had a storage capacity of about ten thousand to twenty thousand (10–20K) characters of data in the main memory.

The ENIAC was a gigantic computer weighing about thirty tons and taking some fifteen hundred square feet of space. It embodied some nineteen thousand vacuum tubes and used an enormous power of 130 kilowatts. Its contemporary computers had the same characteristics and consumed enormous electrical energy. Their primary use was for scientific and mathematical calculations.

In 1947 transistors were invented by physicists at Bell Laboratories, but it was not until the late fifties and sixties that transistors were widely used as the essential component of the computers replacing vacuum tubes. Unlike vacuum tubes, transistors used solids as the medium for electronic functions. They were much faster, far smaller in size, and more reliable and, above all, required much less electric power. The operational speed had multiplied, rising to 1 million instructions per second; it performed at microsecond speeds (one-millionth of a second per instruction). The main memory capacity had increased to sixty-five thousand (65K) storage locations. Beside being transistorized (known as solid-state) this generation of computers had operating systems, time sharing, and languages.

The integrated circuit, invented in 1957, entered the structure of computers in 1964.[23] It created a new generation of computers. Generally speaking, an integrated circuit (IC) is a very small silicon chip (about one–two-hundreth of a square inch) with capabilities of many transistors and other circuit components. The use of integrated circuits sharply reduced the size of computers, multiplied speed (10 million additions per second), and substantially enhanced the memory capacity (in excess of 10 million storage locations). This was the era of minicomputers, which became popular by the mid-1970s.

By the late 1970s, increased density of integrated circuits resulted in Large Scale Integrated (LSI) circuits. Consequently, the physical size of computers was further reduced while their performance increased. This was, and still is, the era of microcomputers. Because of the fantastic capacity of LSI, multiprocessing, multiprogramming and virtual memory concepts became an integral part of computer design. *Multiprocessing* refers to using more than one central processor in the system. *Multiprogramming* means using paging (partial processing) and entering a variety of functions or program executions into a specified time limit. *Virtual memory* relates to manipulation of primary and secondary memories to show the apparent capacity of the computer as enhanced. The largest of these computers have a basic memory size of 16 million bytes, increasable to 32 million. Their processing speed varies from 10 to around 16 million instructions per second (MIPS).

There is a new generation of computers under development, and the next few years will witness still more fascinating discoveries in computer technology. Several important areas are seriously under consideration.[24] First is the area of artificial intelligence with the intention of replacing the human mind by machine, at least in certain areas of human function. Advanced computer-operated robots will be a part of this discovery. They may be able to operate some sections of information systems and centers, including libraries. The second area is concerned with combining a series of computer systems and subsystems together for the purpose of distributed processing. Finally, further advancement in very large scale integrated circuits (VLSI) will make possible reduction in the cost of these advanced systems, making them available to the general users.

MICROCOMPUTERS AND SUPPLEMENTARY TECHNOLOGY

An explosion is on the way in the use of electronic information. Sophisticated operating systems have been developed making it possible to connect a variety of devices to a single computer system, multiplying its power and usability. Substantial reduction in price and rapid development of strong and sophisticated microcomputers have multiplied demand for services and have accentuated this usage explosion. The process has become a vicious circle. The upward-moving self-perpetuating spiral of demand induces development of better systems and services, which in turn results in further increasing demand. With the advance of microcomputers more attention is being given to storage capacity, supplementary storage devices, and their interconnection with the main machine.

Microcomputers are the result of miniaturization of computers by using the latest LSI and VLSI technologies. Development of microcomputers has been a boon to the electronic information industry and a means to popularize the use of electronic information services. Despite a fantastic advancement in improving the qualities of microcomputers, the objective is far short of being completed. As expressed by some experts:

> Many LSI chips, such as microprocessors now consist of multiple computer subsystems, and thus really integrated systems, microcomputers rather than integrated circuits .... Physical principles indicate that transistors can be scaled down to less than 1/100th of their present area and still function as sort of switching elements with which we can build digital systems. By the late 1990s it will be possible to fabricate chips containing millions of transistors.[25]

One of the most important aspects of electronic information technology has been the development of mass storage devices. Magnetic tape is among the early types and has one of the highest storage capacities. However, due to its sequential access, its usefulness in on-line storage systems is limited. Punched cards, which have been used extensively in data processing, are another sequential access type and have the drawback of not being suitable for convenient on-line manipulations.

The rapid increase in the use of on-line services has given rise to popularity of random access devices in information processing. Most commonly used devices include magnetic disks, magnetic drums, and floppy disks. There is also the Computer Output Microfilm (COM). Data from the central processor are reflected into a microfilm recorder that is connected to a film processor. The output is either on microfiche or microfilm. The process is preferred in storing archival materials.

DATA DISPLAY

The new generation of computers is more and more oriented toward usability with comfort and ease. Ergonomics, which is a human-oriented design technique, has been instrumental in bringing about improved appearance and use facility of computers and other electronic display devices.[26]

Teletypes, which are alphanumeric terminals, constitute some of the most common terminals. They have a keyboard similar to that of a typewriter and are capable of hard-copy outputs.

Cathode Ray Tube (CRT) terminals do not have hard-copy output facility but are becoming popular because of two reasons. First, they have much better visual images and capability of multicolor graphics; second, they allow attachments that give them capability of hard-copy production.[27]

Printing technology is witnessing rapid developments. There are over one thousand different printers on the market today using a wide variety of techniques. Distinguished among these are laser printers capable of printing over a hundred pages per minute.[28] In general, printers are improving in quality of printed products and variety of typefaces as well as speed.

Finally, optical character recognition (OCR) has seen tremendous developments. This is a process by which a variety of devices are employed to read in data without typing. Libraries and other information centers are now using electronically sensitive wands or light pens to record details of readable materials. Increasingly libraries and other information centers are using the Universal Product Code (UPC) concept in recording checked out items. For example, information about the item is prerecorded on a UPC label pasted on the item. When lending, prerecorded reader and item details are matched by using a light pen and automatically recorded in the main storage system.

INFORMATION TELECOMMUNICATION

Combining computers with telecommunication networks in recent years, as explained in more detail later on, has provided for astounding results. It has fantastically facilitated the transfer of information within small and large institutions, among organizations at the local, regional, national, and international levels. Researchers in different institutions are now able to exchange related information; financial institutions, by using the system, effect electronic fund transfers; electronic mail, the latest development in office automation, allows information to be transmitted regularly to other locations; satellite-computer connections make possible transborder data flows to faraway distances.

Different means of communication are employed in effectuating this information-communication system. These start from interconnected telephone systems, terrestrial microwave, and optical fiber cables and extend to satellites. Cable television (CATV) is another medium gradually but effectively entering the information-communication scene.

Software refers to programs that command a computer to perform specifically designated functions. It is a very important and essential supplementary component of a computer without which a general purpose computer is a useless collection of electronic and electromechanical components.[29] Functionally computer software may be divided into four basic categories. First is the interface function, by which the interconnection of incompatible hardware is facilitated by software. This appears to be one of the most difficult aspects of systems management. Second is the access function, which facilitates user machine interface. Third is the multiple use facilitator function, by which several users can use the same system simultaneously. Finally there is the programmer's tool function, through which programmers are provided by utility programs employed as editing devices.

In a much broader sense software may be placed in two categories. First are the operating system programs including system control programs (SCPs), communication control programs, data-base management systems and utility programs. Operating systems are the most significant and crucial. They are a set of programs designed to manage, direct, and, in general, operate computer software. The second category includes the application program, produced by programmers to perform specifically designated functions.

INFORMATION-COMMUNICATIONS SYSTEM

The history of development of human societies, particularly the last few centuries, reveals that major changes in information collection, storage, and distribution have had profound effects in institution structures and societal functions. The introduction of new information systems such as printing, telegraph, telephone, radio, television, satellites, and finally computers has revolutionized the information technology and has had revolutionary effects on societal structures, institutional organizations, and human interactions.

The current linkage between the communication and computer systems—and phenomenal changes it has caused in the structure of information system—is having an enormous effect on the use of technology in production, entrepreneurship, market operation, education, public policy, and even social habits and interactions.

It is impossible to predict exactly what changes will occur in information technology in the near future. However, it would be illuminating to look at the possibilities based on the current discoveries, developments, and trends, which may suggest the variety of choices that may ultimately make for good or evil.

The combination of two major technologies forms the foundation of the current information system. The first is a high-speed, broad-base, and reliable communication system employing satellite, telephone, microwave, and cable television systems. The second is the computer system, with the rapid proliferation of very inexpensive compact yet powerful hardware and software.

The combination of these two technologies allows individuals to interact directly with one or more computers, by having access to enormous data bases and a variety of problem-resolving softwares. The users are able to amplify their memory, intelligence and mental process through a rapid, convenient and economical access to a wide range of information products and services. These services, products, and information supplied are collectively referred to as network information services (NIS).[30]

The most revolutionary aspect of this merger between communication and the computer system is the availability of network information services in the user's home or office. It allows a very flexible choice in locating hardware, software, or data bases, access to libraries and other information systems and ultimately to the marketplace. All these suggest radical changes in communication systems and institutions and sharp reorganization of tasks and resources, production, sale, and delivery of goods and services.

Through the network information services it is possible for individuals as well as institutions to affiliate with each other over vast distances and be linked in networks that have no particular existence but are the outcome of innumerable nationwide or global system networks or "infrasphere."[31]

The use of network information services has started in business corporations and is rapidly developing in the areas such as teleconferencing, electronic mail, and message systems. It further expands to word-processing systems and distribution of data processing through satellite communications, corporate security, and environmental monitoring systems. One recent study concludes that by 1990 as much as 50 to 70 percent of all intracompany communications and services will be electronically carried out.

ORGANIZATIONAL STRUCTURES IN PRODUCTION OF GOODS AND SERVICES

In general, the geographic location of the principal components of a corporation strongly influences many organizational relationships. The new technologies tend to free organizational designs from many of the old constraints because the network information services are able to link together people, resources, tasks, and management in many different configurations, making possible coordination and control of dispersed functions.

In the corporate world it is already far more economical to take work to people than people to work. In many areas of production, particularly those of information services, experiments are being carried out by choosing some workers to work at home, with computer terminals linked to the employer's information network. As the number of such workers increases, corporations will, necessarily, tend to become radically and uniquely decentralized. These small production facilities, located where the employees like to live, will easily be tied together by the linkage of telecommunication to computers. This arrangement, without loss of coordination and integration, will allow much flexibility in operation and work design and arrangement.

The new information services provide for an ideal production facility. They substantially provide added value to existing services. Production resources can be pooled together to a grand extent to achieve economies of scale; production information available can lead suppliers to concentrate on products where they have a competitive edge and swiftly moved from one line of product to another as the market demands change. The same advantage is also available to the producer of the products. Furthermore, the availability of such an information system will enable small producers to produce custom-tailored products meeting the individual user's specifications.[32]

The information industry itself will be the major beneficiary of this new production system. These will include firms such as publishing, software production, engineering, banking, insurance, accounting, employment and credit, public health, legal counseling, and so on.

Other industries will acquire a high flexible production process enabling them to produce to order rather than for inventory, in other words to custom produce many items that are now mass produced while sustaining the economies of scale.

PRODUCTION AND MARKETING

The network-information services enormously facilitate transactions between producers and consumers. The usual marketing elements, such as product advertisement, video catalogs, location of sellers and purchasers, ordering, billing, instant purchase, payments, accounting and delivery, consumption of wholesale and retail transactions, and mass distribution all will materialize through the communications network. When products can be displayed on the home terminal screen according to demand of the consumer and products are selected, purchased, and paid for all electronically, the whole system of traditional sale, wholesale as well as retail, through personal contacts will be extremely diminished, if not totally abandoned. Because this marketing process facilitates and accelerates sales and distribution unmatched with any other existing means, buyers are now matched with sellers, employees with employers, professionals with clients, producers with suppliers, and so on.

EDUCATION

In the field of education, the impact of the computer and communication is also being felt even though the widespread use of computer-assisted instruction allowing highly individualized instruction has not yet been materialized. However, scattered efforts in this direction have begun, and new systems are being developed.[33] These systems allow students to learn directly in interaction with computer systems such as tutorial instruction, student-initiated inquiry, student-computer dialogue, simulation games, drill, and practice.

When the system is developed further it could be delivered to the homes, revolutionizing the educational process by delivering educational materials and instruction at home and making it much less expensive and more convenient compared to the traditional and conventional forms.

The organizational structure of educational systems and libraries would also go through a radical transformation. The current physical, organizational, procedural, and administrative structures of the schools will be less and less suitable to serve the purpose of education and satisfy the accelerating educational demands of the future. It will easily be possible to deliver educational programs electronically at home or in a local station, from quite remote locations, to students far more efficiently and conveniently than requiring them to leave their hometown to attend a special educational institution, living in a crowded campus and rushing from one classroom to another. The future educational systems likely may not require the physical presence of professors and instructors, which now forms the basic foundation of such an institution. Yet students will be able to have contact with the brains of outstanding scientists nationwide and benefit from their knowledge and varied approaches.

Individuals will be able to take educational courses any time they desire and at any institution they are offered and receive cross-institutional degrees or transfer all the courses to their desired institution and receive their degree. This advancement in the educational process will now also entail a standardized examination process that will tend to guarantee a quality education.

LIBRARIES AND INFORMATION DELIVERY SYSTEMS

Individuals will no longer be restricted to their local library as a source of documented information; they will be able to use the resources of other libraries long distances away, nationally or internationally.

THINKING COMPUTERS

Some three decades ago, after a handful of experts at MIT began the quest for a computer that could think like a human being, such a machine has emerged from the realm of fantasy into the marketplace.

Achieving artificial intelligence (AI) is the purpose. It may range from talking cameras and intelligent ovens to emotional computers capable of anger and ambition. These are all possibilities now. Artificial intelligence refers to a computer that can imitate the way the human brain reasons. It is estimated that within two decades machines with electronic brains will be a part of almost every car, home, and office and all production and service institutions.[34]

As one expert comments "Ten years ago, this whole field was out there in the cold, in the woodshed, with researchers begging for grants; now, artificial intelligence is being used, commercially, for the very first time. It is still quite primitive. It is not divinity in a box. But it's pointing at what's coming down the road."[35]

For example, a computer software program called Financial Adviser introduced to the market is claimed by the producer to have the analytic abilities of not one but many high-priced MBAs. At the same time, using the adviser requires no special skills. All the user needs to do is supply the machine with information necessary about a company plan, such as building a new plant, introducing a new product, or investing in a risky prospect. The Adviser is even capable of making international product market analysis. For example, in relation to a new product introduced to the Adviser it may ask the user, "Do you believe your product enjoys a competitive advantage others do not?" If the answer is "yes," the computer may respond "Shall I tell you about those of Japan and Taiwan?"

Simply, after all information about the new product or policy has been fed into the machine, it tabulates, analyzes, makes graphs, takes into account the inflation factor, taxes, and other economic elements, and then makes recommendations about a course of action.

So far, what the computer cannot do is make the decision. It does not replace the human mind. It is simply a tool to free managers to use their talents for more creative functions. This and other artificial intelligence machines are generally different from an ordinary computer because they are able to digest information with an enormously complicated language called LISP. This language computes symbols rather than numbers and letters and is punctuated with a score of parentheses to the extent that the experts in this machinery jokingly refer to LISP as Lots of Idiotic, Stupid Parentheses. The symbol actually stands for List Processing.

It has been commented by some professional users that having the Adviser is like having a team of experts at one's disposal; it answers some questions one wouldn't even have thought of asking.[36] It must be noted that the general public still fears the notion of computers that have the ability to think and reason.

COMPACT DISCS

The compact disc (CD) uses digital technology to create a sound far superior to that of traditional phonograph records. The new technology delivers almost perfect pitch replication and stereo separation without any of the scratchy background noise that occurs when a turntable needle touches a record. In CD technology nothing ever touches the disc except the concentrated light from a laser. Sound signals, in the two-digit language understood by computers, are etched into a disc as a series of microscopic pits.

When the disc is placed inside the player, a laser light is focused on the microscopic pits and is reflected to an optical sensor, which converts the signal into digital zeros and ones. These pulses then pass into a microprocessor, which decodes the digital language into sound.[37]

Contrary to the size, weight, and portability of turntables, there are CD players on the market measuring five by five inches on the surface and one and one-quarter inches in thickness. As with any other electronic gadget, as the sales increase, the price decreases. The same applies to the cost of discs.[38]

The sound technology does not stop here. It moves forward. An exciting development in CD technology is on the way. This is a new system that allows users to present graphics from the discs on their television screen or computer monitor. A CD-like device for computers can now store 450 million characters of information, enough to fit the *Encyclopedia Britannica*. It is expected that soon the user will be able to hook his CD player right up to his computer. The compact disc so far is the most revolutionary audio breakthrough.

THE VIDEO REVOLUTION

Video technology is on the verge of a revolution that promises better picture quality, previously unimaginable features, and consistently better values.

The quantum leap in technology is seen most clearly in the advent of the digital television set. It is able to convert the analog signals it receives into the binary language understood by computers. The units constructed by Japanese firms permit viewing a picture within a picture. It can show two stations simultaneously, one station and a videotape, or a station and a computer file.[39] One with the most dazzling displays, which is entering the market, is capable of showing nine stations on one screen at the same time and can display nine sequential pictures in a freeze-frame effect.

Some units are equipped with a "home-management helper" that flashes reminders and dates programmed by the user. It also allows users to block out shows that they do not want their children to watch.

The industry has already shown its prowess at shrinking TV sets to shirt-pocket size. Technology is now heading toward a large-screen direct-view set. Previously, only rear-projection models, whose pictures tend to be fuzzy, could be so large. At the same time, a linkage between video and audio is developing where audio-video systems combine hi-fi components with television sets. They consist of compact disc players and video recorders with a remote control device that regulates the entire system.

An expanding number of firms now sell videocassette recorders that use eight-millimeter tape, as opposed to the standard half-inch size. This sharply reduces the size of the VCR systems. It also decreases the size of video cameras. The phenomenal developments in this area have brought to the market a camera-recorder combination system about the size of an ordinary paperback book. Furthermore, it is possible now to watch a videotape on any of several television sets in the house or even on more than one set.

INFORMATION-DELIVERY SYSTEM

Advancement in information technology has revolutionized the search system for collecting relevant information. Through computerized indexing methods one can now retrieve bibliographies on virtually any subject in just a few minutes.

However, when a bibliography on a topic is collected access to the main literature is still cumbersome. Information technology has not advanced to the stage that one could have instant or easy access to a copy of the materials contained in the bibliography. We can find out instantly whether or not a document exists, but we cannot have instantaneous access to it. This is especially true when the source of the document is another country.[40]

The effect of interlibrary loans, concerning the rapidly increasing level of demand, is unsatisfactory, time-consuming as well as costly. Though some advanced libraries have streamlined this process of delivery by using computerized data bases, it is quite expensive to resort to it.[41] It is estimated that each year some 20 million documents are obtained through various interlibrary loan systems. The number is expected to multiply in a few years.

With the rising costs of delivery, search for a more economic and efficient method of delivery seems to be imperative. The solution appears to depend on development of the electronic document-delivery systems. But it must be economically feasible and standardized in electronic formats and codes. One relevant technology in this regard is videotex. It uses the television set as a display terminal for computer-based information services.[42] However, currently the cost of modifying television sets of videotex is too expensive while the resolution of images, particularly graphs, is quite poor. Furthermore, only a few lines of the text are shown on the screen at one time, which makes reading slow and tedious.

These facts illustrate that electronic document delivery systems are not yet effectively, efficiently, and economically available. However, several systems are at the proposal and development stages through which machine-readable documents would be electronically transmitted to a center to be printed or relayed to the consumer's computer.[43]

These proposals are mostly in a conceptual stage, and many problems, including that of cost, must be ironed out. Besides technological problems there are other obstacles, such as belief that conversion from print to electronic publishing would be profitable to the enterprises; regulation and protection of copyright of electronic information; international agreements for transmitting of information; acceptable forms of the new electronic information by users; and willingness to pay for information.

Once these obstacles are overcome there will be an accelerated movement toward complete conversion to electronic information transfer. Arriving at this stage, under the current circumstances, is at least a couple of decades away. Not only would one have access to electronic journals, but one would not need to subscribe to complete journals but to a selective dissemination-of-information service and receive only the information of particular interest.

Once people in all parts of society have rapid electronic access to information, its use and demand will multiply. As the information technology reaches the stage of general-public use, need for individual information storage or libraries will tend to disappear, since it will be unnecessary when it will be easily and cheaply possible to receive information or documents needed anytime from centers of information.

Libraries will turn into broader and more complex information centers. They will be packed with computer hardware, storing electronic documents and data. There will practically be no users present in the library, since all needed information can be retrieved electronically through home or office terminals. Libraries will be equipped with facilities for receiving, storing, and electronically transmitting all kinds of information. Librarians will become data-base administrators and electronic communication specialists.

NECESSITY FOR DEMOCRATIZATION OF INFORMATION-COMMUNICATIONS SYSTEM

The right to free expression and the right to knowledge are actually being endangered by the way communication technologies are used and controlled today.

Particularly, it won't be more than just a few years before most expressions of information necessary for knowledge will be available mainly through these electronic technologies such as two-way cable television and the interactive print systems known as two-way teletext or videotex. By then, both of these technologies will be incorporated in a home communication system, most likely through a home computer terminal.

The result is the availability at home of an incredibly vast amount of information and extensive intercommunication possibilities. One will be able to order up printed information appearing on his video screen, and if one desires, one can get its photocopy printout. It will allow one access not only to the library reference materials but also to the original material of one's need. Furthermore, it would allow two-way communication with all those whose terminal is connected to the system. At present this home communication is possible through the two-way cable system among subscribers.[44]

In the near future, on the selection of the subscriber, materials from newspapers, magazines, and other periodicals and even books will be delivered to the subscriber through the screen. Any part may be transcribed by the subscriber's word processor for his personal use. All these with all the convenience they bring will cost a fraction of what they cost now through conventional printing and distribution systems.

The more extended this electronic information system becomes, the more important becomes the question of who will control the content. If the control becomes monolithic, then the public receives information according to the desire of the controller. Such a monolithic content control system could run by the state, a media conglomerate, giant corporations, et cetera. In any case, the information is controlled and freedom of press, as well as expression, is lost.

In technologically advanced societies this control can be materialized by manipulating the information technology by taking advantage of public awareness. The nature of this high-tech information system makes it easy for the state or other powerful institution to exercise control over its content. If the government runs this electronic communications system two questions arise: first, should the government put the information into its own videotex system; and second, who would have access to this government-run system. Governments using this advanced electronic information system have been trying to answer these questions.

In Sweden the telephone and telecommunications system Televerket, which is operated by the government, is not to control content. In France the law separates the electronic delivery system from its content. The government delivery systems such as two-way cable television and interactive videotex are leased to providers of information as well as entertainment. The system operates as a delivery agent similar to that of conventional telephone operation.[45] In the United States, despite the more advanced stage of electronic technology, there is no clear direction established regarding this critical issue. However, the trend is alarming. The profit motives have led cable systems and media firms to attempt in gaining control over the electronic distribution system as well as its content. Without public policy and regulation, the quality and extent of information to be delivered will fall under control of the delivery systems and clearly lead to the loss of freedom of information as well as the reduction in sources of information.

The crucial question that arises is how to provide a system of information where the providers as well as the receivers of information and entertainment would have an equal opportunity of access to the distribution system. Simply put, how can the monopoly and control of either system be avoided? Monopolizing of the market in either area of delivery or content by giant conglomerates would lead to a de facto control of information. There must be a framework established by a public policy that, first, separates the content technology from that of distribution and second, provides for diversification in both areas in a manner so that at no time either the content or delivery would be controlled or even influenced by giant market forces or public institutions.

In the United States the control of information has reached an alarming and seriously critical stage. On the one hand, Congress has given complete control of broadcasting to radio and television systems. The station managers decide what the public would hear or see through their facilities. Consumers are provided with no right to intervene. On the other hand, cable companies are trying, by using all political muscle at their disposal, to make sure that the public does not get access to their system. They are driving for deregulation of cable systems, possibly through a federal law, so that cities could not require public access channels from the cable system or prescribe that certain number of channels open to be leased by the outside providers. They want complete control of all channels.[46] This would mean a practical elimination of unprofitable services such as educational programs, library reference services, and news and many other public-interest services. The danger and magnitude of this control by the cable system are better visualized if one considers that their few channels of the current time will multiply to several hundreds in a few years and content will expand enormously, including national and even local newspapers and magazines, books, and a score of other printed information, which is now freely available to anyone. Thus through control of their system the cable companies could block a newspaper's or other publisher's access to the system. The cable system, and not the public, determines what kind of information goes into the channels and to what extent. The cable companies can then effectively restrict public rights to free speech, press, and information.[47]

It is obvious that in order to prevent the occurrence of this terribly suppressive system, there should be a structural regulation by which, on one hand, the distribution system will be accessible to everyone and, on the other, the production of content, be it information or entertainment, be highly diversified and dispersed.

NECESSITY FOR DEMOCRATIZATION OF INFORMATION

By providing a new form of communication system, new organizational structures, new production process, new form of marketing, and new educational system, the new information system tends toward a complete restructuring of individual interactions and their daily functioning. So it is quite dangerous to allow the system to evolve on the basis of profit motives and commercial interests. It can easily be a monstrous means of exploitation. The system must be designed and regulated in a way that no user is exploited and everyone has an equal opportunity of access to information and to realization of its benefits and at the same time everyone shares the costs of operating the system to the extent of the benefits received. However, certain services of important social benefits such as education and health care must be made available to all, without economic burden.

NOTES

1. Alfred R. Berkeley, "Millionaire Machine," *Datamation* 27 (August 1981), pp. 21–22.
2. Daniel Bell, *The Coming of Post-Industrial Society* (New York: Basic Books, 1973), preface.
3. *Datamation* 27 (January 1981), p. 14.
4. For examples, see Fritz Machlup, *The Production and Distribution of Knowledge* (Princeton, New Jersey: Princeton University Press, 1962), p. 14.
5. NATO, *Advanced Study Institute on Perspectives in Information Science* (Leyden: Noordhoff, 1975), p. 14.
6. A. P. Garvin, *How to Win with Information or Lose Without It* (Washington, D.C.: Bermont Books, 1980), p. 60.
7. Susan Artandi, "Man, Information and Society: New Patterns of Interaction," *Journal of American Society for Information Science* 30 (January 1979), p. 16.
8. R. K. Ackoff, "Management Information Systems," *Management Science*, 14 (1967), p. B147-B156.

9. Marc Uri Parat, *The Information Economy* (Washington, D.C.: Government Printing Office, 1977), p. 172.
10. Ibid., p.1.
11. For more detail, see Fritz Machlup, "Sciences of Information: Looking Over the Fences," in *The Information Community: An Alliance for Progress: Proceedings of the 44th Annual Conference of the American Society for Information Science* (Washington, D.C.: ASIS, 1981), p. 6.
12. Forest Woody Harton, "The Paperwork Reduction Act of 1980—Reality at Last," *Information and Records Management* 15 (April 1981), p. 10.
13. See, for example, Michael Korek and Ray Olszewski, "Telecom: The Winds of Change," *Datamation* 27 (May 1981), p. 160.
14. See, for example, Information Industry Association, *The Business of Information Report* (Washington, D.C.: Information Industry Association, 1981), p. 29.
15. For tremendous growth regarding personal computers see Everett T. Meserve, "A History of Rabbits," *Datamation* 29 (September 1981), p. 190.
16. Rita Lombarco, "AIM Looks at NICE V," *Information and Records Management* 15 (June 1981), p. 35.
17. The White House Conference on Library and Information Services, Washington, D.C., 1979. *Information for the 1980s* (Washington, D.C.: Government Printing Office, 1980), p. 21.
18. "Informatics and Society," *UNESCO Journal of Information Science, Librarianship and Archive Administration* 2 (January-February 1980), p. 3.
19. Harry D. Huskey, "Computer Technology," *Annual Review of Information Science and Technology* 5 (1970), p. 73.
20. John W. Mauchly and J. Presper Eckert jointly invented and built this prototype.
21. Saul Rosen, "Electronic Computers: A Historical Survey," *Computing Surveys* 1 (March 1969), pp. 7–36.
22. William Davis and Allison McCormack, *The Information Age* (Reading, Massachusetts: Addison-Wesley, 1979), pp. 67–70.
23. Martin O. Holoien, *Computers and Their Societal Impact* (New York: Wiley, 1977), pp. 14–47.
24. Mark D. Zimmerman, "Japan Throws Down the Computer Gauntlet," *Machine Design* 54 (February 1982), pp. 22–24.
25. Carver Mead and Lynn Conway, *Introduction to VLSI Systems* (Reading, Massachusetts: Addison-Wesley, 1980), preface, p. v.
26. James Martin, *Design of Man-Computer Dialogues,* (Englewood Cliffs, New Jersey: Prentice Hall, 1973), pp. 3–7.
27. Frederick W. Miller, "CRT Terminals Get Smarter, Cheaper," *Infosystems* 28 (September 1981), pp. 101–106.
28. Williams, "Information Technology," p. 114.
29. T. A. Dolota, *Data Processing in 1980–1985* (New York: Wiley, 1986), p. 34.
30. Burt Nanus, "Restructuring the Information Ecology," *National Forum* 53, no. 3 (Summer), p. 17.
31. Ibid.
32. Burt Nanus, "Restructuring the Information Ecology," *National Forum* 63, no. 3 (Summer 1983), p. 18.
33. For example, the PLATO system, which has been developed jointy by the University of Illinois and Control Data Corporation.

34. Suzanne Wetlanfer, "Thinking Computers No Longer Science Fiction," *Wisconsin State Journal,* January 19, 1986, sec. 5, p. 1.
35. Philip Cooper, Chairman of Palladian Software, Inc., *ibid.*
36. Ibid.
37. Manuel Scheffres, "Compact Discs Now the Hottest Sound in Town," *U.S. News and World Report,* June 17, 1985, pp. 62–63.
38. The price of a CD player has been reduced from around $1,000 in 1983 to under $150 at the present. The price of a disc with up to seventy-two minutes of playing time, which cost over eighteen dollars originally has been reduced to thirteen dollars.
39. "Quantum Leaps: The Video Revolution," *U.S. News and World Report,* June 17, 1985, p. 63.
40. Eugene Garfield, "Document-Delivery Systems in the Information Age," *National Forum* 63, no. 3 (Summer 1983), pp. 8–10.
41. Commercial document-delivery systems are now being developed such as the Institute for Scientific Information's Original Article Text Service (OATS), which can be ordered through DIALOG's DIALORDER service or the ISI Search Network, et cetera.
42. An example is the Prestel system, commercially available from British post offices since 1979.
43. One example is the proposal by the Commission of European Communities. It combines library systems with electronic document delivery. It is called Automatic Retrieval of Text from Europe's Multinational Information Service (ARTEMIS). It proposes the use of magnetic tape to store the full text of documents and then transmits them through telephone wires to computers at designated centers where the text would either be printed electronically or relayed directly to the consumer. Article Procurement with On Line Ordering (APOLO) is another project proposed by the European Space Agency. Here documents that are located through the bibilographic databases available by Direct Information Access Network for Europe (EURONET/DIANE) could be ordered through its telephone network. These documents are to be transmitted via satellite systems of the agency to printing centers. Another project proposed by a group of publishers is Article Delivery Over Network Information Service (ADONIS), where journal articles would be stored on video disks. The computer would locate the requested article and produce an original copy and mail to the requester. It would also be able to transmit documents on line or by satellite to the printing center closest to the requester.
44. John Wicklein, "How to Guarantee Diversity in the New Communications," *National Forum* 53, no.3 (Summer 1983), pp. 14–16.
45. Ibid.
46. Lynn E. Brown, "High Technology and Business Services," *New England Economic Review,* July-August 1983, pp. 5–17, p. 6.
47. Ibid., p. 8.

Chapter Three

Uses of Information and Its Societal Impacts

ON-LINE DATA-BASE SERVICE

On-line data-base service consists of searching computer-stored and computer-readable data at a distant terminal. Computer-stored data are referred to as data base, which is collected information relating to specific topics in health, economics, scientific matters, and information of general interest, indexes, bibliographies, and so on.

In on-line data-base service the user makes contact with the desired data-base computer through a telecommunications network. By using a designated query language he is able to make contact and search for and retrieve relevant information. It has taken nearly two decades to develop the on-line data-base service. Several technological achievements were needed to make on-line data-base service conveniently and appealingly possible. Of course the first technology needed was data bases; this simply means storage of computer-readable sets of information. Other technological developments consisted of low-cost but powerful computers, low-cost, high-capacity disk-storage instruments, fast and reliable computer terminals, and low-cost communication means for linking the user to the data-base sources.

Of course, the usability of the information system depends on the extent of availability of information sources or data bases, accessible through on-line systems. Progress in this area has been very promising. Between 1980 and 1985 the number of data bases in the United States have increased fivefold from 450 to over 2,200 served through more than 250 on-line systems.[1]

The number of data bases is expected to approach four

thousand by the end of 1990.² At present there are several major forms of data base. *Reference data base* refers the user to the source of information sought. *Bibliographic data base* refers the user to a document. *Full-text data base* contains records of the complete text of the item sought.

The advance of microcomputers, hard disks, and other storage devices has facilitated the transformation of libraries to electronic service systems. It has made libraries able to receive information from outside data bases, store and index them, and thus build their own data bases. This is known as the *downloading* process. Yet use of full power of the microcomputer is open to a great deal of innovation by those who produce and distribute information, those who use on-line services, those who produce computer programs, and other information professionals.

All these phenomenal developments in the advancement of microcomputers are due to developments in speed and the capacity of semiconductors in the form of microchips. This capacity is measured by RAMs (random-access memories), which can store thousands of bits of data on a single chip.

There are two principal kinds of semiconductor memories, *volatile* and *nonvolatile*. Dynamic RAMs (d-RAMs) are the most favored. They fall into the volatile category. This kind of memory loses its data unless constantly refreshed by electrical inputs. The term *dynamic* points out the fact that the memory, in order to be prevented from vanishing, must constantly be charged with microelectric pulses. *Random-access* indicates the ability to reach each memory cell at will.³

It seems that ideally every user would prefer nonvolatile memory. It needs to be noticed that nonvolatile memories cost considerably more and often do not permit immediate data revision. Therefore, it is used more extensively where there is no need to alter the inscribed data such as in electronic games and certain consumer products.

Dynamic RAMs, despite their volatile nature, are the most widely used of all memories. Not only are they much cheaper, but they allow the advantage of immediate erasing of stored data and replacing it with new information. They are also favored because they have the highest storage density, lowest power consumption, and fastest speed. They are also small in size and low in price, with ever increasing storage capacity.

The most popular d-RAMs in the late 1970s and early 1980s were 64K. One K refers, roughly, to a thousand storage cells. About 1970 Intelligent Corporation introduced its 1K d-RAM chip, which contained 1,024 cells. Today 256K is on the market with over 256,000 memory cells in each tiny chip.[4] Each of these cells consists of a storage transistor, or capacitor, that holds the tiny electrical charge and a switch transistor that lets the charge in and out. There are some six hundred thousand active devices in a 256K, in a silver silicon the size of about one-sixteenth of a square inch. Efforts are being made to advance the chip storage density to 1 million. It is likely that this will be achieved in a few years. Obviously an increase in chip storage capacity broadens memory applications, which in turn helps to increase the memory capacity and usability of the microcomputer. A single 256K chip, for example, has the capacity to store ten thousand telephone numbers or fifty-two hundred words. At the same time, increased memory capacity multiplies the sharpness of pictures and graphics and provides for faster access to stored data and better retrievment of information. 256K also offers other unique features such as the "nibble" and "ripple" modes. These are ways of retrieving data in bigger dips than one bit at a time. Furthermore, the chip will enable manufacturers to build cheaper, more reliable, and more powerful computers and a variety of other electronic devices.[5]

The most recent and somehow revolutionary development has been a chip that contains no individual transistors or data storage cells. Instead, one of the material layers in the chip serves as a depository of tiny charges put there from above by microscopic electron guns firing beams of electrons.[6] As its inventor explains, a beam drives a "nail" into the target, then the nail is removed except for its tip and the structure relaxes back to where it was before. The nail tips become data bits that can be detected by the electron beams.

Since no transistors or cells are needed to store the charges, the capacity of this kind of chip is limited only by the smallest number of electrons that can be detected in a stored charge.[7] The relevant initial devices, now under development, are being designed to store over 4 million bits of data—sixteen times as many as the 256K. The designed chip has other advantages besides its huge storage capacity. Unlike d-RAMs, it won't lose its data when the electricity is cut off. It provides incredibly fast access to data—5 million times faster than the present disk memories. Therefore, these new chips could eventually replace not only d-RAMs but also disk memories, greatly improving the functioning of a variety of electronic devices.

The inventor even foresees the future chips, based on the same concept, as having the storage potential of four hundred megabits (400 million bits).

Several other firms are trying to develop a conventional one-megabit d-RAM, which is not expected to materialize for a few years.

Alton O. Christensen, the inventor of the electron chip, is not, however, the inventor of the basic idea. The notion of storing charges by means of electron beams, emitted by a big vacuum tube serving as an electron gun, grew out of research at MIT's Lincoln Lab in the late 1960s. Some Lincoln scientists formed a company, Microbit. The purpose was to develop a memory device based on the vacuum-tube technology. It came to naught. General Electric also worked along similar lines without results.

Christensen carefully studied these failures and decided that the only way to make such a memory economical would be to use semiconductor technology. After two years he succeeded in microminiaturizing the electron guns. Now hundreds of microguns can be embedded in a silicon chip. These microguns, tiny, inverted pyramids etched in silicon, have been tested successfully, and a demonstration of the complete device may come soon.[8] The company expects volume production of the four-megabit RAM to start soon.

Despite over some two thousand data bases in the commercial market, providing specialized information on a wide variety of subjects, the industry is still in the stage of infancy.[9] No doubt the industry will continue to grow quite rapidly. Supportive of this prediction is the revolution in microelectronics, which continues to make the cost of purchasing computers and receiving computerized information more and more affordable. At the same time, the increasing power and speed of microcomputers along with rapidly developing possibilities of designing sophisticated programs and the need of business, professional, and educational organizations tend to encourage and accelerate the use of computers.

Data bases are capable of providing specialized information with an unimaginable speed. Because of the speed, depth, and breadth of information contained in them and the ability to match and reorganize information, data bases have become extremely helpful and, in many instances, indispensible to professional individuals and organizations. Data bases and other electronic libraries have a powerful and compact filing system in which they can index and code every individual word for cross-reference use. For an inquiry regarding a term the computer can give the user all articles on the subject and relevant cross-references. However, in each inquiry the user must be aware that the word he uses might appear thousands of times in a single data base. The user must learn to specify the question in order to avoid being overwhelmed with data irrelevant to his purpose.

Some data bases don't deal with words but provide statistics, often in the form of tables, charts, and figures, and some go beyond presentation of statistics and provide for expert interpretation of the data aimed at assisting institutions in forecasting the future.

Currently two major problems stand in the way of consumerization of electronic information. They are the cost of electronic data and the ease of obtaining it. The videotex might be one answer. It is an interactive transmission that provides data retrievable in a slower but cheaper and less complicated method. However, it may take a few years until it takes a broad commercial form.

DATA BASES IN EUROPE

Study of data bases in England, France, West Germany, and Italy shows that there are differences between these countries regarding the availability, accessibility, and distribution of data bases.

Data bases owned or administered by the government tend not to be free anymore but offered and sold close to the market prices. At the same time, a growing number of privately owned firms offer data bases, mostly compiled through the use of public sector sources. However, these firms are finding it hard to compete with the lower prices tendered by the public sector.[10] Government market prices undercut those that a private sector would likely charge because the former have, economically, the advantages of the hidden subsidy element.

In England most of the public sector producing data bases provide free access to data stored on magnetic tapes. These are placed at the disposal of private data-base producers with no charge for the information. There is, however, a charge for cost of the tapes. Costs are higher to the users since royalties have to be paid to the public producer of data.[11] Currently, these private data-base producers provide data bases in a variety of areas, such as balance of payments, employment and earnings, financial statistics, index of production and cyclical indicators, main economic series, national accounts, prices (retail and wholesale), and production accounts. However, other host computer data-base producers who purchase information from this original private contractor can repackage the data into an already existing data-base for in-house use or on-line external sale for profit. Thus the great advantage of the British system is that any person or firm desiring to make use of publicly produced data, for private or commercial purposes, has free access to information as long as the required royalty fee is paid.

The public sector in France has invested very heavily in information technology and services either as full or part owner of data-base firms or through granting of large subsidies. A substantial part of the publicly accessible data bases are produced by the public sector.[12]

The French Central Statistics Office, INSEE, is a leader in Europe in relation to the creation of data bases on French socioeconomic information. While the British Central Statistics Office is primarily concerned with serving the government agencies, INSEE tends toward a balance between serving public and private sectors.

Currently the service of data bases for private users, which are organized and run by private or public hosts and data-base constructors, are made accessible on a strictly commercial basis.

In West Germany the first electronic data-base plan was launched some twenty years ago by the government. Currently public agencies have a monopoly on information. This has left very little room for the private sector to act. It is virtually excluded from using any data produced by the public sector for the purpose of data base construction or acting as host for public data bases. Furthermore, on-line services offered to the users carry price tags that no private firm can beneficially compete with.

A number of public on-line vendors, besides offering German publicly owned data bases, also host some major European and American data bases.[13]

In Italy there is no crystallized public information policy. However, a great sum of money is directly or indirectly invested in supporting several public or semipublic firms.[14] They provide for a variety of information services, including commercial, financial and fiscal, demographic, legal, directory, and a variety of statistics.

ELECTRONIC PUBLISHING AND INFORMATION DISTRIBUTION

Electronic publishing is done through the application of computers and other electronic devices. Such publication is, at the present, in electronic devices such as magnetic tape or disc, optical disk, or microchip. The spread of its current and future influence is paramount.

Currently computers are used for photocomposition, which permits printing on paper without the conventional and slow process of typesetting. This electronic process has been most helpful in printing indices, abstracts, and indexes by virtue of their enormous size and high costs. Besides print-on-paper, the machine-readable data bases used in the publication process are also available on magnetic type for a variety of applications.[15]

Also emerging are completely new publications exclusively in electronic form, consisting of data collection as well as indexing services. Some professional journals are emerging now in pure electronic format, and the trend is to replace the existing print-on-paper publications with electronic type.

Transformation of publications to electronic form allows room for multiplication of information and a variety of combinations. Such developments have caused and will continue to cause the expansion of the type of information service affected by electronic publishing such as Selective Dissemination of Information (SDI)[16] or Document Delivery Service.

Electronic publication has rapidly expanded from those exclusively scientific and technical in nature to the areas of social services, business, and the humanities. Following the increased appeal of the electronic services in academic libraries, the public libraries are now being affected as more and more materials of general interest are becoming electronically available.[17]

As the videotex system advances, various types of electronic publications are available through home or office terminals. Currently these are available in the form of videocassettes or videodisks. However, different types of electronic publications are increasingly available through home computer terminals from different information centers. With the decreasing cost of home computers and increasing access to them, there will likely be a great impetus to the use of electronic publications by the general public. The exciting side is that society is evolving from a communication pattern, primarily based on print-on-paper, to one largely electronic. Economic considerations appear clearly to favor electronic publishing, particularly in that technological progress is likely to continue to reduce the cost of distributing information electronically. The process of transition will further accelerate through the rapid spread of home computer, videotex, videodisk, and other new technologies.

Despite the fact that printed books have aesthetic appeal, easy browsability, and portability and can be randomly selected, they are entirely static in both text and illustrations. Particularly, they cannot be easily reorganized or updated.

Even though most of the existing electronic publications present information originally available on the paper-print form, the future content of the electronic publications will likely be highly dynamic and versatile. With the ever-changing levels and contents of knowledge and information, it will be possible to have immediate access to texts and materials as demanded by the requester. For example, the electronic textbook on a subject will have as many versions as there are users, yet will be recognizable by the individual instructor or student. The textbook used in the beginning and the end of a course may not be the same, due to continuous updates of the related information.

The world of periodicals will be revolutionized by the employment of electronic printing. Packaging and distribution of journal information will see dramatic changes. It will make no sense anymore to subscribe to a specific set of journals. One could subscribe only to information from the contributions accepted by a wide range of electronic data bases. One wonders if, with such access to data bases, electronically printed journals could persist in having a meaningful use or benefit. Instead of having specific books and journals in electronic forms, the libraries will evolve to be computerized data-base centers, providing information as individually requested. Thus they could present countless forms of books on chemistry, physics, and any other subject exactly as requested. They also can provide the requester with a variety of recipes of a specified food.

TECHNOLOGICAL LITERACY

Currently, as it has been explained before, the new communication technology has been developing and rapidly advancing under the labels such as teletext, videotex, viewdata, data base and other devices and processes. With these phenomenal developments, the society is faced with the important question of how these are going to be used and who is going to control them.

If today, through electronic publication and storage, the content of information is controlled by a particular group or institution, then the future of free expression is quite dim. The only hope to avoid this situation is through public awareness of the process and public demand for openness in preparing the content of the information.

To make such a demand possible there is definite need for public education on this subject. The advance in microchips and computer technology as a whole in the past two decades shows its exponential character with ever-accelerating pace. It seems obvious that with the lack of public literacy concerning electronic technology and the lack of advancing this literacy at the same pace as technology develops further, a small group would tend to appropriate it and use it, by employing experts, for individual or group purpose, more likely to the detriment of the public benefit.[18] One needs to be aware that in this age of electronic technology the standards of literacy cannot remain static and must move along and be updated and modified as the old technologies are refined and new technologies are discovered.

One also needs to notice that in order to illuminate a society, the real aim of publication is dissemination of ideas, thoughts, and information. It needs to be pointed out that this medium is not the message per se. The medium only conveys or displays the message. The message is the substance, the content, to be conveyed or displayed. It consists of the ideas, thoughts, knowledge, information, story, and so on. It is the work of a writer, inventor, innovator, producer, painter, or photographer. The crucial question is as to how this content is processed and how the pieces of knowledge or information are put together, molded or remolded, stored, and finally placed in the public domain. In general, the content is quite independent of the process and the format that is the manner of display. Until now the media have been books, magazines, newspapers, and so on. Despite the rapid development of electronic technology, the paper medium has still remained predominant. However, our society is moving toward an all-out electronic information system with an incredible and uncontrollable speed.[19]

The number of personal desktop computers has increased from 1.5 million in 1981 to over 18 million in 1986. Nearly one-fourth of these are in homes. With the ever rapidly decreasing price of a decent programmable computer and its availability at discount stores and rapidly increasing exposure of the younger generation to electronic media, primarily through video games and then required computer education in many schools (middle schools as well as high schools), promises the very fast multiplication of desktop computers. Today having a home computer is not a fad but a trend toward its permanent and dominant place among home facilities. In the near future, most likely by the end of the century, it will be as indispensible in most homes as a refrigerator.

It is already a known fact that the use of desktop computers in business, public offices, libraries, and schools has been growing rapidly. Today many millions of employees work daily with video display terminals as clerks in tens of thousands of firms, as executives, experts, analysts, and reporters, not counting the rapid development of these computers in educational institutions by students as well as scholars. Enhancing this trend toward acquiring home computers are processes that are developing to bring home related information that was not available before. For example, Compu-Serve Information Service as well as the Source Telecomputing firm are now offering selected parts from newspapers such as the *New York Times, Los Angeles Times,* and other publications through computer to home and office terminals.[20] Publishing companies are following the same trend by producing electronic software that offers far more than a book could on the same subject.[21] These are usually in the form of videotex or interactive videodisk.

It seems quite obvious that a short time from now, the vast array of services provided by these companies would find it necessary to provide home terminal access.

There are high motivations in rapidly increasing interest in electronic publishing. There has been a substantial increase in the fixed cost of conventional publications, the price of paper in particular.[22] Added to this is the cost and complexity of the physical distribution of printed materials.

This upward spiral of cost trend is in contrast with the dramatically decreasing cost of electronically stored information. The rate of this decline is incredible.[23]

The magnitude of this change from printed to electronic storage becomes evident with the facts that by 1990 it is expected that all major and medium-sized industries and educational information institutions and a substantial number of governmental offices will have one computer terminal for every two employees in addition to many millions of home terminals. The wide variety of services unavailable today that could be achieved through this advanced system cannot be foreseen easily, yet it would be phenomenal.

In the computer era of the near future the true test of literacy will tend to be the ability to manipulate the information stored in computer devices, quite similar to the way printed information source materials, such as indexes and reference materials, are manipulated today.

The economic and technological components of the future communication process will tend to come together with the cultural changes necessary for adaptation and widespread use.

COMPUTER-BASED EDUCATON

Historically speaking, human memory and printed materials have been the sources of information and vehicles toward achieving wisdom and knowledge. In the last two decades, the computer and rapidly developing associated programs and data bases have revolutionized the sphere of collecting the dissemination of information. Associated computer programs, when applied to data bases, organize and display information for the acquisition of knowledge by the users. If applied to the educational system, this still rapidly advancing technological achievement is expected to bring about fundamental changes in teaching and other educational processes.

It is important, however, to recognize that this new technological communication system will not change the content of the knowledge available now through the libraries and other sources of knowledge. It will change the manner in which the knowledge is received, stored, processed, and transmitted.

Today universities use mass lectures as the basic educational tool. In a lecture class, the individual student has very little chance, if any, of direct contact or communication with the teacher. Computer-based education (CBE) is capable of producing the opportunity of one-on-one teaching relationships of many centuries ago but in enormous proportion. Computer-based education is actually using computers in teaching students by realizing a mass production of one-on-one educational relationships. Many thousands of students can benefit directly from the knowledge of many teachers in an independent manner.[24] The new information technology is capable of providing an automated individual teacher surrogate for every student. The evolution of microcomputers with increasing capacity and decreasing cost tends to accelerate further this revolution in the educational process.

Computer-based education "uses a computer program to emulate an excellent, extremely patient teacher who is equipped with a very sophisticated blackboard. The program communicates with a student in a conversational dialogue made, employing high resolution, electronic displays of text, numerics, and moving graphics."[25] Videodisc technology developments promise the possibility of integration of picture and sound into the program. Computers that respond to voice commands or to a finger pointed at the screen are no longer the stuff of science fiction and will be available in a few years.[26]

The student will sit at a televisionlike computer set using a keyboard for communication with the program and a printer to reproduce on paper the program materials appearing on the screen. The microcomputer will execute the desired educational programs stored on a magnetic disk device or yet on a better and more sophisticated medium, not yet visualized today.

More important, as communication technology advances further, the student will be capable of connecting the terminal to remote centers of information where vast and various course materials are stored under individual course programs, with the technical possibility of combining two or more programs together or to supplement them with further information, annotations, or explanations as desired by the student.

Incidentally, it must be noted that the term student in the future information society would have a much broader meaning than it embodies today. The process of search, research, and progress will be a lifelong and continuous one, embracing every working person and most nonworking individuals. The educational system will be nothing similar to what we have today. Except for the primary levels, education and work will be incorporated into one system, giving education a lifelong continuity as part of the work process.

The advanced educational system will require the student to participate actively in the learning process by performing immediate calculations, answering questions or responding and interacting by new means not practical today, but at the threshold of creation and innovation. The advanced interaction between the student and the computer system will reinforce and facilitate the learning of presented materials while allowing the student to progress at the desired pace.

Operation of a computer-based educational system will require contact with a human character. However, the role of the teacher will be more that of manager-consultant. Non–computer-expert faculty members will be necessary for updating and revising the automated programs and for creating new ones.

Computer-based education may not substantially alter the demand for faculty members but will definitely change their instructional role and functions. This type of educational system not only increases the instructional quality and productivity of students, but also those of the faculty. The instructor will be able to manage the instruction of more students with much less effort. The computer will be doing the bulk of teaching, testing, and grading. However, the instructor will devote more time to other academic pursuits, such as research, writing, and producing or revising of instructional materials.

For the faculty members involved in teaching acquiring a certain amount of technical knowledge will be a necessity. Currently many faculty members, affected by technophobia, are not favorable to technology-based instruction methods. However, the increasing use of the computer method, as all other technologies, will gradually lessen this reluctancy to join the trend, as a result of pure necessity if not any other cause. Despite all the fears of the new machine, understanding and use of computers for instructional purpose do not require acquiring computer technical knowledge. With easy-to-use manuals and disks, a person of average intelligence can become quite well acquainted with the use of computers in a matter of a few weeks.

For a more complex use of the computer, such as text-and-graphics-editing programs at the current technological level, competency can be acquired within some 200–240 hours of structural training and practice.[27] Some of the required skills are those of communicating with a computer, programming in a computer language, and operating an editing-utility program somehow similar to that used with a word processor. With rapidly improving technology of the use of necessary hardware and software, using electronic materials by the computer nonprofessionals will become much easier.

Computer-based education is increasingly being used in training programs of business and industry.[28] It requires that universities should start a systematic plan for installing and developing computer-based education programs. With great interest of business and industry in using the system, the universities must plan to graduate students in a variety of disciplines who will be familiar with the system and its use.

For these and other direct educational reasons it seems absolutely certain that universities will increasingly and rapidly install and employ computer-based education in their educational processes. Effective and efficient education as the product of the system will oblige the universities and faculties to accept and adopt it.

Ultimately the use of the program will descend to secondary and elementary school levels and computer-based education will embrace the total system of education.[29]

THE SOCIETAL EFFECT OF INFORMATION AVAILABILITY

It is claimed that six thousand to seven thousand scientific articles are written each day and that scientific and technical information increases 13 percent each year.[30] It was estimated in 1982 that in three years the total volume of information would have multiplied four to seven times its 1982 base.[31] Today this mass-produced information and the knowledge derived from it are of inestimable value and a driving force in modern society's socioeconomic and political development.

It is also pointed out that while in 1900 only about 3.7 million in the United States were employed in the information sector, in contrast to agriculture, industry, and service, by 1980 this figure had increased to 44.6 million. As the percentage of the work force, this represented 47 percent in 1980 against 12.8 percent in 1900.[32]

It is astonishing to notice that it took a little over a century for Western societies to move from an agrarian society to an industrial one, while it has taken only a little more than three decades to evolve from an industrial society into the information society. Today in the United States nearly 50 percent of the Gross National Product is derived from information-related activities.[33] It is not, therefore, surprising that there is a growing tension in how this already enormous and yet rapidly growing resource should be viewed and managed and as to how public interest will be protected and individual rights and democracy will be preserved.

For more than a decade there has been a growing debate on whether information should be considered as a commodity to be purchased from and sold in the market or whether it should be regarded as a public service accessible by all members of society. Obviously, the private business sector, expecting profits, considers information as a commodity in the marketplace while others, particularly those in the public sector, view information, at least a good part of it, as public service beneficial to all and thus subject to no economic burdens.

Needless to say, certain classes of information are of a private and personal nature and thus may rightfully remain under possession of the individual or institution having access to it. For example, a new industrial or managerial process may be regarded as a private property. However, one needs to consider that information has a value that transcends pure economic worth. There is no clear-cut understanding of the borderline between private and public ownership. Neither is there any process or regulation established to determine the interest of private and public sectors regarding to rights to information.

It has been pointed out that as those who create or manipulate information become aware of its market value and profitability, grounds for conflict arise.[34] Some 160 years ago, the public nature of information was expressed by James Madison through his statement: "People who mean to be their own Governors must arm themsleves with power which knowledge gives."[35] Today, more likely than ever, people believe that "the free exchange of ideas, the preservation of contrasting points of view and intellectual freedom itself, are best protected through the public sector provision of information."[36]

It is quite clear that a free democratic society depends on a fully informed citizenry. To achieve this end, all citizens must have access to information that is timely, reliable, and objective, and thus no citizen should be restricted from access to information by monetary impositions.

These views were clearly voiced in the White House Conference on Library and Information Services that convened in November of 1979, which proposed that a national information policy that would "guarantee all citizens equal and full access to publicly funded library and information services needs to be established."[37]

In 1981 the American Library Association stated that a democratic government has an obligation to make available to its citizens the results of its actions, including its information-collecting activities and its research and development efforts.

The association recommended to Congress that in the development of information dissemination policies and procedures, it should establish the principle of free and equal public access to the data collected, compiled, produced, and published in any format by the government of the United States.[38]

In contrast to these tendencies toward achieving freedom of information, the private sectors consider any information produced by private capital and effort private property and thus marketable on the basis of supply and demand. Based on the U.S. Constitution and the country's capitalistic tradition, this claim appears to be sustainable. However, the private sector is not satisfied unless the government stops producing and disseminating information that can be produced by the private sector. This tendency is, of course, open to argument and is objected to by the formerly stated institutions and many others.

These individuals and institutions do not regard most information as a commodity in the marketplace. The U.S. Congress, seemingly following this line of thought, has consistently required many federal agencies to disseminate information to citizens. Today a vast and broad range of information is disseminated by government agencies to the public, most of it free of charge and the rest for a nominal charge.

It has been pointed out that the reason government often does not charge for its information services is that it considers them as serving an important societal interest and, furthermore, because the recipients are taxpayers who have already paid once for its preparation and dissemination.[39]

In 1982 a task force of the National Commission on Libraries and Information Science (NCLIS) conducted a comprehensive study regarding the public and private aspects of information. After studying the views from both sides, the task force recognized that there is an increasing awareness of information as something of economic value, as a commodity, as a tool for better management of tangible resources, and as an economic resource in and of itself. However, it pointed out that information is essential in order to achieve democracy and that the government should take a leadership role in creating a framework that would facilitate the development and faster use of information products and services.[40]

While in certain areas that government provides and disseminates information, it cannot be fruitfully argued in favor of the private sector, there are areas where no dividing line between the public and private nature of the information is evident. This situation arises when there is an interdependency between the two sectors because of funding, contribution, and increasing economic complexity in providing information. It has been pointed out that the boundaries are becoming less and less clear and one can no longer distinguish between the public and private sector. Government and private institutions have become interdependent in information production through government contracts and grants, advisory bodies, information sharing and repackaging, and the widespread use of information technologies.[41] Therefore, it beomes unrealistic to consider some suggestions made to the effect that the private sector keep information as a marketable commodity and sell it for profit and public agencies, which are funded by the government, provide for and disseminate information to the general public they are ready to serve.[42]

It is clear that the continuing controversy between the public and private sectors revolves around perceived economic value of information. However, it seems logical and, for the purpose of democracy, essential that information affecting the public welfare and social justice ought to be provided for and disseminated free of charge. This necessarily would fall within the responsibilities of the public sector.

In supporting this view it seems appropriate to cite the basic principle sustained by the majority and summed up as follows regarding information services rendered by the National Library of Medicine. It is "that scientific information about health is a national resource for the public good. The Federal Government supports biomedical research not to satisfy the intellectual curiosity of scientists but to develop new knowledge that ultimately can be applied to health care. The publication and dissemination of this knowledge should be considered an extension of the research process.[43]

ECONOMIC AND SOCIAL USES AND BENEFITS

There are a variety of socioeconomic benefits to be gained as a result of advances of electronic information and communication technology. Among these are the coordination of socioeconomic activities, reorganization of the industrial operation, unification of service systems and substantial progress in infrastructure. However, the most profound and significant benefits relate to sociocultural aspects.

Commercial firms are already experimenting with computers to help them sell everything from paint and hair coloring to shoes and eyeglasses. Mass retailers, facing their toughest competitive environment in years, are discovering a new and incredible sales instrument, the computer. Major chains have already hired full-time experts to search for ways to sell with computers. In the process, these mass retailers have added another term to the computer vocabulary, namely *transactional terminals*. It refers to computer screens that help close a business transaction as opposed to those that simply provide information. An explosion of computerized merchandising in retail stores will occur as soon as new technology becomes affordable. It is the way of the future, and by one estimate there will be fifty thousand transactional terminals working in the marketplace by 1990.[44]

Given current population trends, retail sales are expected to grow at an excruciatingly slow pace in the next several years. According to Marketing Science Institute's study, the average retail sales growth through 1990 will be only 2.3 percent per year.[45] Furthermore, the marketplace has been flooded with new players, including "off-price" merchants and specialty stores selling clothing and toys, as well as electronic products. One management consulting firm calculates that there is 50 percent more retail selling space in the United States than is actually needed.[46] That means that to survive merchants will have to steal customers from their competitors. Computers may come in handy. For example, one cosmetics firm has taken its electronic make up system to large stores in several major cities. The high-tech machinery has drawn far more new customers into the stores than typical promotions. The new electronic system overcomes the reluctance of many women to have their faces made over in the store. The work is electronically done on an image of the customer's face projected on the computer screen. On a split screen the customer can compare four different suggested make up treatments at one time. The system currently costs about forty thousand dollars.[47]

Another example is a computer Magic Mirror that produces a full-body image of a person standing in front of it. First, the reflection of the customer's face appears on the mirror. From the neck down the computer takes over, shaping a figure that conforms to that of the customer and on which it projects any number of outfits the customer desires to see.[48] The customer can try on as many as ten different outfits in a time limit of one minute. Presently, after seeing several images, the customer narrows down her choices to one or two, which she then tries on in the conventional manner. In the future, after consumers have developed confidence on computer projections, they may not deem it necessary to actually try on the outfit. This is the time that the computer order sales will flourish. Consumers can examine the outfits on the images projected in the screens of their home terminal, make selections, and order and pay for the merchandise without the necessity of leaving their family room. But such developments, though very possible, are years away. One recent experiment with this system showed an increase in sales of 700 percent.[49]

There are many other ways that computers have entered the marketing process. A computer can show a customer a graphic of every new model car put out by a company and let the customer compare any model he is considering with similar cars by other automakers and help the customer decide whether it is better to finance the purchase or pay cash. A paint company can use a computer that measures the light frequencies of a color sample and concoct a formula that allows a dealer to mix paint to match it exactly. For a selection of eyeglasses from among several thousand styles a computer, after receiving a customer's facial characteristics and favorite colors, is able to narrow down the customer's choice to a relative few that the customer should try on. The use of computers in retail marketing expands to many areas of retail business. Currently the cost is the main element preventing the widespread of its most advanced systems systems in trade. As the costs are reduced, more and more firms will adopt the use of newly developed systems to enhance the sales volume.

In France citizens now bank, shop, read their morning papers, and maintain anonymous friendships through Teletel. This is a national videotex system that has been transforming French business and culture since its introduction in 1981. Videotex is the process of sending and receiving texts and graphics primarily over telephone lines between a central computer and a terminal or personal computer. Videotex is not unique to France, but Teletel, a project created and operated by the French Postes Telephones Telecommunications (PTT), the state-owned monopoly that controls the nation's postal and telephone services, is the world's first successful mass-consumer videotex system.[50]

In a mere five years desire for the videotex has swept France. Currently there are over 2 million in use in households and businesses throughout the country. Each unit is known as Minitel and consists of a keyboard, screen, and modem, an instrument that translates telephone signals into computer-readable graphics. The PTT owns the terminals and issues them free of charge to selected customers and for an eighty-five franc (about twelve-dollar) monthly charge to business customers. For the French government and industry, the sophisticated Minitel network is a profitable enterprise with virtually unlimited growth potential.

Not surprisingly, commercial firms elsewhere are scrambling to follow the French lead in videotex. Several early forays into commercial videotex in the United States have failed. However, major American communication firms are continuing investment on videotex and redesigning the systems.

The greatest success of Minitel has, so far, been among home owners who have been drawn to the system by its most unusual feature, le Kiosque, which is the old name used for the corner newstands usually located at the intersections.

In Paris the modern Kiosque provides more than two hundred separate services that enable consumers to read updated news synopses, browse through paper and magazine headlines, and communicate with other customers, all without leaving their home. Users only pay for the time they spend on le Kiosque. The charge goes to their monthly telephone bill. The service providers keep about 60 percent of the revenue, and the remainder goes to PTT. Services provided through le Kiosque account for more than half of the country's Minitel use.

Many of the services provided through le Kiosque are owned and operated by French newspapers and magazines. Initially, many newspapers voiced concern that Minitel would cut into their readership. However, it has worked as a publicity device, widening the recognition of the newspapers and increasing circulation. With its twenty-four-hour operation le Kiosque has also proved to be complementary to the newspapers' conventional print operation. This occurs especially when important news misses the print deadlines. It can readily be made accessible through le Kiosque.

The success of the Minitel has moved the French newspapers to not being content with offerings, ads, games, and news headlines, but going after developing new methods of employing videotex. For example, a discussion program on current issues, led by a well-known expert or celebrity, in which hundreds of individuals could participate simultaneously from their home.[51]

Satellites have become a mainstay of the information revolution, which was triggered when the computer and telecommunication technologies gradually merged into one. They have become vital for long-distance data transmission and broadcasting over large areas.

Currently the U.S. space shuttle is the major means of launching satellites into space. However, the European Space Agency (ESA) has entered the competition. It has produced the Ariane rocket, which has opened up encouragement of commercial prospects for the European Ariane launches, produced and marketed by Arianespace and owned by shareholders from eleven ESA member countries. Arianespace began its commercial career in 1984 by putting an American satellite, the *Spacenet 1,* into orbit. It has booked a total of twenty-four launchings of some thirty satellites to be accomplished by the end of 1998. Over half of Arianespace's customers are non-Europeans, including many American groups.

French firms have dug in among the ranks of the world leaders in new communication technology. They have made their mark in areas such as digital public telephone exchanges, fiber-optic systems that transmit data by laser pulsars through a glass-core cable, and smart cards, now poised to revolutionize the retail banking industry. In a more artistic vein, INA[52] and its industrial partners are developing exciting new uses of computer-generated images (CGI) for television advertising and movie industries.[53]

France has also emerged as Western Europe's leading space power and the pilot of a joint European venture that has produced the Ariane satellite launches, the only significant commercial challenge to the U.S. space shuttle program. By 1995 the French and their European partners hope to send their own space aircraft (code-named Hermes) on its first manned flight around the earth. It is designed to carry up to six astronauts with a 4.5 ton payload. It would be smaller than the U.S. shuttle because heavier payloads would be launched separately by the *Ariane 5*. France is driving for the third position in space, behind the United States and the Soviet Union.

France has already launched the first of four SPOT remote sensing satellites into a polar orbit from the Kourou space center in French Guyana. The SPOT is capable of providing more precise data for cartography and surveys of natural resources and environmental and land use than the U.S. Landsat, its only rival.[54]

A joint French-German direct broadcasting satellite (DBS) project is meanwhile setting the stage for an audiovisual revolution in France, which now has only six national TV channels. TDF, the French public broadcasting authority, has its first DBS satellite operational. It has doubled the supply available to 18 million French households with a total of 22 million TV sets. With agreement on new technical standards, this and its German counterpart should reach 200 to 300 million Europeans, offering programs with sound tracks in the language of their choice.

Television without frontiers is heralding significant change in geographically fragmented Europe, and the information revolution is breaking up old notions about distance and space. For example, Frenchmen are suddenly warming to armchair banking and shopping through the Minitel and smart cards. According to an official report, two-thirds of the French people are now enthusiastic about or interested in computers. The percentage far exceeds that of the United States.

Experts link the trend with a crash program initiated in the 1970s to modernize the French telephone network. This program has led to rapid expansion in the field of high-speed data transmission, including interaction product. As a result, the videotex has expanded far more in France than in the United States or Japan.

French banks and the post offices have agreed on standards for credit cards. The Bull computer group's smart card, tested extensively in several small French, Norwegian, and American cities, has been a success. Home banking, now in an experimental phase, will soon be a reality in France. Using a secret identity code entered on the chip, bearers may make payments from their personal bank accounts through the Minitel, pay for their grocery purchases, and make phone calls from public booths.

Experts in Europe and the United States believe that the French-invented smart card will have a bigger impact than the personal computer. The card is being tested by some American credit card groups.

However, there already is stiff competition between American, Japanese, and European firms regarding all segments of the telecommunication market. French companies are also pushing the advancement of the art of computer-generated images (CGI). They are trying to develop high-quality but cheaper three-dimensional (3D) CGI for the television, advertising, and movie industries.

Interactive videotex, as a fantastic educational device, is attracting more attention. Efforts are being made to establish the world's first computerized data bank for radio and television broadcasting. This audiovisual medium now covers between 350,000 and 400,000 hours of French language programs, and sales of digital copies to several American TV networks is now a possibility.[55]

PROSPECTS AND POSSIBILITIES DURING THE NEXT DECADE

The integration of digital technology has caused the unification of transmission and contents of information systems. On a nationwide electronic information network digital integration will make available a wide range of activities to be coordinated irrespective of distance and complexity of required services. The use of on-line computers will vastly extend from their current uses in business and industry to other areas such as education, entertainment, and most important of all, the services related to daily family life and general services. Socioeconomic activities will closely be tied to and associated with the electronic information-communication systems.

Reorganization of the industrial operation based on digital electronic systems appears to be vital in a competitive market system. Even in a monopoly system, adherence to this technology will be a requirement. Automated production will go far beyond the current stage, which is primarily concerned with the mechanical production process, to include management and supervision and individual services to the workers while at the workplace. An electronic workers' grievance resolution process will be possible in which the workers' grievances will be received by the grievance computer terminal, studied, analyzed by detailed and exact consideration of working conditions, and respond back to the workers. The working conditions will be automatically corrected according to the findings of the grievance resolution system.

Of course, to improve productivity a shift to advanced electronic technology will be required in order to minimize the resources and energy inputs and maximize added values. But technology will not be solely concerned with this aspect of production. It will also turn to the workers' well-being at the workplace. High technology will make it possible for reducing the full load of workers far below forty hours per week. This will allow the workers extra hours of leisure time while at the workplace, with creation of entertainment centers, which will nourish the workers mentally and physically and give them ample time for leisurely social acquaintances with one another at the workplace.

Unification of services as a byproduct of digital technologies enables identical processing of data and facilitates communications in various formats. Distinction between services that were once considered separate and different are disappearing; information and communication systems are being molded into one.

Regarding the effect of electronic information-communication technology on cultural development, one only needs to look at the revolution brought about in the entertainment area by the development of audio and video tapes. Historically speaking, each new development in information technology has caused the enhancement of culture in the affected society. The introduction of paper and the invention and development of printing methods were an era of revolution in information technology. The combined information-communication revolution under way as a result of electronic technology is incredibly powerful. Its consequences on cultural development appear to be beyond imagination.

Changes in industrial operation through technological development invariably results in certain workers becoming incompetent within the new system and thrown out of work. The question arises as to how to transfer workers from the old systems into the new ones. What comes to mind first is reeducation. Currently this is a difficult and costly process. The reeducation process also is not appealing to many workers who otherwise would have liked to be reeducated. Computerized training is more likely to facilitate this training process. However, it requires training of the workers to use computers as training media. Such a reeducation process also needs upgrading available data bases, and creation of new ones. Currently information produced each day is far beyond the capability of society to digest it. But the problem is not that too much information is being produced; the sheer volume of production makes it quite difficult to locate the desired information under the current dispersed system. There is need for a centralized and easily accessible information-communication system, where each individual, upon registration of the type of information he needs, can obtain precisely what is desired. Data bases should be developed and upgraded with this concept in mind. The method should provide an easy access to desired information. There should be developed a unified and simplified process of search and screening of data not beyond the understanding and convenient use of common people.

Regarding the fusion of service systems, without appropriate legislation and regulation, users will benefit little from information technology that integrates different types of services. Here we are talking about the choice between monopoly and equal opportunity of access to information. The concept of free competition will not solve the problem, since giant corporations will have market factors to suppress competition by small firms. In a technological capitalist market there is no such thing as free competition. Lions kill and eat their prey, and jackals take care of the leftovers. It is the job of legislation and the state to prescribe the framework for democratization of information-communication systems and enforce it. The government should strive to protect the public nature of the information-communication systems.

From the national scene, liberalization should extend to international information services. One step toward achieving this goal is through legislation. Currently the issue appears complex, but after democratization of information services on a national base, its phenomenal public benefits from all social, economic, political, and cultural viewpoints would induce national democratization within other technological societies. This movement ultimately will result in international coordination, since it would be the cheapest way to extend national information services beyond national capacity. For example, France, instead of creating data bases about many facets of American life, including its technology, can simply retrieve desired information from relevant data bases in the United States. The smaller the nation and its technological resources, foreign resources become more attractive and beneficial through the international coordination of the information system. It may be interesting to notice that developing countries could become the greatest beneficiary of the information-communication systems of the industrialized societies. Countries not being able to establish their own advanced information systems may receive all kinds of desired information by retrieving it from the sources available in developed countries. It appears to be some kind of reversed colonization, which they deserve after centuries of donating their resources to developed countries. By reverse colonization it is meant that new developing nations can freely and cheaply tap the phenomenal technological and other resources of developed countries just by installing in their country the information retrieving systems.

As through colonization in the past, developed countries benefited from the immense resources of developing nations for their own industrialization and economic development, now developing countries can retrieve and use much more immense resources of developed countries for their own social, economic, and political advancement.

As under the old colonization, the developing countries were powerless against the dominant power of the colonizing countries. Now the old colonizing countries will be powerless against the power of developing nations to extract and use vitally valuable information from the developed and democratized information systems of the advanced countries. In the long range, access to this great variety of all valuable information, which has been the result of many years of hard work and spending of phenomenal sums of money by developed countries, may prove to be more valuable to developing countries, compared to the resources lost under colonial exploitations.

The service systems have already become vastly internationalized in certain areas. Today a single satellite can provide communication across one-third of the globe. In the near future, the satellite coordination will make this availability global. Today, with the use of a small dish antenna, an individual receives access to hundreds of international entertainment and information channels. Those who air the program cannot prevent such use. This will even be widened in the near future by advances in satellite as well as antenna systems. A receiving satellite of a developing country can easily retrieve information worldwide for national use without going through building highly costly systems for collecting and producing these services, programs, and information. A fundamentalist Muslim would say this was "Allah's will to make Satan nations work and produce for the benefit of good Muslims." Consider what this would do for socioeconomic, political, and cultural development of usually isolated developing countries.

With all these fascinating expectations, it is a mistake to embark in integration of social and economic systems through information-communication networks without first thinking of the possible negative side effects that it may entail.

Electronic coordination of socioeconomic activities, if improperly managed, could well lead toward a highly controlled and regulated society. This could happen if the operation of the network or networks falls into the control of a specific group, rather than remaining in the public domain. Today business, government, and other private organizations gather and store information about individuals, as well as construct data bases and control their use. It is expanding into vital areas of life concerned with an individual's freedom. For example, if electronic publishing is controlled by a small elite, capitalist or political, the whole area of freedom of press becomes seriously violated. The controlling groups may simply publish what they want people to read or see in audio or video forms. It will end in a tightly controlled and conditioned society.

Therefore, it appears essential that steps be carefully taken so that the system will remain under public control rather than fall into the hands of a group, whether private or public.

A CONCLUDING OVERVIEW

The purpose in this chapter has been an attempt to present a macro-collective overview illustrating some of the important aspects of the information-communication system. Most of these have been the result of employment of electronic devices, particularly the digital system. Operation and use have been presented in a variety of relations such as information resources and data processing systems, information centers and libraries, data bases, information marketing and uses, and the roles of educators, government, and commercial firms. All put together, it presents a telescopic view of computer-based information society.

In some three decades information industry has advanced incredibly and the environment of information processing has reached a very dynamic and dazzling stage. As the system continues to develop, information centers expand and multiply and the volume of electronic information develops incredibly; the fundamental and pressing question of accessibility receives increasing attention. This is a serious question not only under the present state of industry and corresponding systems, but more so in the future, when most, if not all, of the vital information necessary in the daily process of individual as well as community life will be accessible through the electronic information system. This question extends from the domestic and national scene to the international sphere. Currently, despite bilateral and multilateral negotation possibilities, development of international agreements has been quite slow and the systems, in their transborder operation tendencies, have been facing conflicts and innumerable difficulties. So far, the United Nations has served as a forum for presenting disputes and corresponding problems. It has structural facilities to deal with problems arising out of transborder data flow. Most notable of such agencies are the United Nations Educational, Scientific and Cultural Organization (UNESCO) and General Agreement on Tariffs and Trade (GATT).

Developing trends in information technology points to the fact that the newer computers will be distinctly reduced in size, more powerful, faster, and easier to use. The performance of electronic information networks will further improve despite the fact that intersystem connections may continue to be an impediment for a time. Microwave and satellite data communication, which have facilitated long-distance interconnections in recent years, will further expand the sphere of international information-communication systems.

Electronic automation in production industries, business firms, offices, and homes will advance rapidly with the increasing proliferation of information sources and processing means. The integration of word processing, electronic mail, fascimile transmission, computer graphics, and microcomputers have already started a revolutionary process in business, education, and other institutions and will continue to do so.

There is a large scale of capital investment in information and communication technology, particularly in the United States and France. Through these allocations of capital, ingenious concepts are being discovered, crystallized, and developed into tangible products. It has been through these discoveries that the hardware industry, a vital component of information technology, is experiencing increased sophistication despite continuous miniaturization of components. As the computers become smaller and less costly, an increasing number of individuals are capable of owning and operating one. Many small institutions, such as libraries and other information centers, can now effectively turn to electronic automation by using microcomputers.

With rapidly increasing use of microcomputers and multiplying user interest the demand for software has sharply increased and will continue to increase. Many daily institutional routine functions, such as accounting, inventory control, statistical analysis, the mailing process, et cetera, are now available in software form on the market. Ease of use is affecting the consumption of information enormously. The expansion of the market is exponential, and well-designed softwares are nearly guaranteed public acceptance and use.

The importance, value, and effectiveness of information-communication systems heavily depend on the availability of information desired. Consequently, there has been a strong drive for formation of data bases, private as well as public. Through data communication lines these data bases, however remote, can be conveniently reached. Of course, if so desired, materials retrieved by the user can be transformed to printed form.

Accessibility of information is still a problem, but the future appears bright. This is mainly because human factors and problems relate closely to computer literacy. While methods of information processing and data communication are being perfected, user access and the method of access do not receive due attention at the present. More likely, this attitude will change and serious attention will be devoted to user access.

The problem of convenient accessibility becomes more acute when there is enormous societal and methodological information placed in electronic data banks; each day the volume is increasing to the extent that pretty soon data banks will embody most of the information now available in printed forms. The experts in the field claim that the new systems designed and produced are "user friendly." However, many personal computer softwares are considered by the users quite complicated, even incomprehensible. This claim has been definitely valid in regard to systems designed in the seventies and early eighties; however, the problem has not been resolved yet to the satisfaction of nonprofessional users.

Another problem relates to that of cost. A good volume of information in private data banks is not readily available to users of public information centers, such as libraries, because of the cost. It seems that this problem will tend to be more acute as more and more information moves into data banks, out of printed forms, and into the domain of private institutions.

Finally, information concerned with personal and private matters needs to be guarded against unauthorized access. However, this may not include so-called sensitive information under the guise of national security or otherwise. In a democratic society, no such information must be kept from public access. Citizens should be informed totally as to how their government operates.

Currently, introduction of new services and products corresponds to acceptibility of those by users. It also depends on the extent of similar products and services available on the market. The outcome depends on market interaction and the latter on marketing research. This type of marketing research relates mainly to the data collection and analysis of developments in electronic information products and services. Since the services are client-oriented, such market research is intended to assist decision makers on the feasibility of introducing a new product or continuing those already on the market. In a democratic society the content of market research will be quite different, since the customer of the product, or the user of information, will have access to all information regarding all products and services through a single information system, that of the Technodem.

Currently, the management of information resources is also

a very significant issue. The extent of coordination and management of information technologies within an institution, as well as among institutions, determine the extent of productivity. To accomplish high productivity, a variety of relevant information technologies need to be reorganized toward providing for a collective and systematized information service, both in public and private sectors. Currently this may require the establishment of a certain coordination system aimed at encouraging appropriate coordination and preventing unnecessary duplication of services and avoiding conflicting interests. In a democratic information system, however, this will not be a problem, since society will be dealing with one centralized and dispersed electronic system where information and services are automatically and without human interference coordinated, analyzed, and produced according to the specific demand of the user.

The total picture of the democratic information system, the Technodem, is much larger than the sum of its component parts. The system designers look beyond bits and bytes into developing a better interaction and response among hundreds of millions of computers attached to the system, feeding it with new information and retrieving from it information desired, relating to every aspect of life. While the system is under control of no one, yet it is served by thousands of technical experts, innovators, and designers all dedicated to its advancement, betterment, and ultimate perfection. The Technodem holds the key for a societal democratic system, for human knowledge of self, nature, and environment, for human understanding and cooperation, for human material and spiritual well-being, and finally, perhaps more important, for human, societal, and world peace with prosperity.

Before starting the description of structure and functions of the Technodem, we need to look into the efforts and attempts toward democratization of information-communication systems and the future prospects. These are presented in the next chapter.

NOTES

1. Carlos A. Cuadra, "The Microcomputer Link: Online Database Services and Local Electronic Libraries," *National Forum* 63, no. 3 (Summer 1983), pp. 23–24, 32.

2. For information about available data bases see *Directory of Online Databases*.

3. Gene Bylinsky, "Semiconductors: The Next Battle in Memory Chips," *Fortune*, May 16, 1983, pp. 152–55.

4. Ibid., p. 152.

5. Below 100 nanoseconds (billionths of a second) compared with the 150 to 250 nanoseconds required by most 64Ks.

6. "A Cheap-Memory Chaser Pursues the 4,000 K Chip," *Fortune*, May 16, 1983, p. 155.

7. Ibid.

8. Ibid.

9. Gerald Lanson, "Databases," *National Forum* 63 (Summer 1983), p. 20.

10. Luciano Daina, "Public Data Banks in Europe," *European Research* 12 (April 1984), pp. 84–87.

11. One of the important public producers of data bases is the Central Statistics Office (GSO), which has given exclusive rights to distribute GSO data in electronically readable form to users to SIA Computer Services, a British company but a subsidiary of the French CISI group.

12. The French National Research Council along with Pascal has the largest bibliographical data base generally available for use. The main private host firms handling publicly produced data are fully or partially financed by the French government. Among the host firms for official data are G. Carn, GISI, Sligos, and GISI Echo. CISI also markets OECD, CSO, and EEC data bases.

13. For example, the German Institute for Medical Documentation and Information, DIMDI Inka/Fachsinformationszentrum Energie, Physik, Mathematik Gmbh.

14. Among these firms are CERVED, sustained by the Chambers of Commerce and banks, which has acquired monopoly in the business area. It is operated commercially and is by far the most successful. SARIN, with the largest videotex library, provides detailed demographic data and directory services and is aiming to produce a total marketing information service. SIPE Optimation, a host and database constructor, belongs to the state-owned Banca Nazionale del Lavoro; among others, it produces financial and fiscal data bases. ITALGIUR has produced very comprehensive legal information; and ISTAT the Italian National Statistics Office.

15. F. Wilfrid Lancaster, "Electronic Publishing: Its Impact on the Distribution of Information," *National Forum* 63, no. 3 (Summer 1983) pp. 3–5.

16. This is the use of the computer to provide up-to-date knowledge, a service by which the latest bibliographic and other information is contrasted or matched with the individual requester's demands or propositions.

17. Currently these are restricted to indexes to popular magazines, the text of newspapers and magazines, and some general reference materials.

18. Benjamin Compaine, "The Evolution of the 'New Literacy,'" *National Forum* 63, no. 3 (Summer 1983), pp. 10–12.

19. Jack Egan, "Publishing for the Future," *New York Times*, August 16, 1982, p. 10.

20. Benjamin Compaine, "The Evolution of the 'New Literacy,'" *National Forum* 53 (Summer 1983), p. 12.

21. For example, Houghton Mifflin's production of an interactive videodisk

version of Roger Tory Peterson's bird-identification books. There are scores of publishing firms working along this line, such as Times Mirror Company, Knight-Ridder, and CBS, which owns several important publishing firms. Ibid.

22. The price of paper increased by 200 percent between 1970 and 1981 far more than twice the rate of increase for all commodities. Ibid., p. 12.

23. The decline in price has been an average of 25 percent per year for the last three decades and more likely will continue to decline in the next decades.

24. John H. Painter, "Approaching Computer Based Education: How Will the University Respond?," *National Forum* 63, no.3 (Summer 1983), pp. 20–22.

25. Ibid., p. 21.

26. Gerald Larsen, "Databases," *National Forum* 63, no. 3, p. 19.

27. Painter, "Approaching Computer Based Education," p. 22.

28. For example, some airlines, such as United and American, are using the system for pilot-training programs. In personnel training, learning centers of Control Data Corporation, equipped with computer-based education systems, are being used by business firms. Larger industries are using the system for increasing personnel productivity (Ibid., p. 22).

29. For more information on the subject, see Alfred Bork, *Learning with Computers* (Bedford, Massachusetts, 1981 Digital Press, Educational Services, Digital Equipment Corporation).

30. John Naidbitt, *Megatrends: Ten New Directions Transforming Our Lives* (New York: Warner Books, 1982), p. 24.

31. Ibid.

32. Daniel Bell, "The Social Framework of the Information Society," in *The Computer Age: A Twenty-Year View*, eds. Michael L. Dertouzos and Joel Moses (Cambridge, Massachusetts: MIT Press, 1979), pp. 163–211.

33. Kent A. Smith, "Information as a Commodity or Public Good," *National Forum* 63, no. 3 (Summer 1983), p. 27.

34. A. K. Kent, "Scientific and Technical Publishing in the 1980s," in *The Future of the Printed Word: The Impact and the Implications of the New Communications Technology*, ed. Phillip Hills (Wesport, Connecticut: Greenwood Press, 1980), p. 163.

35. James Madison to W. T. Barry, August 4, 1822, *Writings of James Madison*, ed. G. Hunt (New York: G. P. Putnam, 1900–10), p. 87.

36. *Public Services Plan for Public Libraries in Montgomery County, Maryland*, FY 83-88, May 1982, p. 10.

37. *The White House Conference on Library and Information Services*, Washington, D.C., final report, 1979, p. 42.

38. Council of American Library Association, San Francisco, California, *Council Document 71.2*, July 1, 1981.

39. Lawrence S. Robertson and Robert F. Aldrich, "Dissemination of Information," in *Issues in Information Policy*, ed. Helen A. Shaw (Special Publication, National Telecommunication and Information Administration, U.S. Department of Commerce, 1981), pp. 5–18.

40. National Commission on Libraries and Information Science, *Public Sector/Private Sector Interaction in Providing Information Services* (Washington, D.C.: Government Printing Office, 1982).

41. Karen B. Levitan, "The New Information Hybrid," *ASIS Bulletin* 7, no. 4 (April 1982), pp. 25–26.

42. F. M. Blake and E. Perlmutter, "The Rush to Use Fees: Alternative Proposals," *Library Journal* 102, no. 7 (1977), pp. 2005–10.

43. Martin M. Cummings, "Medical Information Services: For Public Good or Private Profit?," *Information Society Journal* 1, no. 3 (1982), pp. 249–60.

44. David Pauly and Carolyn Friday, "Computers Make the Sale," *Newsweek*, September 23, 1985, pp. 46–47.

45. *Newsweek*, September 23, 1985, p. 47.

46. *Newsweek*, September 23, 1985, p. 46.

47. The system is used by and is available through Elizabeth Arden, Inc.

48. The system is being used by L. S. Ayres and Company.

49. The experiment was carried out by L. S. Ayres by putting the entire Liz Claiborne spring collection on the system at three of its stores. The system was leased for $135,000. The Magic Mirror is a French invention and is distributed in the United States. Currently the high price of the system limits its use to very large firms.

50. Nadine Epstein, "Et Voila! Le Minitel," *France Magazine*, nos. 4–5 (Summer 1986), pp. 71 and 75.

51. Ibid., p. 75.

52. Organizations corresponding to abbreviations are as follows: ESA: European Space Agency; CNET: National Telecommunications Research Center; INA: Institute National de la Communications; CNES: National Center for Space Study (France); and DBS: Direct Broadcasting Satellites.

53. Marie Joannidis and Jan Kristiansen, "Telecommunications: Its Irreversible Impact," *France Magazine*, nos. 4–5 (Summer 1986), p. 69.

54. Joannidis and Kirstiansen, "Telecommunications," p. 71.

55. Ibid., p. 72.

Chapter Four

Technology and Democracy

The implications of the advanced information-communication system for democratic societies have largely been overlooked. The issue requires specific attention from the socioeconomic and political standpoints and from the viewpoint of the effects of this rapidly developing technology on industrialized as well as developing societies.

From a political viewpoint, responses to information technology may fall into two categories. One may be called the counterutopian model, where it is felt that the new technology is inevitably dominated or controlled by a small political clique. It forms a power elite that is capable of maneuvering and manipulating mass information and thus mass sentiments and opinions. From this standpoint, any control or domination of the masses by this high-tech electronic media is considered evil and in favor of a totalitarian society.[1]

Thus the key issue is not the quality of hardware or software but rather ownership and control of information and communication systems.

The second view is of those who have been critical of the information-communication systems as another culmination of the imperial capitalist state with monopolization of the means of advanced information and communication technology. The speculation, which is also sustained by Marxists, is that under this system ideas will be managed and manipulated by a small economic elite.

Both sides, whether capitalist or Marxist, are thinking in terms of traditional thoughts and institutions. The bitter differences are in totalitarian implications against economic class domination of a computer-oriented world. But there is serious doubt as to the relevance and persistence of traditional political forms in a society that traditional modes of expression and life have mostly become obsolete.

The assumption under either concept is that no positive political good will evolve from the control of the new information-communication technology.

One area of major concern relates to the printing process, which will substantially be affected by a shift of production from paper print to videotex formats. This has been a matter of grave concern that not only has worried literary and scientific people who worked in the information-communication area but also has occupied the thoughts of political and other leaders of advanced nations. It must be noted that this shift in printing technique does not necessarily mean a decrease in the use of conventionally printed materials, such as books. In fact, surveys of the last two decades show that despite the development of electronic printing, the printing and sales of books have substantially increased.[2]

Despite this fact it is too early to conclude that this trend of the last decade will continue in the future when people will become better acquainted with electronically printed materials and when ways and means for individualized use of such materials are devised and made possible. On the outset, in spite of the facts showing to the contrary, it appears that the use of electronically printed materials will prevail.

Development of electronic information and communication systems within a capitalistic society like the United States would have the potential of seriously hampering democracy unless the following conditions are materialized: (1) the phenomenally increased amount of information through the use of new technology, particularly those affecting democratic norms, is made available to the public at large; (2) encouragement and provision for active participation in vital areas of this new technology (these areas primarily relate to sectors of information having an effect on the maintenance and enhancement of democratic goals and processes from social, economic, political, and cultural viewpoints); (3) the corresponding capacity for confirmation and verification of information; (4) the public rather than privileged nature of electronic information; and (5) restructuring of the information system in a manner to guarantee the materialization of the above stated conditions.

Some discussions about the relationship between the new information technology and democracy perceive recent development in science and technology as favoring elites, manipulating masses, exploiting the poor, and enriching the wealthy. Some others emphasize its positive aspects and counterbalancing effect. However, ultimately it is the manner by which the new information and communication technology is handled that would determine whether it would serve as a promoter and protector of democracy and its ensuing freedoms or would become a harbinger of totalitarianism and suppression.

Compared to the previous forms of communication, modern technology provides for a modular, gridlike pattern of information storage and retrievability, such as those possible by videotext, which allows for a much wider level of choice and decision. These are roughly ten thousand active possibilities available through broadcast teletext at any given time.[3] These may range from a variety of shopping and travel information, movie, concert, and theater programs, and commercial and industrial news to all kinds of library information and educational programs. The videotex, as one of the new forms of interactive communication, allows a higher level of storage, retrieval, and utilization of data to a much larger number of people. The use of videotex permits each individual or firm to have at his or her disposal as many as ten thousand different forms of information. This broadening of the amount of information available through new technology substantially enlarges channels of choice and decision making for individuals, extending them to areas previously available only to the elite and giant firms.

The individualization of information, as well as the collectivization of thoughts, is now possible and probable. The democratization process will require policies that would provide for a competitive information environment. The essential requirement is democratic participation in the information process and not monopolization of the sources of ideas.

One dynamic aspect of modern communication technology is that it encourages active rather than passive public participation. It allows a higher level of interactional involvement. The uses either can confirm or disconfirm exactness of information, test propositions, and even arrive at comparabilities not envisioned by the original source. In general, confirmation refers to consideration of factual rather than interpretive information. The acts of verification and confirmation, which currently is an exceptional event within the domain of specialized elites, will likely become an unavoidable part of the daily life of ordinary individuals.

In the interactive videotext area, the move is toward multiplication of images, which will tend to stimulate a deeper computer involvement. Beyond verification and correction of information, it will allow the capacity to relay information from the user back to various centers and data banks with which he is in communication.

In the political arena, such developments will make it possible for individuals to vote through a decoder-equipped terminal in contact with receiving computer centers. This interaction may be extended to expression of opinions in local council meetings, state assembly and national congressional meetings, and hearings, all through electronic media.

The activities of local councils and courtrooms and other governmental agencies and board meetings of commercial institutions will be received, seen, heard, viewed, and responded to on appropriate occasions by individuals through home or office terminals. One will be able to register almost instantly his personal points of view in relation to matters at issue. These technological developments will encourage and enhance individual participation in many aspects of the societal process, and citizen passivism will gradually transform itself to dynamic activism. The substantive as well as procedural democracy will be enhanced and ultimately attained by the electronic linkage of individuals to private as well as public organizations in the community at regional, national, and international levels.

As a result of the new technology the availability of the signals that individuals are able to transmit by cable or telephone tends to make them eager to have their views expressed on local and national issues. The scope of interactive videotext participation tends to add rather than subtract from the concept of an informed and involved citizenry. Such possibility increases as more home computers become available and used. Not everyone may constantly want to be involved in every aspect of public decision making but its certain possibility is definitely to enhance participation.

The expansion of democracy is not incompatible with diminution in specialization. The new technology, while it offers abundance, facilitates rather than hampers a check on a specialist. Like academic life, which has become increasingly specialized, new developments in information technology tend toward servicing of a highly refined clientele with particular interests. This is being done in a variety of ways, using a plethora of techniques. For those not comfortable with electronic information technology the good news is that hard copy text will surely remain, at least for quite a while, a primary source of ideas and knowledge. In effect, the new electronic technology does not cause a diminution but provides an addition to the potential for the printed materials by offering a definite value-added attribute to the reading of book.

The presence of the television screen in home and office has permitted new linkages to electronic information systems. It is difficult to envision the way people will apportion their time in this new world of technology and how many will be excluded. Fabulously expanded options that the new information technology makes available will cause a new paradigm to evolve relating to the manner by which the individual will decide about apportioning his time to its use. One may reach the assumption that democracy will dissolve under the weight of a large scope of choices and decisions. This may lead toward centralization in contrast to pluralization. The main problem is the emergence and evolution of a technology that tends to resolve the problem of access and retrieval of information it has to offer, only with a much higher rate and level of abstraction and sophistication than ever before.

The problem, politically significant during the coming years, does not correspond to the amount of available socioeconomically important information, but relates to the way of discovering and gaining access to the value and significance of such a large reservoir of data. With the plethora of technical options that has been made available, there is a fear that society may fall behind in proper processing of information. In general, democracy operates properly according to a set of commonly accepted guidelines and procedures. Democracy is not amenable to pure choice within the framework of a normless external environment. The potential for complex problems within the new technology exists not primarily because of its totalitarian capabilities but because of its anarchic consequences. The phenomenal multiplication of options enormously increases chances for normlessness and anomie. First, there is no common computer language or protocol able to synthesize the ever-increasing number of data bases available through a variety of sources. The result has been the emergence of problems in evaluating quality on a scale without precedent. A serious problem is that unprecedented rapid developments in new technology cause the current ways and means of ascertaining the quality of performance or of information to become outmoded, if not obsolete. The enormous problem expected is that there may not be experts adequate to the task of screening such a phenomenally large volume of information and data. Yet these are only some of the enormous problems the modern society confronts in the near future. Democracy requires freedom of access to information. Besides these technological problems, there is the vital question of blockage or prevention of access. The question becomes even more complex when, as it is expected, access becomes more important to society than ownership of information. New problems arise if proprietary considerations yield to those of availability and access to information.

The relationship between the new technology and democracy is so close that the extent of information available to ordinary citizens determines the extent of proper operation of the system. Studies of the new information technology have made evident the existence of a generational gap. The older generation, for which printed materials is a symbol of status, achievement, and proper understanding, is facing the young, for whom the videocassette, videotext, and video games constitute paramount means of conveying information as well as understanding it. The heroes of the old are the authors of books and novels, while those of the young emanate from the electronic screen. However, despite the fact that the video machine may be a dominant force affecting cultural transition and transformation, while in an airport a person may well prefer to buy a paperback book rather than carry a videopack in his knapsack. However, the information system of the future may well depend on cost-benefit outcome. Currently it is still cheaper, easier, and more marketable to place paperback books on a newstand than videopacks or related software.

However, the situation may change rapidly as a result of miniaturization of electronic machines by development of microscopic computer chips. Furthermore, the relationships between democracy and the new technology are neither uniform nor mechanistic. Nationalism may conflict with a wide use of information technology having foreign origins in many rapidly developing areas. Antidemocratic constraints may be masked with hostility to foreign ideas, influences, technology, or other scientific systems. A tightly knit control over the new information technology may occur as a result of the intense desire for national autonomy. Such controls over the flow of information may be justified with the intention to protect the society on account of national security, privacy, or economic independence. But at the same time the need for socioeconomic developments may require maximum participation in the international exchange of information and ideas.

From a democratic standpoint, resources restraining the distribution and disbursment of information, whether they are imposed by a nationalistic regime, military clique, or political-economic elite, are considered negative. But the greatest impediments to democracy and massification of information come from the creators and proprietors of information and ideas. It is claimed that the intellectual property or any kind of new or newly organized information belongs to creators and author and they have a right to control their own creations. They argue that autonomy is necessary in order to maintain integrity, protect their interests, and recover the cost.

The debate is on the right of public access to information versus the recognition of proprietary claims. At the same time, there is no question that the notion of property rights and confidentiality of information, if broadly sustained, can definitely become a powerful restraint on the process of democratization. In fact, everything from the legal protection of privileged information and data to monopolistic industries has a substantially dampening effect on the broad use of information and data. On the one hand, those who demand access to information claim the right to know as an essential condition of democracy. On the other, public agencies claim the right to information as part of their obligation to ensure so-called responsible operation in order to meet policy goals and to maintain law enforcement and national security in the public interest. Yet more serious and restrictive measures come from the clique between proprietors of information and data. To them information is an economic commodity and thus should remain under the control of its rightful and legal owners. Ownership, of course, is an individual right in capitalistic society. It may not appear so restrictive as long as it is open to plurastic competition. But this is not the situation regarding the new information sources. A great bulk of it is already under the control of a very few giant economic institutions, and the trend is toward a further concentration of information in the hand of a few. Of particular importance is that this increasing control not only is in relation to sources of information and data but also extends to the means of information distribution.

Another concern that affects the consciousness of society and thus its tendencies toward a democratic way of life relates to the deep ambivalence within science about its cognitive and practical dimensions. Is science the pursuit of truth for benefit to society as a whole or the pursuit of profitable knowledge? Is it a carefully disciplined process for human well-being or a professional instrumental occupation? The regretful reality points to the fact that there have been significant changes in the social and societal role of science and diversion in the importance of research. Economic interests have succeeded in dominating social benefits. The new technology enlarges on the one hand the possibilities of a greater access to new information and data and thus widening practice of democracy, on the other a greater limitation to accessibility of information, which tends to narrow down opportunities for practice of democracy. Simply, the new electronic information technology heightens the awareness of democracy as a way of life, but it does not in or of itself lead to either egalitarian or dictatorial systems.

The plethora of new developments in information-communication technology provides a potential for democratic expression far beyond whatever existed before. The extent of public access to information is a main problem of democracy that has initiated struggle between economic and intellectual classes. The former is seriously inclined to manage and manipulate the technology for its own economic goals, while the latter emphasizes the accessibility of information for public benefit. Continuation of the current situation leads toward a point where a sophisticated but small portion of the population has acquired capability to manage the new information system, thus forming the ruling elite, while for the entire other stratum of people the technology remains like an eternal mystery. These become the plebeians of the computerized culture. Whether this contradiction develops into another class struggle or establishes a new way according to which society is benignly stratified remains to be seen. However, it should be noted that the uneven distribution of hardware and software, resulting in uneven access to information, is a development in contradiction to democracy.

By considering the fact that democracy can exist and persist only in a highly educated and conscious society, the computer literacy adds another dimension to the currently existing problem of literacy. It must be noted that technology, whatever its state of evolution may be, does not automatically open or close opportunities. It increases the options and thus causes increase in opportunities as well as in hazards. However, the new technology provides potentials for the inclusion of even larger numbers of individuals in the mainstream of socioeconomic and political democratic participation. These involve not only political but, more important, socioeconomic and technical challenges.

Toward these formidable democratic aims, under the current highly unjust elite class control of information and educational resources, and low level of literacy of words, let alone of technology, our chances of success appear very bleak.

As to the former, it may suffice to point out, as an example, that five New York based multinational financial institutions own controlling shares of stock in the nation's three largest information sources, namely, CBS, ABC, and NBC.

As to the subject of illiteracy, 25 million American adults

cannot read the poison warnings on a can of pesticide, letters from their children's teachers, or the front page of a daily paper. An additional 35 million read only at a level that is less than equal to the full survival needs of society. Together these 60 million people represent more than one-third of the entire adult population. Eighty-five percent of juveniles who come before the courts are functionally illiterate. Half the heads of households classified below the poverty line cannot read an eighth-grade book. Over one-third of mothers who receive welfare support are functionally illiterate. The United States ranks forty-ninth among 158 member nations of the U.N. in its literacy level.[4] This places the country not only below all industrial nations but also several less developed countries.

Yet more frightening is the lack of substantial efforts to remedy the situation. Together all federal, state, municipal, and private literacy programs used in the nation reach a maximum of 4 percent of the illiterate population. At the current level, direct federal allocations represent about $1.65 per year for each illiterate. The importance of the danger of illiteracy to the future of democracy cannot be exaggerated, because today the number of identified nonreaders is three times greater than it was sixteen years ago. The nation is at risk.[5]

With all these facts, the central challenge posed by the new technology is how to reduce technical illiteracy and the number of individuals for whom the computer is mysterious machine and a menace. The problem of illiteracy is far more serious in the area of electronics than that of words.

In the world of information technology, while democracy widens the horizons and opportunities offered by the new technology, it must tend to increase greatly the number of individuals involved. This requires properly planned and executed mass technical education.

Democracy is not simply concerned with options and choices for elites; it demands a social responsibility to bring the largest total of eligible adults into the framework of socioeconomic and political decision making. At the present, this problem of the new technology and democracy has not begun to receive proper attention. Yet it appears that the issue of democracy in the next century will receive its heaviest challenges at this level of mass participation and technical literacy.

THE NEW TECHNOLOGICAL ELITE

Probably the most important cause for the rise and spread of democratic values in Europe and the United States during the seventeenth through nineteenth centuries was the destruction of the gap in sociopolitical culture between the masses and that of the ruling classes. The invention of the printing press caused a significant growth in popular literacy. By the middle of the eighteenth century the public literacy had reached a level to support a variety of newspapers and periodicals gradually expanding from the larger cities to the smaller towns. The advance of literacy and print provided for the spread of information nationwide, causing the demystification of both religious and political privileges of the ruling classes. At least, one of the cultural gaps between the common men and the aristocracy was closed.

The movement was further enhanced by the expansion and improvement of roads and postal systems and the consequent invigoration of economic and commercial conditions of smaller towns. The outcome was a gradual sociocultural enrichment of a large segment of the population. The living experiences became more varied and richer and ever getting closer to those of the ruling classes, causing the social rationality of the lower classes.

The increasing participation of the common man in commercial, governmental, and professional activities provided a rich variety of experiences similar to those of the elite. Demystification of the processes of law and government, plus the spread of egalitarian and republican doctrines, provided the grounds for public contest to the elite rule. These feelings were increasingly expressed through organized means of popular contest.

With no doubt the advance and spread of technology such as the printing press and expansion of roads and communication means contributed to increasing public awareness, consciousness, and closing up the knowledge gap between the lower classes and the elite. However, as technology advanced during the second half of the nineteenth century and the twentieth century, its control by the economic and governmental elites has caused a new gap between the people and their rulers. Thus the new technology has contributed substantially to the erosion of democratic ethos.

It seems that the old cycle is renewing itself as the evidences point to a growing separation between ruling and lower class culture in the United States. This separation is particularly enhanced by the accelerating growth of technology and the increasing influence of the concept of *laissez-innover*. There has been a substantial lack of literacy relating to understanding of the social and political character of the new technology. The widening gap is affected heavily by public ignorance in rapidly developing technical language and enormous difference created between the language of technologists and managers and that of the common man.[6] This new language of social and technical institutions is divorced from the general population.

Thus the managerial and administrative processes, with their highly technological complexities, become the domain of the national technical elite and the expression of their vital personalities. In ideology as well as in reality and appearance, these managers tend to separate and isolate themselves from the rest.[7] The primary and truly creative role in the social processes corresponding to technological developments is thus reserved for a scientific and technical elite. However, this elite is controlled by a very small monopoly economic elite, which not necessarily discovers and organizes the new technology but controls it.

For these reasons and realities, it appears obvious that the most important step toward establishing a democratic society is democratization of information systems. As has been made obvious, whoever controls the electronic information system has the tools to control the society as a whole.

TOWARD DEMOCRATIZATION OF INFORMATION SYSTEM

One may look upon the modern information system in two different ways. On the positive side, one may visualize technologically instant access to desired information through an appropriately and effectively managed system. On the negative side, one may consider that for the necessity of the use of advanced technology to seek and retrieve information, only comparatively small expert groups will use the available information while a large number of subgroups will remain without access and cause societal impoverishment in general. The rich will become richer at the expense of the rest of the society, which will get poorer.[8]

It is assumed that information is a product that can be collected, classified, stored, retrieved, and disseminated like most other products, that it can be objective and organized in terms of its accurate connection to reality and its effectiveness in results, and that accessibility of information alone tends to equalize its use. This line of thinking does not provide any move toward democratization of information. From a utilitarian point of view, it tends to make information less and less usable to more and more people. The sole availability of information does not make its use democratic when an overwhelming majority of people do not use it for a variety of reasons. People may not know how to use it, what is actually available, or how or where to get the desired information. It also makes a lot of difference whether the access is economically affordable or at least feasible.

The prime requirement for democratization of information is that it should not be considered primarily a market commodity but a public service. It must be responsive primarily to a kind of information in line with the public wishes and desires. Democratization of information is also a process that requires providing common means for public education regarding the use of information technology, the object being the use of high-technology information system.

The second important aspect of democratization of information relates to the kind of information needed to be collected and stored. As mentioned above, this must be in line with the public wishes and desires. This is the clue.

The typical information system today is aimed to provide for a particular body of information as defined and desired by experts. But experts altogether form a small group of individuals quite different from ordinary people. Furthermore, expert information is understood to be based on empirical and factual findings. Consequently, it is assumed that the information collected is the correct way of looking at a given situation. Thus a very basic ground is ignored, namely, that different people from different backgrounds and different places see the world differently.

It is, furthermore, ignored that information is the outcome of observations by human beings who exist at particular points in time and space, come from particular backgrounds, and have particular aims.

When objectivity becomes a guiding factor in formation of information, it tends to remove the richness of human situations; the facts are presented without appropriate context, isolated and disjointed.[9]

The third aspect of democratization of information relates to the means by which users are allowed access to information. Currently these means are prescribed by the experts. They classify the information as they see fit; they select the key words and isolate topical entry points without regard to general ability of users to search and find the desired information. These experts in devising the access means simply ignore the principle that it is at the subjective level that a person is able to connect with observations made by another in order to be able to judge whether such observations will be useful. Therefore, it seems only appropriate that the entry points allowing users access to information need to be based on the subjective means by which people choose to go about seeking and using information—that is to say the different ways people look at situations attempting to make sense of them, the different kinds of questions they ask, and the different ways they conceive themselves in the need of desired information.

A fourth aspect of democratization of information is concerned with the study of the users. Generally, the information system users are studied through the normative approach, though with an intention to make the system more responsive. As a result, the system has been employed by only a small subgroup of potential users, likely those at the level of the experts who devised the system. From the experts' viewpoint, nonusers are less educated, lack motivation, and are unprepared to use the system. Therefore, experts underestimate and stereotype nearly all groups of average citizens.[10]

Information sharing between individuals in a broad manner depends on new innovations within the realm of possibilities and increased efficiencies, with efforts being focused on the subjective or human aspects of societal life. This approach may be considered the scientific humanization of information. Increased efficiency more likely will accompany increased effectiveness. With a large segment of public in mind, cost-benefit analysis may ultimately end up on the public side, rather than favoring the use by small expert groups. The information system must be adapted to users rather than requiring users to adapt to it. What is required is to take the information system out of its present hodgepodge situation and subject it to a scientific systematization under which neither inputs nor outputs would be, or can be made, subject to control by a few individuals or groups. Information will flow in and go out of the system through public participation as a whole. The scientific design of the Technodem is aimed to provide for such easily accessible democratized services. People serve the Technodem and the latter, in turn, serves the people. The Technodem is the depository of all societal information, and people are at ease in referring to it for their informational needs. The Technodem contains all the information. and each individual has access to all. At this stage people are advanced to a level of human excellence where they trust and respect one another and consequently have developed a trust in the Technodem as their major essential, indispensible instrument of virtually all societal interactions, whether they are of an economic, social, cultural, or political nature.[11]

DEMOCRATIZATION OF INFORMATION AND THE ISSUE OF PRIVACY

At least in the early stages of democratic society, access to information is not absolute and total. Some areas, though quite minor proportionally speaking, are and must remain exceptions. The most important of these relates to personal information. However, it must be understood that as democracy advances and democratic society matures, all these restrictions will be voluntarily eliminated; more and more individuals will make their personal data available to access. In a fully advanced democratic society there will be no limitation whatsoever relating to access to information. There will be no personal information that would deserve hiding. Of course, we also have stated that there will be no information relating to so-called national security that will not be publicly accessible. This is based, obviously, on the application of the principle of equality of opportunity. It is also necessary in bringing about more sentiment of frankness, which is needed in moving other societies toward democracy.

Toward this goal, it becomes necessary that we take a look upon the current status of privacy of information and developing problems as the use of electronic information expands.

ELECTRONIC INFORMATION AND PRIVACY

Concern over the potential misuse of files containing personal information and the threat this poses to individual privacy have been receiving increasing attention in recent years. Several countries, including Austria, Denmark, England, France, Iceland, Luxembourg, Norway, Sweden, and West Germany, as well as the United States already have certain data protection legislation in force. Some others, such as Belgium, Finland, Italy, the Netherlands, Portugal, and Switzerland, are in the process of legislation affecting transborder data flows.[12]

Essentially, the purpose is to reconcile two fundamental objectives: on the one hand, the protection of personal privacy regarding the electronic recording and storing of personal data and, on the other, the commercial and managerial advantages of development and use of databanks.

Electronic privacy is both a difficult and novel concept that, like many other modern concepts, eludes precise definition. The essential notion of privacy per se is that there are aspects of one's life that one may legitimately seek to protect from outside intrusion. These aspects of privacy are differently affected as a result of one's nationality, age, personality, and circumstances. There are times when one needs solitude and others when one needs the comfort of one's friends. There are times when one needs the intimacy of communication with others close to one and other times when one needs to maintain one's reserves. One needs to be able to keep to oneself one's thoughts, feelings, beliefs, doubts, hopes, plans, fears, and fantasies. These are known as the private aspects of life because of the individual's wish to be able to make personal choices, without hindrance, as to the extent one wants to be let alone. However, this right cannot be considered absolute. One is born into society, where one enjoys the benefits and thus has to accept the responsibilities emanating from belonging to that society. The right to privacy clearly has to be balanced against wider social needs, because an unqualified right to privacy would be incompatible with the concept of society that is based on social participation, interaction, and coexistence.

However, the importance of privacy right is evident by its inclusion in national constitutions and in important international documents. The United Nations Covenant on Civil and Political Rights, as well as the Universal Declaration of Human Rights, declare that no one shall be subjected to arbitrary interference with his privacy and everyone has the right to the protection of the law against such interference. Also, the European Convention for the Protection of Human Rights and Fundamental Freedoms recognizes everyone's right to respect for his private and family life, home, and correspondence.

At the national level, the constitutions of a variety of nations recognize protection of privacy. For example, the French and West German constitutions recognize privacy right and tend to protect it under the "right of the personality." The concept is further elaborated under French parliamentary legislation embodied in the 1970 Civil Code. It declares that "everyone has the right to respect for his private life." Determination of the meaning of privacy, however, is left to the judicial branch.

Privacy is, more or less, a novel and contemporary concept. Early societies gave scant attention to an individual's life away from public scrutiny. The earliest constitutional provision concerned with the protection of privacy appears to go back some two hundred years, as reflected in the Fourth Amendment to the U.S. Constitution. It prescribes as follows: "The right of the people to be secure in their persons, houses, papers, and effects, against unreasonable searches and seizures, shall not be violated, and no warrants shall issue, but upon probable cause, supported by oath of affirmation, and particularly describing the place to be searched, and the persons or things to be seized."

It seems that increasing concern for individual privacy is related to the growth of industrialization and urbanization. It has been argued that privacy has been relatively threatened by the new and changing urban life-styles and is further affected by the development of the welfare state requiring that personal data be disclosed for consideration of eligibility for welfare programs. The rapid advance in technology has substantially simplified access to personal data by electronic storage of individual information in data banks. This new technology not only allows for collection, storage, and easy access to personal data, but it also provides opportunity for its misuse and abuse. Governments, as well as commercial institutions, have shown an increasing appetite for personal data. Within the private sector, there is a flourishing interest in collecting and storing personal information used for a wide variety of commercial purposes, from consumer credit to market research.

However, it is governments that pose the most potent threat to personal privacy. They have the right to demand personal information. It is easy for them to collect information for one purpose and use or misuse it for another. In fact, data collected by one department of government is often interdepartmentally transferred for other uses. Most government requests for information are considered justified and legitimate. They are intended to operate for the good of society and thus receive public cooperation. One might consider this also true regarding the private sector. Individuals voluntarily submit detailed personal information to banks, credit unions, and employment agencies with expectations of financial aid, employment, or other personal benefits. However, each time such information is disclosed by any individual, the personal impression is that the information will be used exclusively for the specified purpose and will not be subsequently used for other purposes or released to other institutions. Any abuse of these two principles, simply any unauthorized use of personal information, will be considered a threat to privacy.

The new information-communication technology has substantially increased concern about privacy by the corresponding increase in the possibility of threat to it. Modern computers possess infinite capacity for data processing and readily achieved cross-checking of data obtained from different sources. More recent developments of memory clips allow the received information through cross-checking to be stored permanently, thus causing ever increasing data banks on personal information.

The fear of privacy is not confined only to the area of legitimate activities of public and private sectors where the release of personal information by the individual is usually voluntary or at the least without an individual's objection. The problem also relates to the more covert methods of discovering personal information. There has been growing public concern about intelligence-related files and records held by a variety of police and other institutions, particularly those concerned with national security matters. These are mostly noncriminal files stored in regional and national computer centers. It is understandable that the very nature of security information gathering dictates a certain measure of secrecy. Recognizing this fact is to concede that traditional safeguards for those who disclose personal information may not be upheld or insured in these cases. Therefore, it is not surprising that it is in these areas, mostly excluded from data protection legislation, that the public finds the most sinister threats to individual privacy.

In general, the term *privacy* relates to individuals' right, need, and desire to keep some details about themselves concealed from others. Based on this general definition, the privacy debate has focused on the protection of personal information, particularly what is released to public agencies. The issue has become the individual's ability to control the circulation of information relating to him,[13] his right to determine when, how and to what extent personal information is communicated to others.[14] Therefore, the debate has been concentrated on the specific issue of handling of personal information by private as well as public sectors. Thus the invasion of privacy is related to the way personal information is treated and the need to control, through special legislation, the modern electronic data banks that are strictly concerned with personal information. Obviously the government's constitutional responsibility to protect individual rights clearly justifies the use of stronger remedies regarding the public sector than the private.

DRIVE TOWARD LEGAL RESTRICTIONS

All the technologically advanced countries have experienced pressures of different degrees to introduce some kind of personal data protection legislation. In some, such as Belgium, Denmark,

France, Luxembourg, the Netherlands, Sweden, and West Germany, it was proposed that the collection of personal information be restricted to the central population census. In Sweden and the Netherlands the concern was created as a result of the computerization of census information and in Luxembourg by the establishment of a state data processing center. Accordingly, the impetus centered on the extension and integration of the public electronic information systems. These pressures, however, were almost invariably developed by the concern over possible future abuses rather than by any abuses that have already occurred.

However, specific and visible safeguards were demanded by those who campaigned for civil liberties. They were not satisfied by simply placing their trust in public agencies or accepting general codes of conduct as substitutes for specific and legally enforceable legislation.

The introduction of information protection controls is not, however, restricted to the protection of civil liberties but extends beyond those to political, administrative, and commercial considerations. In some countries, such as France, information protection measures have been instigated by the government, without response to pressures from the outside, for the ensued administrative benefits of computerization to the state and the long-range benefits accrued from electronization of public record systems. In West Germany the establishment of controls paralleled the lightening up of procedures for public servants and the imposition of severe antiterrorist procedures. To alleviate the political impact of these measures, it was expedient for West Germany to protect civil liberties in other areas through appropriate legislation. Commercial considerations have also been factors in encouraging public legislation measures. At a time when information technology promises strong growth prospects, protection of business interests relating to transborder data flows may be a significantly powerful stimulus in encouraging legislative action.

Concurrent with these national developments, international organizations such as OECD of the European Community and the Council of Europe have also demonstrated an interest in the effect of the electronic information systems on civil liberties. Since the early seventies, they have attempted harmonization of standards of practice. OECD, though not primarily concerned with civil liberties, has been concerned, since shortly after its inception in 1960, with the economic potential of free flow of electronic information between member nations. This interest necessarily brings into consideration the issue of privacy and ensuing legal implications. As a consequence, for example, OECD organized a seminar on the effect of electronic information systems on privacy in 1974,[15] and in 1976 an international panel of experts drafted a set of principles on transborder data flows that was also concerned with the issue of privacy. This draft was a forerunner for Guidelines Concerning the Protection of Privacy and Transborder Flow of Personal Data, which was adopted by the OECD Council in September 1980. The guidelines focus on eight principles, which include limiting the amount of collected information, ensuring accuracy and quality, ensuring the restriction of use to the specified purpose, requiring adequate safeguards for the secure storage of personal data, allowing individuals access to check the validity and accuracy of personal data, and requiring the accountability of those involved in the operation of or having access to data banks in the system. Currently the guidelines have been accepted by all OECD countries except Australia, Canada, and Ireland. It is needless to say that the guidelines have been influential in shaping and reshaping data protection legislations in several countries.

Of the three international organizations, the Council of Europe has developed the strongest record in relation to civil liberties. In 1977 a committee of experts was assigned the task of preparing a convention regarding the transborder data flows. The outcome was a document titled the Convention for the Protection of Individuals with Regard to Automatic Processing of Personal Data. This convention and the OECD Guidelines are the most significant international documents on the protection of personal information. The convention is to be legally binding when ratified by five of the member states. It has been signed by Austria, Belgium, Denmark, West Germany, Greece, Iceland, Italy, Luxembourg, Norway, Portugal, Spain, Turkey, and the United Kingdom. So far, it has been a considerable influence in encouraging corresponding national legislations in several countries. In general, these legislations cover the scope of control, methods to be used, the extent of powers of the corresponding regulatory authorities, the extent of subject access, control asserted by the individual, and the manner of financing.

The legislation protecting transborder data flows currently exists in Austria, Canada, Denmark, France, West Germany, Luxembourg, New Zealand, and the United States. This protection is in the process of becoming legislation in several other countries, such as the Netherlands, the United Kingdom, Belgium, Finland, Greece, Italy, Portugal, and Switzerland.

Among these, the French legislation appears to be the best in illustrating the association between public concern with privacy and the state's keenness to utilize new technology.

All the countries having data protection legislation have a similarity of approach. In general, it is agreed that controls should cover manual files. There is a universal agreement on the principal controls to be embodied in the legislation. These, in general, relate to the prohibition of transfer and storage of a certain class of information, some being subject to special conditions or exemptions; control over the accuracy, completeness, and relevance of information; control over transfers of information; control over the period for which information can be stored in an active file; control over the physical security of records; and an individuals' access to details stored relating to him and his right to challenge such stored information.

The main differences relate to the method of protection controls. A central agency is the favored option. It is in the form of a central board in Denmark, France, and Sweden; the Federal Commissary for Data Protection for the control of the public sector and Data Protection Representative for the private sector in West Germany; and data protection registrars in Britain. However, the French legislation is unique. It provides for stronger controls in the public sector compared with those prescribed for the private sector. In one sense, this reflects the importance of the public sector and an attempt to encourage the introduction of more public-sector electronic information systems. Any collection and storage in the public sector must be authorized by the National Commission for Data Processing and Liberties. Those with the intention of data storage in the private sector must declare their intention to abide by the provisions of the law.

It is of no doubt that the rapidly developing information

technology will require periodic revisions of the existing legislations in order to update them to accommodate new situations and circumstances. This in itself is a significant burden on the legislature and the executive branch. From this standpoint, the French system stands out. In contrast to the apparent weakness of data protection legislation in other countries, the French system is also unique. The National Commission for Data Processing and Liberties has proved to be a forceful agency of control over the public electronic information systems. As a result, there has been a little opposition to the increased public use of electronic information. For example, when a new plastic identity card was planned, the commission recommended that only the sex of the holder should be identifiable from the card and obtaining other information should be made impossible. It also rejected that the card could be readable by computers. The new socialist government in 1981 decided not to proceed with the effectuation of the proposed cards. Another example relates to the planning of the 1982 census. The commission recommended that individuals should be allowed access to details concerning their personal data, if such intention was declared by them on census day. It also recommended that no additional questionnaires should be attached to that of the census and strict safeguards should be provided to preserve the anonymity of information gathered for statistical purposes.

The emergence of information protection legislation over the past decade has been the consequence of the increasing public awareness of the importance of privacy. All this legislation has attempted to reconcile two essential goals. While preserving civil liberties, they have attempted to exploit to the fullest extent the administrative as well as commercial benefits of the progress in electronic information-communication technology. Governmental attitudes have been motivated to minimize the threat to privacy in order to smooth the way for orderly development and use of the new technology without impediments.

International pressure and guidelines have been influential in shaping national legislation and regulations. A review of enacted as well as as proposed legislations reveals a remarkable degree of similarity among countries and conformity to international standards.

The momentum accomplished has been quite significant.

Even countries that do not yet have data protection legislation often adopt certain forms of self-regulation or impose certain procedures for protection of certain specified areas. In general, however, self-regulation has given way to external controls. There are still substantial problems remaining unresolved, such as those concerned with law enforcement and national security. A specific issue of concern has been the rapidly increasing use of home computers. For the time being these have been specifically excluded from legislative protection in some countries, such as Britain.

It is clear that the advents of rapid changes in information-communication technology will make the review of the existing legislation necessary. Several countries, including the United States, have already revised earlier legislation, and several others are in the process of doing so. In general and so far, administrative and commercial considerations have motivated governments to conform to guidelines established by the international organizations in order to provide a certain degree of personal privacy in transborder data flows.

INTERNATIONAL ASPECTS OF ELECTRONIC INFORMATION SYSTEM

In 1982 the United States government embargoed certain strategic information exports to the Soviet Union by American corporations. This decision alarmed some foreign governments that had vast amounts of various data stored in the United States. They became concerned as to the serious implications entailed if the United States for certain political or other objectives would embargo export of information to the countries involved.[16]

Even though the transborder data flow (TBDF) is in its infancy, tremendous amounts of data are presently being transported internationally. Not all of this concerns big economic firms, and by no means not all are economic and business data.

Consider, for example, the town of Malmo in Sweden. Its fire alarm system was linked to a data base in Cleveland, Ohio. When a fire alarm in a building in this Swedish community went off, the computer in Cleveland supplied the fire department in

Malmo with information about the size of the building and its current use, its structural materials, whether dangerous products were stored in the building, and other vital information. This information was transmitted by satellite within seconds, possibly faster than a local telephone call to the fire department in Malmo would if the fire were discovered instantly.

There is a growing uneasiness among many countries when they think about the great quantity of information that is transmitted out of the country either by governments or multinational corporations. These situations, in addition to political and other reasons, have already led some national governments to restrict the sending, processing, or storing certain types of information abroad.[17]

The United States and several European and Latin American countries have laws enacted to protect individual privacy against unauthorized transborder data flows. Some require the registration of all computer systems that store any personal data or prohibit outside transmission of any data when the individual is identifiable. Yet others have established agencies to monitor the personal data collection and storage and some allow individuals the right to review and modify any data about themselves if inaccurate. Finally, some governments prohibit the transmission of personal data to countries that do not have protective laws similar to those of the country of origin. Recent national tendencies toward such restrictive measures affecting transborder data flows are mainly the result of extraordinary advances in information technology that have vastly increased the volume of data that can be stored in and transferred to many parts of the world with an incredible speed. The concentration of this extraordinary attention to transborder data flows is mainly due to the linkage of computers to advanced electronic telecommunication systems. Thus restrictions usually exclude the older conventional media of international communication such as telephone, telex, or postal services. This exclusion is understood through congressional documents that describe the term *transborder data flows* as referring generally to transmission of data from computer to computer, using telecommunication circuits across national borders.[18] According to the United Nations report in 1982, in a narrower sense transborder data flows take place through transnational computer-communications systems. These are arrangements whereby one or several sophisticated computers in one or several countries are linked to affiliated computers in other countries and through them (or directly) to remote terminals.[19]

Even though nonelectronic media are currently excluded from transborder data flows regulation, it is possible and probable that situations may arise in the future that may justify including this sector also within an overall TBDF regulation. As stated in the U.N. report, this sector of nonelectronic media not only may include telephone, telex, and postal activities, but also portable devices such as magnetic tapes, discs, punched cards, and similar devices mailed or even sent by a carrier across borders.

Since the developed societies have the technology for advanced transborder communication, the rest of the world depends on them for much of the needed or desired information. Among advanced societies the United States is far advanced in producing the hardware necessary for TBDF as well as storing and transmitting data.

Nearly all firms doing business abroad are obliged to use data that must be sent across national borders. It includes transmitting and receiving orders, production, marketing, financial and personnel data, and labor and credit information. Financial institutions, such as banks, require a continuous flow of information regarding international financial transactions, credit situations, and currency fluctuations. Any restriction on the free flow of this information can impede not only the immediate decision-making process but also important long-range operational planning.

The debate on the regulation of transborder data flows is mostly the consequence of division of the world into technological haves and have-nots. The questions, growing in number and concern, include privacy, technical, economic, and political issues.

PRIVACY

An important area of conflict relates to the subject of privacy. It originates primarily from the incompatibility of national laws. It is not unusual to find the privacy law in one country in direct conflict with that of another. For example, American pharmaceutical firms frequently test drugs abroad. The Food and Drug Administration requires that the firms must supply it with personal histories and results of those tests, regardless of the place they were carried out. A good number of such tests are conducted within several European countries whose privacy laws prohibit the transmission of personal medical information abroad. A few even prohibit processing medical data on identifiable persons even if they are the firm's own employees. The potential problem for such firms is evident.

Continuous efforts are being made to establish certain privacy standards applicable to transborder data flows. One example is a draft of voluntary guidelines by the Organization for Economic Cooperation and Development. This draft has already been accepted by several countries and a score of private firms. Another example is the treaty on privacy standards prepared by the Council of Europe and ratified by several member countries.

Inscription has been suggested to be a satisfying remedy to maintain privacy. This is done by the use of a code system. It is not, however, free of problems. The United Kingdom, for example, seemingly has a law enabling the British Post Office to read any message it transmits, including electronic transmissions. It appears that the post office would have the right to know the content of the coded messages.

While the privacy laws relating to individuals are supported by many countries, the issue arises about its extension to legal persons such as corporations and research organizations. Such an extension entails a host of new and complicated questions. For example, what would be the situation in those countries that allow individuals to review electronically stored information about themselves? Can a corporation demand to review information about itself that is stored in its competitors' computer systems? This is only one of the many serious questions.

TECHNICAL ISSUES

The main technical issues relating to transborder data flows include the continuing assignment and proper use of radio waves for transnational communications and the appropriation of geostationary orbits in space for the use of satellites.

The use of a geostationary orbit is a recent phenomenon. It is an orbital location in near-space on which a satellite travels around the earth with the same speed as that of the rotation of the earth, or once every twenty-four hours. In this way the satellite appears to be stationary in relation to a designated point on the earth's surface.

This orbit is preferred for several reasons. One is to provide for a worldwide communications system. Only three satellites properly placed will be capable of relaying signals to and from the entire surface of the earth. For this purpose the preferred orbital spots are limited. Consequently, those few countries with the technical capability to launch satellites into space are rushing to claim these preferred orbital spots. At the same time, several of the remaining nations, which do not yet have the capability of launching geostationary satellites, are demanding that appropriate spots in the geostationary orbit areas be reserved for their future use. The conflict is rising over this issue, since the current users consider such appropriations for future use uneconomical and somehow a waste of presently useful orbital spots. Another use of the geostationary orbit is to provide for domestic or regional educational and communication purposes. This, of course, is not much of a problematic issue, since each country claims its sovereign rights to the space above its territory. India, for example, has such a satellite, which is mainly being used for educational purpose and for increasing the rate of literacy among its population.

Another major technical problem relates to the issue of standardization of computer and telecommunications machineries, equipments, and supplies, at least for the purpose of accommodating transborder data flows. Some countries, for reasons of their own, refuse to go along with standardization policies. The lack of standardization prevents firms in developed nations from entering certain foreign markets. When they decide to enter such a market, the necessary adaptations are very costly. The multi-standard electronic communication systems may also affect the speed and convenience of transborder data flows.

A favorable phenomenon relating to transborder data flows is the existence of the International Telecommunications Union

(ITU). The major task of the organization is to deal with the technical problems relating to international communications. The recent technological advances in international communications, including fiber optics, television, computers, and satellites, have substantially increased the importance as well as complexities of the organization's technical tasks. Unfortunately, added to this already difficult work has been the emergence and increase of nontechnical issues such as privacy, national security, economics, and cultural and even political independence.

These new nontechnical entanglements in addition to increasing number and speed of advances in electronic communications technology have multiplied the workload of the ITU. Many of these issues, while demanding rapid solutions, require studies by the organization that may extend quite a few years into the future. However, ITU is an important and valuable organization with the capability to deal with some of the complex technical issues relating to transborder data flows.

POLITICAL AND ECONOMIC ISSUES

Transborder commercial and other activities require that a certain amount and certain class of data be sent out to be stored in another country. Many countries are uneasy about sending data abroad for processing and storage. The situation becomes more delicate and sensitive if the data have any relation to security or military matters. The situation becomes more of concern if the means and technology for telecommunications are within the domain of the foreign government or private firms controlled by it.

For example, the American Defense Department has been concerned that the United States should not become dependent on foreign institutions for providing vital telecommunications equipment or services.[20] If the United States, the country most advanced in telecommunication systems, is so much concerned about the security of information, the strong concern from the part of the less developed countries becomes well understandable. The imposition of restrictions in transborder data flows on these grounds appears, at least for the time being, justifiable.

Another problem arises from the structure and operational processes of the telecommunication systems and industries. In some countries, including the United States, domestic competition is encouraged in telecommunications and computer services and the corresponding manufacturing industries. However, in most of the countries, including several in Western Europe, telecommunication activities are assigned to postal, telephone, and telegraph companies (PTT), which are controlled by the government. PTTs usually have a monopoly on telecommunication services. They control the use of domestic facilities and thus have a choice in determining which foreign competing services will have the advantages of using the country's domestic facilities to be linked to the international network for transborder data flows purpose.

Under such controlled systems it becomes possible for the government to use its regulatory power and legislative authority to discriminate against potential foreign competitors in favor of its own electronic services. For example, such government may require that all potential users, domestic or foreign, must purchase and use locally produced equipment. If imported equipments are allowed to be used, the government may require the payment of high tariffs for imported equipment in order to boost the market for domestic telecommunication products. In Brazil, for instance, government approval is required to purchase telecommunication equipment. A permit for imported products will not be issued if the equivalent of such equipment is produced domestically. Furthermore, in order to help its own telecommunication systems and provide more demand for services rendered by its domestic PTT, the government may increase rates for users of privately leased lines, as the case is in West Germany or like in Japan, which restricts the use and interconnection of privately leased lines.

Another issue arises as to the nature of information either as a publicly accessible good or as a private marketable commodity. Several countries, including the United States, view the international transmission of data as an extension of freedom of information. Accordingly, they are in favor of the least possible restrictions. Some other nations, including France, have come to view information as an economic commodity. In France it is argued that information services, as they develop, become increasingly a significant part of economic activities. Consequently, information is considered some kind of man-made national resource. Thus, like any other economic commodity, information can be sold, bought, taxed, subsidized, monitored, or regulated. If this idea is accepted substantially by this group of countries, its effectuation may entail to highly obstructive regulations such as imposition of tariff and nontariff restrictions and governmental attempts to register and monitor all data bases and to tax transborder information flows by private firms involved in international commerce. A much higher burden is likely to fall upon firms providing transborder information transfer facilities and services. They are to find themselves unable to compete because of the barriers established and imposed by the government, affecting transborder transmission of data to their subsidiaries, affiliates, and other firms relating to production, finance credit, marketing personnel, et cetera. They will suffer by encountering a variety of information transmission obstacles within these countries. This concept is, at the least, a potential problem for companies whose activities involve substantial transborder transfer of information.

It is becoming increasingly urgent for the private sector to recognize the legitimate concerns of governments. If the private sector does not demonstrate sufficient sensitivity and understanding of government concerns, most likely governments will move in and take action to resolve problems from the public viewpoint. Commercial organizations and other firms may find it difficult to comply with those regulations. At the same time, governments must try to understand the types of data and information the private sector needs to transfer out of the country for appropriate and effective operation. If governments fail to understand the requirements for appropriate transborder data flows, they may enact and implement measures that may cause greater problems than those they are supposed to resolve.[21]

TECHNOLOGICAL DEMOCRACY AND PRIVACY

Looking toward the future, where the establishment of technological democracy would become a possibility and a central system of information-communication system, will be established similar to that of the Technodem proposed in this study, many of the existing problems will be straightened out automatically because of the nature of the system.

It is considered that the society, including its information-communication system, will operate through the application and effectuation of the principle of equality of opportunity. On this base, the information system will be controlled by no specific groups but by the whole society through individuals and through all kinds of its institutions, social, economic, political, and otherwise.

The information will be fed continually into the system by millions of individuals and institutions and will be revised and updated automatically by the system itself. Consider that all terminals—private, public, commercial, and noncommercial—will be connected together under the control system of the Technodem. As will be described later, the Technodem system in its local, regional, national, and international structure is very similar to the telephone network system of today. Each terminal becomes connected to its destination terminal or center through the whole system network by feeding a designated code of the destination. This code, like a telephone number, has an area code and then the code of the destination point. To connect to computers in other countries, the code proceeds with the country's code again, similar to telephone country codes.

Consequently, with the overall access of individuals and firms to either home or office terminals and through these terminals to information centers within the Technodem, state actions through legislation or otherwise will be ineffective in restraining people from having access to all necessary information, including personal data. However, such freedom of access does not necessarily imply that there will be no protection against unauthorized use of personal data. The creation and use of a personal electronic identification card in properly codified manner will offer near complete protection against disclosure of personal data. It is needed to categorize personal information into two classes. First is information that is a matter of public record, such as birth, marriage, employment, et cetera. Since this information is a matter of public record, it can be received through reference to public or institutional files in the same manner that it can be done relating to any other matter of public record. Of course, for an individual or firm to collect such information about an individual would not be easy even through the electronic system. It would be time-consuming at least, since an individual's personal information, such as his place of birth, marriage, employment, education, et cetera, is recorded in different places and one has to know these place first in order to search for the individual's records. This, to say the least, would be time-consuming even through an advanced and centralized system such as the Technodem. It is in the individual's personal data form that all this information and much more of a more personal nature are registered. It is a document of collective information that is personal and subject to privacy and requires protection.

It is possible even now to place all personal data of a person on a small disk not larger than one square inch, if this disk is placed in a transparent plastic card with a specific code number. If an institution wants information about an individual, the only source of information will be the personal file of the Technodem, which is not open to anyone but the individual himself, and the other source will be the personal file of the individual in his electronic ID disk. If the individual places his ID disk in the appropriate slot provided for it in a computer terminal and types or conveys the code of the institution concerned with his personal data, his personal data then will be accessible to the institution for observation, evaluation, or investigation. These data will appear on a disk in the institution on a special disks provided for this purpose, from which the information will be automatically erased after a short period of time or upon the electronic signal of the owner. Sustaining personal data beyond this time will be illegal and subject to heavy penalty unless it is expressly permitted by the individual himself. Transfer of personal data, in full or in part, from one institution to another will be prohibited unless permitted by the individual or directly disclosed by him to the other institution. Since there would not be much of the welfare functions in technological democratic society, such as social security, food stamps, retirement systems, et cetera, much of the need for mass transfer of personal data will be eliminated. As has been mentioned in other parts of this book, this codified ID disk will also be useful in the electoral process when a person can vote by inserting his ID disk in a computer terminal and then, after giving the electoral code in local, state, and national elections, register his vote. It would also be used in commercial areas when individuals do their purchasing through the computer and also desire to pay through the computer.

Currently a great deal of personal information becomes available through the census agencies. Of course, the conventional process of census by the means of written questionnaires reveals each individual's identity as well as detailed personal information about him and his family. This personal information, being public, is often used and abused by the government as well as the commercial firms for private benefit. Under the Technodem information-communication system, the need for personal data protection will be minimal and marginal, since to a significant degree personal information will be protected through the nature of its collection, storage, and retrieval for census purposes. Personal information, for the most part, will be self-protected, since individual information will be fed to the Technodem through home terminals without personal identification. These will be stored at the local, regional, and national centers. The personal data of each individual will be revealed only to him or through him to others on a limited manner, as explained before.

Census information will be collected by each individual feeding to his home terminal all the census information by using his ID code rather than his name. This information will be collected and stored at the local, district, regional, and national levels, providing detailed, up-to-date, and accurate statistics and information about any related subject matter. The data will be updated automatically by the system itself, since it will be receiving continuous information about any change in an individual's status, such as marriage, new birth, death, employment change, educational progress, et cetera. The remaining minor part will be fed to the computer by each individual by his answering specific questions asked by the Technodem. Individuals not responding will be asked to do so repeatedly until they complete the request. It must be also noticed that a good part of this information that is added by the individual to his personal data will be automatically extracted and incorporated in the census information. So there is very little, if any, that the individual can add beyond what he has fed to his personal data and what has been inserted to his personal data by the Technodem such as conviction, traffic violations, and other delinquencies of public record. In all this process, the individual's identity will remain anonymous not only to the private sector but also to the public sector and none will have access to personal data without the individual's permission and only the individual will have access to his personal data by using his ID code through insertion of his ID disk into the computer. The reason that the individual will remain anonymous in relation to his personal data is that they are fed to the computer by the individual personally and stored on his individual data file within the Technodem system, without passing through any public or private hands. The individual simply inserts his ID disk in the slot provided for in the computer. This connects him to his personal data file. He then, through the computer, gives any additional information about himself, which is added to his personal file in the Technodem as well as into his ID disk. His ID disk is also updated if the computer file has some additional information, such as a traffic violation, which is not on his ID disk. Thus, any time an ID disk is inserted into the computer, it gets connected to the individual's central data file and is updated automatically.

Each person at the time of birth or acquiring residence in a country will be issued an ID disk with a specific code number. The child's ID disk will carry all initial personal information about him, and a new resident in a country must submit his ID disk of his previous country. All the information from this ID disk will be transferred to his new ID disk, and the old disk will be destroyed. If the previous country did not use computer ID cards, then the person will be questioned for personal information that will be inserted in his new ID disk. Of course, the individual may be required to show police and health records. These are all during the early stages of technological democracy.

In this way and under such a system, transferring a personal data, whether domestic or transnational, will depend on the individual's consent and no regulatory legislation will be required. At the domestic level, there will be harsh punishment for the abuse of the system and keeping or transferring personal data without the concerned individual's consent. This rule will apply particularly to institutions such as banks or credit agencies, which for certain financial transactions may require access to personal data. Of course, as explained before, the disclosure of data will be temporary; disclosed personal data will be erased automatically after it is used for credit, personal, or other purpose. The using institutions will not be allowed to keep personal data files on any person, whether customer or employee. However, if personal information about an individual is needed, he may be contacted through his home computer or otherwise to disclose his personal data for a new observation. An individual may also allow an institution to keep a copy of his personal file. Such consent must be a permanent part of his file. However, personal data information relating to such individual cannot be transferred to the sources outside the agency. It is obvious that by allowing a firm to keep a permanent file on his personal data the individual voluntarily waives, to that extent, the protection of his or her personal data.

It must be noted that the level of abuse of personal data will be minimized in a technological democratic society. In the private sector, since the profit motive will be removed, the level of abuses for commercial purposes will be reduced substantially. At the public level, since law enforcement will be an open public function and since any covert intelligence activities will be prohibited, the governmental interest in having access to personal data files will be nearly totally eliminated. Law enforcement agencies, however, may refer to the Technodem to find out whether a suspect has any criminal background. If so, only that aspect of the individual's personal data will be disclosed. In fact, this is not a particular disclosure of a person's personal data, since any criminal action, whether it has been ended in conviction, acquittal, or dismissal, relating to each individual is also matter of public record. In fact, the law enforcement agency is asking the Technodem about criminal public records of an indicated individual.

It is expected that all advanced countries using electronic information systems will find the self-protective system of personal data appealing, less costly, and more convenient as well as efficient and thus strive to adopt it and cooperate with other countries using the system.

TOWARD TECHNOLOGICAL DEMOCRACY

As the facts illustrate, the current status of the information-communication system, whether domestic or transnational, is quite chaotic. Yet the decisive role that technology plays in all these interactions is of no doubt. Dramatic developments during the past three decades have demonstrated the increasing burden imposed by rapidly developing technology on socioeconomic as well as political systems. However, most corresponding problems have been, and are more so now, in socioeconomic spheres of activities. Technology has become an indisputable part of the societal system. Recognition of this fact will allow better identification of the opportunities as well as obstacles emanating from technology. It will attract serious attention to the proper and systematic incorporation of technology in societal structure along with social and economic systems.

No other aspect of technology affects the societal structure and function as much as the information-communication one. For the future well-being of human society we need to concentrate our efforts toward proper structuring and operation of this aspect of technology. The difference is between totalitarian dictatorship and democracy.

In developed countries of Europe as well as in Japan, the centralized direction of communication systems by the government has allowed for faster decisions and actions. This approach may well cause these countries to move ahead of the United States in their information systems during the coming decades.

All industrialized countries are moving into a new era of information. They have proceeded from agricultural societies to industrial ones and now are moving into a society whose new patterns are rapidly emerging. The agricultural era emerged during several thousand years, the industrial era during several hundred; the new information era will emerge in a few decades. This does not leave much time for systematic planning and organization. A philosophy responsive to this era is badly needed, but by the time such philosophy is crystallized, another era will mature, more likely in a haphazard manner.

What accelerates the emergence of this era is the phenomenal developments in the information system. The United

States has been the primary incubator of the advances that now move the world toward that information era. But the United States has a serious problem in maintaining the edge in the transition into the new era. Its lasting influence depends on its ability to transform its political and social conditions in the coming years through masterful designs and strategies, comparable to its technological developments. This requires a philosophy-of-information age with its design of equitable social, economic, political, and technological developments, with its objectives of the future information society, and with its presentation of the process to proceed toward such objectives.

It is clear that this is going to emerge as a technology-based civilization with the evolution of almost incomprehensible and extremely complex information and communication systems. As the area of communication develops, the production of goods will diminish in favor of the production of the information services. The heaviest burden will be upon the political system. It is either democracy or authoritarianism. With the power of the information-communication system there will be no middle ground. Whoever controls this system also controls the sociopolitical system.

TRANSITION TO AN INFORMATION-BASED SOCIETY

Considering the United States as an example, the information systems currently are concentrated in the hands of and dominated by a small group of large corporations. These are actually the producers as well as operators of the basic information and communication systems.[22] They are building the high-technology infrastructure tending to crystallize the basic pattern for the coming information economy. This information economy, which is expected to be well emerged by the end of the century, will be based on the information services required by the institutions that have become the primary users of these new high-technology systems. The primary users among these appear to be financial, health, educational, and insurance institutions as well as the public sectors. Nearly all institutions will see a rapidly developing trend toward automated office operations.

Along with these developments will be an accelerating mass

consumerization of high-technology information services. Compared to this stage, the current communication-information systems are relatively primitive. In a span of probably a couple of decades, the advanced information and communication resources now available mainly to large private and public institutions will extend their availability to homes as well as small institutions. They will provide services concerned with daily chores of family life and needs.

In several European countries, England and France in particular, there are networks that already supply thousands of homes and offices with a wide range of computerized information services. Each system consists of the telephone, the television set, and a "black box" attachment and is linked to hundreds of data bases that provide a tremendously wide range of information. These are received on the television screen simply by dialing the appropriate center through the telephone. The fee is added to the telephone bill of each unit at the end of the month.[23]

At present this is a one-way information system. In the near future, but only in countries where the information service has been democratized, all subscribers will be allowed to develop their own mini data banks or just bits of original information and send these, through their computer terminal, to the central data banks. This information will then be available, through the central system, to other subscribers. In this manner, every person or institution will be his or its own data collector and contributor to the whole system. The system, which is an ultimate form of democracy, will be, for the first time, unmediated by any authority, whether public or private, and committed to an open, continuing, and self-updating information process. It will provide for all forms of education covering all areas of knowledge and extending to a vast array of areas and subjects unthinkable at the present. The current educational resources will be comparatively miniscule. Of further importance of availability of such educational resources is that the future system of education will be a continuing one rather than belonging primarily to a particular stage in life, as it is at the present. With this new information technology, continued learning will have a profound substance in an educational environment that will provide a stunning dimension to knowledge and creative thinking. All these developments will be discussed in more detail when we consider the study of the

Technodem information system of the future technological democratic society.

When we refer to the immense development of creative thinking we actually are talking about the immense possibilities of inquiry, search, and research, not only by scientists and experts but by anyone wishing to do so. The inquiry and research will be highly simplified. The machine, the computer, with access to unthinkably large amounts of resources and information, with exact methods of inquiry and analysis in its disposal, will do 95 percent of the research job that today only a few people are able to carry out. As we will see, the Technodem will connect each home or office terminal to all information resources available not only in one society but worldwide. Thus our understanding of equality of opportunity, freedom, individualism, and democracy as a whole, along with the incredible advance in our creativity, will all present a new dimension, a new and fascinating era and society.

The big question toward this kind of society is whether we will continue using the information technology for maximization of profits and exploitive private gains or will use it with a clear perception of socioeconomic needs, environmental protection, and preservation of natural resources and, above all, for a corresponding emotional and spiritual life that these dimensions will create. Our success in this direction will depend on the degree to which we lead the new information technology and on the extent that it corresponds with human values and answering human needs. The simplified question is whether we can finally have a really civilized society.

Toward this aim we need to move away from the use of information systems for maximization of material gains and concentrate our efforts and attention on humanistic targets. We need an alternative direction in which we can begin to consciously distinguish our choices in the emerging information environment. In a simplistic expression, the choice is between democratic, humanistic ideals and authoritarian technocratic operations currently derived from the control and use of the information system. The danger is magnified manyfold by the fact that the new information technology has been able to amplify intelligence dramatically in the minds of those who have access to it. One main problem is that the information technology is pulling us toward a transformed society faster than we can understand our direction. Major policies in this transformation process are not set by the government, industry, labor, or universities. Although all of these are important factors in the process, they are under the influence and instruments of a small financial community. Collectively, this group at present has control over the main structure and use of the information system, primarily for maximization of material gain.

The transformation process demands a new kind of awareness in order to take an appropriate democratic and humanistic direction of the relationship between technology, economic and social needs, and a political system to encourage and support it.

Technological democracy thrives only when there is equality of opportunity from social, economic, and political viewpoints and when members of society share enough information, beliefs, and assumptions to function together in a rough consensus toward these aims. The overriding concern should be the pattern by which influence is exerted and information becomes effective on a popular basis rather than on a centralized authoritarian fashion. Such a process demands collectivizing human intelligence by encouraging technological dialogue based on shared information and leading toward consensus on strategies for surviving and thriving as individuals in a democratic and humanistic society.

If technology continues to be mainly under the domain of a small group of special interests and remain under their rigid and narrow use for group benefits, it will tend to stratify the society further and lead to social and political alienation and unrest.

The promising aspect of the new information technology is its enormous capacity and capability to expand democratic and humanistic options. However, this can be possible if responsibilities and rewards of the system are shared by a large segment of the population, gradually approximating the whole population. This would mean progress toward equality of opportunity, an individual-centered perspective where information technology plays the principal role.

The special appropriation and misuse of the information system at present is an obstacle to proper understanding of the phenomenal liberating potential and democratizing dimensions of the information technology. The stumbling block to realizing this potential is technological illiteracy, which creates a disturbing tendency to retreat from the implications of the new information processes. The result is to forego the possibility of a viable technological democratic society.

To attain each of the various stages toward a democratic society there is a need for a process that will develop a level of literacy apt to stimulate creative use of the information machines by nontechnical and ordinary individuals.

Today technological development is a universal motto. It usually carries the title of modernization. It supercedes any other socioeconomic or political ideologies such as socialism, capitalism, or communism. Technological development has become a universal catalyst, with continuing and accelerating transformation in every aspect of life with which it comes in contact. It has turned into a universal dream, particularly among less developed societies, and a gospel that pronounces the common desires of human beings.

In this forward-moving process of technological development, the American example stands as a major force.[24] The drama is that while America is entering the era of information technology after a full conventional technological development, less developed countries are obliged to plunge into the modern information system despite their immature technological development. This urge toward development and use of information technology complicates the conventional modernization process.[25] It is a desire to get involved in high technology without having appropriate technological foundation. However, despite all its complications, the spread of information technology promises a substantial change in world order. It will tend to open a stunning global dimension to learning and knowledge turning into a powerful civilizing and democratizing force.

Attaining this stage of consciousness depends primarily on what the society does as a whole. The purpose must be the development and application of information technologies vital to moving toward a democratic society in the United States and abroad. Unfortunately, at present there are no such emerging strategies. Presently, the high technology is used on haphazard, unstructured decision-making processes driven primarily by economic forces. The problem is twofold. First, there is no definition or understanding of the concept of democracy as an independent and complete ideology. What is thought of democracy is primarily in a political sense accompanied by other economic ideologies such as capitalism or socialism. Thus a proper direction toward a democratic aim and future is absent. Second, the high technology, information technology in particular, is owned or controlled by a small economic elite and its supporting government. People as a whole do not have either control, input, or appropriate benefits emanating from the use of high-technology information systems.

There is no such concept or formula to guide us into an uncertain future where there would be enhanced intelligence capability along with greater social ambiguities. What is primarily needed is a proper formula for democracy and then a proper popular and practical information system. This has been our purpose in this writing.

NOTES

1. Irving Louis Horowitz, "Printed Words, Computers, and Democratic Societies," *Virginia Quarterly Review,* August 1983, p. 620.

2. In 1970, when the impact of the computer began to reach major proportions, 36,071 books were published and the sales amounted to 2.9 billion, while in 1980 over 45,000 books were published, with a total sales of 7.0 billion (ibid, p. 622).

3. Ibid., p. 624.

4. Jonathan Kozol, *Illiterate America* (Garden City, New York: Anchor Press/Doubleday, 1985), pp. 4–5.

5. Ibid., p. 5.

6. Consider, for example, *Dictionary of Political Science,* edited by Joseph Dunner (New York: Philosophical Library, 1964), comprising of 585 pages; and the *International Relations Dictionary,* by Jack C. Plano (New York: Holt, Rinehart, 1969), 337 pages. There are similar dictionaries for nearly any specialized field, such as engineering, economics, psychology, computer science, et cetera. *Black's Law Dictionary* (St. Paul: West Publishing Company, 1972) is nearly two thousand pages long.

7. John McDermott, "Technology: The Opiate of the Intellectuals," *New York Review of Books,* July 31, 1969. Also Teich, pp. 130–63.

8. Brenda Dervin, "More Will Be Less Unless: The Scientific Humanization of Information Systems," *National Forum* 63, no.3 (Summer 1983), pp. 25–26.

9. Ibid., p. 25.

10. For more details see: Brenda Dervin, "Mass Communicating: Changing Conceptions of the Audience," in William Paisley and Ronald Rice, ed., *Public Communication Campaigns* (Beverly Hills: Sage Publications, 1981), pp. 71–88. Brenda Dervin, "Communication Gaps and Inequities," *Progress in Communication Sciences,* vol. 2, Brenda Dervin and Mel Voigt, eds. (Norwood, New

Jersey: Ablex, 1980), pp. 73–112.

11. For a detailed explanation of the Technodem see chapter 5.

12. Colin Mellors and David Pollitt, "Legislation for Privacy: Data Protection in Western Europe," *Parliamentary Affairs* 37 (Spring 1984), p. 199.

13. A. R. Miller, *The Assault on Privacy* (Ann Arbor: University of Michigan Press, 1971), p. 25.

14. A. F. Westin, *Privacy and Freedom* (New York: Apheneum 1967), p. 7.

15. See OECD "Policy Issues in Data Protection and Privacy," *OECD Information Studies* 10 (1976).

16. Ibid., pp. 212–213.

17. James Basche, "Information Protectionism Across the Border," *Conference Board* 20 (September 1983), p. 38.

18. Ibid., p. 39.

19. For example, by a 1980 Bank Law, the government of Canada required all data originating in Canadian banks to be processed in Canada unless its processing elsewhere is specifically approved. A 1978 Brazilian regulation required approval from a Coordinating Commission on Data-Processing Activities for establishing a transborder data flow (TBDF) system. Currently the task is being carried out by the Special Secretariat for Informations. The number of restrictive regulations relating to transborder data flows has steadily increased since 1978 (ibid., p. 41).

20. Ibid., pp. 40–41.

21. Ibid., p. 41.

22. Ibid., p. 43. The statement is according to a February 1983 report by the National Telecommunications and Information Administration.

23. Ibid., p. 44.

24. Among these are global multinational corporations such as IT&T, IBM, ITT, RCA, GE, and CBS.

25. Wilson P. Dizard, Jr., *The Coming Information Age,* 2d ed. (New York: Longman, 1985), pp. 6–7.

Part II

TECHNOLOGICAL DEMOCRACY

Chapter Five

The Future Use and Control of Technology

TOWARD A DEMOCRATIC INFORMATION SYSTEM

Technology can be devastatingly evil if controlled by a small group and operated for its benefit. It can be a tool of exploitation and subjugation never envisioned before. Its enormous power over the daily life of individuals can be turned against them and create an incredibly monstrous authoritarian society. Since a technological power system can be encountered only by a better technological system, rivalry and race for domination between the elite-controlled technological systems tend to drag the human race to the brink of extinction. Each system tends to tighten its domination over people, transforming society into an inescapable modern slavery system controlled by the means of technology. This technological slavery is of the worse kind. In appearance the individual may feel free, but in reality he is hooked to the system from many directions. He has no way out if he desires to live within the technological society.

    This situation happens when the information as well as the production technologies are controlled by a small elite. Under the current situation in advanced countries, the United States in particular, where the substance of technology is controlled by a small elite, society tends toward such a technological authoritarian system. For example, in the United States, as has been demonstrated before, a small monopoly capitalist group controls the information system, such as television stations, radio networks, and most of the published information materials.[1] It also has monopoly over production technology through controlling the giant production and finance institutions.² As technology advances, through its use by the elite as a suppression instrument, individual freedoms are suppressed systematically. Consider, for example, the electoral process before the first television debate of the presidential candidates in 1960 and those of 1968 and thereafter. The media work for the elite and inform the public in a manner acceptable to the elite and in conformity with its interests. The media support only the candidates of the two major parties, since both of these parties serve the interests of the elite and the difference between their candidates is mostly cosmetic and for public consumption. Every president in recent decades has been the servant of the economic elite, if not a member of the group himself.

The only way, the sole hope for democracy, lies in the control of technology by the people as a whole rather than by a small group. Technology must be democratically owned, controlled and used.

Capitalism was a societal development encompassing and enhancing the process of industrialization. Though it was highly undemocratic, exploitive, and discriminatory, through the accumulation of capital it caused the rapid advancement of technology. But as technology progressed, the evils of capitalism became more stringent through the use of more advanced technology to tighten exploitation and discrimination.

When society passed through the stage of industrialization and reached the era of postindustrialization, capitalism became monopolistic. In order for the capitalist group to hold the status quo, it had to resort to its technological power to control the capitalistic oriented socioeconomic and political setup. But the advance of technology and its operation also required better and better educated masses. Currently though the elite tries through control of the information and educational system to prevent or at least retard the enlightenment process. Public consciousness takes root mainly through activities and teachings of a small intellectual anticapitalist-futurist group. Consequently, as the pressure of the monopoly capitalist elite to maintain power increases, the public consciousness about the situation develops further. It comes at a moment in history when capitalism has to leave the stage and technological democracy take its place.

This occurs through a social revolution by the employment of the theory of the general strike.[3] Since the capitalist elite and its instruments of power, including the state, control the use of technology, no violent uprising has a chance to succeed. It can be suppressed easily by the state military and local police forces, all at the service of the capitalists. But when people as a whole stop working, the economic system immediately disintegrates and along with it goes the political system. A point in favor of this general strike is that in a highly advanced society, the production and distribution processes are highly specialized and the whole operation of economy depends on the supply of energy and available distribution systems. If through a general strike workers in the energy and transportation areas or a specific sector of production stop working, the collapse of the economy occurs in days. The government will be placed under no condition to persist or continue operation. People can then ask for a constitutional convention to get rid of capitalism and establish a new technological democratic system based on the principle of equality of opportunity.

The first requirement for the new system would be the democratic control of the use of technology in information, production, and distribution areas. There cannot be a true democracy without first achieving this goal. Once this goal is achieved, socioeconomic and political democracy will follow. The most important factor in helping to achieve technological democracy is the democratic use of information technology in a systematic manner. We have labeled this coherent information system the Technodem. What is being presented here is not extraordinary and needs not to wait for a decade or so to be invented and developed. The technology necessary for the operation of the fantastic system of information and communication, this pillar of modern technological democracy, is already in existence. What is really new about the Technodem is the way the existing information technologies are put together and managed.

The Technodem actually is a more systemized and nationwide system of data collection, processing, and dissemination. It is new in that it has been placed in public domain. On the one hand, information is fed into the system by every individual and public and private institutions, and on the other, everyone and every institution has access to all the information stored in and analyzed by the system. The Technodem is the backbone of democratic technological society. It is the information system without which technological society cannot function properly. It is the symbol as well as the instrument of democracy, provider of opportunity for all, grantor of freedom, protector of individual values, dignity, and power, destroyer of giant public and private institutions, and a staunch instrument of decentralization and transfer of authority to individual and local private and public institutions.

The current state of technology, the way it is used, controlled, and abused in advanced societies, is regrettable. In capitalistic societies it has been controlled and directed by the monopoly capitalist production institutions and their supporting state agencies. Thus technology has been used primarily for profit and for its maximization. We have already demonstrated the negative and ever-increasing destructive effects of the use and control of technology for profit purpose by the production elite and by the state for the protection and preservation of the elite interests.

The situation is not much better under the socialist system. Here technology is controlled by and used according to the wishes of a small political elite, which controls the means and the processes of production and distribution. Though technology may not be used primarily for profit making and its maximization, it is, however, used to secure and maintain the power and status of the political elite. Consequently, the negative aspects of technology, though somehow diminished, are by no means eliminated.

Under some of the existing advanced systems, capitalistic as well as socialistic, the working people and the public as a whole have nothing much to say about the use of technology. Technology controls not only the production process but also the daily life of every individual, and the elite—corporate elite under capitalism and political elite under socialism—controls the use of technology.

With this technology's dominance over our daily life, as long as it is controlled by a small elite, no substantial progress toward a democratic way of life can be made possible. This is the main difference between an advanced technological society and those less developed. Whoever controls the technology controls the societal system. This is the modern type and the most monstrous elite rule. Through the use of technology, there is nearly an absolute tyranny in the economic sphere, which expands to the social structure and ultimately encompasses the political process.

Thus democracy in a technological society is possible only when technology is governed by the people as a whole rather than by a minority elite. This is why the democratic system of the future may be properly called *technological democracy*.

For moving toward a technological democratic society the control of technology must gradually move out of the hands of the monopoly capitalist group and into the hands of the working class. Unlike monopoly capitalism, where a very small group of capitalists control and benefit from technology, the major beneficiary under the new system is the public as a whole and the working class in particular.

Now let us see how this change of hands and decentralization takes place. Once workers start to receive shares of ownership of the means of production, in a manner that will be explained later, technology, which is probably the most important factor among the forces of production, starts to be owned by the workers. As the workers continue to increase and accumulate their ownership shares of the means of production, they continue to increase their voice in the use of technology. Once they take over the majority of the membership of the board of directors and other decision-making bodies of their firm, the control of technology within the firm falls into their hands.

As will be demonstrated later, once the workers take the control of their firm of employment, they tend to run it independent from the parent company. For example, in the case of Safeway Food Corporation, its twenty-four hundred supermarkets, its food processing plants, et cetera, will all tend to become independent once the decision-making body in each of these component institutions falls into the hands of the workers. Thus gradually the large production institutions become highly fragmented. Decentralization of the production institutions necessarily entails decentralization of technology used by these giant institutions. Before decentralization, all available technology was directly under the command of the parent company, in this case Safeway Food Corporation. After decentralization, each newly independent firm takes hold of its own technology. Thus high decentralization of technology is the outcome of the application of the principle of equality of opportunity to the area of capital and capital ownership. For the benefit of society and control of the negative effects of technology this transformation is a very significant achievement. It is an achievement resulting from the application of a democratic theory, with an enormous effect upon the environment and society.

Under the new system, control of technology is purely and totally in the hands of the private sector. It takes two different directions: a centralized, yet dispersed, national information system, and a highly decentralized and dispersed technology of production of goods and services.

THE NATIONAL INFORMATION SYSTEM: THE TECHNODEM

The current possibility of a national or international information and communication system labled here as the *Technodem* is no longer a fantasy, dream, or utopia. It can be realized with the currently existing information and communication technology and refined in a matter of one or two decades.

The Technodem is a nationwide network of electronic communication and information that can provide any desired information any place in the country and can connect individuals and institutions anywhere within the national or international territory it covers. It operates like the current telephone network, except that it also supplies the desired information in written displays in the computer terminal or in audio-video forms on the screen. Development of various technologies has made the availability of this high-tech information and communication system possible.

The first development is the progress in electronics, which has been increasingly and astonishingly shortening physical distance. For example, a single communications satellite launched into a geostationary orbit is capable of headlining communication over an area as large as about one-third of the earth's surface.

Optical-fiber cables offer fantastic advantages compared to electrical transmission, by having a much wider bandwidth with much less loss of signal strength.[4]

The second is that of remarkable progress in digital technology with a trend toward digital integration of all kinds of communication and information systems. Quite similar technologies now can be employed to handle every kind of information and communication. The integrated digital systems that are now being developed and used offer the same degree of support for all kinds of communication, whether it is a speech, written text, or even gestures. This is a revolutionary concept with the potential of handling all the modes of communication that human beings use when conversing face to face.

The third is the massive potential and storage capacity of computers, microcomputers in particular. Many complex and complicated tasks now can be carried out by microcomputers. Larger, ultra-high-speed supercomputers can carry out hundreds of millions of matrix calculations per second. Currently these are used in information centers and are also available on a time-sharing basis for a variety of extremely complex and powerful uses.

The fourth, but not the least, is the availability of rapidly developing electronic information sources retractable through computers. It provides the users easy and immediate access to the data resources.

The combined development of computer networks and data bases will make it, not very far from now, possible for anyone anywhere to retrieve, feed into the system, or exchange any type of information desired.

The fifth is the rapidly developing office automation as a result of the availability of microcomputers at progressively lower prices. An outstanding feature of this process is that materials produced in a word processor in one office will no longer have to be printed and copied for mailing to another office. The material can be transmitted electronically from one word processor to another through a teletex system. The new electronic methods of producing, editing, storing, and transmitting information will be a normal way of working and doing business. This will substantially reduce the time and paperwork required for the same results obtained under existing conventional systems of communication. One of the rapidly developing relevant areas is electronic publishing through the use of word processors. Today it is already possible to produce, edit, and print sheet music in the same way other texts are produced in a word processor.[5] The publishing industry is going through a thorough revolution in its production process.

Of course, last but not least is the introduction of electronic devices at home, including microcomputers, which have been discussed before. As illustrated in figure 5-1, the Technodem is a two-way information service system that is fully computerized. It is the most beneficial contribution of technology to human society. Continually useful, new, and modified information is fed to the terminals within each unit of production of goods and services all over society. These are then automatically transferred to the local centers. They are checked against existing information, filtered, modified, and then made accessible to the regional centers and from there to the central computer system. The central unit, which has access to information of a similar nature or category nationwide, checks and verifies it. If it finds the information is new, it then records it.

No computer unit in each production institution, which is located at the bottom of the information service hierarchy, would report anything that is already available through the Technodem. Because, each production unit has access to all information available through the Technodem. Any new information fed into the unit terminal, which is connected to the Technodem through local centers, will reject the information if it is not new; at the same time it will signify where such already existing information is stored within the system. Thus if the "new information" is already available through the Technodem, it will be known and such "new information," which is not actually new, will be discarded.

Besides its use in production of goods and services, through local centers every household is connected to the Technodem by a terminal computer. So a vast amount of information stored in the Technodem is available to every individual in society. At the same time, all data about each member of the family and information regarding the family as a whole is available to the

Figure 5-1. The National Information System: The Technodem

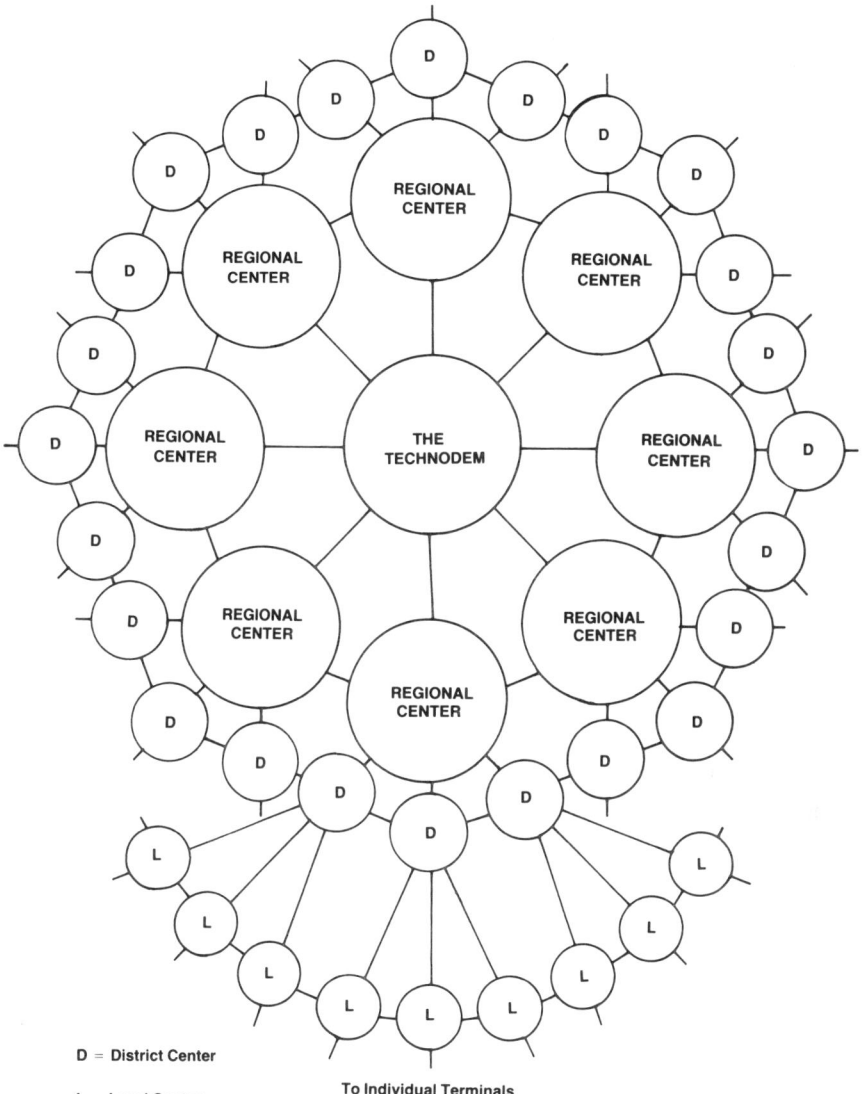

D = District Center
L = Local Center
To Individual Terminals

Figure 5-2. Local Structure of the Technodem

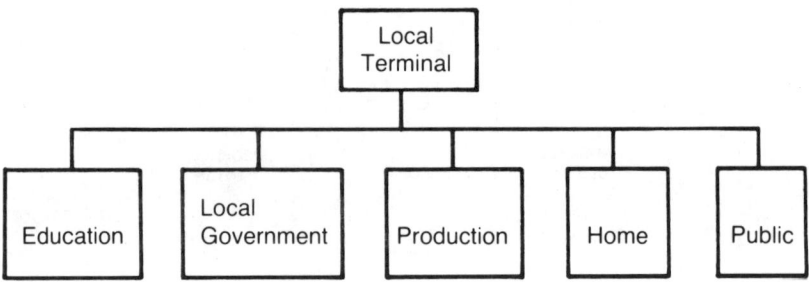

1. Central terminal in each educational institution connected to the terminals within the institution providing access to educational programs produced or available.

2. Central terminal connected to other terminals in different departments or offices providing information relating to local government functions, rules, and regulations, also providing for public participation in the decision-making process.

3. Central terminal in each production institution connected to terminals in different departments and offices within the institutions.

4. Personal terminals located in each home.

5. Terminals located in public places (similar to public telephone system) to be used by persons who need immediate access to a terminal.

Technodem through each family terminal. Each household pays a small fixed monthly fee for the use of the Technodem to a local center, similar to what is currently paid to the telephone company. Figure 5-2 illustrates the structure of the local system of the Technodem.

The Technodem is a two-way system of information: upflow and downflow.

INFORMATION UPFLOW

Each individual, family, and institution of production of goods and services carries a data disc about one square inch in size embodied in a plastic rectangular computer ID card (CID) with a specific computer code. Each disc embodies detailed information about the individual, family, or institution. Within each household, this information is fed to the terminal by inserting the CID card into a slot provided for this purpose. The same applies to each institution. In this case, the CID card contains basic information about the institution. Each time a CID card is inserted into the computer terminal, it is also automatically updated. For example, if a person had left one job and was employed in another place, since this information is totally available to the Technodem, through the corresponding employers, the individual's CID card is automatically modified and his new employment and its specifics are added to his personal data disc. It is the same if the individual changes his residence, achieves certain educational goals, or receives a promotion. Part of the information, which is public record, will be accessible to everyone. But personal data that are private remain confidential unless one has access to the individual's CID card. Each disc card carries a computer code, similar to the Social Security number of each individual or business identification number of each institution. Without this code, even though personal data of each individual are stored in the Technodem, it will remain confidential and will not be accessible. Thus in order to receive confidential information about an individual or institution, one has to give to the computer the name of the individual or institution and the pertinent code.

As information fed to the individual and institutional computers moves upward to local, district, regional, and national levels, it is analyzed, tabulated, processed, and stored. This allows the person access to phenomenal statistical data at the local, district, regional, and national levels. The Technodem thus becomes a source of vast information never achieved before and, more important, always updated and immediately available to the inquirer upon request.

Therefore, the upflow of information is highly, and nearly totally, decentralized as well as dispersed. It starts from each independent individual or institution at the bottom of the social strata and moves upward to the center of the Technodem at the national level. The input of information is continuous, reflecting every change and interaction in society, and through the immediate availability of information it also, in turn, continually affects changes and interactions. This makes society on the whole highly dynamic, a stage never achieved before.

Thus in gathering information for public use no single group or combination or groups or government agency has control or even influence over what is being gathered. This advanced technology of information system makes it highly democratic.

INFORMATION DOWNFLOW

As stated above, while information is being fed into the individual and institutional computers, it continually moves upward to local, district, regional, and national levels. At each level, the information collected on each subject is categorized, processed, and tabulated and ready to be used at that particular level. It is also transferred to the upper level and processed and tabulated at that level. Thus at the national level we have all kinds of national statistics and national information available through the central system.

For example, if we want to know the rate of exchange for a dollar in European countries, classification of a specific position and its salary ranges by the national office, number of children born during the past day, the text of a specific law just passed through the national legislative assembly, job availability on the market in a certain specific field or profession, and millions of other examples of national level information, we can get it from the central system through our computer terminals at home or in the office. If the inquirer is in Region A and wants certain information about Region B, his computer through Regional Office A is connected to Regional Office B and he receives the information relating to Region B. If he wants information from district other than his own and that district is within his region, he can get direct contact with that district through his computer by dialing the code of the intended district. If the district is outside his region, then he goes through the regional office by dialing the specific code of that region and the intended district located there. If the information relates to a locality other than his, if that locality is within his district, he can get direct contact by dialing the computer code of that locality. If the local system is out of his district, then he dials the district code and then the local code to get contact with the intended locality.

Simply, communication within this whole national system of information is very similar to the telephone system and the area codes we use for long distance calls, except that instead of an individual at the other end of the line, we deal with a much more knowledgeable machine, the Technodem. These communication code numbers are different from the CID card codes. The latter are confidential, while the former are available through a directory similar to that of the telephone, except that it is electronic and can be retrieved from the computer by dialing the name of the area, institution, or individual.

Therefore, each individual through his computer has access to all kinds of information available at any place in the country. By this computerized arrangement, no central office or group or governmental agency has neither control nor influence upon availability of any information to individuals or institutions. Everything is controlled and automatically processed by the system and made accessible to the inquirer by the computer.

Thus, despite the fact that the Technodem is a centralized information system, gathering of information and its dissemination are highly decentralized and dispersed. Here again, high technology makes this vital process in the daily life of individuals, institutions, and society highly democratic, a stage of democracy never achieved or possible before. The Technodem is the foundation and backbone of *technological democracy*.

SERVICES AVAILABLE THROUGH THE TECHNODEM

It is practically impossible to enumerate the services available through the Technodem or try to describe its vital contribution to daily life and to individual and societal development. The few examples described below illustrate the incredible magnitude of the capacity of the Technodem to serve humanity. An interesting and unique aspect of this high technology is that the individual does not have to leave his home or office in order to get these services, whereas today he has to travel long distances to go to different localities to be able to get only a fraction of the service or information available through the Technodem.

1. Education Services

Each household will have access to immense sources of educational information from preschool all the way up to the highest educational level. For example, the outline of every course will be available to each individual through the home unit; a person may choose to start a course at the first-grade level, take a eighth-grade social studies, physics. U.S. history, advanced algebra, and thousands of other courses. While studying such a course, a student is able to ask questions from the Technodem and receive explanations. Of course, all educational materials are prepared by competent scholars and fed into the Technodem system. At a higher level of knowledge, different schools of thought in a field are available for comparison and analysis. This will particularly be true in the area of social sciences, which is and will remain the most complex and increasingly important of all sciences. Furthermore, examinations for each course are carried out through the computer. They are corrected, graded, and recorded in the individual's academic record, stored in the computer of his local educational institution. Thus each individual will have in the possession of the computer an accumulated record of his education and achievements coded to that individual and accessible to others only by permission from the individual through a temporary decoding process through the use of an individual's CID card.

This system will revolutionize the total educational process. First, it will make available to each individual updated educational information at every level of knowledge or discipline, twenty-four hours a day. Thus an individual may spend his daily hours for learning according to his own choice. Second, the current classroom education and instructions will become obsolete and discarded. Laboratory work, for study or research purposes, will be carried out through the computer by using the latest available facilities. Experimental research work will still be carried out through traditional research institutions, the results being fed continually into the computer and thus made available to the public and other scholars. Third, the system will be used by individuals as an enormous encyclopedia, covering every area of knowledge, updated at all times. Fourth, new educational institutions will be created whose jobs will be to prepare courses in every subject area and at different levels within that subject area and feed those to the computer, thus making the knowledge available to the public. Fifth, for the preschool and the first stage of general education up to the eighth grade physical institutions and instructors will be used. However, this type of education will be heavily supplemented by computer education, particularly in doing homework and seeking study aid. Sixth, the system will serve as an enormous library and provide the individual with all the services currently available through a modern library except that the services will be far more comprehensive, more extensive, and easily accessible. This is a democratic educational system, providing equal opportunity for all, which never existed before and could be achievable only through the use of a high-technology information system such as the Technodem.

2. Medical Services

A data bank regarding medical information, including preventive medicine, health, and diet care, will be provided and be updated continually by medical task forces, each consisting of experts in a specific area of medical knowledge. All will be made available to each individual through his home terminal. Each person may examine his own health condition by feeding into the computer symptoms of his illness or discomfort for the purpose of diagnosis. He then receives a response about his condition and possible alternatives, which he may continue to narrow down by giving more facts and asking additional questions. For simple discomforts, allergies, et cetera, the individual may get prescriptions for drugs and instruction about using them from the computer. The computer will also disclose the side effects of each drug. If the computer finds the situation serious, it will then suggest possible diagnoses and will advise seeing a physician. The computer will be equipped to respond to questions regarding the nutrient or other effects of fruits, vegetables, grains, et cetera, upon the body and health of the individual, particularly if the individual gives the computer his vital statistics such as age, height, weight, sex, blood pressure, et cetera.

In brief, the Technodem will serve as an ever-ready medical aid that keeps the individual conscious of his health condition and provides the individual with guidance in taking care of his health. The possibility of many illnesses will be discovered without reference to a medical expert and will induce the individual to see a doctor. The computer will also make an analysis of all drugs and outline their beneficial effects and negative side effects. The same will apply to all foodstuff. The computer will also provide a list of physicians in the area, with their specialities. The individual will then receive a copy of the computer analysis from the printer of his computer and take it with him to the physician. The Technodem will be specifically useful for children, the elderly, and those who shy away from seeing a doctor or are reluctant to disclose their physical ailments.

3. Legal Services

Most of the services rendered by attorneys will be available to each individual through the Technodem. These will include information and commentaries about the laws, court decisions, and administrative rulings. The computer will provide a copy of any legal form needed by an individual, such as a lease form, an affidavit, a financial loan, a corporate charter, and thousands of other forms, with appropriate information about completing each form and procedures to be followed. It will also have a list of attorneys within the area, with their specialities. If the individual asks the computer about a certain illegal act, it will explain the law applied to the situation, including a previous legal history of such violations by others. It will also propose the steps to be taken to resolve the problem, which may include seeing an attorney. The Technodem will also be used extensively by physicians as well as lawyers, since it can supply all information available through a medical or law library and much more. Physicians will receive analysis and advice from the Technodem about the illness of their patients, drugs to be used, and procedures to be followed to cure the illness. Lawyers as well as judges will receive all kinds of necessary information, even suggestions of decisions, from the Technodem about each specific case. This will be possible because the Technodem has the legal history for each offense, including past applications of pertinent laws, court interpretations, most recent rulings, et cetera.

4. Product Services and Market Information

In technological democracy, the Technodem will be the prime tool of marketing as well as shopping and purchasing. One must pay special attention to understand the simplicity of highly complex processes of marketing and distribution effectuated through the Technodem.

Marketing

Nearly all kinds of advertisement currently used will gradually be discarded, because through the increasing use of continually updated information available through the Technodem to the consumers, all advertisement will be outdated and obsolete.

As society moves toward technological democracy and the Technodem develops, gradually production firms will desire to submit their catalog of items to the Technodem. When a consumer asks for a product, the computer will show the item on the home screen and give specifications of the product and the price.

Thus the current system of commercial advertisement will lose its effect and be discarded. A substantial amount of capital that is spent on advertising today will be saved, causing a significant reduction in product prices. The tremendous amount of capital saved by abandoning advertisement will then be channeled toward production of goods and services. This will also eliminate the annoying advertisements on billboards on the side of highways, in newspapers, and on radio and television, because through the home computer an individual, for example, may investigate the kind of restaurants in the area, their specialities, and their menus. He may then choose which one he desires to go to.

Each locality, based on size of the community, will have several public information centers, each with several computer terminals where newcomers and tourists can get information about hotels, restaurants, apartments and houses for rent, and any other needs.

Shopping and Purchasing

This system of computerized shopping applies to retail as well as wholesale transactions.

For example, if a person wants to purchase a cassette player with special specifications, he will feed to the home terminal the name of the item and the specifications he has in mind. The computer will respond by listing different brands available on the market. Though specifications for each may not be exactly what the customer desires, he has to make a choice from among several presented to him. The individual may ask the computer which one of those presented at his desired price range is the best buy and why. He may then ask which stores in the area carry that item. The computer will list all local stores having the item available. The customer then calls the store and makes the purchase, which is delivered.

In technological democratic society there also will be little use for money as we know it today. Most transactions will take place automatically through an advanced credit system that transfers funds from the customer's computerized bank account to the seller's account. Each account holder will receive a monthly computerized statement that will show all transactions, deposits, and transfers. In addition, through use of a CID each individual will have immediate access to his account, including recent deposits and payments, on the screen of his home terminal. He can then make any transfer of funds he desires, which will be recorded in his monthly statement of account. For making payment for the purchased item the consumer will give the computer the computer code of the store where he purchased the product, plus his bank code and account number. The amount equal to the purchase price will then be transferred from his bank account to the store's account. In the advanced stage of technological democracy, no monthly bank statements need to be sent to individuals, since each individual will have access to his acount statement through the computer.

5. Library Services

Each terminal will have access to the Technodem's library. There is a vast variety of information stored in the Technodem, including areas of literature, history, science, technology, art, music, sports, et cetera. Imagine the information held today in the Library of Congress and expand it several times. Currently such sources of knowledge are not available to everyone but to small groups of scholars and researchers. Through the Technodem, everyone will have access to this information. As a result, the library systems existing now will become obsolete and gradually be discarded. The new local and regional libraries will be electronic and to that extent a part of the Technodem.

The immensity of information available through the Technodem is beyond comprehension. For example:

1. A person wants to see all available works of Picasso or Renoir. These will be available in full color on the screen, with specific commentary on each item of work of art, when the viewer requests.
2. A person wants to visit the Tower of London. He will

be given the historical background and will be exposed to all its treasures and points of interest.
3. A person wants to hear the 1983 New Year celebration in Vienna performed by the famous Vienna Philharmonic Orchestra or wants to hear and view the repertoire of such ceremonies for the last twenty years.
4. A person wants to watch the 1980 Wimbledon men's tennis championship match, 1984 world soccer, or 1964 football championship game.
5. A person wants to view the movie *Cleopatra*, with Richard Burton and Elizabeth Taylor.
6. A person wants to view the national Democratic party convention of 1976.
7. A person wonders what is new in genetic research.
8. A person wants the weather forecast for the next seven days in Chicago, London, Moscow, et cetera.
9. A person wants to learn about Einstein's theory of relativity and its use.
10. A person wants the story of Mother Goose and its origin and background.
11. A person wants Japanese soup recipes and information on how to prepare them.
12. A person wants to learn about the invention and development of the automobile.
13. A person wants to learn about outer space and what is a black hole.
14. A person wants to know what is the latest in artifical heart transplants, how is it transplanted and how it operates.
15. A person wants a brief review of U.S. presidents and a detailed review of the Truman presidency.
16. A person wants to read a certain article in the *New York Times* of January 18, 1933.
17. A person wants a bibliography of recent publications on DNA or air piracy.

Of course, these can all be copied through an advanced VCR that is connected to the terminal set or can be transcribed through a word processor attached to it. At the same time there will be no need to copy any of the programs, since each will be accessible through the terminal any time it is desired. Only materials to be used for research purposes, such as a bibliography, may need to be copied.

Of course, as it was described under "Education," the Technodem will make available to each person instruction on any subject matter at any level desired. This may be beginner tennis, high level physics, or biochemistry instruction or instructions regarding the maintenance and repairs of household items such as plumbing, electrical wiring, water softeners, refrigerators, heating and cooling systems, et cetera.

6. Entertainment

The Technodem will have in its library an immense collection of material for entertainment, such as movies from its silent stages to the most recent productions; concerts, operas, ballets, documentaries of all kinds, whether historical or relating to the nature of things or outer space, sports of any kind, with championship matches, et cetera. Each individual will find a variety of items according to his taste and for his enjoyment.

7. Job Market and Placement Service

Placement services available through the Technodem to every individual are unique, and it has never been possible to render them before. Every institution that has any open position feeds it to the computer through terminals available to it.

An individual looking for a job or desiring to change his current occupation or place of work may ask the computer for open positions in his desired field or location. He immediately receives a list of such positions in the desired location. If there was none available in that specific area, then the computer will give openings closest to the desired area. Or the individual, if he has no preference of a specific locality, may check the openings on a regional basis. Each opening has a computer code number presented on the screen. The applicant, after selecting one or more of the open positions, gives the code number of the position to the computer, plus inserts his personal computer data card (CID) in the computer.

Immediately the terminal in the personnel department of the corresponding institution extracts and transcribes the applicant's personal data. The personnel department's computer then studies it, comparing the applicant's qualifications to those of other applicants. Then using the applicant's CID, the computer informs the applicant of the results and his ranking compared to all the others. The message is transcribed by the applicant's computer. An unusual benefit of this process is that the applicant finds out, immediately after his application for the job, about his position compared to the other applicants and thus the likelihood of getting the job. If his standing is not promising, he may then apply for other jobs without waiting for the final results from the one already applied for. After the deadline for filing an application, the final decision is made by the institution and is communicated to the applicant in the same manner. The communication is transcribed by the applicant's computer. The institution may decide to interview the top two or three on the list. If the answer is negative, the applicant then applies to the place of his second choice and so on until he is offered a job. If the applicant does not receive a response for his application within a reasonable time, using the code number of the position applied for, he communicates with the employer asking for an explanation.

Consider the tremendous amount of time, red tape, and money saved compared to the present procedures that one has to follow while seeking employment.

8. Communication System

The Technodem provides for a super communication system never available before. It substantially eliminates communication by the postal system as well as telephone. Though the individual is charged for each communication, the cost is much less than for postal services or long distance telephone calls. The reason is that this is a nationwide centralized system capable of providing for a superadvanced and instant interpersonal or interinstitutional communication, and furthermore, there is no profit to be gained. For example, if a person is sending a message and the receiving terminal is busy transcribing another message, this individual's message is stored in the memory of the receiving unit and transcribed when its turn arrives, a service that the current telephone answering devices are not able to render. A great advantage of this communication system to the postal services is that regardless of distance the message is received instantly, rather than in the day or more needed by airmail. Also consider the tremendous amount of manpower, buildings, materials, transportation, and other resources saved. All these can then be diverted to be used for more beneficial production of goods or services.

It must be noted that unlike postal communication, where the individual must know the exact address and zip code of the receiving party, or telephone communication, where the party must have access to a telephone directory, in the Technodem system the computer has the needed information for communication purposes. For example, if A wants to communicate with B, he gives B's full name to the computer. Immediately B's computer code number appears on the screen. If more than one code number is received, it means that there is more than one person with the same name. Individual A then gives the name of the city or area where B resides. Immediately the extra codes disappear and the individual has access to B's code. By giving B's code to the computer, A is connected to B's terminal and can start communication. The individual may also store in the memory of his computer the names and code numbers of the individuals or institutions he usually contacts. This serves as a personal computer communication directory, similar to the personal telephone directory individuals use today. In these cases no search is required and the individual need only give the computer the area code and the code number of the person or firm with which he wants to get in contact.

In the advanced communication system of the future, B will personally appear on A's screen and the communication can be carried out orally. If B was communicating with someone else, A could leave a transcribed message for B to contact him when he is available. This technology is not far off and will be available in a decade or so.

Thus daily communication, personal as well as business, is a very important part of the Technodem services. Thinking of the enormous volume of such communication, one may doubt the capacity of the Technodem. To comprehend this, one needs to consider that in actual operation the Technodem is highly decentralized. For example, within a locality, e.g., Chicago, for local communication purposes people and institutions use only the local system. The rest of the Technodem is not involved. The same applies to regional communications, e.g., the Midwest. In this case only the regional system is involved. The basic function of a regional system is simple. It connects the involved local systems together. For example, if a person or an institution in Chicago wants to communicate with a person or an institution in Detroit, the function of the regional system is to connect the Chicago system to the Detroit system. So the main functions of communication are carried out through the local systems. If the communication is interregional, then the Technodem makes the connection. Most individual communications are local, such as contacts with the city government, schools, utility companies, shopping centers, local social and service organizations, et cetera. Most of the production institutions' communication is also local. These are small service institutions and retail businesses. Most of the larger institutions' communication is regional. These comprise the bulk of daily communication, and in none of these does the central system of the Technodem get involved.

Thus when we say the Technodem is a centralized information system, we must make a distinction between the daily communication process, which is highly decentralized, and the interregional communication, when the Technodem gets involved and interconnects the regions in question. Thus in this situation its only function is to connect the two regions together.

In fact, in operation the system uses area codes and is quite similar to the telephone system currently used except that it is far more advanced and much cheaper.

In the areas of general information services of nationwide interest such as library, medical, legal, and educational services, the system is highly centralized. Yet gathering of information for these services is highly decentralized and achieved through many expert task forces for accuracy and neutrality. This decentralized system also keeps information gathering out of the hands of the small elite, which may tend to manipulate the information.

Thus the central operation of the Technodem is purely a technical function and no employee is involved in dealing with substances of the information supplied by the system. This is simply because the important aspect of control relates to the preparing and feeding of information to the Technodem. In this regard, local or scientific information is prepared by the local or scientific task forces, each consisting of a carefully selected group of experts, by the academic or scientific institutions, on the subject matter of information. Many vital statistics and data are gathered automatically as soon as information is fed to the system by an individual or an institution. These include areas such as population, elections, economics, production, housing, and employment and thousands of other areas. Nearly all the data used is fed to the computer by individuals, institutions, or agencies at the local levels and then processed at the district, regional, and national levels. This process makes an elite control or influence impossible.

Thus the collection of data is highly decentralized, and after, in each locality, the information is fed to the computer, it is the computer that tabulates them at the district, regional, and national levels without any human function involved. And when the information is needed, it is the computer, without human involvement, that provides it.

Furthermore, a substantial bulk of information is supplied by the production and distribution firms by feeding the data to their own computer terminals, which become available to interested parties through the Technodem. This information must be verifiable by the company documents, files, and accounts. Since the operation of the firms will be electronic, this purpose will be achieved by connecting the firm's computers to the Technodem. This will be a requirement in democratic society, as will be discussed later. In this regard, hundreds of thousands of firms supply much vital information relating to production, finance, employment, positions, their classification and corresponding salary ranges, organizational structure, and function; products, product description and prices, employment, ownership, work regulations, and so on.

District computer centers tabulate and store all this information, available to regional and national centers. District computers also are able to give information requested by anyone regarding any or a collection of firms within the territory or a specific subject area. The same information will be accessible by terminals in other regions by going through the Technodem.

Thus when we are talking about a highly centralized information system, we are not talking about a centralized control of information but a centralized system of electronically controlled information services. Even a great bulk of national information will be supplied to the Technodem not by one, but by a variety of the national institutions independently. For example, the Economic and Production Council will provide information relating to the frameworks established for position classification, pay system, capital distribution and return, natural resources, and environmental use or preservation.

This information is fed regularly into the computer terminals of the council and its subordinate agencies, and through these they are transferred to the Technodem. The information and data are kept updated.

In the same manner, the National Health and Education Council provides information and data regarding the educational system, its structure and operation, curriculum, general rules, and requirements. The same applies to health care and welfare rules, principles, and framework of operation. The International Affairs Council and Foreign Affairs Department supply an immense volume of information regarding economic, sociocultural, and political aspects of other nations in addition to relations between the nations in each of these areas, including the foreign relations of the United States. The Judicial Council supplies information regarding the national laws and regulations, final court decisions on matters of regional and national conflicts, criminal and civil punishments and information and data regarding prisons, prisoners, and prison work regulations. The National Legislative and Coordination Assembly provides information regarding the approval of reports submitted to it by all the above stated agencies, the legislative process, the latest status of bills under consideration, and their passage or failure.

The same applies to all agencies of the national government, including the Executive Council and the Defense, Foreign Affairs, Finance, and Judicial Departments. Thus collection of information at the national level is highly decentralized and dispersed and out of the control or influence of a particular elite.

All this immense information is accessible to every individual through his home or local public terminals. The only thing he needs to do is ask for his desired information through his computer terminal by using the specific code from the code directory or asking the computer for the desired code if he has no access to such code.

9. The Electoral Process

In general, there are two kinds of political democracy: popular and representative. In popular democracy, all eligible citizens participate in the policy-making process as well as in choosing their leaders. Since this kind of democracy was not possible in a country which was large and populated and since it was neither possible nor practical to refer to people frequently for major policy-making decisions, representative democracy was invented. Under this type of democracy people, as a whole or as groups, choose a few representatives for a definite and limited period of time and those representatives, within that determined period of time, make policies on behalf of the people.

Framers of the U.S. Constitution were well aware of these two kinds of democracy. Since the American territory, comprising of the previous thirteen colonies, was very large and the means of communication and transportation were slow, achieving popular democracy was impossible despite the fact that this kind of democracy was more desirable. Therefore, the framers chose representative democracy as an alternative for the system of the new government. Accordingly, they established a congress (comprising of elected representatives) and also an elected chief executive. States and later on the European countries followed suit.

But as Western societies became industrialized and technology advanced, the representative democracy, though maintaining its appearance, lost its essential quality as being the representative of all the people. Through the control of capital and technology, the economic elite and its corresponding pressure groups took over the electoral process. So today the people, if they choose to vote, do vote for the candidates who, through intricate technological and financial processes, are preselected by the economic elite and its instruments of power.

The result is that the so-called representative democracy today in reality does not represent the people as a whole, but represents the ruling elite—an economic elite in the United States and political elite in the Soviet Union—and serves its interests. Neither of the two is actually democratic. The same applies more or less to other industrialized countries.

People still believe that popular democracy on a large scale is, if not impossible, impractical and highly burdensome. Furthermore, it is claimed that even if it is allowed, it cannot produce fruitful results because people as a whole are ignorant of the issues and incompetent of making proper decisions. None of these claims is authoritatively sustainable in relation to the future.

The Popular Electoral Process

At the present stage of high electronic technology it is possible that today a person can carry an electronic computer as large as a wristwatch and vote yes or no or abstain several times a day within a specific time limit designated by the government or smaller institutions. All these votes can be recorded, tabulated, stored, and announced at the local, district, regional, and national computer centers in a matter of minutes. A very important aspect of this kind of popular election or decision making is that no human hand is involved in its processing and tabulation and all is carried out automatically by the computer system, the Technodem and its subcomponents. In the age of the Technodem, when each individual will be able to carry such electronic devices and, furthermore, will have access to computer terminals at home or office or within his vehicle, not only will each individual be able, at any time, to participate in the electoral and decision-making process, but he also will be able to answer a score of questions relating to the subject of a specific decision. The contention of public ignorance will be of no importance since, on the one hand, in technological democratic society every individual will be highly educated, particularly in relation to public issues, and on the other, the size and variety of public issues will be highly decreased and a large sector of them will be institutional or local.

A very important aspect of this kind of process is that it

substantially diminishes the effect of organized interest or pressure groups, since each individual is able to make his choice of leader or decision at complete privacy and secrecy. After each electoral or decision-making process is recorded and tabulated, each individual has access to its results and analysis through his home or other public computer terminals. It must be noted that because of the highly decentralized nature of technological democracy, most of the important decisions are institutional or local. There will be only a few decisions of regional or national importance. Individuals become a very important and essential element in the operation of production as well as local systems and in management of their affairs. This is the meaning of a true and technological democracy, achievable only through the availabilty and use of the high technology information system.

Education for Political Democracy

The second argument for popular democracy is that the ordinary citizen is ignorant in regard to the structure and operation of the system and the complex subjects of decision and thus incapable of meaningful participation.

To challenge this claim one must notice that democracy can take place and be maintained only in a society that is highly educated. In this sense, education does not refer to engineering, computer science, or accounting and so on. These are technical or special training programs and do not contribute to individual knowledge about human society and its operation. Education meaningful to the democratic process for the advancement of civilization and for understanding and fostering human values relates to the areas of history, humanities, and the normative aspects of social sciences.

From this viewpoint the United States, among the advanced societies, is substantially illiterate. The emphasis in education has been placed on technical and professional training in order to enhance productivity and thus maximize exploitation and profits. Education relating to human values and social organizations that causes enlightenment and enhances the civilized quality of society is systematically and intentionally eliminated as required curricula. The elite want better producers rather than better thinkers. Advanced thinkers, if they are allowed to materialize, obviously and by necessity would reject the unjust system of capitalism and its inhuman consequences and rise against it. Thus, from the rulers' viewpoint, this social element so dangerous to the continuation of capitalism must not be allowed to materialize. This is why, among advanced societies we are near the bottom in the level of civility. We pay lip service to human life and human values. Our production institutions fire hundreds of thousands of workers without thinking what happens to them and their families.

Our government suppresses many Third World nations through economic domination and by supporting dictatorial regimes that demonstrate sympathy toward the interests of the American economic elite within their system. For the same reason, our government is adamantly anticommunist, since the primary function of ideology, wherever it takes root, is to eliminate capitalism. It is because of this lack of proper education and enlightenment, and development of national ignorance that people's destiny has been taken over by a very small group of economic elite, which has been able to manipulate the political process to its benefit, carefully hidden behind the facade of representative democracy. Millions of people live in poverty and despair in a society of plenty and alongside centimillionaires. Millions perish for lack of medical care and hundreds of thousands are massacred by the instruments of elite in order to maintain the existing power structure and profit level. Consequently, if citizens are properly educated, they will be well able to determine what kind of policies are sound, just, beneficial, and appropriate to them and their society as a whole.

The Electoral Process Through the Technodem

In a technological democratic society, there will be no need for campaigns, which are actually an elite propaganda, a waste of time for citizens and money for society, for the following reasons:

1. Each elective office has a position classification, as does any other occupation in society. Thus getting the

job is no longer a popularity contest as practiced in the United States, where the process of election involves a good deal of propaganda and deception through commercial and media image building. The candidate must be, primarily, qualified for the elective position based on the job description and the education and experience required to hold the position. Whether an elective position is local, regional or national, it will have its job description and required qualifications.

2. The personal data of every candidate will be released from confidentiality and will become available through the Technodem system to each individual. The data will reveal all one needs to know about the candidate's family, education, achievements, and experience. Furthermore, such a candidate's past experience in different institutions is a public record and will be available and verifiable through the Technodem. Each voter may check to find out about the candidate's achievements at the workplace, which will reveal a good deal about the candidate's true characteristics, ideological directions, responsibility, and accountability. If the candidate had held any elective office before, all his records of behavior as an elected officer can be investigated through the Technodem. These are the facts of the candidate's life, qualities, and experience. Anything beyond this is propaganda. If an otherwise qualified candidate has been outstanding in his performance, the likelihood is that he will do the same under the new position.

3. The continuation of this system of investigating a candidate will cause the individuals who run for elective offices to maintain a clean and outstanding achievement record. Furthermore, it will discourage individuals from running for an elective office if their educational background and experience do not qualify them to hold the office. The candidacy of such individuals will automatically be rejected by the computer, which has access to their personal data and achievement background.

Despite the advanced technological system in the United States, no such true factual specifics and broad information about a candidate are available to the voters today. The voters' information depends heavily on what the candidate's agents supply and on the media, which is under elite control, through its ownership and financial sponsorship, and thus the information is always prejudiced one way or another, more or less. The media also are mainly concerned about the campaign process because of its commercial value, rather than the facts about the personality or philosophical directions of the candidates.

Thus if we eliminate campaigns, we come down to finding the best qualified person from among many candidates for the job. One must notice that in a technological democratic society, based on the above process and services available through the Technodem, the need for political parties will disappear totally. Imagine how much the nation will gain if the time and efforts of millions of party workers, for a campaign period of more than a year in presidential elections, plus billions of dollars spent on campaigns—presidential, congressional, and gubernatorial—will be saved. The Technodem provides opportunity for such enormous savings of manpower and money.

Under the new process:

1. A person desiring to run for a specified office will announce his candidacy. Let us say a person is running for the highest office, for example, membership in the National Executive Council. Let us assume also that the job requires at least thirty years of regular education background, experience at least in a regional governmental position, and strong background in international education, with proficiency at least in one major foreign language.[6] The candidate-to-be must first consider his qualifications before announcing his candidacy.
2. The announcement of the candidacy is through the Technodem. The candidate simply feeds his name, personal data code, and candidacy, with specifications of the office, to the Technodem. First, the Technodem will immediately check the qualifications of the individual against the requirements of the position. If the candidate does not have the minimum qualifications required, his name and candidacy will automatically be rejected and discarded from the list of candidates. Second, if the candidate is qualified, his name and qualifications will be tabulated along with those of the other candidates and

his name will be placed in the appropriate place on the list. The tabulation of the candidates' scores does not depend only on personal data. Past service and experience, through information supplied by personal data and all service records in every institution they worked, will automatically be examined by the Technodem and added to their scores.

3. Enough time will be given to voters to examine the records. Of course, the Technodem has already examined the qualifications of all the candidates and has ranked them accordingly in three categories: education, experience, and personality. However, each voter is free to vote for the candidate of his choice. Based on advanced education and consciousness of the voters about the requirements of the position to be filled, it is more likely that the voters would prefer to choose the best qualified person.

4. An election day and hour will be announced. During that hour every eligible citizen will vote, simply by recording in his home or car terminal "yes," "no," or "abstain." A person can vote regardless of where he is in the country, and he can vote only once, since his name code in the Technodem will reject any subsequent additional vote. In a national election this is no problem. A person living in New York but in Los Angeles at the time of election can vote there. In order to vote, the voter first inserts his personal data card into a slot in a terminal that is accessible. At home this will be his home terminal, in a car this will be the car terminal; elsewhere it will be a friend's home terminal, an office terminal, or a public terminal. Once he inserts his ID card into the terminal, his identification will be recorded. Then he will vote. His vote will immediately be recorded and transferred to his local center in local elections, to district centers in regional or national elections, respectively. No voter can vote more than once in each election. If he does, since the computer already has in its record that he has voted, his second vote will be rejected, but his improper action will be recorded in his personal data file. This will necessarily discourage any person from trying to vote more than once in each election. In the case of local elections, only those eligible can vote. Sup-

pose there is a mayoral election in Madison, Wisconsin. The candadites, and date and hour of elections have been determined and announced. During that election hour the computer will accept only the vote of those persons who are residents of Madison, regardless of where they are at the time of voting. A voter's residency, of course, will be determined as soon as he inserts his ID card in the computer terminal anywhere within the national territory. Since there may be more than one local or district election within a specified election hour, each locality or district will have an electoral code, which is printed in the code book. A Madison resident outside Madison and desiring to vote in the Madison mayoral elections will give the code to the computer wherever he is and then insert his ID card and vote. His vote, through the local code, will be transferred to the Madison computer center and will be tabulated with the rest of the votes. This is a fantastic achievement toward a true democratic process. A citizen's voice is heard and the vote is counted, regardless of where he is at the time of policy making or election. No elite or pressure group can interfere or influence such an election or policy-making process.

Of course, this kind of true democracy is possible because of the availability to every citizen the use of high-technology information system. This is what *technological democracy* is all about.

THE TECHNODEM AND THE PAY SYSTEM

In describing the services of the Technodem it is important to remember that not all the information is stored in the central brain, but only that of general interest and of use to everyone regardless of the place of residence. Much information of local and regional interest will be stored only in local and regional information centers. However, since these are connected to the Technodem, they will be available to everyone within the whole system. Thus if one wants to purchase a stereo set and wants to know what is available on the national market, one will use the

Technodem through one's home terminal. After one choice is made, in order to find the closest place that carries the chosen item, one will ask the local or regional information centers. One will then, through one's home terminal, get in touch with the closest store carrying the item and will order it. If one needs nursing service, one will need to use only the local information center. After the purchase is made, one feeds one's bank account code, the price of the item, and the company code to the computer. The cost of the item, including the delivery charge, if any, will be transferred from the customer's bank account to that of the company. The item will then be delivered. If no such service is available in that locality, the computer will indicate the closest locality that provides such services. The Technodem is supported by a monthly payment for each terminal set held by each household, business, or institution. For example, fifty dollars per month appears to be a very reasonable fee to pay for the use of many available services and information. This will provide the Technodem with an annual revenue of more than $100 billion. Besides paying for its operational costs, a substantial part of the revenues will be allocated to research on further technological developments and innovations in order to advance and refine the structure and operation of the Technodem. The excess amount of the revenues will go to the Public Consumption Fund. These functions are supervised by the Technodem Operation Council. The Technodem and its branches will also charge fees for businesses that want to feed into the Technodem their catalog of items for sale. There shall be a standard form for this, e.g., description, prices, delivery cost, if any. The consumer is able to look at all similar commodities presented by different firms on the screen of his terminal set, compare qualities and prices, make a choice and order, and pay through his set and the item will be delivered to his place of residence, or he may choose to go and see the merchandise and purchase it personally. He may make more than one choice of company and then go and see each item and make his final choice. Or, giving the computer his desired specifications of the item and the price range he is ready to pay, he may ask the computer which of the available makes would be the best buy. The computer will designate the choice. All this will eliminate the need for print, radio, and television advertising, printing and distribution of catalogs, et cetera. It will provide substantial savings for business firms. It will also save time for consumers, while allowing them access to all varieties of the item to be purchased in the market. Currently a consumer does not have this chance. He either has access to a catalog of certain major companies or goes to the market searching different stores for the item he intends to purchase.

For entertainment a consumer will have access, through his set, to huge libraries of films, concerts, operas, comedy shows, plays, games, excursions, documentaries, et cetera. The payment for such access will appear on the corner of the screen. The viewer will allow, by giving his bank code and account number to the computer, the amount to be charged to his account. From the amount paid by the user a certain prearranged percentage, e.g., 15 percent, will automatically go to the account of the Technodem and the rest will be transferred to the account of the owner of the program, show, or movie. This will, first, provide, for a prompt payment; and second, eliminate billing, check writing, mailing services, et cetera. These and other services provided by the Technodem will cause the elimination of all television networks and stations for two reasons. First, the services and programs provided by the networks will be made available to the viewers through the Technodem; second, there will be no desire by the business to sponsor TV programs, since consumers more likely will receive their information from the Technodem, which will include not only the goods sold by one company but goods sold by all companies selling similar products. However, the importance of television networks may remain in the area of the news and live programs. The question will be whether it will receive sponsors and whether the network can sustain itself economically. Society may end up with either one or two public television networks to keep people in contact with the local, regional, and national news and international affairs, despite the fact that all these can also be available through the Technodem. The advertising business will be extremely diminished in size. Their main job may be reduced to advising businesses as to how to present their items in the Technodem or assisting them in doing so. Because of all the media channels available through the Technodem, all conventional antenna systems or cable TV industries will be eliminated. More likely, each community will have cable-antenna systems consisting of one large antenna system connected to all homes and businesses. A household may have more than one terminal or one terminal and several screens, the receiver having the capacity to handle incoming of more than one program or information. Satellite systems will play a very significant role in this new network of communication, information, and entertainment.

For businesses one central terminal in the industry or department may handle several office terminals. Society will also get rid of all advertising billboards, which now occupy roadsides. Newspapers and magazines can feed the news and editorials to their computer, to be picked up by the Technodem, and through the local, regional, and national centers individuals can get hold of local, regional, and national news. Important local news of national interest is also sorted continually and instantly and incorporated in the national center for national consumption. This may tend to eliminate or sharply minimize the need for published newspapers or magazines, causing substantial savings in human and natural resources, equipment, buildings, and other facilities.

To have access to the news, the individual feeds to his computer the identity of the news center, e.g., *Washington Post,* by using a computer code, which he can get from the code directory at home or through his terminal. Then immediately his computer is connected to the intended news center. The individual then asks for the kind of news he wants, e.g., the Middle East situation, general national news, and sports or specific news related to a specified date in the past. The requested materials appear on his TV screen. Or if he wants video news he may ask for, e.g., ABC news, using the same process and the proper computer code. More likely, the audio and video broadcasting networks will sharply change in their structure and functions to comply with the new high-tech information system of the Technodem.

Each time an individual connects his terminal to any of these centers, his own computer code is entered at the accounting sector of the destination, whether it is the *Washington Post* or ABC network, or any entertainment firm. The individual is then charged for the use. As the individual uses the newspaper or video news center, the amount of charge appears at the corner of the screen and the viewer gives the computer his bank code and account number and the bill is automatically charged against his bank account. His monthly statement from the bank will show all the charges. If he does not desire to pay when using the service, at the end of each month he receives a computer printed bill that he pays in the same manner he paid the paperboy or his cable TV, or he may allow this to be charged to his bank account.

Furthermore, each time that he gets in contact with his desired news center, his balance of account with that center is shown on the corner of the screen. In the long run, as a result of acculturation, individuals will pay on the spot what they owe, allowing it to be charged to their bank account, and gradually monthly billings will be eliminated and the institutions will only bill those who are behind in their payments, e.g., beyond thirty days.

Financially, this will be beneficial to the news consumers because currently they pay for all materials in the newspaper. But through the Technodem, they pay only for the news they want and not for the whole cluster of news, in some of which they have no interest. Furthermore, the cost will be far less than at present because, first, there will be no profits made; second, there will be no need for capital spending on the printing and processing equipment; third, there will be no physical distribution to individual customers and thus a very substantial cost of marketing and distribution will be eliminated; and, finally, human resources previously used for these purposes can be averted to more beneficial and fruitful services.

MUSIC, FINE ARTS, SPORTS, AND THE PAY SYSTEM

1. Available through the Technodem

An immense amount of music, concerts, operas, and plays will be available through the Technodem and the user pays a very small amount for whatever he uses. Through the Technodem, part of this income is paid to the producers of the program used, which is then divided among the producers of and participants in the program, as illustrated in explaining the salary and compensation. Those participating in the production of the program, whether it is a rock concert, opera, play, or baseball game, receive pay within the range specified by the national position classification system. The range of this pay, like in any other occupation area, is based on the level of education, skill, and experience. It never exceeds the level of the highest annual pay of, e.g., forty-five thousand dollars.

This is sharply in contrast with the current situation, when an actor or actress may receive one or more million dollars for a movie, a popular band may earn far over a million dollars a year, or a top-rank tennis player, baseball star, or football player amasses over a million dollars a year.

In technological democracy, none of these individuals will receive above the maximum wage prescribed by the national classification pay system. As we will see, in the equitable society the highest pay is around three times more than the lowest pay. So if the lowest full-time pay is fifteen thousand dollars per year, the highest pay will be forty-five thousand dollars.

This pay system embodies every position in society, including garbage disposal men, actors, musicians, engineers, doctors, and lawyers as well as famous sports personalities. That is why the cost of using the Technodem for recreational purposes will be far, far less than what people currently pay to see such programs, and in most cases they don't get the quality performances that they expect. The Technodem will offer such quality, with much wider variety and choices. The cost will be minimal.

2. Live Programs

In the first place, live programs will be extremely popular, since these will be the areas more and more people will choose as their profession and, since people will be well educated in these cultural areas to enjoy them, their interest in such events will increase sharply. Second, people will have more leisure time.

Since they will spend a good deal of time using the Technodem for the purpose of their daily needs, e.g., education, work, shopping, et cetera, they would like to get away from it and get out to see a live program or sport event.

Third, when the current pay schedule is sharply reduced and more and more people seek to work in these recreational professions, the cost will be minimal. Instead of paying ten to twenty dollars for a concert or play as the case is now, one may need to spend only one to four dollars to attend an opera or one to two dollars to see a sports event. The price at movie houses will be also sharply reduced to a fraction of the current rate, since the participants in the production of a movie are compensated based on the amount of time they have spent in production corresponding to their salary schedule. For example, if a participating actress is famous and popular, her pay will be around the top bracket of the pay schedule, e.g., forty-five thousand dollars per year. If she has spent six months in production of the program, she will receive only $22,500. The film company will receive what it has cost to produce the film. The company may do one of the two things or both of them at the same time in marketing its production.

The first choice for the film company is to market the product itself through renting it to the movie houses. Of course, in this case the company moves away from its artistic work and gets involved in advertising and marketing. If production is of high quality, it will bring money that may far exceed the total cost of production, marketing, and distribution. In this case, through annual accounting reports the excess amount is reported and paid to the Public Consumption Fund, which is responsible for public services such as health care and education.

The second choice will be to make the film available by its computer terminal to the public through the Technodem. The cost will then be recovered by charging a fee to the users. Income beyond the cost will go to the Technodem. Finally, the company may choose to send the film to movie houses first and after a period of time feed it into the Technodem. Or it may decide to do both at the same time.

Considering the fact that through individual marketing and distribution the company occupies itself in a kind of function that has no extra income for it, the company may find it more convenient to sell the production to a distribution company and go about producing another program.

Naturally, as a result of sharply reduced costs of production, the fee at movie houses will be reduced sharply. The fee must be enough to pay for the cost of operation, plus a small amount paid to rent the program. The rented rate of films will be reduced sharply in proportion to the reduction of the cost of production.

Consequently, for all these reasons, there will be a phenomenal surge in attending fine arts and sports events, which will create employment for a large sector of the population. It will also demonstrate the highly civilized quality of the nation and exert liveliness and dynamism into the nation's cultural life.

NOTES

1. For more details, see Michael Parenti, *Democracy for the Few,* 4th ed. (New York: St. Martin's Press, 1983), pp. 182–83; and Peter Brosnan, "Who Owns the Networks?," *Nation,* November 25, 1978, pp. 561, 577–79.

2. See Parenti, *Democracy for the Few,* Chapters 2 and 3.

3. For more on the theory of general strike, see George Sorel, in *Communism, Fascism, and Democracy,* by Carl Cohen 2nd ed., (New York: Random House, 1972), pp. 297–302.

4. Hiroshi Inose, "Social Benefits of Information Technology," *Economic Eye,* March 1985, pp. 407.

5. The system has been developed by a Stanford University research group.

6. Regular education means the continuing education concurrent with the work that will be required if one wants to advance to the higher positions or maintain his present position.

Chapter Six

Essential Principles of Technological Democracy

INTRODUCTION

The main responsibility of philosophers, students, and other men of knowledge is, by taking into account the past theories of utopia, to recreate a long-range vision for the world and adamantly embark on reenacting it. If by employing the knowledge left for us by the past utopians we don't succeed in providing a rational coordination of impulses and thoughts toward restructuring the past utopias, for probably centuries our civilization will be degenerated into a state of chaotic minor excitements.

Unfortunately, today the technological society as a whole, including nearly all its young people, is unable to conceive of any vision of the future, though many are not satisfied with the welter of minor excitement.

With over twenty-six years of university teaching experience behind me and with background in technology, economics, law, and political science, I have been unsuccessful in getting students to grasp the speculative writings about utopias by Plato, Bacon, and Moore or Marx's utopia of communism, the term students hear continually on radio and television programs and read over and over in magazines and newspapers without a true comprehension of it.

For years I have repeatedly asked my freshmen and sophomore classes the following two questions. The first question is: "Who dislikes communism?" In answering this question, everyone raises his hand. The second question is: "What is communism?" No one responds. The third question is: "How can you dislike a concept or ideology when you don't know what it is?"

After my insistence on response, one or two would respond that communism is an evil system, a harsh dictatorship. What could be more away from the truth. It is not the students' fault. It is the faulty system of education they have gone through.

I remember when I finished high school in Iran I already had taken two courses in philosophy and knew quite a bit about the ideologies of capitalism and communism. I also had studied three languages and spoke them fluently. One was French, in which in a period of six years I had read a great deal about Western philosophy and philosophers, writers, and poets. Fifty-five percent of Soviet elementary school children study English starting at fifth grade. How many of our students study Russian? My point here is not our lack of concern in teaching Russian to our children. It is through the knowledge of language that one has the opportunity to get acquainted with literature, culture, and socioeconomic and political concepts of another nation and understand its values and the meaning of its aims.

The response of upper-level classes is no better to my questions. Except for about ten in a thousand who take a course in political theory, the rest are plunged in the same total ignorance.

If they had studied the subject, they would have known that communism, though utopian, is the most perfect democratic society ever described: a stateless, classless society where everyone voluntarily works according to his best capability but receives, also voluntarily, only according to his needs. Of course, when I describe this to my students many eyes become wide open with a clearly apparent sense of disbelief. They are not to blame; they had never heard such a statement about communism.

When students talk of a communist dictatorship they are unaware that they are talking of the process of reaching the stage of communism: through proletarian dictatorship envisioned by Marx and through the dictatorship of intelligentsia as prescribed by Lenin. Neither of these is relevant to communism, which is the objective. In the early 1970s, the people of Chile, through democratic election, chose Marxism as their objective, bypassing the dictatorship stage. In Italy the Communist party during the last two decades has taken over, one after another, the municipal governments of most of the major Italian cities, all through the democratic process. By its action the party has repudiated the dictatorship process of the ideology prescribed by Marx and Lenin and is proceeding toward Marx's communism through democratic means.

As technology advances, the need for such ideological and futuristic concepts increases in exponential scale, because technology has greatly widened the span of options and at the same time has made the choice a necessity. While through science and technology we can realize the results of alternate choices, we could hardly find out what it is that we really want. We have almost lost our ability to decide subjectively, out of the domain of technology, what we want. Thus through science and technology we have created power to destroy our enemies with enormous efficiency, yet we have made no real effort to analyze what it is that separates us from the Soviets or, at least, develop a cost-benefit analysis of coexistence. The general public's ignorance may end up to be very costly, if not totally destructive to our civilization.

Only a nation conscious of its present can hope for a bright future. It is about time, before it is too late, to ask ourselves, "Why must per capita consumption always increase in order for us to be a healthy society? What do we get for it, except the depletion of our finite resources and a tremendous amount of junk and garbage, including the atomic and toxic waste that threaten the healthy continuation of our civilization? Are we really happier, healthier, or closer to some ideal state of societal life?" Shouldn't we ask ourselves why many of the early societies have remained in a relatively balanced relationship with the environment for many centuries? Why in these societies was social life highly organized and rewarding and was there a lot of leisure time to devote to pleasurable pastimes such as conversation, literature, and art? Shouldn't we use technology to provide us with such a pleasureable life rather than employing it for wasteful production and destruction of our environment? Shouldn't we use technology for freeing men and women from dull, irksome, distasteful, and uninspiring work and for enlarging opportunities for more cultivated, enjoyable, and creative pursuits?

We may sustain the philosophy that man's spiritual welfare is closely linked to his material circumstances and to perfect man we must perfect his material circumstances. But this concept by no means implies that we overproduce everything. The concept simply means the satisfaction of man's material needs. But it is also unfortunate to notice that technology is used to overproduce, not primarily to answer man's material needs, but to amass profit for its users. So it is used for a very unhealthy and wrong purpose. Isn't it time for us to pay attention to the fact that material abundance alone is not enough to create a healthy society, rather, it is the equitable way wealth is distributed among members of a society. Over 24 million people are very poor in the United States, and over 40 million lack essential needs even for a subsistence living. Yet the United States is materially the most abundant society. At the same time, this is a society with some of the highest rates of crimes, accidents, homicides, and mental stress. Thus material abundance alone does not inevitably lead to spiritual peace of mind, happiness, and pleasure. A healthy society means a state of physical, mental, and social well-being, and material abundance has not produced it. With emphasis on material production the technological human community has lost a good deal of what made social life worthwhile, warm, delightful, rich, and human.[1]

A comprehensive, equitable, and satisfying concept of the future is badly and imminently needed, a concept that would provide an overall standard for judging the more obvious and immediate use of technology for societal equilibrium, with equitable distribution of its fruits among all. This aim cannot be achieved if technology is used primarily to profit a small group in its attainment of power and wealth, because it has already become clear that the material successes of the spirit of capitalism enormously enhanced by the use, or more truly misuse, of technology has not been the outward and visible signs of inward and spiritual grace; it has not caused social justice. Technology in the wrong hands can be utterly dangerous to and destructive of human prosperity, happiness, dignity, and freedom.

THE DEMOCRATIC ORGANISM AND ITS COMPONENTS

In technological democracy, society does not consist solely of individuals. Society composed of persons can apply to any kind of society, from primitive to technological. There is another ingredient that distinguishes technological society from the previous ones, and that is the high technology affecting every aspect of life from home, transportation, and work to leisure and recreation.

Technological democratic society is yet sharply distinguished from technological society through another important and essential ingredient, namely the equality of opportunity. Thus there are at least three basic components that together form the organic structure of technological democracy: people, technology, and equality of opportunity. Elimination of either of these three components from life's process will cause the elimination of democracy. Simply, no single component can provide for democracy without full use of the other two. Each must be aware of the full capacity and capabilities of the other two. An individual is necessary to operate the system. But this is a special kind of individual. He is well aware of the other two components. He knows all about the essence of technology and its role; he is also deeply committed to the principle of equality of opportunity. This required span of knowledge makes him a high-quality being that the world has never before encountered in masses. He is self-conscious, eager to learn, and well informed of social and technological norms as well as democratic principles. His knowledge is not limited to the normative aspects of life, but he knows how to employ, apply, and operate all these norms in practical aspects of life. Without these qualifications, no man can fully and meaningfully participate in materializing technological democracy and fully, or at least substantially, enjoy its fruits.

Technology as the second component of democratic organism is mostly a self-operating organ that facilitates and substantially helps the materialization of the contributions of the other two components.

One of the essential requirements for a democratic process is freedom of information. This can be only possible to a full extent through a high-technology information-communication (Technodem) system. This is another reason that democracy can be achieved only in a high-technology society. There is no need to mention the overwhelming importance and influence of electronic technology at the current time on the political electoral process. However, compared to the information system of the future with its role in bringing about democracy, the current systems are primitive. In a technological society, a true democracy without high technology is unthinkable as well as impossible. It is for this reason that technology constitutes an indispensible component of the democratic organism in modern society.

The third and most important component of the democratic organism is the principle of equality of opportunity. This principle does not intend to provide for a society of equals in the absolute sense. It leads toward an equitable society where each person is equal to another with the same level of knowledge, capability, and experience.

As the highest principle and component of democratic organism, equality of opportunity is permanent and universally superior and, at all times, controls the exercise of any human authority whatsoever. All other principles of society concerned with human rights are derived from this superior principle. They are supplementary to it and cannot alter it. These principles are to be obeyed only when they are consistent with the principle of equality of opportunity to which they are always subordinate.

By nature of this supreme principle and under the protection of its application, man has a right to preserve his life, liberty, and property during the full span of his life.

Equality of opportunity is a sacred right that serves as a foundation for all other rights. When a man renounces this right, he renounces all his rights and liberty emanating from this right. It might be rightfully assumed that by doing so he renounces his duty as a true human being. In a modern, nonbestial society such renounciation is incompatible with human nature, as man has been born free. It deprives him of his freedom as well as ensuring essential moral norms. By doing so, he also renounces mutual obligation, which is one of the essential requirements of equality of opportunity, because it is not an individual principle but a societal one. The application of equality of opportunity requires multiplicity of individuals. The opportunity of one has to be compared with and evaluated according to the opportunity of the other and usually those of many others. Democracy can flourish when one respects this principle in relations with fellow workers or citizens. The common benefit to which each individual's rights are subordinate is a benefit in which each person has a share. Each individual's good is a part of the common good.

Equality of opportunity is thus a very important societal obligation in democratic society. During the early stages of technological democracy one may, based on one's discriminating and exploiting character inherited from the previous ideologies to which one has been long subject, be obliged to follow and abide by the principle of equality of opportunity as the supreme law of the land. One may even be forced to comply. But as democracy progresses and democratic principles become general and ordinary norms of society, individuals become acculturated and accustomed to these norms and not only tend to comply with their application but believe deeply in them and become ardent advocates of them, including, of course, the most important of all principles, the equality of opportunity. In a democratic society, the fulfillment or full development of an individual's characteristic is possible not in isolation from but in association with all members of one's community. It becomes the persistent impulse of every rational being to move toward a life of harmony, rather than conflicts and contradictions.

The common good includes the good of every individual and postulates free scope for the development and perfection of every individual. This is the very outcome of the application of equality of opportunity.

In an advanced democratic society, the collective activities of an institution or community do not proceed by coercion or restraint but are the result of freedom and general consent. They are based on voluntary association and willing participation. The common good of society and its members can be realized in its fullness only through the common will to adhere to the principle of equality of opportunity. The benevolent despots, fatherly aristocrats, and liberally elected governments all paid lip service relating to the common good of individuals and society.

Making the rights and responsibilities of every citizen real and dynamic and extending to the whole society are possible through the effect of democratic organism and the contribution of its organic components to the fullest extent. Such fulfillment is only possible when members of a society, by their own feelings, are strongly drawn toward the system. In the organic conception of democracy, there's no room drawn from the imperfect ideologies of the past—capitalistic, socialistic, communistic, or others. It is only through a democratic system that the ideal society is conceived as a whole, a society that lives and flourishes by the harmonious growth of its component parts, each of which, in developing on its own directions and in accordance with its own characteristics, tends to further the development of other components and society as a whole.

The progress of a society and that of its members are not separable from one another. The development of society is a result of the expression of deep-seated forces of democratic norms that come to materialize only through an infinitely slow and cumbersome process of mutual adjustments. A basic force in democratization is understanding that progress is not a matter of mechanical contrivance, but depends on the enrichment of mind and spirit, in democratic principles and materializing them through meaningful and vigorous actions.

To gain and maintain equality of opportunity and ensure freedoms, man has no choice but to submit to democratic organism. It is the only hope of humanity to free itself from the yoke of powerful and tyranical economic institutions that rule men and have created and maintained political and social organizations to subjugate them.

The democratic organism is not a system established by an agreement reached between members of a society. Its nature is absolute and ever existing. It is the ultimate system. A society submits to it by simply discovering it. It is a system under which all people live according to its norms and demands. The difference with other systems is that it is truly and totally democratic. It causes the flourishing of associations, as a result of which the whole strength of society is enlisted for protection of the individual, community, property, and nature.

Though equality of opportunity is absolute and permanent as a component of democratic organism, it is also the primary source of utility and abundance for all. It embodies utility in the largest and broadest sense. The term *utility* does not correspond only to material things in life, but those nonmaterial as well. Equality of opportunity is not only the source of a broad spectrum of liberties for the individual, but also the source of happiness for him and for society as a whole. Its utility, in every direction of application, is always supportive of what is just, moral, and good.

Equality of opportunity provides for many kinds of rights and freedoms for the individual. It affects all individuals within society. It thus serves the common good of all, which is the outcome of collective effects of individual rights and liberties. Therefore, the individual rights and liberties are not, and cannot be, in conflict with the common good. Since the common good is inclusive of all individual rights and liberties, thus no individual rights and liberties can exist apart from it.

It may appear that the individual is being made too subservient to the principle of equality of opportunity. Though the values of equality and freedom outside the principle of equality of opportunity can be argued and criticized, no such criticism can be reasonably sustained regarding the latter. Within the realm of reason, everyone would accept its universal democratic and beneficial effect. Equality of opportunity is per se neither equality nor freedom, but it provides grounds for both, equality based on knowledge and experience, freedom so broad that it cannot be fully expressed but is possible to enjoy.

TOWARD TECHNOLOGICAL DEMOCRACY

Apart from the United States and the countries with Marxist-Leninist systems, the rest of the countries that have advanced beyond the feudalistic system have a mixed economy. Of particular interest for our purpose are those in advanced industrial stages, such as those of Western Europe and Canada. The production process in these countries is capitalistic and based on maximization of profit. This is true regardless of whether the capital is owned by the private sector, as is the case in all of these countries in different production areas, or owned by the public sector, as is the case relating to some main industries in some of these countries. For example, coal production, the largest industry in England, has been publicly owned since its nationalization in the late 1940s. Its operation, however, is capitalistic, since it is based on profit and its maximization. These industries may be characterized, at best, as examples of *state capitalism,* where capital is owned by the public at large and is controlled by the state on its behalf and where the operation is concerned primarily with making a profit and tending to maximize it, and where all the operation depends on the market economy. Thus, from a production viewpoint (the most important distinguishing factor between capitalism and socialism), the countries that have nationalized some of their industries but operate them in a capitalistic manner cannot be called socialist. In general, countries identified as socialist are those that have adopted broad social welfare services, with emphasis on certain specified areas, such as health care, education, housing, transportation, old age benefits, and unemployment compensation. Nearly all Western European countries fall within this category, with varying degrees of socialization of these basic individual needs. Despite this fact, the basic character of these nations remains capitalistic because of their capitalistic mode of operation. However, one may justifiably argue that by taking drastic steps in social welfare services and using the surplus value received through their capitalistic mode of operation to maintain and enhance these services, these countries are moving gradually toward socialism. Therefore, since despite their progress in installing extensive social benefit programs, none of these countries have reached the stage of socialism and since capitalism is the prevailing mode of production, they may be called *mixed capitalism* at best. One important positive character of these systems is their advancement primarily in political democracy and, to a certain degree, in economic and social democracy. Despite the above mentioned distinctions, these countries remain within the sphere of the capitalist mode of production.

PREVAILING POWER SYSTEM

From the above explanation it can be concluded that there are two dominant systems in the world today. First is the capitalist system exemplified by the United States and Japan and, to a lesser degree, by the Western European countries and Canada. Second is the socialist system represented by the Marxist-Leninist socialist Soviet Union and, with some variations, China and Eastern European countries.

Both systems, whether capitalist or socialist, are authoritarian in which the major public and economic policies are made by a very small elite group. In the United States, a little over seven thousand persons form the ruling capitalist elite, and as has been demonstrated, the political democracy practiced is geared to maintain and support the elite interests and is used as a facade for certain claimed freedoms, which are nonexistent in reality.

In the Soviet Union, the system is controlled by a very small and select political elite. Though there is more social and economic equality of opportunity than in the United States, it is not inherent in the system itself but granted by the ruling elite in accordance with the framework established by the Marxist-Leninist theory as interpreted by the elite.

Therefore, neither of the two systems enjoy a true democracy where the operation of the system, socially, economically, and politically, will be in the hands of the people as a whole. One problem with and essential requirement of establishing and maintaining a true democratic system is that it can be possible only in a highly advanced and well-educated society. Both Marx and Lenin visualized this fact. Marx's democracy was to be attained when a highly educated society, after advancing through a proletarian dictatorship, would reach its ultimate technological stage, which would be stateless and classless.

DEMOCRACY AS A SYSTEM: AN INTRODUCTION TO TECHNOLOGICAL DEMOCRACY

By this point it is hoped that the reader has realized, through our documented presentations, that despite some two centuries of effort to establish a more just society through democratic means, today there is no single nation in the world where democracy has been established in its true sense.

During the last two centuries, political democracy has been the center of attraction by practitioners for the main purpose of establishing a legitimate system to maintain property rights and capitalism. The U.S. Constitution was framed with this main purpose in mind.

It was not until after the Second World War that attention

was given to the reality of the situation. It was during the past three decades that monopoly capitalism, which had its roots in the late nineteenth and early twentieth centuries, established its firm grip on the American economy and, through that, on the economy of many Third World countries. Similar developments, though in a less dramatic manner, were followed by other industrialized countries of Western Europe.

The uprisings in the United States of the sixties and early seventies were the first organized reaction against the monopoly capitalist group and the state that protected its interests. The uprisings failed for two different reasons. First, since they took a violent form, they legitimized forceful and brutal state action to suppress them. Second, and more important, while the primary aim was to undo the existing "establishment," there was no other suitable alternative envisioned to replace it. Some had suggested socialism as a substitute, but this received no support for two main reasons. First, people were uneducated in regard to societal philosophical ideas and visualized socialism as another evil system. This feeling was of course enhanced by decades of indoctrination by the capitalist system about the evil nature of socialism. Second, socialism as practiced then by some Western European countries was not what the theory intended it to be. It was just another kind of capitalism, maybe not as bad.

However, the hold of monopoly capitalism on the economies of the United States and other countries during the last decade has increased phenomenally.[2] It has also been during this decade that different scientists and philosophers have paid increasing attention to erosion of individual rights and liberties under *technological monopolistic capitalism.* It must be noted, as it is presented in the preceding chapters, that technology that is controlled by the economic elite has played a significant role in this process of subjugation.

Our attempt in this chapter is to introduce in brief a philosophy of the future society that, as all trends indicate, all advanced societies are moving toward and inevitably will attain it. This is the theory of a true democracy never described before. This is a democracy as a system embracing all aspects of societal life, whether economic, social, or political.

Since this is a brief introduction to a very complex societal theory, it will be necessarily and properly so open to many questions, answers to which may not be clearly evident, thus open to adverse criticism.

This deficiency is the result of the fact that the attempt here is a brief, rather than a detailed, presentation of the theory. However, by no means does this brevity signify that the concept is poor or is based on a weak and shaky foundation. The theory is quite solid and valid. For any question in mind the reader will find a lead, even in this brief presentation, if he reviews the materials carefully and impartially.

Before starting to advance the theory of *technological democracy,* it seems appropriate to clarify the meaning of certain terms that are used here. Among these the clarification of two terms are most important: *democracy* and *equality of opportunity*.

DEMOCRACY

Under technological democracy, this term is looked upon as referring to a system embracing not only the political components of society but also its social and economic spheres. The term *democracy,* in its true and full meaning, means political, economic, and social democracies all put together as a system. All these parts are interdependent. If any of these component parts are missing, democracy is defective to that extent and a true democracy does not exist.

In the United States, for example, there is no economic democracy and social democracy is substantially missing. This makes the existing political democracy highly defective and, in many respects, meaningless. The lack of economic democracy is evident in control of the economy by a small group of monopoly capitalists, the exploitation of the workers and consumers, and the economic class stratification. The lack of social democracy is visualized through the practice of racism, and sexism, lack of appropriate educational opportunities, lack of health care, housing, transportation, adequate old age benefits, et cetera. Thus there is very little, if any, meaningful democracy in the United States.

In the Soviet Union, democracy is highly defective because there is no political democracy. The political system, despite its electoral process, is controlled by a small elite of party leaders.

However, there is more economic and social democracy than in the United States. In the economic sphere there is a more equitable distribution of wealth despite the fact that people are exploited. But apart from the defense expenditures, a substantial part of the surplus value gained is spent for the causes of socialism, such as education, health care, housing, transportation, recreation, and old age benefits. These are social benefits financed through the system that rules. People have nothing much to say and have no power to cause desirable changes. Democracy is thus highly defective.

Technological democracy, therefore, is a societal system by itself quite distinguished from the existing systems of capitalism and socialism. It extends to all aspects of the societal life. Its understanding is quite simple, since its operation depends only on the application of one principle (equality of opportunity) to its other two components (the individual and technology). Accordingly, it becomes of utmost importance to understand the meaning of the term *equality of opportunity*.

EQUALITY OF OPPORTUNITY

The simple meaning of the term is that every individual in technological society must have equal opportunity of access to social, economic, and political means. However, its application is not so simple; in fact, it is quite complex and requires particular attention to the meaning of the term. As we progress in definition and analysis of our theory of technological democracy, we will receive gradually increasing knowledge of the meaning of equality of opportunity and a better understanding of it. Once we master ourselves through different applications of the term, it will become quite easy to grasp its meaning and its manner of application under each situation, be it economic, social, political, or technological.

Some Aspects of Application of Equality of Opportunity

The manner in which property is produced, owned, and used determines the economic structure of society and to a substantial degree its social and political characteristics. Productive forces constitute land and natural resources, capital, technology, and labor. In modern industrial society, capital is the most important source of production. Though by itself capital is not productive, through the use of capital one can employ all other forces, including labor, for productive purposes. Thus those who have access to capital, to the extent of their access, hold power within the producive system as well as society as a whole. If most of this capital is owned or controlled by a few individuals or firms, then the production process and other superstructures in society are dominated by these few. If the capital as a whole is owned and controlled by the majority of the people, rather than by a few, then the other productive forces as well as the political and social system are governed by the majority of the population.

Therefore, one of the imperative conditions for democracy is the equitable distribution of capital among the people, along with highly dispersed control over its use.

How can we bring about the equitable distribution of capital? There are two ways to achieve this objective, both of which must be applied concurrently.

The only thing required is the application of the principle of equality of opportunity. This principle, in an economic sense, means that no one in technological democratic society should gain opportunity over others through accumulated wealth except for savings he has made through his own labor. Based on this principle, no one can be enriched through inheritance or through receiving material goods or capital without a comparable compensation. Such enrichment will disturb the equality of opportunity by increasing one's opportunity, without personal efforts, over that of others. Any amount of wealth received through inheritance or bequests immediately places the receiver at a higher level of opportunity. The level of higher opportunity received by such enrichment is directly related to the amount of wealth received. Thus inheritance or bequests of large amounts of wealth is the main reason that keeps wealthy families in control of the means of production for generations. Therefore, the application of the principle of equality of opportunity prescribes the *prohibition of unjust enrichment*. For example, if this principle is applied in the United States, in a matter of a few decades, as the members of wealthy families die, their wealth will be transferred to the public treasury and the economic and political powers of these families will disappear. This principle of the prohibition of unjust enrichment continues to apply even when society has reached the stage of technological democracy, because any free transfer of wealth at any time upsets the concept of equality of opportunity. The application of this principle will eliminate the accumulation of wealth in any family, since whatever is accumulated during a lifetime of an individual reverts to the public upon his death. It must be noticed that the concept does not prohibit individual accumulation of wealth.

Second, social surplus or profit is an unjust enrichment, since the capitalist receives it without compensation but for free, through the exploitation of labor as well as consumers. As we also know, appropriation of social surplus by the capitalist is the main source of accumulation of capital and wealth. Thus the application of the very concept of equality of opportunity prohibits the appropriation of social surplus by the capitalist since such appropriation enhances the opportunity of the capitalist to the detriment of that of the labor. Accordingly, in technological democratic society profits are not allowed. If in certain cases, particularly in early stages of democracy, because of trade with other nations or market conditions making profits is unavoidable, such profits are reported at the end of each fiscal year and returned to the public treasury.

It has been argued that profit is the main inducing factor in productivity and without profit there would be no incentive for productivity. This is a very false assumption because first, under a capitalist mode of production, the main producing factor is the labor force, which is deprived of such incentive, since laborers do not benefit from the profits. Those who do benefit from profits form a small minority class of nonproducing capitalists. To increase productivity and thus the profits they are obliged to impose inhuman and harsh pressures upon labor. Therefore, as a whole, there is no incentive in the capitalist mode of production, but forced production in order to produce high profits for the capitalist. Second, incentive is a factor that induces the worker to produce more and better-quality products. If there is going to be no profit made by the capitalist, the laborer will receive, in addition to his wages, what is labeled as social surplus or profits. In other words, laborers will not be exploited for profit purposes. This factor alone will necessarily increase the workers' incentive to work harder. Thus under technological democracy there is a high level of incentive for productivity that is nonexistent under capitalism.

Consequently, by the prohibition of unjust enrichment in a capitalistic society like the United States, the accumulated wealth of the capitalists, monopoly capitalists in particular, tends to disappear in two ways. First, it is lost through prohibition of inheritance and other unjust enrichments, such as establishment of trust and free bequests. Second, the capitalist loses his main source of accumulation of wealth by the abolition of profits. He can no longer create appropriate surplus values.

Thus in the period of transition from capitalism to technological democracy the capitalist class tends to disintegrate and then disappear, while the wealth and its control tend to be distributed equitably among the working class. Along with these changes society tends to become more dynamic because of increasing incentive allowed to the workers. The level of productivity and the quality of production tend to increase, reaching their maximum level when society reaches the stage of advanced technological democracy.

The Socialist System and Technological Democracy

The application of equality of opportunity in a socialist system like the Soviet Union would have a reverse effect on the ownership of the means of production. Under technological democracy, all of the means of production are owned and controlled by individuals. Under the Soviet socialist system, the means of production and distribution are all owned by the public and controlled by a small group of the Communist party leadership. Thus the individual worker is deprived of the ownership as well as control of the means of production and his employment opportunity is dependent on government "whim." Application of the principle of equality of opportunity would bring about several changes. The first and most important one would be returning the ownership and control of the means of production from public to private hands. The manner of this redistribution among the workers, and as to who gets what, is presented later through discussion of the labor force. Another change is the elimination of centralized bureaucracy, which is discussed when we consider the status of the state under technological democracy. A third change is the elimination of political dictatorship, which is being maintained now under the dominance of the Communist party leadership.

One important and positive point relating to this transformation in socialist countries is that in these countries the control of the means of production and distribution, as well as natural resources, is already in public hands and they don't have to be taken away from the capitalist elite ownership, as the case is in the United States. Thus while in a capitalistic society, like the United States, transformation to technological democracy will go through a period of transition that may stretch into several decades, in a socialistic system, like the Soviet Union, the whole transformation may take only a few years.

CAPITAL AND CAPITAL ACCUMULATION

Capital will still be one of the important forces of production in technological democratic society. However, its characteristic will be quite different from its counterpart in a capitalistic or socialistic system. In a capitalistic society accumulation is through appropriation of the surplus value and added value through exploitation of labor and consumers. In a socialistic society the accumulation is the result of exploitation of labor through forced appropriation of the proceeds of production by the government.

In a society under technological democracy the accumulation of capital is a direct result of savings by the labor force. These savings are the result of surpluses left after each individual laborer spends his earnings to satisfy his and his family's needs. In other words, this accumulated capital is not the result of any kind of exploitive process, but the outcome of labor's work. Returns from its use also are not through exploitation. Furthermore, its ownership ends with the death of its owner. Thus there is no continuing accumulative system, since no accumulation extends beyond the owner's life.

Moreover, there is a very important distinction between the capital accumulated under the capitalist system and that accumulated under technological democracy. The capital accumulated under a capitalistic mode of production is the result of the appropriation by the capitalist of the surplus value materialized through the exploitation of labor. This is, therefore, an "unfair accumulation" forming a "malignant capital" that tends to empower the capitalist further and subjects the workers for more exploitation; whereas the capital accumulated under technological democracy is through savings by the worker from his earnings. It is a "fair accumulation" forming a "beneficial capital" that causes more prosperity for the working class and provides income and security for their old age, after retirement. As we will see later on, under technological democracy there are neither retirement programs nor Social Security benefits for the retired and elderly people, except for those who are disabled or handicapped.

Therefore, since the capital is accumulated by the working class as a result of their own labor and it is a "beneficial capital," it is justified if it receives reasonable returns from its investment, which will directly benefit the individual worker holding the capital. First, the capital could be loaned for which the owner receives a fixed rate of return similar to the interest rate under capitalism. Second, it could be invested, for which the investor receives shares of ownership of the firm corresponding to the amount invested. Returns from such accumulation could be used for the purpose of providing for more comfortable living conditions or could be saved for a better life after retirement. Each worker also has another automatically accumulating source of capital in shares of ownership he receives each month along with his wage. As will be explained later on, this capital cannot be transferred or expended. It remains intact until the owner dies. It then reverts to society to be used in the same way by the new generation.

THE WORKING CLASS UNDER TECHNOLOGICAL DEMOCRACY

Technological democracy eradicates the gap between the capitalist and working classes. Actually, it eliminates distinctions between these two classes and gradually molds them into one. For the first time in modern production history, the worker becomes involved in the whole process of production, having input as to what is going to be produced, how it is going to be produced, and what is going to be done with the product after it is produced. Alienation of labor, a major cause of social contradiction and the struggle of masses, is eliminated.

This new mode of production is attained by the application of the principle of equality of opportunity. First, the very concept of equality of opportunity does not allow any kind of exploitation, which is currently practiced under either the capitalist or socialist mode of production. By its very nature, exploitation of any kind increases the opportunity of its beneficiary to the detriment of the exploited. Thus a continuous exploitation causes a continuous rise in the level of opportunity of the beneficiary, ever widening the gap between the level of opportunity of the exploiting and exploited parties.

To avoid this kind of exploitation, the worker must receive full compensation for his work. This means that after the worker is compensated, there will be no surplus value left for the capitalist to benefit from in the form of profits.

Second, there is no equality of opportunity when the form and process of production are decided without input from the part of the workers and when, without their participation in policy conception and formulation, they are forced to produce products whose production they did not consent to. This, however, does not mean that in technological democracy all the workers in an institution should collectively participate and make decisions as to what they want to produce and how they want it to be produced. This simply means that these two decisions must be made by appropriate and qualified representatives of the workers who are also part owners of the capital of the firm.

In analyzing these situations we must bear in mind that equality of opportunity is not an abstract principle. As we have explained before, it is a principle subject to relativity, based on reason and reasonableness. Opportunities can be expected to be almost exactly equal when the qualifications of two persons are exactly the same, including their intelligence, education, and experience. This would be a rare case, if possible at all. Therefore, the equality of opportunity is judged taking into consideration all productive qualities of the individuals with reasonable evaluation and nearest proximation.

Opportunity levels are of two kinds: *initial* and *gained*. The initial opportunity level is based on each individual's natural competence, without counting the effect of outside factors such as education and experience. From this viewpoint, the opportunity level for each individual is different from all others. This level is determined by the level of mental and physical capabilities of each individual at the time of birth. Thus individuals are not born with equal opportunities. As they enter the world and face outside factors, educational opportunities in particular, and as by these contacts they increase their knowledge and thus competence, they reach a higher level of opportunity. This is a stage of *gained opportunity*. Therefore, even if a person is born at a lower level of opportunity, he may increase the level of his opportunity through seeking knowledge and experience This makes the availability of education and experience imperative for increasing and equalizing of the opportunity level. If the opportunity of education and experience is available to some and not to others, then the level of opportunity of the beneficiaries will rise faster than that of the others. Therefore, though individuals start life with unequal initial opportunities, they can move up their opportunities to equalize them with those with a higher initial opportunity. However, each individual has a ceiling in his level of opportunity. This ceiling cannot be surpassed and can be attained only by the maximum use of one's capabilities. These different opportunity ceilings among individuals establish in each society what we may call *opportunity classes*. The crucial point in technological democracy is that everyone within each opportunity class should fully enjoy the equality of opportunity with others within that class.

Thus by full availability of educational opportunities people are able to raise their level of opportunities to the level they may desire. This attained level may not be the optimum possible for further improvement is available, but the individual, with his own free will, choses not to improve it further. This tendency may not be desirable in capitalistic society, but will be quite common in technological democratic society, where materialism does not dominate the life and happiness is not determined in material terms. Consequently, individuals are classified according to the level of opportunity they have achieved based on their education, experience, and personal desire. They form administrators, engineers, lawyers, accountants, computer scientists, technicians, economists, and different echelons of white and blue collar workers. Each individual's competencies are examined and certified by an appropriate institution. This certification determines the levels of opportunity available for each individual. Currently there is this kind of certified classification, though it is fragmented, disorganized, and often discriminatory. For example, there are elementary and secondary school certifications, college certifications (bachelor's, master's, and doctoral levels) in a great variety of areas and disciplines, certification in a wide variety of technical specialties, et cetera.

Let us see now how this class system of opportunities is transferred into the production process. In actual operation of production, opportunities have a hierarchical structure that is based on different levels of competence required to carry out a great variety of jobs. There are positions for top-, middle-, and lower-level managers, professionals, technicians, specialists, and skilled and unskilled workers. Each level within the individual opportunity class has a matching level of positions within the hierarchy of the production process. The competency and performance required for each of these positions have been prescribed in detail, and all the positions are classified according to the level of competency required. Currently there are such position classifications in both capitalist and socialist countries, but it is fragmented and uncoordinated, with an unequal framework of formulation. For example, in the United States we have position classifications within the national as well as state bureaucracies. Also, many businesses and other institutions have their own position classification systems. For public positions the individuals are examined regarding their competence, which also determines their level of opportunity. In technological democracy, position classification is universal and it is within each level of opportunity that equality of opportunity must apply in providing positions for all those within that specific level.

According to this process of application of the principle of equality of opportunity, there cannot be discrimination within each level of opportunity. Equality of opportunity in employment will apply whether the applicant is male or female, a black, a Mexican-American, a Native American, or a member of another group.

Besides initial opportunity and gained opportunity, there is also what we may call *lost opportunity*. This occurs first when a person is deprived or denied the opportunity to raise the level of his competence and consequently raise the level of his opportunity, such as if a person is deprived of or denied the opportunity to educate himself. This is one of the characteristics of a capitalist society, like the United States, where at the lower levels of education, elementary and secondary, the poor sectors of society are provided with educational opportunities far below those of well-to-do and wealthy sectors. As a result, poor and minority groups are denied the chance of appropriate high-quality education, depriving them from raising their level of opportunity. Second, lost opportunity occurs when a person, because of exploitation, is not granted equal opportunity in employment. Again, this is a characteristic of a capitalist society like the United States. Poor and minority groups are denied employment opportunities granted to rich and nonminority groups. Suppose individuals A and B, both college graduates with the same academic achievements, look for employment. A's father is a wealthy corporate executive; B, on the other hand, comes from a poor or minority family. A, because of his father's connections, will have a variety of available positions to choose from. B, however, will have difficulty finding a job, and if he is finally able to find it, it will more likely not be within his specialty or a suitable one.

Third, the lost opportunity may be the result of wage discrimination. For example, women and minority members in the United States are paid much less than other workers for the same kind of job.

In each of these situations, when the discriminatory practice is carried out for an extended period of time the continuous loss of opportunities widens the gap between the deprived group and the rest of the working class. It results in a undemocratic class stratification.

While lost opportunity is a major characteristic of a capitalist society, it does not exist under technological democracy. In the period of transition from capitalism to technological democracy, it is up to the system to see that those subjected to lost opportunities be compensated, moving them gradually to other levels of opportunity. The intention must be to close the gap between the highest and the lowest levels of opportunity. The differentiation between the opportunity levels must tend to correspond to differentiation between the levels of competence.

In this process of change, during the transition period the differentiation in the opportunity levels for employment must be based purely on competence and experience and not on wealth and residually attained power and status. Once society reaches the advanced stage of technological democracy, capitalists are automatically eliminated, their power and social status disappear, and opportunities tend to be based strictly on competence and experience.

SHARED OPPORTUNITY AND EMPLOYMENT RIGHT

An outcome of the principle of equality of opportunity is the right of every individual to employment. This simply means that if an individual loses his job or is not able to find employment corresponding to his level of competence, he is denied the employment opportunity that he is entitled to, while his working fellows enjoy that opportunity. Under this circumstance, there is no equality of opportunity present between those who are employed and those who are not. To remedy the situation the system must provide the unemployed individual with an appropriate employment opportunity. By an "appropriate" employment opportunity it is meant that the person must have a position corresponding to his level of competency so that his skills and experiences can be used fully and productively and his pay schedule corresponds to his level of opportunity.

Shared opportunity signifies a situation where there are unemployed workers and there are no open positions available for their employment. By the very fact of being unemployed with no jobs available their opportunity has been lowered, compared to their fellow workers who are employed. To equalize these two different opportunities and bring about equality of opportunity, the working fellows must share a small part of their employment opportunity with their unemployed fellows. For example, looking upon this issue in general at the national level, let us assume that there are 100 million workers on the job and upon graduation from different educational and training institutions an estimated 2.5 million individuals enter the job market. Let us consider the extreme situation and assume that there is no job available on the market for any of these newcomers. If this happens in a capitalist society, like the United States, all these people would remain unemployed and become welfare recipients, demoralized, and a burden upon the society. Under technological democracy, if each of the working persons gives up one hour of his forty hours per week—that is, if he works only thirty-nine hours and receives pay for thirty-nine hours instead of forty—there will be 100 million work hours released, providing for 2.5 million new positions, which will accommodate all the newcomers in the job market. Sacrifice of one hour's pay would hardly affect a worker's financial situation or daily family life and obligations, while it would provide a means of livelihood for 2.5 million new workers and their families. The workers who sacrifice that one hour in actuality do not lose all the pay for that one hour, because otherwise the government has to support 2.5 million unemployed and their families through its welfare funds, available through the imposition of taxes on the working people. By using this process of "shared opportunity," the principle of equality of opportunity continues to prevail and full employment is maintained all the time. There is no need to tax working people in order to raise revenues to support millions of unemployed and their dependents. There is no layoff of workers during a sluggish market situation. By the application of the concept of shared opportunities all the workers of a firm will remain on the job. Instead of layoffs, the hours of work for each employee will be reduced with the corresponding pay. All workers will work several hours less than their full-week work hours. In essence, everyone will be partially laid off. For example, let us assume that a firm has ten thousand employees and has to lay off one thousand workers or 10 percent of its total working force. If instead of laying off these one thousand workers, the firm reduces the weekly work hours by 10 percent, it will not need to lay off anyone. If we assume that each worker works forty hours per week and the work load is reduced by 10 percent, each worker will work thirty-six hours and will get pay for thirty-six instead of forty hours. As a result, there will be no layoffs and all the workers will keep their jobs. Doing it any other way will be contrary to the principle of equality of opportunity. At the time of recession, this will resolve the most serious problems of unemployment. In financial terms, this means that billions of dollars, which otherwise would have had to be used for unemployment compensation and welfare payments, will now be channeled into the production process to help the economy and recovery. This self-nourishing financial process actually tends to eliminate or make highly unlikely the occurrence of recessions or depressions.

As we will see later on when we discuss market operation, inflations and recessions are very unlikely under technological democracy. Two of the main reasons for this optimism we already know. Under a democratic system, since there is no drive for profits, prices remain quite stable and, because of shared opportunities, there is always full employment.

THE WAGE SYSTEM

At every level of work hierarchy, compensation is based on the level of required competence and experience. Competence is determined by the level of education corresponding to the responsibilities of the position, and experience is based on the relevant knowledge and expertise acquired through time at the workplace. The general level of compensation is determined through a general position classification at the national level. The work system is divided into different classes and within each class into different levels.

There is a National Economic Council, and under its authority there is a National Position Classification Commission. As the operating tools of the system, this commission classifies all available positions provided by computerized data and establishes the level of competence and experience required for each position. This appears to be a difficult task. It is not so. Under a national computerized information system (the Technodem) as discussed before, information about all jobs in the country and duties allocated to each is easily collected. An assortment of the positions and classification is all carried out through this computer system and made available to the commission. Of course this national position classification does not attempt to specify in detail every available position. The classification is general yet thorough and specific at each level. It also establishes the general level of pay and compensation for different classes of position within each level. This is all the commission needs to do. From there on, the system of positions and compensations is updated each year; nearly all the work is done by the computer. The commission's functions will relate partially to resolution of specific problems relating to classification and wages.

Each production or service institution establishes its own position classification and pay system, according to the general classification system established by the national commission, available to it through its computer terminal. A computerized copy of such document is submitted to the regional office of the National Economic Council. This copy is fed into the Technodem to check the accuracy of the classification and pay system, comparing it with the standards established by the National Economic Council. Any deficiency is reported, and the corresponding institution is directed accordingly to correct its position classification and pay system. In more advanced stages of democracy, each institution will feed its position classification and pay system directly into the Technodem. They will be checked automatically against the nationally established framework, and deficiencies, if any, will be pointed out by the computer that must be corrected by the institution. These deficiencies will be reported electronically to the regional office. The most important point in this system is that while the national authorities establish a framework for position classification and pay systems, they do not go ahead and do the actual classification or assign the actual compensation for each position. All these responsibilities are transferred to the local individual institutions, which are better equipped to classify them with allocations of appropriate pay for each position. Thus the enormous bureaucratic system of doing work at the national or regional level is eliminated by transferring the task to individual institutions.

The execution of this system is much simpler and less burdensome than the system currently used in industrial societies. Its great benefit is that it provides for equality of opportunity through a uniform system of classification and compensation and it eliminates the bureaucracies of the present civil service commissions (national, state, and local) and similar agencies within industries and other large institutions that operate such systems. A further benefit is that it extends the scientific classification system to every production institution in society, regardless of size, including those self-employed.

CHARACTERISTICS OF THE PAY SYSTEM

With taking into consideration that pay for each position strictly corresponds to the level of competency and experience required for that position, the pay system under technological democracy has two major characteristics. First, compensation for each position consists of two parts: a cash payment, which we may call a wage, and payment in stocks of the employee's firm. However, the cash payment must be sufficient to provide the worker with a convenient living condition. Projecting this minimum pay to the current economic condition of the United States, we may dwell in the vicinity of an annual income of $15,000, or about $7.50 per hour. In addition to this wage, each employee also receives a certain number of shares of stock in the firm. In order to determine the amount of stock that each employee must receive, it must be taken into consideration that the accumulated amount of these stocks within thirty years of employment will be appropriate to provide a return sufficient for sustaining a convenient living condition, at least at the level of the median wage paid. One must notice here that there is no inflationary process in technological democracy, so the value of the unit of money received will remain stable for years and more likely for decades.

Stock allocations take place each month, concurrent with the salary payment. The result is a gradual transfer of capital from capitalist to working class to the effect that, after a period of time, all capital is transferred to the workers and there is no capitalist involved in the production and distribution process.

Thus one of the major distinctions between the capitalist mode of production and the democratic mode of production is that under the latter, despite a total private ownership of the means of production, there is no separation between capital and labor. Labor owns the capital and thus governs the policy-making and management process, two important factors in the production process from which labor is totally detached under capitalism.

Monthly allocation of company stock to workers has several purposes. First, it transfers ownership of the means of production from capitalists to workers. Second, it causes an accumulation of capital for each worker, returns from which bring additional income to the owner during his working years. This income gradually increases corresponding to the increase in the amount of stocks. Third, by the time of retirement the return from accumulated stocks is sufficient to sustain a comfortable retirement. The main purpose of this stock allocation is to provide each individual with an independent retirement and old age benefits. This is a substitute for the current Social Security and retirement benefits. The major difference is that under the American capitalist system, the control of Social Security funds is in the hands of the government and retirement funds are controlled by the leadership in private sectors. A retired worker depends on monthly payments from these two resources. Furthermore, while the worker is heavily taxed for this purpose during all his working years, the amount received is nowhere sufficient to provide for a comfortable living condition, nor is he guaranteed to receive payment during his retired life. Under technological democracy each individual is the holder of his source of income for the duration of his retired life. He depends on no one for his support; he is the owner of the capital accumulated not through exploiting others, but through his own labor. It is this capital that contributes to the demands of production while providing enough income for a dignified, individualistic, and independent life for its owner, the retired worker. As will be explained later, this retirement is formal and actually the person never retires from being productive.

To protect this comfortable old age living for the workers it is imperative that the stocks earned by each worker remain in his possession for the period of his life. For this very important purpose, these stocks must be nontransferrable. However, in order to diversify stock ownership, these nontransferrable stocks are exchangeable with other nontransferrable stocks available on the stock market. For example, a worker who works for Company A and receives stocks of that company as part of his monthly pay may desire to exchange part of his stocks for nontransferrable stocks of Companies B and C. Since many workers working for different firms would also like to diversify their nontransferrable stocks of their company, a worker of Company A will have no difficulty exchanging his stocks for that of other companies in the open market. The value of nontransferrable stock of each company is determined by the value of transferrable stock of the same company on the stock market.

One may argue that since these stocks are nontransferrable, ownership is not complete. Considering the purpose of these stocks, this argument is not valid, because these stocks are given to the workers, first, to transfer capital from the capitalist to the workers, second, to provide an additional source of income for the workers during their working years, third, and the most essential, to provide for a source of sufficient income for the workers after they retire. If these stocks were transferrable, it would have been possible for a worker to liquidate them in the market and spend the proceeds. In this way, he would have destroyed his source of maintenance during his old age. He would also have relinquished his ownership of capital. Since, under technological democracy, there is no welfare assistance, except for those who are disabled, if such a worker liquidates his stocks, he may not have sufficient income to maintain himself. Furthermore, public assistance to such a person would be contrary to the principle of equality of opportunity, since by liquidating his stocks and spending the proceeds he consciously has harmed his equality of opportunity and by receiving welfare assistance he would be unjustifiably using the money earned by others for his support. Finally, nontransferrable stocks have all the benefits of ownership, except being transferrable. The owners receive return from them, and they are as valuable as transferrable stocks of the same company. Furthermore, one must note that most of the investment capital will be in the form of nontransferrable stocks and thus most of the stocks in the stock market will be of the nontransferrable kind. The philosophical idea behind this is that the capital, as a means of production, does not belong to anyone but to society as a whole. Each person during his lifetime becomes the custodian of some of it and enjoys the benefits accrued from it. When the person dies, since there is no inheritance under technological democracy, the capital he owns is transferred to the public treasury and gradually passed on to the next generation. Nontransferrability of the stocks guarantees to every worker a share of ownership of capital; it materializes the equitable distribution of the means of production and distribution among all the members of the working class.

THE WORK SYSTEM

Under technological democracy, there is a general education program that every individual is required to complete. As is explained later, when we discuss education, this general education is somehow similar to the system of general education presently applied in socialist countries like the Soviet Union.[3] It consists of a four-year preschool education (ages three through six), a four-year elementary education, and a four-year secondary education. We consider these grades one through twelve. This is the most important part of each individual's education and enormously effective in determining the future competence of the work force.

Work starts at the age of fifteen. However, the individual works only part-time. There are two sides to a worker's life. First is his development as a human being necessary to prepare him as a conscious participant in a democratic society. Here the purpose of a worker's education is to develop and advance him as a *democratic person*. Such a person is deeply devoted to the principle of democracy, equality of opportunity in particular, in every aspect of the societal life. In order to achieve this high human quality the person needs a broad education in humanities and nonprofessional aspects of the social sciences as well as the natural sciences. A person needs a deep understanding of the purpose of being, truth, honesty, one's place and rights within the society, one's attachment and respect to the nature and environment, and one's unselfishness in social, economic, and political spheres of life.

To develop as a democratic person one has to understand, through education, practice, and experience, the complex meaning and application of the principle of equality of opportunity, because it is only through the application of this principle that the socioeconomic and political framework of each individual's life is determined, expansion of one's freedoms occurs, and their limitations are distinguished.

The core part of the education required to understand these democratic values is achieved through an individual's general education extending through the twelfth grade. Education, however, is continued beyond this level and through all the working years of each individual. As part of this continued education, along with a technical and professional education, each worker will be required to take each year a certain prescribed number of courses in the areas enhancing his general and cultural knowledge, including his knowledge of democracy as applied in daily life.

The other side of a worker's life is related to his work, his professional knowledge, his proficiency, and his productiveness. His education in this regard starts when he enters the labor market. There are two aspects to his education. First, a formal technical and professional education which will continue through one's working years until retirement. For example, if a person wants to become an electrical engineer, he will start his formal higher education as soon as he finishes his twelfth-grade general education. Each worker starts his professional education part-time when he starts to work and continues thereafter while working. The first six years he works part-time, and after that he works full-time for a period of thirty years, after which he retires from formal employment. As will be illustrated later, by no means does this retirement indicate the end of an active and productive life.

During the first six years, after graduation from the twelfth grade, the individual continues his education almost full time, let us assume the equivalent of thirty college credits per year, including eight weeks of the summer. Within six years this amounts to 180 credit hours of education, far beyond what is required now for receiving an engineering or other professional degree. After this period of six years, when the worker assumes a full-time job he is required to study at least the equivalent of six college credits each semester (two three-credit courses). One of these two courses relates to his professional area in order to keep him up-to-date in his field, and the other is the liberal arts area, to give him a better understanding of self and society and also to provide him with a better means of enjoyment of life.

This is the course of the individual's formal education, which continues at least up to the time of retirement.

The other aspect of a worker's education is experience. Experience at his workplace teaches him how he can turn his scientific and professional knowledge into efficient and productive action. Experience with the institutions of society outside his work teaches him how to use his knowledge in the social sciences and humanities to better serve his fellow citizens and his society as a whole.

MOBILITY

In technological democracy, an individual is free to terminate his employment in one institution and seek employment, within his level of competence, in other institutions. Or he may desire to move to another class of work or profession. For this purpose he must channel his continued education toward his desired field and complete the requirements for the level of competence necessary for his desired position. It must be noted that education is provided free of charge, day and night. An individual desiring to change his field of occupation may be obliged to take courses in addition to those required from each worker.

SALARY RANGE AND COMPENSATION

The minimum salary for a full-time job is based on the amount necessary not only to accommodate the basic needs such as food, housing, clothing, transportation, and recreation, but to provide for comfortable living conditions. Based on the current standards, we may assume an income of $15,000 per person ($7.50 per hour) for this minimum pay. It is obvious that jobs requiring higher and more specialized education or harder physical work would pay a higher salary. As the years of experience and further education are added to a worker's initial level of competence for a full-time job, his salary increases accordingly. But at no time does a worker's pay exceed three times the minimum wage.

Let us assume, for example, that the minimum wage for full-time employment is fifteen thousand dollars; the highest salary would be around forty-five thousand dollars. If we consider the economic conditions as those of the United States at present, an annual income of fifteen thousand dollars will be sufficient to provide an individual with comfortable living conditions as far as the basic needs are concerned. Consider that there is no individual taxation under technological democracy and no property tax to cover the cost of educational institutions. Thus a fifteen-thousand-dollar income is equivalent to about twenty-two thousand dollars under the current federal, state, and local tax systems. One must also consider that there are no Social Security deductions and no expenditures for the worker's health care, his education, and that of his children. Furthermore, each worker receives an equivalent of about five thousand dollars per year in company shares, from which he also receives benefits. On the other hand, an income above thirty-five thousand dollars would be sufficient to provide for a comfortable life with much higher standards. Here again, since the worker does not pay taxes and receives free health care and education, his thirty-five-thousand-dollar salary plus returns from his accumulated capital compared to the current standards in the United States would be equivalent to nearly fifty thousand dollars.

It is obvious that while most workers start their full-time employment at the level of fifteen thousand dollars, many others with higher levels of opportunity, receive an initial salary higher than this minimum. Since through required continuing education and increased experience the level of competence of a worker continually goes up, so does his level of opportunity and income. The extent of increase in competence determines the amount of increase in salary one receives. This principle applies to all levels of competency. Technical and professional learning can never stop, because in technological society one easily becomes obsolete without updating his knowledge. Remaining at the same level of knowledge is equivalent to decaying in competence. Such behavior will cause lowering of one's level of opportunity and thus the level of one's income. This is why continuing education is necessary and required in technological democratic society. Technological society cannot progress or even sustain itself without properly educated and conscious citizens.

RETIREMENT

When a worker reaches the stage of retirement, he is a very highly educated and well-experienced person. Thus by no means does retirement mean idleness, particularly when a person is in his early fifties and still has some fifteen to twenty years of dynamic life to pursue.

First, as a person of high education in the liberal arts with years of experience in the operation of technological democracy in its economic, social, and political spheres, one would be highly qualified to fill political positions. As will be explained later, the elected government officials are volunteers with no pay; only their expenditures are paid on a per diem basis. Elected line officials, such as governors, are exceptions. However, since these positions require high qualifications, a broad knowledge of society, and deep acquaintance with the principles of technological democracy, newcomers to the labor market are not qualified and retired individuals are well suited for the job. Since nearly all elected political positions will be part-time and the essence of the work will be carried out by full-time specialists and technicians, those at the later stages of employment, if otherwise qualified, may seek political positions by choosing to work part-time and spend the rest of the time on political matters. However, they will be reluctant to do so, since part-time work will affect their salary and retirement benefits.

Second, retired persons, because of their high qualifications, will be in demand for lecturing and consulting, particularly if they continue their education after retirement.

Third, again because of their high knowledge, retired workers may involve themselves in research and writing. They may concentrate on subjects in their technical or professional field. They may choose subjects relating to social or economic aspects of technological democracy, drawing from years of experience, as well as research.

Finally, a retired person may not wish to do any of these. He may desire to devote the rest of his life to art, music, literature, travel, or further study of nature and the environment, or he may desire to start a business of his own by investing his savings and forming partnerships.

In doing any of these choices, with the exception of the latter, a retired person has plenty of time for travel, sports, and recreation, since he is the sole determinant of his own time schedule. He may make his work and recreation plans as he desires. He has a steady income from his accumulated nontransferrable shares; he is totally on his own as a truly free and independent individual. The retirement period is, in fact, a dream of life, with security, creativity, and freedom to do as one wishes with one's money, body, and mind. Furthermore, retired people are the holders of a good part of the investment capital in society through the ownership of their accumulated nontransferrable and transferrable stock of production firms. In fact, the retired workers are the largest per capita owners of capital in the technological democratic society. All these put together make retired workers highly respectable individuals in the community. The slogan in technological democratic society may well be that "I work and improve myself as an individual with the hope of arriving at the heavenly stage of retirement." This becomes even more desirable when individuals retire in their early fifties and have many years of dynamic life to look forward to. For some, this period may be more expanded than the period of their working years.

In a capitalistic society, like that of the United States, as it has been presented above, the capitalist controls the economy. Through a continuous accumulation process, the capitalists increase their power and authority over the state to the extent that, under modern technological monopoly capitalism, the capitalist class controls or at least highly influences state activities directly concerned with capitalistic interests.

The matter of the power struggle has become more complex in favor of the capitalist class, where no single state has neither the authority nor the power to regulate or investigate the total operation of a multinational corporation.

Furthermore, while the state is responsible to its citizens and rules with their apparent consent, a multinational corporation is an autocratic system ruled not by its shareholders, as it should have been according to its charter, but by a self-appointed and self-perpetuating board of directors holding, collectively, only a small fraction of corporate shares.

Under a socialistic system, like that of the Soviet Union, the state is controlled by a single political party, that of the Communist party, and the party is controlled in turn by its leadership. Like members of the board of directors in a corporation under the capitalist system, members of the party leadership are elevated to their position by initial and senior members of the ruling body of the party.

The Soviet constitution, like that of the United States, prescribes a government by a democratic process. But the execution of this electoral process is controlled tightly and supervised by the party through its instrumentalities. Consequently, the government ends up being governed by a few who hold positions of leadership within the party.

In a socialist society it is this small political elite that, through holding the authority of the state, maintains control over the national economy. The continuing advancement of technology has provided the state with means of further tightening its control over the means of production and distribution.

Thus it is the state that, through its control of the means of production, determines what is to be produced, how it is to be produced, and how the proceeds are to be appropriated or distributed. This mode of production is in direct opposition to the fundamental socialist principle that all means of production belong to the people as a whole and shall be used by them to produce and these products shall be distributed among all to each according to his needs.

In a sense, because of its dominance over the means of production, the socialist state appears to be more autocratic and more bureaucratic than the state under capitalism. Actually, under socialism the capitalist and the state have merged as one and the workers are exploited to the extent desired by the state, with no recourse.

Of course, it may be claimed that under socialism people receive a great deal of social benefits not available under capitalism, such as free health care services, free education, and highly subsidized housing, transportation, and recreation, as well as substantial old age and retirement benefits. But all these benefits, taken that all are provided, are granted at the pleasure of the state and not by a democratic process.

Consequently, under both capitalist and socialist systems individual freedom has remained at the mercy of a very small group, which controls the means of production and distribution. Neither system has allowed the individual opportunity to develop according to individual desire but by subjugating him to the norms and requirements of the prevailing capitalistic or socialistic mode of production. In this manner, the state has increasingly imposed limitations on an individual's freedom of choice and action and thus has deprived him from full development of his faculties.

All this suppression has occurred because the individual, under either system, has been deprived of equality of opportunity. Under both systems, as illustrated in previous chapters, the state has played a substantial role in installing and maintaining the subjugation process. Individual life under either system is highly exploitive.

The main objective in a technological democratic system is to allow opportunities for individual freedom and dignity in a way so that no one is exploited economically, socially, or politically. To accomplish this goal, as we have seen, control over the means of production and distribution must be taken away from the small group that controls them and be returned to the individuals within the working class. This purpose is achieved through the application of the principle of equality of opportunity and the prohibition of unjust enrichment. Through this process, capital and control of the means of production are transferred gradually from the controlling capitalist or socialist group to individual workers. By application of the same principle, as we have also seen, any kind of exploitation becomes prohibited and eliminated. Accordingly, no profits are to be made through the use of productive means and individual workers collectively, through their representatives, take over the policy-making process of production and distribution.

Consequently, in a technological democratic society, the role of the state becomes quite distinguished from those under capitalism or socialism. Like every individual in society, the state is obliged to abide by the principle of equality of opportunity. As a result, first, the state cannot keep anything secret or confidential. Every individual has equal opportunity of access, mainly through the Technodem, to governmental archives and information sources. If secrecy were allowed, it would increase the opportunity of the state to the detriment of the public, which would be contrary to the principle of equality of opportunity. Thus technological democratic society has an open and very small bureaucracy. This openness extends to every corner of its operation, including that of the national security. This may seem very inappropriate and irrational under the current situation of international relations, but as will be explained later, such external relationships in technological democracy cannot be anything but open. Any other way is in conflict with the principle of equality of opportunity and tends toward exploitation and subjugation of other nations. Second, in technological democracy a major part of public functions are transferred down to the individual production firms. Other parts, such as maintenance of law and order and supervision and enforcement of the principles and standards governing the production process, are entrusted to local and regional governments; there is no line function left for the national government except defense and foreign affairs. As we will see later, the defense establishment is also highly curtailed, because in technological democracy the essence of strength is not in military might and weapons but in the strength of its citizens' minds and commitment. No conquering force can rule a technological democratic society without being assimilated into its norms and culture in a short time. Thus any conquering force will soon be conquered by the conquered society. In essence, then, there is no need for military forces. Elimination of the military establishment will mark the disappearance of the greatest evil that have haunted humanity and its well-being for centuries.

To many, this allegation may be idealistic and utopian. These are people who have failed to study and understand the essence of technological democracy, the depth, force, and effects of its founding principles, and the causes that may induce military action under such circumstances. We cannot judge or evaluate the characteristics of technological democracy by employing our current values. We must rise and place ourselves on the proper plateau of knowledge and understanding before we start making judgments about the values of technological democratic society. Proper judgment requires a thorough knowledge of facts, which are ascertained through appropriate education and comprehension. Faulty judgments are often the result of haste and shallowness. One thus ought to be careful in making judgments, particularly concerning the future of humanity.

Consequently, if the state and its government have no line functions, there will be no need for the kind of vast, wasteful, and expensive bureaucracy that currently characterizes the state under capitalism as well as socialism. The vast amount of capital used for its maintenance will be channeled for production purposes, and at the same time citizens will be relieved from its dominance and burdens.

The state, while having new and extremely important functions, will be highly simplified and much closer to and within easy reach of the people.

NOTES

1. Robert S. Morison, "Vision," in *Technology and Man's Future*, Albert H. Teich, ed., 3d ed. (New York: St. Martin's Press, 1981), pp. 7–22.
2. This increased control is evident from reference to available statistics.

3. For a brief but very thorough presentation of Soviet education, see A. I. Piskinov, "The Soviet School and Soviet Pedagogy in the Period of the Competition of Socialist Construction and Gradual Transition to Communism," *Soviet Education*, February-March 1978, pp. 106–194.

Chapter Seven

The Structure and Function of Technological Democracy

For decades and perhaps centuries democracy has been emphasized as a process by which people freely select their leaders and, through those leaders, express their views and influence the formation of policies. Democracy has been considered a political process only and has never been defined in its totality as a system.

For over two thousand years, since the Greeks crystallized the idea of democracy, this concept has been surrounded by controversy. Throughout most of this period, kings ruled and subjects obeyed. When the idea of democracy was brought to life in seventeenth-century England, it was limited to the socially privileged class. Even the framers of the U.S. Constitution considered popular election mob rule, and accordingly only one institution, the House of Representatives, was made subject to popular election, with suffrage restricted to propertied adult males. In theory, the individual citizen has sovereign power but in practice, the power was safely guarded by those of greater economic means and stability.

Today few Americans are deprived from exercising their voting rights, and the public in general considers the system democratic. But there is more to democracy than being able to vote for candidates, even if there is full participation of those eligible to vote.

Democracy as defined and applied during the last two centuries has meant a governing process, a political process tending to lead toward a substantive democracy in which political equality of opportunity is to be realized. However, this goal has never been materialized.

Today, except for Marxism, there is an absence of contemporary systematic philosophy that attempts to explain the whole socioeconomic and policital situations through generalizations about man, institutions, and his environment.

However, there has been no deficiency of individual political ideas, as visualized by scientists with varying perceptions from different disciplines.

In political science there are Laski's analyses of the evils of economics, the social system, and political pluralism, Weldon's challenge on the ethical implications of traditional political philosophy, Oakeshott's exposition of rationalistic misconceptions in politics, Lippmann's discovery of public policy, Strauss's revelation of the proper nature of political philosophy, Rawl's theory of justice, and Nozick's concept of the minimal state; in sociology, there are Weber's interrelationships between ideology, the social structure, and material interests, Mannheim's sociology of knowledge, Riesman's analysis of character, and Whyte's organization of man; in psychology, there are Freudians such as Alder and Fromm; in law, there are Kelser's basic norm theory and Paund's sociological jurisprudence; in economics, there are Schumpeter's conceptions of capitalism, socialism, and democracy, Keynes's general theory, and the ideas from Hayek, Ropke, and de Jouvenel; in philosophy, there are the various interpretations of the Vienna school as well as existentialism; in history, there are Spengler, Copernicus, and Toynbee; in literature, there are Proust's kaleidoscopic picture of society, Kafka's parables, and the futuristic visions of Orwell and Huxley. The list extends further to business and other disciplines.

Despite all these honest and earnest efforts, no attempt has been successful in defining democracy in its entirety as a system. There is no straightforward set of ideas universally agreed to be the philosophy of democracy.[1] There is no set of writings that can serve as democratic gospel.[2]

Looking at the theoretical and experimental developments of democracy, there is first the *natural rights theory*. Before Christ, Cicero wrote: "We are so constituted by Nature as to share the sense of Justice with one another and to pass it on to all men."[3] Locke,[4] Rosseau,[5] Burk,[6] and Jefferson[7] are the most eloquent proponents of the theory of natural rights democracy.

Second, there is the concept of *utilitarian democracy* or democratic liberalism, whose ideas were initiated and developed with different variations by thinkers such as, Bentham,[8] Mill,[9] Calhoun,[10] Green,[11] Hobhouse,[12] and Dewey.[13]

Third, there are contemporary democratic thoughts attempted by contemporary thinkers, among whom are George Bernard Shaw, Thomas,[14] Hayek,[15] Lindsay,[16] Schumpeter,[17] Mayo,[18] Rawls,[19] and Nozick.[20] Philosophers in this category, by the very nature of complex problems of modern societies, while concentrating on political democracy have been forced to deal explicitly with the economic aspects of societal life. From a variety of economic orders that have been defended, two general trends have evolved. One is *democratic capitalism*, which recognizes the need for some state activity in economic affairs but emphasizes the primacy of individual economic liberty; it presents a conservative defense of the freedom of enterprise. The other is *democratic socialism*, which emphasizes the need for radical socioeconomic reconstruction, greater range of community control, and the cooperative determination of planned economic goals.

Consequently, on one extreme stands the United States, where the political democratic process is used to provide justification for sustaining socioeconomic discrimination and exploitation inherent in capitalism; in the middle of the road is Sweden, where political democracy is attempted to maintain the unstable combination of state and private capitalism; and on the other extreme stands the Soviet Union, where so-called democratic centralism has been made a facade to justify state socialism. In none of these systems has a substantive political democracy materialized. It cannot materialize.

In reality, democracy as an ideology has no relevancy to capitalism or socialism; it is incompatible with both. Democracy is an independent system by itself, of which political democracy is just a part. It has never been defined as a system. Furthermore the democratic system has an important inescapable ingredient, technology, which has not been considered and is not an inherent part of other less advanced systems such as capitalism or socialism. While technology has developed under the latter systems, because of disparity between the level of capitalism and then socialism with the higher level of technology, the latter has never been understood properly and has thus been abused and used to the detriment of itself and the environmment, as well as the society as a whole.

The term *technological democracy,* as it is used here, means democracy as a system. It embraces not only the political but also the social, economic, and technological aspects of a societal life. It encompasses the interactions of society as a whole.

Democracy of this kind cannot occur in any society that is not highly developed and broadly educated. It requires that people understand the democratic principles governing the socioeconomic, political, and technological norms and processes of society. It also requires that they do comprehend the causes and effects of such norms and processes and the philosophy and reason behind them.

On the other hand, such a developed society is also highly advanced in science and technology. Thus democracy and technology are inseparable and democracy as a system can occur only in an advanced technological society in which people are well educated in social science and humanities in order to understand and properly apply and maintain the required democratic principles and norms. Therefore, it would be appropriate if we label this democratic system as *technological democracy.*

SUBSTANTIVE AND PROCEDURAL DEMOCRACY

There are two aspects to this democracy: democratic goals and democratic processes. Democratic goals are those ends toward which society strives. The closer society gets to these goals, the more democracy it attains. There are three basic objectives of democracy. These are: *equality of opportunity* from social, economic, and political viewpoints, *freedom,* and *individualism.* Figure 7–1 illustrates the system.

However, the essential objective of democracy is to achieve equality of opportunity in its full and broad sense. Once equality of opportunity is established, the other two objectives of democracy, namely freedom and individualism, will be ascertained as its consequences. The quality and extent of expansion of these goals mark the degree of *substantive democracy* achieved.

There are two ways of achieving these objectives of democracy, either by force or by democratic ways. It is obvious that to

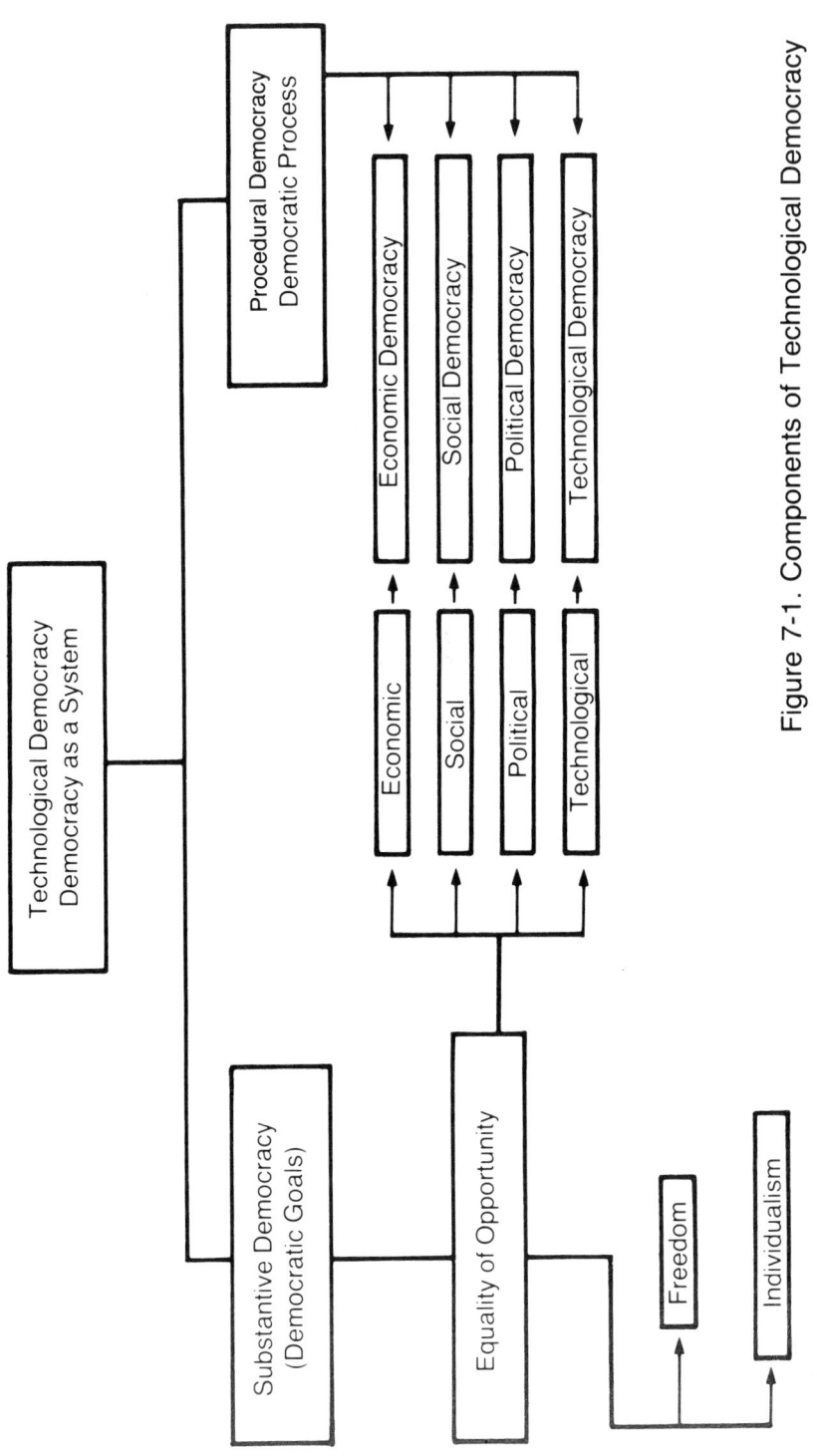

Figure 7-1. Components of Technological Democracy

attain equality of opportunity in a society, all elements against it must be destroyed or eliminated. To use force to achieve this objective means that there will be, for the time being, no political democratic instruments used for achieving economic and social equality of opportunity. In other words, political authoritarianism will be used to materialize economic and social democracy. This seems more suitable to developing countries at least at the initial stage of transition in order to eradicate undemocratic elements.

Once socioeconomic democracy is well established and all elements of nondemocratic systems, such as capitalism and socialism, are eradicated and their relevant norms abandoned, the authoritarianism will automatically be replaced by political democracy by the extension of the application of equality of opportunity from the socioeconomic sphere into the political arena. This inevitable consequence is the result of the fact that the democratic system rests heavily on the socioeconomic equality of opportunity rather than the political equality of opportunity. Once socioeconomic opportunities are equalized, tremendous forces they create will tend toward equalizing political opportunities and gradually bringing about political democracy. Society will then become as a whole a democratic system, a technological democratic society.

Another way of achieving socioeconomic democracy is through democratic political means. But such political democracy cannot be materialized unless either socioeconomic democracy is already established and thus the special interest groups' power has been demolished or at least socioeconomic democracy is being pushed along with political democracy, because in order to achieve political democracy certain prerequisites must be met.

Most of all, to attain political democracy there must be *popular sovereignty*. This simply means people having full authority over the government. Such authority, particularly in technological society, can be achieved through elections. However, such elections must be *free* and *frequent,* both based on the concept of equality of opportunity. Figure 7–2 illustrates these requirements.

First, elections must be free, and in order to achieve free elections, equality of opportunity prescribes certain requirements to be present. One must be free to elect or be elected. Any

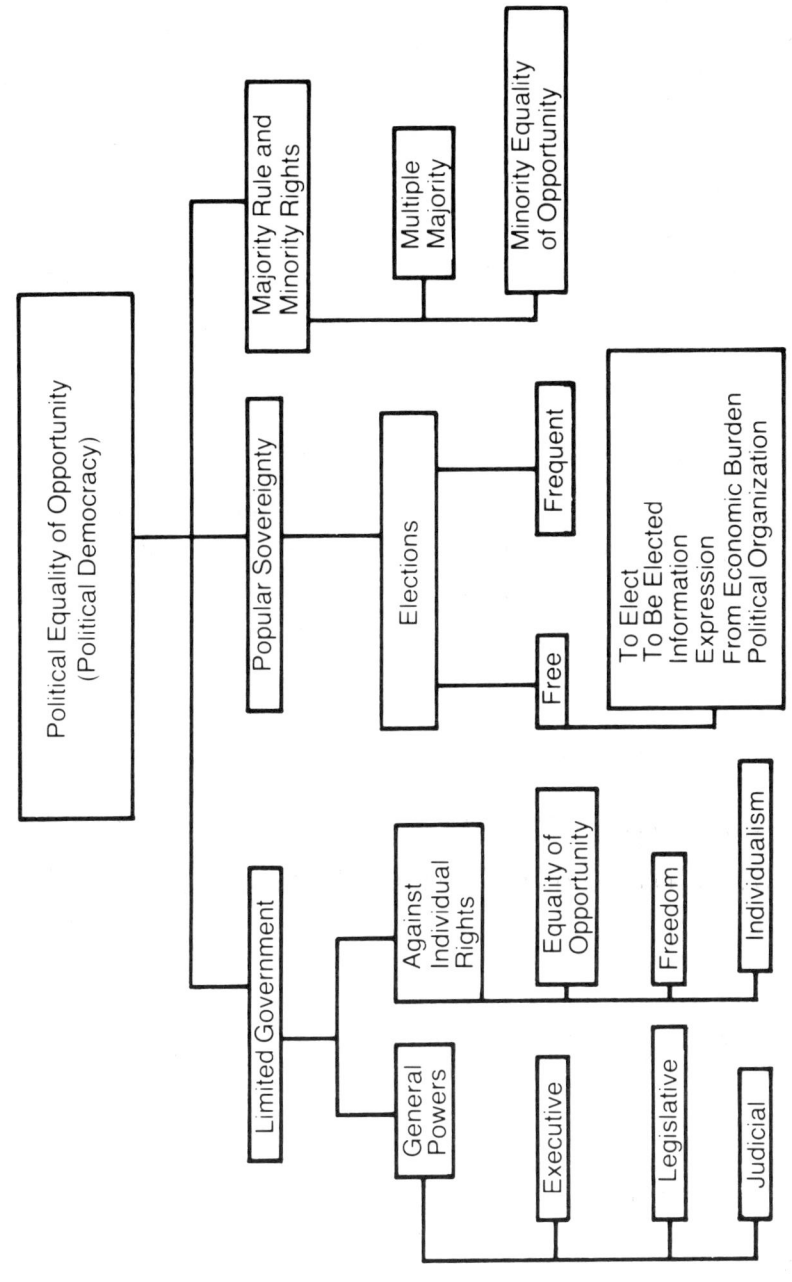

Figure 7-2. Prerequisites of Political Equality of Opportunity

elements hampering this freedom must be eliminated. Thus there should not be any institutionalized political parties, as has been the case in industrialized countries of today. Political organizations were necessities during the early stages of political democracy. But once they were institutionalized, they became subject to power structure and control by an elite; hence they became undemocratic and often reactionary. However, for election purposes there must be freedom for political organization. Such organizations may be formed for electoral purposes only and after each election, once they have served their purpose, will be automatically dissolved. However, since the elections will be carried out through the Technodem, there will be little, if any, use for such an organization. In technological society when, through advanced technological means, people have continuous and immediate access to the government and vice versa, there is no need for institutionalized and permanent political organizations such as political parties, because the main purpose of political parties is to express the ideas and desires of its members for electoral aims. In technological society people can organize and express their views and desires as groups without need of established political parties. And these groups can continually change and reshape their character, ideology, and demands freely and without being entangled in party bureaucracy and hypocrisy. Advanced technology and information systems will allow such changes and facilitate continuous meaningful contact between many divergent groups in the society and between them and the public institutions.

For free elections there must also be freedom of expression. Equality of opportunity prescribes that people be free to express their ideas, regardless of how unorthodox these ideas may be. They must be received, analyzed, and evaluated in light of the principle of equality of opportunity. No idea can be accepted as healthy and useful if it disturbs or adversely affects in any way the equality of opportunity. Thus ideas supportive of capitalism or socialism, though they may be allowed free expression, cannot be accepted, since they tend to destroy equality of opportunity.

Free elections also require free access to information. If people do not have full access to information, they cannot be able to find out and know all about the elected officials and bureaucrats, as well as public policies. And thus they cannot make proper choices and appropriate judgments about their representatives and public policies. Accordingly, if important information relating to governmental policies and functions is made classified and kept away from public access, the concept of equality of opportunity is disturbed, because those few having access to such information are in a better position than those without access to them. Thus in a democratic electoral process there should not be any information withheld from public access. An essential requirement for a democratic system is the total awareness of people about the operation of the system. Democracy is harmed when a bulk of important public information is stamped "Top Secret" or "Classified."

Most of all, free elections require freedom from financial burdens. If the electoral process requires candidates to spend money, then those who have access to more money have a better opportunity to win; thus the concept of equality of opportunity is disturbed. All candidates should have the same opportunity of access to financial needs for the elections. This equality of opportunity can be achieved only when all the electoral process is publicly financed and all viable candidates benefit equally from it. As has been explained, through the electronic electoral process this very important obstacle to equality of opportunity is avoided.

Another requirement for popular sovereignty is that elections must be frequent, so that people have frequent opportunities to check their leaders and their policies. This means that the elected offices must have short terms. However, the term of office must not be too short, e.g., two years, and deprive its holder from proper planning and functioning. Also, it must not be too long, e.g., ten years, to make its holder less sensitive to public demands. The appropriate length of the term of office appears to be six years. In multiple-member bodies there should be a continuity in operation. A more appropriate way to achieve this is that one-half or one-third of the membership be up for election during each term. For example, with a six-year term one-third of the membership will be up for election every two years. This concept of continuity is particularly important since incumbents serve only for one term and cannot be consecutively reelected to the same office.

If all the above mentioned conditions are present, then the

elections are free and frequent and popular sovereignty is achieved.

The second requirement for political procedural democracy is *majority rule with minority rights*. It is a well-known concept that if a single majority rules and makes policies without concern for the rights and demands of the minority there is *majority dictatorship*. It is possibly one of the worst dictatorships, since it is hidden behind its democratic appearance.

Majority rule with minority rights means that while decisions are made by the majority, the minority should be given equal opportunity to participate in the decision-making processes. It should be allowed opportunity of equal participation in debates and voting processes.

The third requirement for political procedural democracy concerns itself with the limitation on state powers in two areas. First, the state must be limited in the area of general powers, namely those of the executive, legislative, and judicial.

On the executive level, under technological democracy, since most of the matters dealing with the individual's daily life will be taken care of within the institution of his work, there will be little, if any, need for the government to intervene. For example, as it will be presented later, each individual's old age benefits will come under his personal control from the day he receives his first pay. Therefore, there will be no need for a Social Security system and its vast bureaucracy. Since there will not be any general welfare program except for disabled persons, the vast bureaucracy administering it will disappear. Furthermore, since there will be no need for government regulation of business and economy, the vast regulatory bureaucracies will be eliminated. Finally, at the national level all departments, except for departments of state and defense, will be abolished. The structure of the defense department, as will be demonstrated later, will also be substantially diminished.

On the legislative level, there will be no need for an extensive national legislative branch, since the matters of national interest will be determined by particular councils or popular legislation, which is quite possible through advanced technology, where every eligible person can vote on matters presented to the people several times during the day through his or a public computer terminal. Thus the whole legislative branch, with its high cost of electoral process and bureaucracy, will be eliminated. There will only be a small legislative assembly with very limited functions, described later.

There will be no need for a national judiciary except for a national judicial council, a supreme constitutional court, a supreme administrative court, and necessary judicial and nonjudicial staff. It will also embody a national law enforcement council that will have coordinative authority over all state law enforcement agencies.

The second area of limitation of state power concerns individual rights. The extension of this power will be based strictly on application of the concept of equality of opportunity and its entailing freedoms and individualism. Again, since most matters concerning an individual's daily life will be taken care of within his workplace and his community and since the solution of his daily problems will be based on the principle of equality of opportunity, little room will be left for the state to interfere with an individual's rights and liberties.

In short, national government will have no line functions except in the areas of foreign policy and defense; regional governments will be concerned primarily with law and order and supervision of the application of the principle of equality of opportunity within the institutions over which they have jurisdiction. Yet, despite these responsibilities, as will be explained later, regional bureaucracies will be highly diminished, since a majority of functions currently undertaken by such governments will not be necessary and will be eliminated.

This is possibly the most important area of limitation on state powers, particularly when it is understood that the individual will enjoy the same opportunity as the state in the case of confrontation and conflict of interest.

ECONOMIC EQUALITY OF OPPORTUNITY: ECONOMIC DEMOCRACY

As illustrated in figure 7–3, economic democracy requires the application of equality of opportunity in four areas: capital, labor, technology, and state.

Figure 7-3. Prerequisites of Economic Equality of Opportunity

- **Economic Equality of Opportunity (Economic Democracy)**
  - **Capital**
    - Prohibition of Unjust Enrichment
      - No Inheritance
      - No Exploitation (No Profits)
      - No Free Transfers
  - **Labor**
    - Ownership of Capital
      - Position Classification
      - Shared Opportunity
      - Full Employment
      - Individual Old Age Benefits
  - **State**
    - Extensive Elimination of National Bureaucracy and Powers
    - Extensive Elimination of State Bureaucracy and Powers
    - Expansion of Authority of Local Government
    - Few National Standards: General Position Classification, Wage System Interest Rates Et Cetera

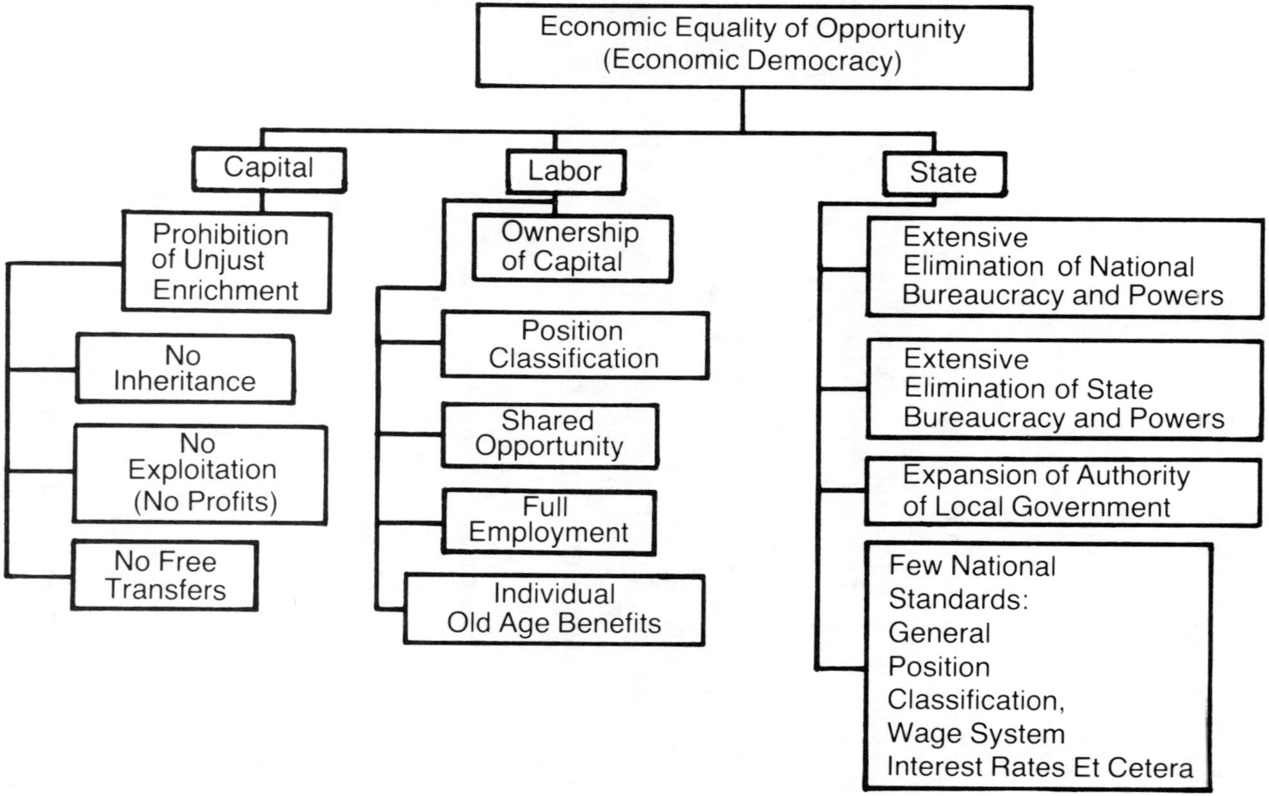

Capital

To democratize the ownership of capital, the principle of equality of opportunity prohibits unjust enrichment. Unjust enrichment simply means that no one receives property without giving in return a comparable compensation and, ultimately, no one receives anything free and without compensation. The application of this concept causes the following consequences:

1. No Inheritance

Since anything received through inheritance is free and without comparable compensation, therefore, it is an unjust enrichment and thus prohibited. Inheritance, to the extent of wealth received, elevates the opportunity of the beneficiary to the detriment of others. It has been a very important cause of unequal opportunities. The proceeds from inheritance will go into the Public Consumption Fund, which will be spent in providing education and health care. The result is that as the rich individuals die, their wealth, instead of going to their heirs, is transferred to the public treasury and spent for the public good. The consequence of this practice is that gradually wealthy families, which enjoyed a very high opportunity under capitalism, will disappear while their riches are used to enrich and enlighten the masses as a whole. In a span of a few decades, society will cease to have any multimillionaires. The ruling capitalist elite will die, and with it will disappear its dominating socioeconomic and political powers.

2. No Profits

Profits materialize from two sources:

1. Through exploitation of workers. The capitalist appropriates to himself part of labor's work without compensation, hence unjustly enriching himself. If profits are eliminated, workers will receive the full benefit of their work.
2. Through exploitation of consumers. If the capitalist

charges a price that is above the full cost of production, then he exploits the consumer to the extent of the price surplus.

Both exploitation of the worker as well as exploitation of the consumer are unjust enrichment and thus prohibited. Both adversely affect the equality of opportunity.

It has been said that if profits are eliminated, there will be no incentive to work. Nothing could be further from the truth. In the first place, workers were those who worked and not the capitalist. Second, if the worker receives full return for his work, in contrast to the partial return he received under the capitalist system, he will have far more incentive to work than before. It must be noted that in advanced technological society the term *worker* applies to any working person within the productive system, from unskilled workers up to top managers.

3. No Transfer of Property without Just Compensation

Any transfer of property without just compensation moves its receiver to a higher level of opportunity, producing unjust enrichment. Thus, for the sake of democracy, it must be prohibited. Certain minor gift items may be excluded from this rule.

The term *property* includes, among other things, any of the following:

1. Physical object or structure
2. Valuable claim such as stocks and bonds
3. Money or other means of exchange
4. Labor

2. Labor

There is a very basic distinction between capitalism and technological democracy. Under capitalism the capitalist controls land, capital, and technology and employs labor from the market. Under technological democracy the workers own and control the capital and all other means of production. Generally speaking, it can be said that all labor is collectively self-employed.

1. Ownership of Capital

The principle of equality of opportunity controls the process of ownership of capital. It is through this principle that the ownership of capital is democratized, materializing the total private ownership of the means of production and distribution to an extent never achieved before.

The process of achieving this goal prescribes that the ownership of capital be gradually and systematically transferred from the capitalist to the workers. For this purpose, while each worker receives a regular wage, he also receives with it a certain amount of the shares of the firm where he works. Thus from the time he receives his first pay he starts to become a part-owner of his firm. As the years pass, the worker continues to accumulate capital and increase his share of ownership. As the big capitalists die, their stock shares revert to the public treasury and from there are offered to the stock market for sale. These are purchased by different institutions, public institutions in particular, and gradually transferred to the workers along with their monthly pay.

After two or three decades, the capitalist class as we know today will disappear and the ownership as well as control of capital become wholly transferred to the workers.

From there on as the retired workers die, their stock shares go to the public treasury, from there to the stock market, and finally are purchased by different institutions and gradually divided among the new generation of workers along with their pay.

This new process of compensating the workers, partially by cash payment and partially by stocks, gives new character to capital. Capital and its accumulation are not the result of profits (social surplus) through exploitation of labor and consumers, but the result of savings accrued from the hours of labor performed by the worker. As such, capital is a cash accumulation of hours of work and thus entitled to a return if it is invested. It is entitled to a return corresponding to the market rate of interest.

For example, if the market interest rate is **10 percent**, the benefit that one hour of work brings to a worker should be allowed to be 10 percent if it is invested in the production process. The National Economic Council will determine this return and adjust and readjust it. This is the same when he loans the money and the return is similar to the interest rate practiced under capitalism. He may invest his savings in stocks. His returns then will be in the form of dividends. Accordingly, as a worker continues to work he receives three economic benefits. He receives a cash pay, which is intended to take care of his and his family's living expenses. He also receives a share of stocks, which helps him to save and accumulate capital. Finally, he receives dividends from the share of stocks he owns, which continue to increase as he continues to accumulate more and more stocks.

2. Position Classification

Position classification is a technology developed for organization, classification, and equalization of similar positions. It accompanies a corresponding pay system for its materialization. Under this technology, positions are classified vertically as well as horizontally. Details of functions and responsibilities for each position are determined and described. The daily expansion of these responsibilities is calculated in a way that fills the daily hours required for full-time work. Horizontal positions are those that require similar levels of skill to carry out job requirements. However, these positions may not be similar in the kind of functions and skills they require. For example, medical doctors, lawyers, and top administrators all require a high level of professional skill, while functionally they are quite different from one another. However, they may be placed horizontally in one category and entitled to the same kind of pay. The same applies to clerical workers. Vertical positions, on the other hand, deal with a hierarchical structure of positions from the lowest level to the highest. Vertically, while positions are divided into categories based on the nature of the required functions, each category is also hierarchically arranged. Thus, vertically speaking, doctors, lawyers, and top executives belong to three different categories of health care, legal-judicial, and management. Vertically, in the health care category, positions start from the lower levels of maids, nurses, paramedics, laboratory workers, and other medical technicians and go to higher levels of interns and doctors. Each of these, in turn, has sublevels within it. For example, there are different levels of nurses, doctors, et cetera. Compensation for each level is determined within a minimum and maximum range according to the level of required skill, experience and complexities involved. Technology of position classification was created primarily for the purpose of increasing and controlling productivity and also for providing equitable pay systems: similar pay for similar jobs.

This technology is not new at all and is being used in every industrialized society by its public sector and by all major and medium-sized and some small private institutions. However, each institution has its own independent classification of positions and corresponding pay system. The national government, each state government, major city governments, and giant corporations each have position classification systems of their own. However, there is no uniformity among these systems and there are injustices. Furthermore, a great variety of small institutions do not have such a system, yet these are the institutions that employ the majority of the working class who are not subject to any standard of pay and are, generally, overexploited.

Under technological democracy, all these systems are brought under one umbrella with the same standards of positions and corresponding compensations. However, such a monumental classification is not done in detail by a central office. This would be an impossible job. The national government through the Position Classification and Pay Commission, a branch of the National Economic Council, establishes a general classification of postions, a system somehow similar to the current national government classification. Then it requires each institution, private or public, large or small, to establish its own position classification and pay system within the framework established by the national classification and pay system. A copy of this classification is sent by each institution to the regional position classification council. The system is put into operation by each institution until it is objected to by the regional council. The systems are reviewed each year by each institution as new technologies develop, certain positions are abandoned, new positions are created, and functions of some positions are revised.

Position classification under one national system has several benefits:

1. It harmonizes and standardizes all available positions, private as well as public.
2. It equalizes the pay system, with similar pay for similar jobs, regardless of whether a worker is a union member or not.
3. It eliminates union bargaining and thus eliminates unionization for economic purposes.
4. It simplifies position and pay classification at the institutional level, since there will be a standardization and updated national model to follow.
5. It democratizes the work system by providing equality of opportunity in similar positions with similar pay.
6. It allows regional agencies to supervise the proper and uniform application of national standards.
7. It bestows discretion on each institution to go about establishing its own job and pay classification.
8. It gives the worker an opportunity to evaluate his position, comparing it with the national standard, and petition first his institution and then the regional classification council in the case of discrepancy. In this way, position classification in each institution is scrutinized by its workers and brought to the level prescribed by national standards.

As will be presented below, the pay system in an institution or a group of institutions may be slightly reduced below the prescribed level by the use of the concept of "shared opportunity." However, such changes will be negligible.

3. Shared Opportunity and Full Employment

The very application of the principle of equality of opportunity requires that those having a higher level of employment opportunity share it with those lacking such an opportunity. Workers who have employment have a better opportunity than workers without employment. If there are no employment opportunities for those unemployed, then those who have employment, in order to provide for equality of opportunity, forego a small part of their employment opportunity by giving up a small part of their work, say one hour per week, and thus cause employment opportunity for their unemployed fellows. This is a requirement for materialization of equality of opportunity in the labor market and is known as *shared opportunity*.

As presented in an example before, if there is a work force of 100 million and, as in the above example, each working person gives up one hour of his weekly work nationwide, 100 million work hours, 2.5 million full-time positions will become available to those who have no employment.

Therefore, those who were employed by sacrificing one hour of pay per week were able to provide jobs for all of the new workers looking for jobs. Of course in practice this is much more complex, since there may be a demand for certain skills and a surplus of others, but these problems are easily resolved by an effective use of the forecasting and information system and by the very concept of supply and demand in the long run. People tend to move out from the areas of surplus into areas of demand through freely available retraining programs.[21] It is important to notice that unemployment in technological democratic society has a different character. Individuals don't wait to finish their professional or technical education and then look for a job. Every individual starts working when he reaches the age of fifteen and completes his professional or technical education while working. So work under technological democracy has a transitory character. Unemployment occurs when a person leaves his job or when a young person enters the labor market looking for a part-time job in less skilled areas that will not be difficult to find. More likely, more than 90 percent of the people looking for jobs will be those terminating their general education at the age of fifteen and looking for a part-time job. The system always tends toward equilibrium.

By this manner, employment becomes an individual right and each person is able to secure employment. Sharing opportunities provides for continuous full employment, causing stability in the market and thus eliminating a major cause of recession.

Furthermore, the inflationary process will also be prevented, since there will be no monopoly industry and no price increases to maximize profits. Giant corporations will automatically be divided into many smaller firms: international corporations will disappear, and competition in the market will be tense, more realistic, and free. This decentralized and dispersed situation will be materialized because once workers receive controlling shares of a giant firm, they will tend to eliminate the superstructure of the corporate bureaucracy, which did not produce anything and also had then lost its unproductive use. Then desire to have voice in the operation will tend toward dismantling the giant corporation into smaller entities in which the policymakers will be directly attached to production process and the worker can feel his voice and power over his institution. The same will happen to the branch or affiliated firms abroad. They would want to be independent, especially when the superstructure in a domestic country becomes abolished. Thus the era of giant multinational corporations will become history as a stage of transition from monopolistic international capitalism to competitive technological democracy. The old motto that "small is beautiful, small is controllable, small is more democratic" will become materialized.

4. Old Age Benefits

Unlike the welfare programs instituted under existing capitalistic and socialistic systems, there will be no retirement or general welfare system under technological democracy. First, each individual will start part-time work when he reaches the age of fifteen. His hours of work increase each year, and in a few years he becomes a full-time worker. From here on, each individual is required to work full-time for at least thirty years in order to provide a sustained and sufficient income for his old age period.

The process works as follows: Let us assume that a worker receives corporate stock equivalent to 25 percent of his monthly pay. Individuals in public service receive stocks purchased by the government from the open stock market. As the individual's pay increases, so does his monthly share of stocks proportional to 25 percent of his salary. We can fairly assume that the value of monthly stock given to each worker to amount, on an average, to four hundred dollars or forty-eight hundred dollars per year. In a period of thirty years he will accumulate a nontransferrable capital equivalent to $144,000. At 10 percent return, this will provide a sustained income of $14,000 per year at the time of retirement. If he saves and accumulates returns from his stocks, after thirty years he will have an additional accumulation of over $160,000 in tranferrable capital. At 10 percent return, this will give him an additional annual income of sixteen thousand dollars.

With a combined income of nearly thirty thousand dollars, a worker who retires at the age of fifty-two will have a quite comfortable life. However, he does not actually retire, but moves out of the general national work force. He may occupy himself with other income-producing functions. This retirement is mandatory for three reasons: first, to provide vacancies to new workers entering the market; second, to provide the retired worker with many years of an enjoyable and intellectually productive life; third, to provide for participation in the political process where required qualifications are high and the service is temporary.

Thus this required retirement is technical. The individual who is highly educated and experienced at this stage of life may get engaged in many different kinds of work, such as art, music, creative writing, counseling, political activities, et cetera. He may also decide to establish a small specialty business of his own or in partnership with other retired workers. He has over $160,000 in capital accumulated, which can be invested. It must be noted that the shares of stock he has received as part of his monthly pay are nontransferrable stock. This is simply to prohibit cashing this stock and spending the proceeds. This stock is to provide income for the worker's retirement years, so it is like retirement funds that the workers now pay to the government and their employers, with the expectation of receiving monthly payments when they retire. Under technological democracy, the individual worker is made responsible for holding and taking care of his own retirement stock. Furthermore, he is allowed to reap the benefits of holding them by receiving annual returns from them during his working years.

Therefore, the individual worker is far better off under this system. He is the direct owner of the means of production while he works and after he retires. When he retires, he is his own boss and a well-to-do person. He does not have to rely on monthly Social Security or retirement checks. His individualism and dignity are enhanced in the community because of his financial independence and his advanced and broad education. At this level of high competence he is also able to enter public life and serve and lead his society toward a better future.

Actually, nearly all elected governmental policy-making members come from this group, since occupying such positions of distinction requires high standards of qualifications and competence. Since top policy-making positions in regional and national government are temporary positions of four to six years, it might just as well fit into the plan for the postretirement period. It would also discourage working people from running for political office, since this will interrupt their working process and financially have a negative effect on their future.

TECHNOLOGICAL EQUALITY OF OPPORTUNITY

In a democratic society, the most important means to bring about socioeconomic and political equality of opportunity is technology and the manner in which it is used.

We have already discussed the status of technology in previous chapters. Here the purpose is a systematic but brief presentation of its role in the democratic system and its effects in materializing equality of opportunity in all other aspects of life.

The first step in this direction is to bring equality of opportunity into the sphere of technology. Figure 7–4 presents the effect of such achievement upon all aspects of life.

Information Technology

From a democratic viewpoint, the most important aspect of technology relates to the information-communication area, where the Technodem plays the predominant role. We have already discussed the democratic operation of the Technodem. In this regard, we know that feeding information into the system is through millions of sources and no single group or groups have

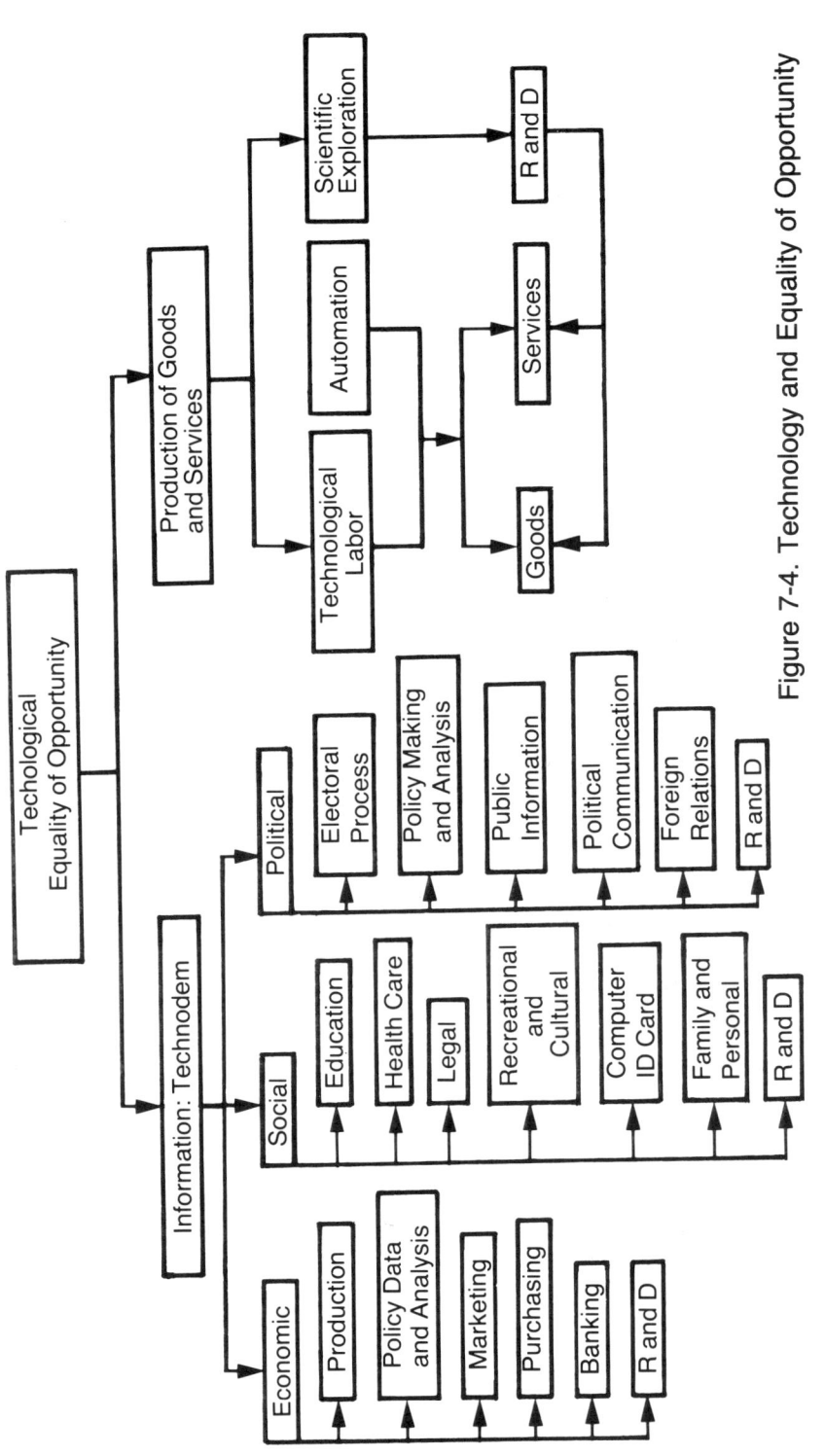

Figure 7-4. Technology and Equality of Opportunity

influence in information gathering. We also know that the system is centralized yet highly dispersed to the extent that all individuals and private or public institutions have equal opportunity of access to all information stored in the system, with the only exception of personal data, which are not a matter of public record, at least in the early stages of democracy.

Economic

In the economic area, this includes all kinds of production data and designs often vital for production purposes. These are all relevant information fed into the Technodem by all production institutions in society. They relate to production of goods as well as services.

The next area is policy data and its analysis. Policies made by an institution or a variety of firms that have been successful can be studied and analyzed for the formation of new or better ones. There is no question about the importance of availability of such information to other production institutions.

Marketing is a vast and important part of the productive economy, and we have seen the vital role the Technodem plays, not only in presenting the products to consumers, but also in analyzing the qualities of products in relation to their prices.

Purchasing is another important area of economic activities that relates to marketing. We already know that the consumers can electronically seek many kinds of a product they want to purchase and go about investigating its quality, compare prices, make a final choice, and purchase or order through the Technodem.

The banking operation will see a major change. Consumers will be able to pay through the Technodem from their bank account for the purchase of goods and have continuous access to their account statements and balance of their account. Monthly bank statements will be a matter of the past. The same transition will occur between financial institutions themselves, and between them and production institutions. The banking system can become nearly fully automatic through computerization and its connection to the Technodem.

Research and development, vital to production progress, will be substantially achieved thorugh the Technodem. In no other place can the researchers have access to such an enormous volume of data, up-to-date information to relevant inventions, innovations, or developments, and, more important, the analytical power and capability of the Technodem.

Social

Education. In the social area, possibly the most important contribution of the Technodem to the equality of opportunity is in the sphere of education, which has been discussed before. Considering the continuity of education, especially beyond the first twelve years of formal education, the Technodem will probably carry the heaviest burden. Nearly all the population in society and, more likely, millions in other countries having access to the system will use it. Education, which is now very costly, will be free to all members of society and will either be free, or for a nominal cost to outsiders. From this favorable economic situation and from the fact that the system is the reservoir of the best up-to-date information and high-quality teachers, there is no reason why people should resort to any other means to educate themselves.

Health Care. We already know that a great amount of information in relation to health care will be available through the system. Among this will be information about diets, food, body care, effects of all aspects of the natural, chemical and synthetic materials on human health, medical information, and consultation regarding general illnesses. The system will provide information and directions for true preventive health care.

Legal. Today most interactions of individuals with each other or with institutions require legal consultation. Many people who cannot afford the cost take the risk. With technological complexities of the future operation of daily life, the need for legal consultation will increase. The Technodem will be a major source of relief, since individuals can get information and necessary legal forms, as well as directions for most of their legal needs.

Recreational and Cultural. Today among the industrialized

countries, the United States in particular, a small minority is educated enough culturally to enjoy artistic presentations, performances, or exhibitions. Even so, in many areas in the United States there are no such performances—operas, ballets, plays, classical concerts, et cetera—available. Those few who are knowledgeable and desire to enjoy have no such opportunity. In large communities such as New York, there are some available, but the opportunities are very limited; first because of cost; second because of space, since in large communities a much larger minority are educated enough to enjoy some cultural events; third, the quality of many performances is quite low, since because of the lack of public education in this regard there is not much encouragement and support for development and refining of artistic skills.

Continuous cultural education in technological democratic society will elevate the cultural events to the level of national consciousness. They will flourish and develop enormously. First, the Technodem will play a significant role in this area of education; second, it will make accessible to the people a wide variety of first-class performances. The public cultural consciousness through the Technodem will also enormously enhance the creation of opera houses, concert halls, and theaters all over society. On one hand, this will provide for the majority of the population an opportunity of access to live performances; on the other, this will be one of the major sectors of societal functions employing a large portion of the workers.

The area of sports and other recreational functions will see similar developments.

Computer Identification Card. The nature and content of this card have been discussed before. It will be a vital companion to each individual. It will be needed in the electoral process for voting purposes as well as determining the candidates' qualifications. It will be needed for employment and any purpose that requires an individual's identification. It will be needed in banking, purchasing, renting, and using of the Technodem for many social and economic needs, such as educational, legal, or medical needs.

Family and Personal. This encompasses a broad area of information including all aspects of technological housekeeping, food preparation, gardening, planting, child care, and a vast area of information that a member of the family may desire for his personal or family use.

Political

We have already seen the enormous role of information technology in the political and electoral process. It also plays a very important role in the governmental decision-making process, particularly in establishing economic and social standards such as position classification, wage system, interest rate, educational standards, and health care requirements. The same importance also applies to use of the electronic-communication system in relation to international affairs and foreign policy process.

The government is also one of the important sources of information. All kinds of information coming from all the public agencies, including decisions, standards, laws, regulations, and judicial decisions, are immediately fed into the Technodem and become accessible to the public.

Another area is political communication, which includes involving the public in the governmental decision-making process or receiving public response to certain decisions made by the government and finally educating the public about governmental policies and programs and receiving input from the people.

The last but not least area concerns relations with other nations. The role of the Technodem in providing for equality of opportunity in international relations has been discussed before. It extends to the expansion of the use of production technology abroad with educational assistance through the Technodem.

Technology and Production

The second area of application of equality of opportunity relates to production technology. Unlike the technological information system, which is highly centralized, technology relating to production of goods and services is highly decentralized. As we have explained before, giant corporations will break into its component parts, each becoming an independent entity by itself. This corporate decentralization process will be the main cause of decentralization of production technology. While in the information area each industry, large and small, is hooked to a highly centralized system of the Technodem, benefiting it and benefiting from it, its production technology is independent from other similar technologies.

Technology in the production area is of two kinds: human technology and machine technology. The labor in technological democratic society will be highly trained and advanced. It won't be inappropriate to call someone a "technological person." This level of individual technological know-how will be one of the three determinants of the level of opportunity of the individual and necessary for his high performance and understanding of technological society and life. No person can work and function properly in this kind of society without the advanced technological knowledge required.

A very important contribution of human technology relates to production processes and corresponding innovations. The process of production, whether it is crystallized and put into effect directly by human hands or computer programs, is initiated by the human mind. Regardless of how far modern computerized technology may develop, the human mind will have the upper hand in establishing the work process. Modern technology will widen and strengthen human minds' contribution to the production process but never totally replace it, except as prescribed and programmed by the human mind. With our lack of knowledge today in relation to the human mind, we are only fractionally aware of the power and capability of the human mind. With further tools of knowledge and control we will attain a greater awareness as to our mental capability. It will dramatically increase and we will have substantial use of our mental power, which has remained more or less idle for centuries. Equality of opportunity to educate ourselves about ourselves and our relations with our work and environment will elevate all citizens to the level of technological people.

The other aspect of production technology relates to machines. Machines are instruments created by humans for production of goods and services. Of course, humans have been able to create machines that create machines. This is done through a process known as automation. Today in most areas of production automation helps human workers in the production process. In more advanced systems automation has taken over most parts of production. It will be possible that in the future many production processes will be totally automated through appropriate and detailed systemwide programming. For example, as we look at the operation of the Technodem, except for the input of information, the rest of the operation, which is immensely wide and complex and involves thousands of areas, is automatic. Yet the system's hardware, software, and communication and energy devices are all produced by the production sector.

Future possibilities in the automation area are fantastic where imaginable. One promising area relates to robotic technology. Yet there are probably areas that are unimaginable today. All these developments will enhance the equality of opportunity of each individual in a technological democratic society.

A very significant area of production technology relates to scientific research and development. This will be a fascinating area from understanding the secrets of creation and life to space science. For the first time in human history, man will start to look upon the universe as a single entity and will start to study, discover, and understand the fine design of the universe and the exact role of every component in its operation and sustenance from atoms, bacterias, plants, humans to planets, galaxies, material universe, and beyond, which in the language of many religions is known as God or the Creator. The great secret of the universe will be known when we discover the essence of the Living Universe upon which all the rest depends, from which all receive life and into which all dissolve and transform.

Less fascinating, but by no means less important, this scientific venture will relate to research and development concerning production of goods and services.

STATE AND ITS ROLE

Under technological democracy, functions of the state are substantially diminished. The main reason for such elimination is that the individual, through his immediate institution of employment, is made responsible for many functions that fall under state authority in industrial capitalistic systems. As the society approaches the more advanced stages of technological democracy, the size of government, because of diminishing need for its functions, will tend toward zero though it may never reach that level of statelessness.

National Government.

Under technological democracy, all line functions of the national government are eliminated except for defense and foreign affairs. The latter two are also substantially reduced:

1. Since the national government will have no function regarding the regulation of business and economy, all current vast bureaucracies of the regulatory agencies are eliminated. This is a very substantial part of the present national bureaucracy in the United States.
2. Since the national government will have no function regarding education and health care, the vast bureaucracies currently relating to these functions are eliminated.
3. Since there will be no national welfare and social security system, the vast corresponding bureaucracies are discarded.
4. The same also applies to the Department of Justice, federal courts, Departments of Commerce, Transportation, and Agriculture, and other federal agencies.
5. The whole Congress and its vast staff institutions are also discarded.

The Structure and Functions of National Government

The traditional representative government and corresponding bureaucracies are far outdated for the fast-moving and self-contained technological society. The political system of society is quite new and substantially different from that of the present. While it is difficult to visualize the exact political system of the future, its basic features can be considered here. In real practice, some modifications may be required.

An important feature to notice is the continuous reduction

in the size and functions of public agencies, as the newly established technological democratic system moves toward its mature stage. At this stage of maturity the government will be diminished to the least important component of the democratic system, reaching, ultimately, the state of negligibility.

Considering the early stages of the system, besides defense and foreign affairs, the main functions of national government are concerned with studying and establishing economic, social, and political standards, all based on the principle of equality of opportunity. Under this new system, there is separation of powers between different branches of government, but these branches and their structure, functions, and relationships are substantially different from those of any existing system. Figure 7-5 illustrates the basic institutions of the national legislative branch. They are as follows:

The National Legislative Branch

This is the main policy-making body of the government and consists of a national legislative and coordinating assembly, economics and production, health and education, international affairs, and judicial councils.

1. National Legislative and Coordinating Assembly. This body has three main functions. First, it gives final approval to regional laws. In this regard, it has amending authority, as it is the guardian of the principle of equality of opportunity. This task is actually minimal. When a regional legislation is made, it will be fed into the Technodem. If any part of this legislation is contrary to or in conflict with the national standards or laws, it will be pointed out by the Technodem and will be corrected by the regional authority accordingly. The assembly also functions to provide uniformity in regional laws when they relate to the application of the principle of equality of opportunity.

The second function of this body is to approve and coordinate the framework for actions proposed by all national councils. The main purpose is to streamline conflicts that may arise from the application of frameworks designed by different councils.

Third, this body receives, amends, and approves the national budget submitted to it by the National Executive Council and

Figure 7-5. The Basic Structure of National Government, Legislative and Policy Branch

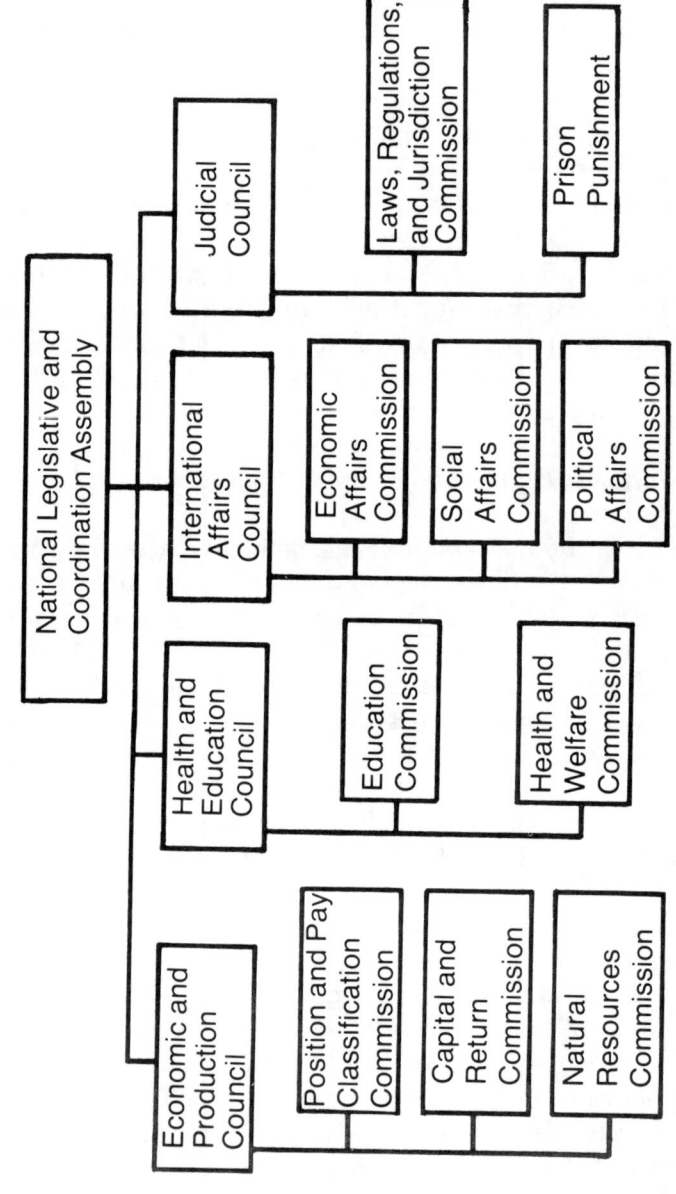

approves the framework of functions proposed by the International Affairs Council for the operation of the executive branch, including defense and foreign relations.

2. The National Economic and Production Council. This is the most important national institution. Its job is mainly to establish economic standards based on the principle of equality of opportunity and enact a framework of regulations for their implementation.

The main functions of the council are:

1. To establish a framework for the rate of return for the use of capital. This is done through a commission and corresponding staff. This is very similar to establishment of the interest rate.
2. To devise a framework for position classification and wages through a corresponding commission and staff.
3. To develop a framework for the use of natural resources and return of the revenues from such use to the public treasury or to the social consumption fund. It must be noted that under technological democracy, the principle of equality of opportunity prohibits the ownership of any part of the natural resources by any individual or institution. All these resources belong to the people as a whole. The natural resource committee establishes a framework for the use of natural resources and lease of land and resources. Any direct revenue from such use will go to the public treasury. For example, oil resources may be leased to an oil company for a determined period of time to explore and extract and market the product. However, the proceeds left after deducting the cost of exploration, production, and marketing will go to the public treasury. This constitutes the market value of oil itself as a resource.

3. The National Health and Education Council. Health care and education in technological democracy are two of the most important services in society. As illustrated in Figure 7–6, they are the basic requirements for social democracy. It is obvious that without a healthy and educated society no progress can be

Figure 7-6. Prerequisites of Social Equality of Opportunity

- Social Equality of Opportunity (Social Democracy)
  - Free Health Care
    - Preventive
    - Old Age
    - Special and Disabled
  - Free Education
    - Preschool 4 years
    - General Education 8 years
    - Continuing Education 36 years
      - Cultural Education 50 percent
      - Professional-Technical 50 percent

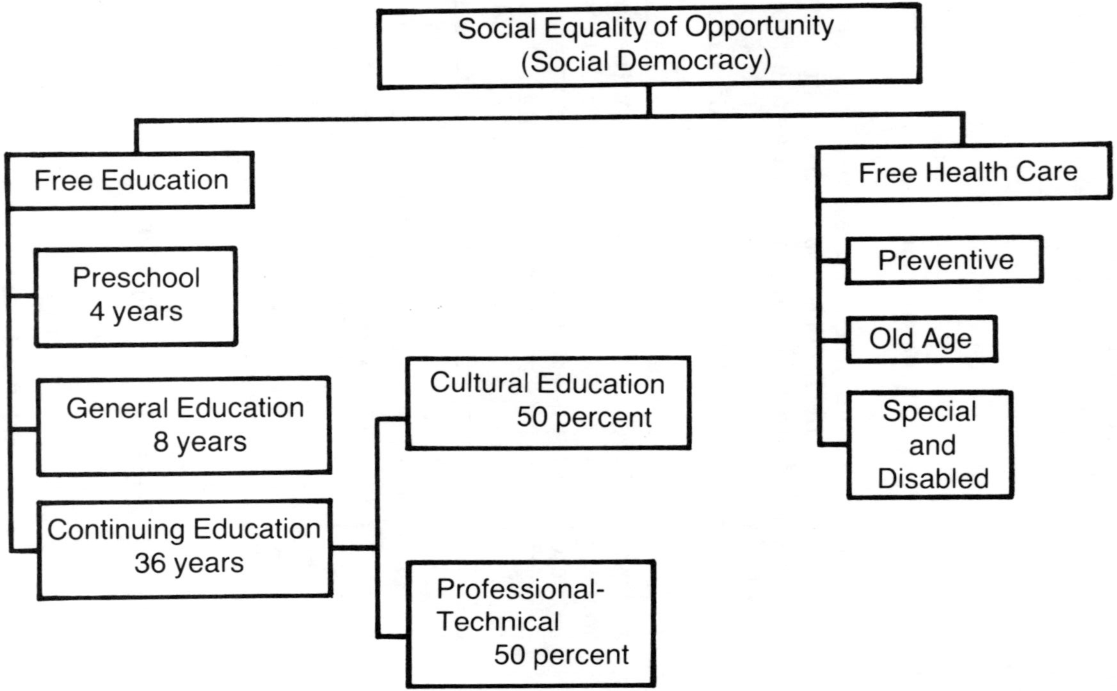

expected. In an advanced technological society also, more than any other, the increase in the level of opportunity heavily depends on the level of knowledge one possesses. This increase in the level of opportunity not only relates to the area of work and production but also to the area of enjoyment of life. For example, one cannot properly enjoy and appreciate an opera, classical music, or modern art unless one has knowledge and understanding of it. This materializes only through education. For these reasons it is imperative that health care and education be fully available to every individual and the work requirement in society be established in a way that continuous education, technical as well as cultural, becomes mandatory as well as desirable. Cultural education must be made mandatory because it is absolutely necessary to maintain and advance a civilized society. Cultural education here refers to the humanities such as art, music, philosophy, literature, history, foreign languages, and the normative aspects of social sciences. The full equality of opportunity can be materialized if health care and education are provided and made available to the public free of charge. The total budget for these two very essential services for the well-being of society comes from the Public Consumption Fund.

The first stage of education is the most crucial in preparing children for life, for its comprehension as well as enjoyment, in a technological democratic society.

Four years of semiformal yet full-time education is required from ages three to seven. It constitutes grades one to four. It is quite similar to preschool education in socialist countries like the Soviet Union, but more systematic and more comprehensive. Eight years of full-time general education is required from ages seven through fourteen. This consists of grades five through twelve and embodies three areas of knowledge: social sciences, humanities, and general sciences, including mathematics each receiving equal attention in the curriculum. Learning at least one foreign language is mandatory starting at grade seven. Every individual starts working part-time and studying part-time from ages fifteen through twenty-two. From there on until retirement, while the job becomes full-time (thirty-two hours per week), each individual is required to continue a part-time education (eight hours per week). The content of this education is equally divided between cultural and professional-technical. The main purpose of this education is to keep one up-to-date in his area of specialty and expand his knowledge into other specialty areas, as well as improve his cultural and intellectual knowledge for a better understanding of human society, for a better enjoyment of life and maintenance of democracy.

However, one is not restricted to this requirement in his education. This is only the minimum requirement, and one remains free to pursue his education further and to advance his knowledge as he desires. For example, one may desire to change one's line of work from one specialty to another. One can easily do so by taking additional classes and acquiring required knowledge. Furthermore, one's education does not stop with retirement: free education is available to everyone for life.

3. Health care. This essential service is rendered through local and regional health care agencies. The framework of their functions and required minimum standards are established by the National Health and Welfare Commission.

Total health care costs will be paid through the Public Consumption Fund. The approach would be preventive medicine. Services will receive great help from the Technodem, through which preventive and general health care and medical information as well as general medical consultation will be available at home to every member of society. Particular attention will be given to individuals with special and permanent health problems as well as the retarded and disabled.

4. International Affairs Council. This council has the important function of establishing the framework for relations of the nation with other nations from social, economic, and political standpoints. These basic policies will be based on the principle of equality of opportunity. With nondemocratic nations the policy will be based on reciprocal opportunity, gradually moving toward equality of opportunity as those nations move toward establishing a democratic system.

However, there are certain areas that the principle of equality of opportunity will govern from the beginning, regardless of the nature of the other nation's system.

In the economic area, equality of opportunity does not allow the exploitation of natural and economic resources of another nation. First, all natural resources of the nation belong to the people of that nation and ultimately to the people of the world. Accordingly, these resources cannot be exploited by any private or public sector.

Any institution extracting material resources must pay to the nation the full value of the extracted resource. An American firm operating in Chile should operate exactly as if it had its operation in the United States, assuming the latter has a technological democratic system. It should take whatever is needed for the costs of operation and pay the balance, which is the price of the extracted resource, to the public treasury of Chile. This concept would encourage the firm not to exploit labor but to pay it wages comparable to the duties of the work. It will cause an increase in real per capita income in Chile.

Labor is another important national resource that, based on the principle of equality of opportunity, cannot be exploited by the outsider. This is important, particularly in the production of goods and services by institutions located in another country but controlled or owned by domestic firms such as those in the United States.

Equality of opportunity also prescribes that well-to-do nations help the poor nations in increasing the level of their social and economic opportunity.

It also prescribes that any other nation in socioeconomic and political relations be treated on the basis of equality and equality of opportunity. One outcome of this, among many, is that no country can give or sell arms to another country where such action will increase the military opportunity of one country over another or become a tool of domination of its people. This is based on the principle that any instrument of killing, if used, deprives the victim of the opportunity of life and any instrument for destruction deprives the victims from their opportunity of property. Simply, any military or nonmilitary action causing death, injury, or destruction of property is contrary to the principle of equality of opportunity. Under the current systems, arms sale is probably the biggest business in the world. No democracy can be achieved through armament. It is inherently undemocratic. It is mainly to sustain the status quo and control the domestic as well as international adverse forces. It is also inherently contrary to the principle of equality of opportunity, particularly at the level of international relations.

Finally, the principle prescribes that citizens of other nations desiring to enter and reside in the country should be allowed to do so without any restriction. Otherwise, such immigrants will be deprived of the opportunities granted to the citizens of the country receiving them. However, in the early stages of technological democracy, where great economic and social differences exist between the host and other countries, such action may have a destructive effect on the system of democracy in the host country. For the sake of survival of democracy, restrictions in immigration need to be lifted gradually as the socioeconomic conditions and education for democracy progress in other countries. The ultimate result of application of the principle of equality of opportunity among the nations is that the national boundaries as we know them today will gradually disappear. As each nation develops toward a democratic system, it will become a sister state with another already enjoying technological democracy. Gradually the national boundaries will disappear, not by force or intimidation, but by the consent of the people involved. We will gradually move toward a universal technological democracy where national contradictions, along with many others, will disappear and a permanent world peace will be achieved for the first time in history. There will be one world government without any line functions but responsible only for establishing the standards required for the operation of technological democracy. As the people become acculturated to the prerequisites of democracy, regional governments will be reduced to their minimum size. Local governments will also be substantially reduced in size and function; they will be primarily responsible to resolution of local and individual problems. Individuals, assuming a much greater responsibility in life, will live enjoying prosperity, freedom, security, and peace never attainable or imaginable before.

ELECTRONIC TECHNOLOGY AND THE THIRD WORLD

With the tremendous pace of development in advanced countries as a result of electronic technologies, developing countries cannot wait or afford to go through the conventional process of development. Beside the comparative slowness of the process, the major problem relates to the cost of development, which developing countries, with the exception of a few, cannot meet. This is particularly true in regard to education and health care, without which no society has a chance for progress. Currently, despite heavy borrowing from the developed countries and corresponding international monetary institutions, the bulk of the population in all developing countries have remained illiterate. The prime importance of education and health care for development requires those countries to find ways of shortcutting the development process despite being financially incapable in a traditional sense.

One sensible way is to use the fabulous resources available through information systems of developed countries with no cost or for a nominal cost. Fortunately, information technology has become universal through use of the satellite communication system. This, along with the incredible developments in electronic information and communication technologies, have been achieved by the scientific and financial efforts of developed countries. In order to benefit from these immense resources, developing countries need only equip themselves with retrieval and storage devices. They can then use these resources either freely or at a nominal cost.

Each country can also have at least one satellite of its own. Several smaller countries may use only one satellite to benefit all. These satellites will be used primarily for education of the masses. Besides general and special education, this will be particularly useful for production training and guidance when illiterate masses can listen, observe, and learn through video programs received through the country satellite despite the fact that they cannot read or write.

This process of acceleration requires a specific governmental system, quite different from the existing systems, that would be capable of moving the developing society toward technological democracy. Among the existing systems, Marxist socialism appears to be most beneficial for the following reasons. First, it is geared to eliminate capitalism by nationalizing all production and distribution means. This automatically eliminates class stratification. Second, it brings about, with a great vigor, socioeconomic equality of opportunity. It provides for free education, health care, employment, highly subsidized housing, transportation, recreation, and old age benefits for all.

Under the present Marxist socialist systems, this is accomplished through political dictatorship. These have been unfortunate situations, because Marxist socialism does not have to be dictatorial in the light of knowledge and means attained since the time when Marx and Engels wrote the *Communist Manifesto*. One should remember the Marxist socialist system established in Chile in the early 1970s through democratic elections. Furthermore, the purpose of the Marxist process will not be to attain communism, which in our opinion is a utopian end, but to achieve technological democracy. So we advocate the use of Marxist socialism for a very different purpose than that intended by Marx.

This seems the only apparent way to accelerate the development process in developing countries toward a technological democratic society. The new national constitution must sanction, and the system, including the government, must effectuate the principle of equality of opportunity. The prime purposes must be:

1. Establishment of a government after the model of technological democracy.
2. Nationalization of all means of production and distribution.
3. Establishment of a twelve-year general education program with no technical education component.
4. Inclusion in this general education the study and experience of technological democracy from the very first grade through the twelfth.
5. Establishment of employment as an individual right from the age fifteen until retirement at the age of fifty-two.
6. Requirement of and providing for a continuous education as part of the employment process. In the early stages of employment, under the socialistic system, this program of education will contain a component for literacy, since the majority of the working class will be illiterate.

7. Expansion of recreational and artistic production along with the production of goods and services.
8. Expansion of roads and means of transportation and communication.
9. Initiation toward establishing a national Technodem.
10. Gradual transfer of the means of production and distribution to individuals as required under the technological democratic theory.

By this process the system will gradually transform itself from a centralized political, economic, and social system into a decentralized democratic one. If properly planned and executed, this transition to technological democracy will, apparently, be achieved within a span of twenty to thirty years. This is indeed a very short time for substantial development toward technological democracy. It is based on dynamic tranformation, with appropriate use of technology, toward a well-established purpose.

In the initial period of this socialism, representatives come from highly educated, small classes who sincerely believe in a democratic system and have a deep understanding of the concept of technological democracy. With the passage of years, as the rest of the society becomes educated, the number of individuals qualified to hold public offices will multiply.

From the very beginning, the term of any public office must be limited to one term (five to seven years) in order to avoid the creation of a new elite and keep the government in the hands of many. Thus a small group of intellectuals will be able to run the system for a short period of time while the concept of democracy takes root and more intellectuals enter the scene to participate in the operation of the system.

In the factual sense, the system starts with Marxist socialism and ends up in technological democracy by gradually returning the means of production and distribution to the people. When all is owned and operated by the private sector, based on the principle of equality of opportunity, society has reached the stage of economic democracy.

This is one incredible opportunity for developing countries to surpass the developed countries, including the United States, by colonizing the latter's information system and employing this fabulous resource for their own development, without any practical cost. Such an opportunity is a unique one and may not happen again in the history of mankind.

JUDICIAL COUNCIL

The council will be primarily concerned with establishing a framework for the jurisdiction of the national as well as regional and local judiciary, their organization and operation. It will also coordinate the standards of punishments for violation of laws with the approval of the assembly. Finally, it will determine the conditions and standards of detainment and work and educational requirements for detainees. Detainment centers, or prisons as we call them today, will all be self-sustaining. Detainees will work and pay for the expenditures of the centers where they are detained. All punishments will accompany hard labor.

Because of the nature of the society and full employment, the rate of crimes will be reduced substantially. The nature of crime also will shift to the area of abusing the principle of equality of opportunity. This, however, will diminish toward zero as the society matures toward the advanced stage of the technological democracy.

The National Judiciary

The structure of national judiciary is very brief. It consists of a supreme court with two divisions: constitutional and administrative, and a judicial staff division, with prosecution and staff personnel necessary for the operation of the system.

Neither court has original jurisdiction, except on constitutional issues created at the national level: each is the court of last resort used only when there are conflicting rulings from two or more highest regional courts. The main function of the courts concerns interpretation and proper application of the principle of equality of opportunity as it relates to the cases. Each of the two courts may have more than one section, depending on the work load imposed upon it. However, as the democratic system matures and the body of rulings develops, there will be less and less need to resolve either constitutional or administrative matters. Figure 7–7 illustrates the basic structure of the national executive and judicial branches.

Members to the national courts are elected from among the members of the regional courts, including their ex-members. The term of office for national courts is seven years. The national courts will each consist of seven members, one to be elected each year. The senior member will assume the presidency of the court.

THE EXECUTIVE BRANCH

This branch consists of a national executive council and foreign affairs, defense, and finance departments.

1. The National Executive Council

As the top executive authority the council replaces the office of presidency or other highest executive office. It consists of seven members who are elected for seven-year terms. Members of the original council are elected with varying terms from one to seven years. Each year thereafter, one new member is elected who replaces the one whose term is expiring.

The senior member of the council becomes president for a one-year term. At the end of this one year the term of his presidency as well as his council membership expires. This eliminates political struggle within the council for presidency. The president presides over the council and acts as the ceremonial head of the nation for diplomatic purposes. He speaks to the nation and the world on behalf of the executive council. The president has no specific powers except those assigned to him by the executive council. All executive decisions and national and international policies are made by the executive council by a majority vote, within the framework established by the Legislative Assembly.

Members to the council are elected from among the regional governors. All governors and ex-governors assemble once a year to elect one member to the National Executive Council. The idea

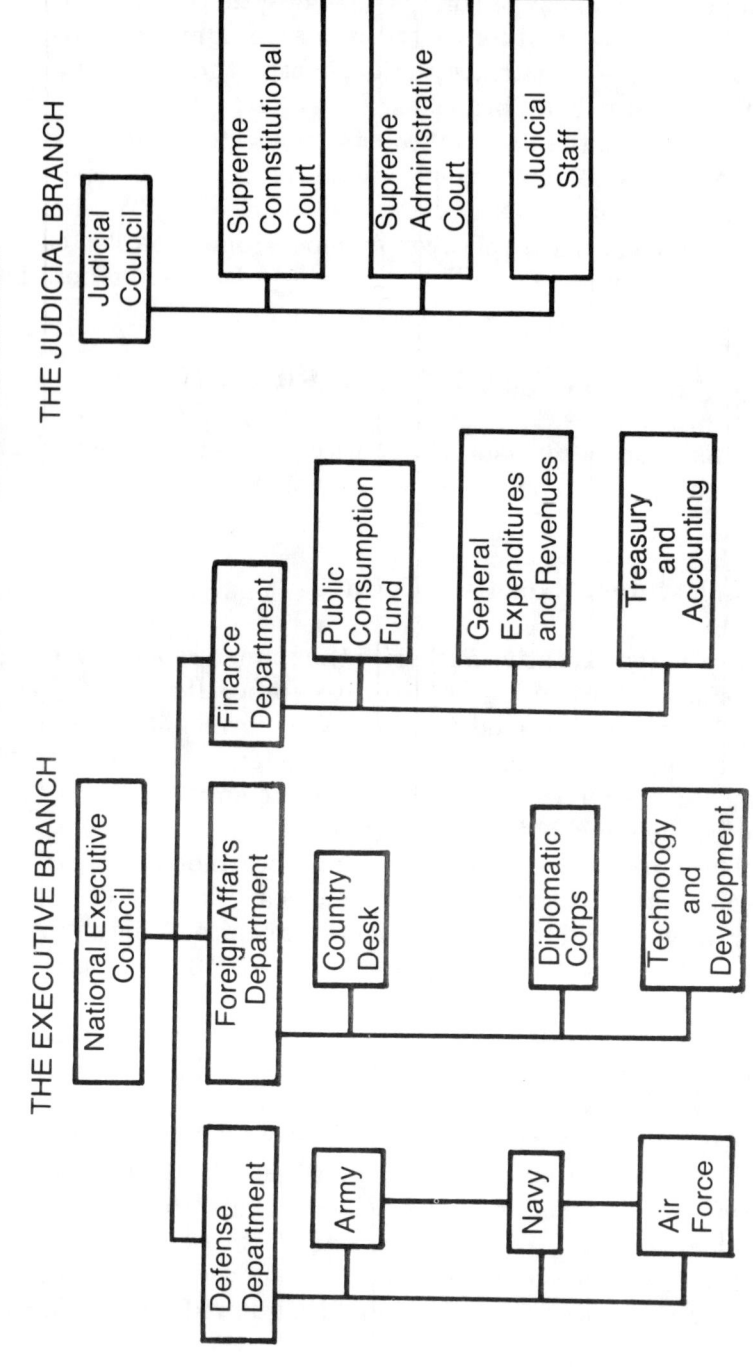

Figure 7-7. The Basic Structure of National Government

behind this process is that a member of the National Executive Council must have experience at the state level, where the action is and where the democratic system is put to operation. The governor gains knowledge and experience regarding socioeconomic aspects of democracy; he also accumulates valuable administrative and political knowledge and skills. These experiences are required because positions at the national level are remote from the line operation since all the domestic services are carried out at the regional and local levels. The national officials must be acquainted with and understand the nature of the public functions at the regional and local levels. The election is for one term only, and no person can be reelected for the same office.

The National Executive Council is primarily responsible for the relation of the nation with other nations from all social economic and political standpoints and executes the international policies established by the National Legislative and Coordinating Assembly toward establishing peace and prosperity in the world.

2. The Department of Foreign Affairs

The basic policies of foreign affairs will be based on the principle of equality of opportunity, particularly regarding the Third World countries. Under current situations of the diplomatic world this approach appears to be absurd. But if we want justice and prosperity in the world we cannot get it through discrimination of less developed nations by those developed, by the United States in particular.

As in capitalism, where a small group of monopoly capitalists controls the societal system, on the world arena also a few powerful industrial countries have enslaved the rest of the world nations mainly through economic exploitation.

A democracy within a nation cannot be meaningful if the nation restricts such system to its own citizens only and practices discrimination in regard to other nations.

A true democracy must have universal effects. A nation adopting such system must recognize the universality of the principle of equality of opportunity. The Third World nations must be relieved from economic slavery. First, all national debts must be abolished to relieve the indebted nations from the impossible burden of paying off such debts. Creditor nations will not suffer much from this action, since they have exploited the indebted nations for decades and some for centuries. Furthermore, as discussed before, the multinational financial firms in the United States will be broken down into smaller firms and their capital will be substantially diminished, since they will lose all their financial holdings in the production sector, whether domestic or foreign. As has been explained, the capital in these firms, as in the banks, gradually will be transferred to the workers.

Second, all subsidiary firms of the domestic multinational corporations in developing countries must be made independent, gradually transferring the capital of each firm to its workers proportional to seniority of each employee. After all, what is justified as being done within a democratic nation in regard to production process must also be justified to be carried out into other nations, primarily in relation to subsidiary firms and branches of domestic firms. There cannot be double standards under a democratic system.

Third, all nations must be granted equal opportunity in international relations. This principle should apply to all facets of diplomatic relations, whether economic, social, or political. This kind of open diplomacy is crucial for peaceful coexistence of the nations. It establishes a rational ground for trust and thus for a permanent peace. The governments not abiding by these democratic norms should be forced out of power by the people and by receiving help from democratic nations. This does not necessarily mean military help. It is the responsibility of a democratic system to provide for equality of opportunity among other nations.

This democratic approach to foreign affairs is the only way that may allow, for the first time, opportunity to developing countries to develop on their own and use their own chosen appropriate technology while benefiting from the technological and scientific knowledge available through advanced societies. It is also the only hope for human prosperity, progress toward a world equilibrium, and a sustained and meaningful world peace.

Currently because of world disequilibrium, peace must be

kept by force, where economically dominating nations, the United States in particular, tend to maintain the status quo through the presence of military power or by supporting despotic Third World systems. Where force is needed to maintain order justice and fairness are absent, so is real peace.

3. The Department of Defense

Military power under the current systems is, generally, needed mainly to guarantee forced domestic tranquillity and international stability. Domestic unrest develops when there is exploitation, discrimination, poverty, and injustice. The state power then becomes necessary to suppress dissent and bring about a forced tranquillity so the exploitation and discrimination can continue and the monopolists could prosper further.

The military power is, furthermore, needed to expand exploitation and discrimination beyond the national borders and into other, less fortunate societies.

Technological democracy tends to eliminate exploitation and discrimination of other nations. Accordingly, once the industrialized monopolistic nation is transformed into a democratic system, its policies toward other nations, Third World countries in particular, will change drastically, tending toward equalization of opportunities. Then need for military force will substantially diminish to the negligible level of an international police force. As the world moves toward economic and social equilibrium, the need for military force will disappear. Accordingly, the size and sphere of activities of this department will be substantially diminished to a small fraction of the current size. The national military forces will ultimately be transformed into a small international police force under the command of the United Nations.

Two important principles must be noted here. First, in order to assist developing countries in getting rid of exploitation and discrimination, the technological democratic country needs to expand its diplomatic relations with those countries particularly in the areas of economics and cultural affairs, rather than tending to increase its military influence.

Second, technological democracy's educational system tends to produce a highly civilized and intellectual society. Such a society need not have a strong military force to defend itself, because it possesses a much greater force, an educated and civilized population. The history of the world has shown over and over that when an advanced civilization was occupied by aggression, it soon was the aggressor that was assimilated into a stronger and more civilized culture and become part of the occupied society. Therefore, a society under technological democracy need not fear occupation by outside forces. It cannot be truly conquered, and it will ultimately subdue and conquer the conqueror.

It must not be mistaken that the United States, while technically advanced, socially and intellectually, by the standards of technological democratic society, is highly illiterate. That is why it has placed its trust in military might rather than in an advanced civilized population, which it lacks.

4. The Department of Finance

This department is responsible for all financial operation of the national system as well as providing funds for two major and essential services: health care and education. It consists of three main divisions: consumption fund, general expenditures and revenues, and treasury and accounting.

The Public Consumption Fund

This is where all funds for social expenditures are deposited and transferred to regional offices according to the framework established by the Social Council. All the revenues from inheritance and profits go to this account and are spent primarily for education and health care. Any surplus remains in the fund's account for future use. If the expenditures exceed revenues, the difference is supplied through general revenues division.

It may be questioned that while technological democracy does not allow profits, where, then do the revenues from profits come from? The fact is that until this democratic system is accepted by all other nations and as long as capitalism is practiced by other nations, profits will be made. It is also because the market system remains, depending on supply and demand. Thus during the transition period from capitalism or socialism to technological democracy profit making is continued. It is diminished as the system approaches technological democracy, and it disappears once full democracy is achieved.

General Expenditures and Revenues

Revenues of this sector are mainly through the sale of national resources extracted by private firms, such as oil, iron, gas, timber, and hundreds of other national resources. It is expected that the revenues from the use of these national resources would far exceed the expenditures and a substantial amount will be left for research, development, and investment. In countries with few or no resources, revenues will be raised through taxation. However, it must be noted that in technological democratic society there is no individual income tax. All taxes are paid by production institutions. Since there is neither poor nor rich in such a society, this form of taxation seems to be just and equitable.

Furthermore, since the size of national government is drastically reduced, its budget is a fraction of the current budget. Thus the rate of taxation is reduced substantially. The revenues from the national resources, as well as taxes, are collected by local governments according to procedures and standards established by the National Economic and Production Council. After taking the local government expenditures, the surplus is transferred to regional government. The latter, after deducting its expenditures, transfers the residues to the national treasury. It must be noted that the local and regional bureaucracies are established under the national position classification and thus their expenditure based on diminished size is quite definite and calculated.

The Treasury and Accounting

This division is where revenues are deposited and expenditures withdrawn. The national budget and accounting system is also a part of this division. This accounting responsibility bestows upon this division the authority to supervise the proper spending of the people's money. This office will particularly check the soundness of expenditure and proper spending and accounting not only at the national level but also relating to regional and local governments by coordination through their accounting office. The regional governor is responsible for supervision of the regional and local expenditures on the grounds of equality of opportunity.

REGIONAL GOVERNMENTS

The national territory is divided into regional areas large enough to justify efficient administration and services and, at the same time, guarantee closeness of people to their government. A population of up to 10 million in the regions that include a metropolitan area seems appropriate. In any case, the ruling principle for the size of a region is that the size of population should justify overhead expenditures for public services. Under this approach the United States will be subdivided into about thirty-five regions.

The basic functions of the regional government are mostly supervisory and include the following: education, health care, law and order, finance, and supervision of the framework established by the national council relating to production of goods and services. Figure 7–8 illustrates the basic structure of the regional government.

Each state has a chief executive who is properly elected. Candidates must have several years of experience in public service at the regional or local level.

In technological democratic society, public service is a profession. Individuals, including those subject to election, must have certain required professional competency for the job. These requirements are determined according to description of responsibilities of each position as determined by position classification. There is no political popularity contest in technological democratic society; however, candidates campaign for the office based on their level of competency.

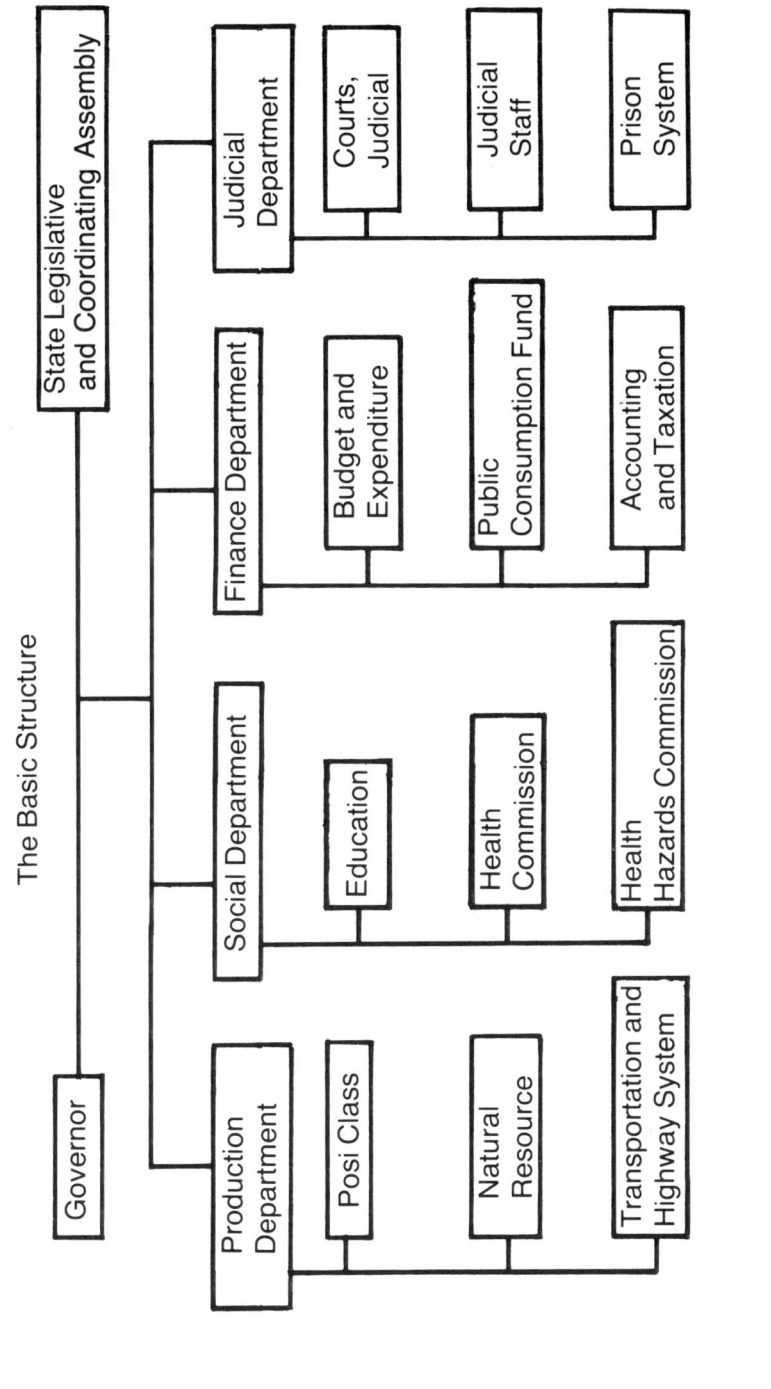

Elections are through a computerized process, as explained before. Each person eligible to vote carries his computer ID card. By inserting his CID card into a computer terminal at home or office he votes "yes," "no," or "abstain." Elections are in two stages. During a designated election date and hour, for example, 10:00 to 11:00 A.M., individuals vote for one of several candidates who are running for office. The results are automatically tabulated, locally and regionally, and announced right after the closing time. If no single person received majority vote, then in a later hour, for example, 2:00 to 3:00 P.M., the same day people vote for one of the three on the top of the list. Each individual CID card once used in an election cannot be used again. The computer will reject. This happens simply because the individual's vote is recorded in his CID card by the special code assigned to that particular election. This technology is currently possible and can be employed in creation of CID cards.

THE STATE LEGISLATIVE AND COORDINATING ASSEMBLY

The assembly has three basic functions:

1. To pass laws necessary and proper for the operation of government as well as protection of human rights all according to the framework established by the national institution and the principle of equality of opportunity.
2. To approve the expenditures and prescribe the sources of revenues.
3. To provide for coordination between different departments of government.
4. To provide for uniformity of local laws and regulations.

The assembly has one hundred members. They are elected at large, ten from each of the ten districts based on proportional representation. The term of office is six years, one-third of the members to be elected every other year. No person can be reelected for the same office.

THE GOVERNOR

The governor is the chief executive. His job is to supervise the administration and provide for coordination. He must be well educated in the humanities and social sciences. He must have several years of experience in the private as well as the public sector. The education requirement is no problem in technological democratic society, since everyone by the age of thirty-five will be quite educated in these areas. More likely the governor will come from among retired persons with much higher qualifications and experiences. The governor is elected for one six-year term only and cannot be reelected to the same office. Departments falling under the supervision of the governor all operate on the basis of a competency requirement for each position and the application of the principle of equality of opportunity. Complaints in this regard, after exhausting administration channels, can be taken before the administrative court.

LOCAL GOVERNMENT

Substantial change in the United States will be in its local government, where, under capitalism, the equality of opportunity is provided the least. The highest class stratification exists in the metropolitan areas, from slums to the split-levels of suburbia, from run-down small businesses of the core city to plush shopping malls of suburbia. Furthermore, the core city is burdened by a score of independent municipalities existing within its boundaries. They benefit from the opportunities provided by the city without contributing to its survival, let alone to its well-being.

The local government will be a single unit covering, wherever possible, the urban, suburban, and surrounding rural areas. The local government must be a sound economic unit and have room for expansion. Many nations have this system which has functioned quite well. The local government will be ruled by an elected council and a manager appointed by the council. Figure 7–9 shows the basic structure of local government. Local public positions are offered strictly on the basis of competency and equality of opportunity. Local government carries the heaviest load of public services. In the utilities area, while it is responsible for waste disposal services, it is also responsible for beautification of the local territory, which includes the preservation of natural beauties.

In the production area, its job is mainly supervisory. It must assure that positions classification established by every private firm is in accordance to the national standards. It is responsible for preservation of natural resources and their appropriate use under the national standards and required regulations.

In the social area, it is responsible for supervising the educational and health care firms and responding to private sector's demands in these respects. Welfare functions are strictly local except when the use of more specialized regional facility is required. Local government is also responsible for control and eradication of health hazards within its jurisdiction and in cooperation with other neighboring local governments when necessary.

In the finance area, it has the major responsibility of collecting revenues from profits of local firms, revenues from the use of natural resources, and institutional taxes when prescribed by the national authorities. It is also responsible for supervision of the Local Public Consumption Fund branch according to the norms established by the National Public Consumption Fund. Its responsibility further extends to its own budget, expenditures, and accounting.

In the area of development, it has the responsibility for research and development, planning, and zoning. The research may involve the feasibility of attracting or establishing certain production, cultural, or recreational firms within the municipal jurisdiction or in cooperation and coordination with the neighboring municipalities. It must be noted that in technological democratic society cultural and recreational functions constitute a major part of production in society.

The judicial system of local governments consists of courts of original administrative and judicial juridictions. These may be quite busy in the early stages of democratization, but their functions will be diminished substantially as the society approaches the matured stage of democracy. The local judicial sys-

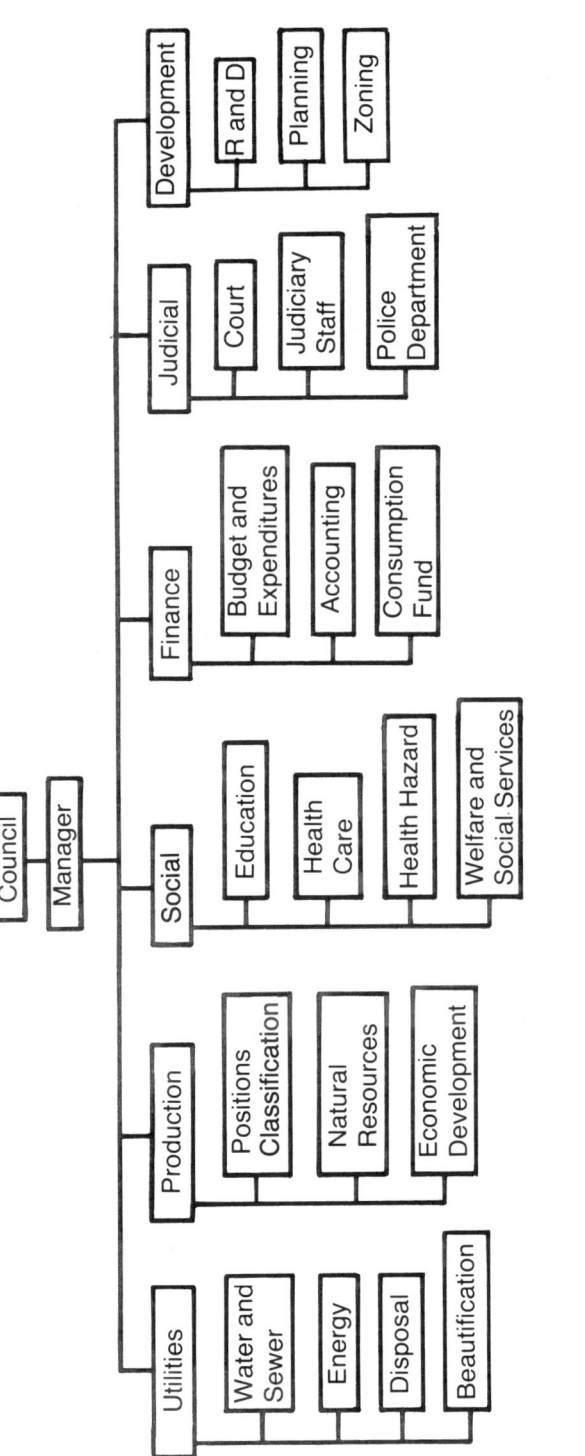

Figure 7-9. The Basic Structure of Local Government

tem is under the administrative control of the regional judicial branch. The judges as well as staff can be transferred to other comparable positions. For example, a judge may be assigned as a public prosecutor based on the necessities of staff allocations within the judicial system. This also applies to law enforcement staff.

Therefore, in technological democratic society the jurisdiction of the judicial system is national. While each local court or police department has jurisdiction within the local territory, the judicial staff is transferrable nationwide and the fugitive from justice can be brought before the appropriate court regardless of where he is found and detained.

When technological democracy develops among other nations and the national borders disappear, the judicial system expands its jurisdiction into other territories. As more nations join the democratic system, the judicial system tends toward a universal one. There will then be one worldwide judicial system with universal jurisdiction.

THE PRIVATE SECTOR

The backbone of the technological democratic system is the private sector and its institutions of production of goods and services. These institutions partially take the place of government, satisfying some of the needs and demands of individuals otherwise satisfied by the government under other systems, socialistic in particular.

Some of the characteristics of the private sector under the technological democratic system are as follows:

1. There is total ownership of means of production—land, labor, capital, and technology—by the private sector.
2. The burden of old age and retirement benefits is moved from the government and production firms to individual workers, thus: (a.) eliminating the individual's economic dependency on others; (b.) guaranteeing a comfortable retirement and living standards; and (c.) eliminating complex and vast bureaucracies

that were charged with rendering these services under other systems.
3. Separation between capital and labor is eliminated by transferring the capital to labor.
4. Operation of production is transferred from capitalist to labor.
5. It automatically causes decentralization of centralized production firms, thus allows workers to control production independently in each institution of a previous conglomerate.
6. It transfers to each individual institution the formulation and execution of position classification and determination of pay schedule, according to the framework established by the national council.
7. It allows access to free education at every stage of life, particularly much needed cultural and humanistic education.
8. It allows access to free health care at every stage of life.
9. It assumes taking care of disabled within each community by community organizations through a nationally determined donation of money and voluntary services. These are included in the local budget.
10. It allows individual exemption from personal income and property taxes, regional as well as national.
11. It provides for security from inflation, recession, and depression.
12. It provides for job security and guaranteed employment til retirement.
13. It allows for early retirement at the age of fifty-two and opportunity to devote many years of the remaining active life to political leadership, and other civic or economic functions.
14. It tends to develop a sense of cooperation and partnership with other fellow workers.
15. It tends to develop a strong sense for domestic and international peace and against militarism and use of force.
16. It tends to develop a strong sense for preservation of natural resources and restraint in the use of non-renewable resources.
17. It tends to develop a sense of respect and dignity

toward fellow humans and a sense of protection of the rights of other living species that share the earth with us and make it livable for all.

OPERATION OF THE PRIVATE SECTOR

Operation and hierarchical structure of the production institutions depend on technological development and the policy of production with the following specifications:

1. The price of commodity is based on its cost, which includes labor, material, marketing, amortization, rent, return on capital, energy, and other incidental costs. There is no profit figured into the cost.
2. It must be reminded that the nature of capital in technological democracy is different from that in the capitalist society. While under capitalist system, the capital belonged to the capitalist, its return had no limits, and its formation was based on profits through exploitation of labor. In technological democracy the capital belongs to the labor and is the product of the work. The return is not from profits but is a justified percentage of the interest rate on the open market. From this viewpoint, it is more like bonds that a capitalist firm would issue to borrow money from the open market. Furthermore, under capitalism the return from capital investment is through exploitation of labor. Under technological democracy, first the return is a fixed amount depending on the interest rate, second it goes to the worker, thus strengthening his economic condition. It must be noted that in technological democracy only individuals can own stock of the production firms. Stocks owned by the firms and government is held on a temporary basis. They are held in trust to be gradually transferred to the workers. Thus no firm can own stock of another firm. Accordingly, all such ownership is abolished and stock owned by the government is transferred gradually to government workers. For the same reason there cannot be any trust funds established

that will extend beyond the establishing individual's life span or will benefit another person or institution.
3. Each institution completes its own position classification based on the framework and model established by the national government. As explained before, the national government through its Position and Pay Classification Commission classifies all predictable positions into categories, groups, and levels describing general job responsibilities for each position and establishing a pay range for each. This will not be anything extraordinary. The U.S. national government today has a position classification schedule for its bureaucracy that embodies nearly all available positions in American society. This needs to be revised and extended a little to include positions not currently within the national system. Revising and updating of this national classification schedule will be not so difficult a task for the corresponding computer center at the national office. The process works as follows. Every private institution after preparing its classification and corresponding pay schedule feeds it to the computer. The computer, which has in its memory a copy of the national classification and pay schedule, compares the institution's schedule with that of the national model and points out disparities, if any. The institution then tries to correct the discrepancies by reallocating job responsibilities. In the case of difficulty, the institution explains the reason why the disputed position could not be matched with those in the national schedule. A computerized copy of the institutional schedule with explanations about non compatible positions is sent to the appropriate local agency. This agency first checks the schedule against the national model in the computer, to see whether there are other discrepancies, and then studies the position under question. In general, incompatible questions are very few and more likely they come up when new technologies are developed and new responsibilities are required. The local agency has authority to modify and approve these new positions after studying them and having appropriate communication or meetings with the in-

stitution's experts. Initially, they are usually approved on a temporary basis. In the case when these positions are new or substantially different, they are reported to the appropriate regional agency along with a computerized copy of the schedule. All new and different positions gathered by the agencies in different regions, each computerized, are then sent to the national council for consideration and modification of the national schedule. At the national level, the computer system simplifies the council's task. The new and diversified positions are studied, and new national samples are created and incorporated into the national schedule. The important outcome of this system is that it prescribes the same pay for similar jobs, regardless of to which institution in the society the workers belong. This provides for a nationwide move toward equality of opportunity in jobs and pay systems. It also eliminates the need for labor unions, since there is no need and reason for bargaining. As a result, the workers save dues otherwise paid to the unions, because they receive just pay, which is established through scientific studies of job responsibilities by a neutral national agency.
4. Differentiation in pay depends on two factors: education and experience. A higher education qualifies a person for higher executive or professional positions. However, differentiation in pay between the highest and the lowest positions is not great. It seems that if one is three times of the other it is justified. This means, for example, if the minimum yearly wage is fifteen thousand dollars, the maximum will be forty-five thousand dollars. However, no one gets to the high levels of management without educational qualifications and years of experience at the lower levels. On the other hand, the worker who receives the minimum salary fifteen thousand dollars gets an annual raise as he furthers his education and accumulates experience. By the time he approaches his retirement age, his salary has increased to a level very close, if not equal, to the highest pay. So continuous education and years of experience are the available ladder for every worker to climb in the pay hierarchy.

This means a person might like to hold the same position for many years.

5. Each institution, when the nature of its production requires, has an agency responsible for studying and reporting the environmental and other hazards of the product as well as the process of production. In the case of large institution, this agency is located within its research and development department (RDD). This study is achieved through technology forecasting and technology assessment. No new product can be produced unless allowed by the local and, in important cases, the appropriate regional agencies. Such a decision is made after these agencies receive the result of studies and findings from the corresponding institutions.

   Larger institutions have a research and development department that is responsible for dealing with three areas: (a.) produce new technologies or improve the old ones; (b.) study the new and old technologies in order to determine the appropriate technology (AT) to be used; and (c.) study the hazards and environmental effect of the new and old technologies and prescribe regulations for the limitation on their use or elimination of the hazards.

6. Based on all of the above stated criteria, production firms in technological democratic society are human-minded, environmental protection–orientated, and conscious of limited natural resources and produce goods and services necessary for public use rather than for profits.

7. Large firms are decentralized and divided into several smaller independent firms. The reason for this is that once the workers one by one elected to the membership of the board of directors in a giant industry's branches or in its subsidiary firms, they would want to separate their institution from the controlling conglomerate. They want to be independent, and they also don't want to pay for the expenditures of a superbureaucracy that would have no production functions once profits are abolished. To clarify this point let us take as an example one of the giant corporations, namely Safeway Stores, Inc., a $7 billion food empire.

It owns over twenty-four hundred supermarkets, one hundred and nine manufacturing and processing plants, sixteen produce packaging plants, sixteen bakeries, nineteen milk and sixteen ice cream plants, four soft drink bottlers, three meat processing plants, three coffee roasting plants, and scores of others. Once employees in each of these institutions start to receive stocks and have accumulated enough to choose their own members to the board of directors or management positions, it is natural that they would tend to operate their firm independent from the parent company. They may still keep their business relations with it but on an independent basis. Thus, in a matter of time, Safeway Corporation will be divided into scores of independent plants and supermarkets. Safeway's board of directors also help conrol Bank of California, General Electric, Wells Fargo Bank, Shell Oil, Pacific Gas and Electric, Caterpillar Tractor, and Southern Pacific Company, among others. Once each of these institutions is taken over by the workers and the workers constitute the majority of board membership, each of these institutions, which are quite large corporations, will tend to become independent from Safeway and other giant multinationals. It is natural that workers would want to be their own boss and make production policies of their own rather than being subject to policies coming from outside their firm. Of course, this is a very healthy result. Its most important effect is the dispersal of capital and technology as well as power. It means the end of concentrated corporate power that dictated economic, social, and political policies under monopoly capitalism.

8. Economic sovereignty. With each monthly salary every worker also receives a certain prescribed amount of stocks of the firm where he works and thus he becomes part owner. Those in public service receive shares of stocks of the production firms purchased by the government from the stock market. As the years pass, the worker's shares of ownership accumulate, giving him an increasing voice in the operation of the corresponding production firm. On the

other hand, as the large capitalist stockholders die, their holdings in all production firms are transferred to the public treasury, in this case to the National Consumption Fund. As a matter of time, in three to four decades, the superrich will be eliminated from the American society. With their disappearance also disappear their economic, social, and political influence. The affairs of society are returned to the people as a whole. While there are no rich, there are also no poor. Everyone, except those disabled, has a job, income, and continuous accumulation of his share of ownership of production means. With disappearance of the wealthy capitalist group and their profit motives, corruption and dishonesty will also be substantially diminished and ultimately disappear. For the first time in world history, the dignity and integrity of all individuals in the society will be recognized and respected.

The economic operation of society will be based on one single principle, namely, the equality of opportunity. The economic return to each individual will correspond to his level of knowledge, skills, and experience. The individuals will move upward in the hierarchy of production based on these criteria only. For this reason, there will be a great incentive in education, which will ultimately cause tendency toward equalization of economic return to everyone in the long run, namely during some thirty years of the work period. By the time of retirement, there will be little difference between the income of a high executive and those who started at lower echelons in the production hierarchy.

While the production process will reward those with higher education in the first stages of employment, the years of experience of other workers, coupled with their continuous education efforts, will enable them to catch up. The level of education and years of experience determine one's level of economic return rather than the kind of his work. Whether a person is a garbage disposal man or a top executive, the position will not be determinant of a person's overall economic well-being in the long run, but his level of education and experience.

Therefore, in the technological democratic society, an individual's continuous education in the humanities and social and natural sciences will lead society toward enlightenment. Humanistic values will prosper, corruption and crime diminish and ultimately be eliminated, and moderation take the place of conflict and confrontation, and militarism along with destructive forces will be denounced. Respect for human life and human rights will extend to other living species on earth. For the first time in the civilized world, human beings will live in harmony with the elements of nature, leading to an understanding of the meaning of creation and sincere and rationalized recognition of the Creator, a Superior Being, not necessarily within the meaning prescribed by the major religious teachings. Ultimately, permanent peace will prevail in a technological society, a society much simplified but much better understood, with a modest but prosperous human life.

THE MORAL STANDARDS OF TECHNOLOGICAL DEMOCRACY

The moral standards of the technological democratic society will be based the same on the single principle of equality of opportunity.

This principle prescribes that one shall not do to others what one shall not desire to be done to him.

One shall not unjustly enrich another, thus causing harm to opportunities of others by unjustly increasing the level of opportunity of the enriched person.

One shall not steal, since this would be unjust enrichment and cause harm to opportunities of one from whom the property is stolen and at the same time unjustly increase the former's opportunity.

One shall not accept bribes or any property without comparable compensation since this will harm others' opportunities against his.

Since levels of opportunities are heavily based on education and education is freely available, one shall continue his educational efforts for all his active life.

Even though tendencies of men and women may differ in

social life, they all shall be granted the same opportunity in all aspects of life. Thus for the first time in world history there will be a true equality between men and women.

In order to enhance and maintain the future of equality of opportunity, all children shall be subjected to a process of required education, namely preschool and general education up to age fifteen. From there on they are independent to decide their own future course in life through appropriate education of their choice.

The principle of equality of opportunity prescribes also that all natural resources belong to all people and to society as a whole. In extreme application of the equality of opportunity, all natural resources belong equally to all people of the world. Thus an oil company cannot appropriate oil resources. It can lease it for a prescribed period of time and extract and market it. However, revenues from the sale of oil, after deducting the cost of production and marketing, will go to the public treasury. Oil companies do not make money out of oil itself. The same applies to all other natural resources.

The extreme application of equality of opportunity also means that other living species have the same opportunity within their particular domain for their life and its pursuit. This simply means that it is unjust to breed and raise animals for the purpose of slaughtering for human consumption. There is enough life-supporting energy in plants, fruits, and grains. One may go even as far as to say that cutting trees for human use is unjust, since trees are living things and should be subject to the same equality of opportunity regarding their life.

The application of the principle of equality of opportunity allows individuals such a broad freedom that the expansion of it cannot be described. Any description of freedom will be imposing limitations on its boundaries. This broad expansion of individual freedom is checked only by the application of the principle of equality of opportunity. One is free to choose and act upon choice as long as such action does not infringe upon the equality of opportunity granted to others. The same principle applies to public officials as well.

Considering all this, if one sincerely looks upon the nature of life in American or any other industrialized society, one would find it utterly barbaric because of increased technological means of destruction of life—human as well as animal—and resources; as long as a man determines the extent of his manhood by the strength of his muscles, he is embodied in his barbarian nature and related to the savage animalistic world. There is no room for such tendencies in democratic society. Reason rather than force prevails. The current society is utterly unjust, discriminatory, and exploitive; it is a kind of modern slavery where individuals are trained to be producers in order to maximize profit margin, rather than be educated toward becoming a better human being, and where everyone is hooked, through credit cards and other credit systems, to the production system. Once he is made a debtor, by being induced to buy now and pay later, there is no easy way for him to free himself. He becomes bound to stay in his job, regardless how much he dislikes it, in order to be able to meet his monthly payments of a variety of debts. In fact, this is economically a slave society for the overwhelming majority of people. The rest are the enslavers, robbers, or scavengers like doctors, lawyers, and bankers, profit makers, all modern licensed *ladrones*. It is sorrowful to attribute these to the society I love, but it is true that the wonderful people of the nation I love are taken over and subjugated by these elements. Nothing can save us except a national consciousness about the conditions of our societal system and its corresponding cleverly devised process of enslavement to which we have been subjected. This consciousness can be materialized only through self-education. There is no hope that our educational institutions under current conditions will be of any significant help. Our educational system is controlled by and is geared to serve the purpose of the ruling elite. The people have to start from scratch developing this consciousness. They must do it on their own. There is no other way. What a beautiful society and peaceful world it would be if the people succeed.

Careful attention to the socioeconomic and political structure of technological democratic society indicates that in its initial stages of development the size, functions, and structure of the political system are substantially and drastically reduced. As technological democratic society moves toward maturity, many political and governmental functions are eliminated or highly diminished. These include those of law enforcement, judicial as well as regular, supervisory bureaucratic functions. Political and public organizations increasingly fall under popular control and gradually, in many areas of operation, lose their political characteristics and increasingly acquire the form and operation like many other social organizations. Therefore, in its ultimate stage of development, technological democratic society tends toward a stateless society where the remaining political institutions from a societal viewpoint become negligible. Most of the institutions, previously considered political, now have become inseparable parts of the social and economic organizations.

NOTES

1. Carl Cohen, *Communism, Fascism, and Democracy,* 2d ed. (New York: Random House, 1972), p. 394.

2. Ibid., p. 395.

3. De Legibus.

4. John Locke, *Second Treatise of Government, 1690* (London: Thomas Tegg, 1823).

5. Sir Ernest Barker, ed., *Social Contract: Essays by Locke, Hume, and Rousseau* (London: Oxford University Press, 1947).

6. T. Dundas Pillans, ed., *Forgotten Truths: Selections from the Speeches and Writings of the Right Hon. Edmund Burke* (London: Liberty Review Publishing Company, 1898).

7. Edward Dumbauld, ed., *The Political Writings of Thomas Jefferson* (New York: Liberal Arts Press, 1955).

8. Jeremy Beremy Bentham, *Principles of Legislation,* 1802.

9. John Stuart Mill, *Consideration on Representative Government* (New York: Harper, 1862); and John Stuart Mill, *On Liberty* (Boston: Ticknor and Fields, 1863).

10. John C. Calhoun, *A Disquisition on Government* (Columbia, South Carolina: State Printing, 1851).

11. Thomas H. Green, *Liberal Legislation and Freedom of Contract,* in *The Works of Thomas Hill Green,* vol. 3 (London: Longmans, Green and Company, 1888).

12. Leonard T. Hobhouse, *Liberalism* London: Oxford University Press, 1911).

13. John Dewey, "The Future of Liberalism," *Journal of Philosophy* 32, no. 9 (April 25, 1935), also his other works.

14. Norman Thomas, *Democratic Socialism: A New Appraisal* (New York: League for Industrial Democracy, 1953).

15. Friedrich A. Hayek, *The Road to Serfdom* (Chicago: University of Chicago Press, 1944).

16. A. D. Lindsay, *The Essentials of Democracy* (Oxford: Clarendon Press, 1929).

17. Joseph A. Schumpter, *Capitalism, Socialism and Democracy* (New York: Harper and Row, 1950).

18. Henry B. Mayo, *An Introduction to Democratic Theory* (London: Oxford University Press, 1960).

19. John Rawls, *A Theory of Justice* (Cambridge: Harvard University Press, 1971).

20. Robert Nozick, *Anarchy, State and Utopia* (New York: Basic Books, Inc., 1974).

21. The educatonal system is continuous, as has been explained before.

Chapter Eight

Technological Democracy: Some Analyses and Conclusions

DEMOCRACY AND EQUALITY OF OPPORTUNITY

The application of the principle of equality of opportunity is a quite delicate matter. Some scientists in the past have tried to describe and analyze it. In describing his democratic "technotronic society," for example, Brzezinski characterized it by the application of the principle of equal opportunity for all but special opportunity for a talented few.[1] This appears to be a combination of a continued maintenance of the popular will with an increasing occupation of the key decision-making positions by individuals of special intellectual and scientific achievements. He argues that the educational and social systems will make it increasingly attractive and easy for those meritocratic few to develop to the fullest of their special potential. While it will be necessary to require everyone at a sufficiently responsible position to take, say, two years of retraining every ten years, the rest of the population will tend to develop a new interest in the cultural and humanistic aspects of life, which will tend to serve as a social valve, reducing tensions and political frustration.

Others argue that equality of opportunity as understood by the former group has little to do with creating a more egalitarian society in the technological age.[2] As they argue, equality of opportunity functions as an indispensable feature of the highly stratified society where equality of opportunity assures that talented individuals will be able to climb into the key decision-making positions, generating the success of new society and its cohesion against popular tensions and political frustration. Thus in technologically advanced societies equality of opportunity will function as a hierarchical principle, in opposition to the egalitarian social goals it is thought to serve. It will indeed become one of the main factors contributing to the widening gap between the cultures of upper and lower classes in technological society.

We intend to repudiate the approach of all these schools of thought to the application of the principle of equality of opportunity. But before doing this we find it important to look, though very briefly, into the characteristics of an advanced technological society.

Some hundred fifty years ago the concept of laissez-faire provided ground for identification of the interests of the institutions of entreprenurial capitalism in the society that they dominated and profited from. Laissez-faire taken as a capitalist ideology provided ground for the cultural as well as intellectual expression of the interests of a specific but small class.

In today's technological society, the concept of *laissez-innover* provides the same ground for expression to a specific class identified as technologists. It is a technological impulse in technological society providing opportunities for the institutions that tend to monopolize technology and profit from it. By free exploitation of technology this privileged class finds a guaranteed opportunity for wealth, status, and power.

This class creates a technological rationality that is as socially neutral today as market rationality was a century and a half ago. It encourages a political and cultural gap between the upper class, those who control the advanced technological systems, and the lower class, those who are subject to control.

To understand the situation properly, we must consider the current status and the nature of technology. We must, first, consider technology an institutional system. Today's relation of technology to monopoly capitalism is analogous to the relation of the latter to the free market (laissez-faire) capitalism of a century and half ago.

Second, the most important societal dimension of advanced technological institutions is social. If left alone, that is to say if we sustain *laissez-innover,* these institutions will tend to be instruments of highly centralized and intensive social control. Technology tends to conquer man and through him conquer nature. Even though there seems an absence of direct controls or coercion, technology demands a high degree of control over the training, specialization, mobility, and skills of the working class. Technical rationality is increasingly employed to organize physical objects as well as human services.

Third, there is very profound social antagonism causing contradictions much more intensive, sharper, and more fundamental than those ascribed by Marx to the condition of the mid–nineteenth-century industrial society. These contradictions are mainly the result of the control of technology by an elite class. The workers are overtrained and underutilized, and their work is tightly controlled by technological means and processes. Technological progress requires a continuous increase in the skill levels of the workers while the advanced technical rationality in the production process does not provide ground for full use of the attained skills. Accordingly, in some sectors the workers are obliged to be highly trained regardless how few of those skills are actually used in the work process. Unlike the nineteenth-century industrial society, in advanced technological society salary and wage increases lose their overriding importance once necessities of life are met and there are ample means of comfort and even luxuries available to the working class. While getting people to work harder requires growing incentives, the effect of traditional incentives such as money, status, and authority has been continually in decline.

If the current situation of class stratification continues, the advance of technology will tend to concentrate authority further in the hands of those who control technology and its managing group. But the advance of technology, information technology in particular, while increasing the required skill, also increases the educational levels of the population on a broader base. This creates first latent consciousness leading to open self-management, both in the workplace as well as in society as a whole. This is one important development in the contradictions inherent in technological advancement. It leads to a profound social contradiction between the highly stratified society of the current technological-capitalist system like the United States and the spread of educational opportunities among the masses. Thus technology tends to create the basis for new and sharp class conflict in modern society quite analogous to the early industrialization era that created the working and owning classes, namely the proletariat and the capitalist.

Accordingly, drive for technological development by the elite—*laissez-innover*—is the most powerful and influential movement toward the demands and program of the technological impulse in industrialized society, which is rooted in its most powerful institutions—government and multinational corporations. More than any other development in the past, this impulse has succeeded in identifying and rationalizing the interests of the most authoritarian elite, which operate under the guise of democracy, in industrialized countries. They also exercise dominating expansion of their policies in the Third World countries.

In the lives of Americans as well as citizens of other industrialized nations, many forces hostile to the democratic values are exerted by those who control the technology and its development. Understanding of this fact requires some comprehension of the fakeness of democratic values and processes in order to grasp the true fact of technological elitism and authoritarianism. The very comprehension of this fact is an important and significant step toward national consciousness leading to understanding the malaise, irrationality, powerlessness, and official violence that characterize life in the United States and other industrial nations. The result may well lead to a politics of radical reconstruction or social revolution.

TECHNOLOGICAL DEMOCRACY AND APPLICATION OF EQUALITY OF OPPORTUNITY

In all discussions above, those who have directed attention and criticism to the application of the principle of equality of opportunity and its implications in causing a democratic society have erred in several ways. The first and most important mistake has been the piecemeal application of the concept. In a highly undemocratic capitalistic society like the United States, if one tries to apply the principle of equality of opportunity to one sector of operation of society, leaving the other areas untouched, it is obvious that the outcome will still tend to comply with the norms of the basic system, in the case of the United States capitalism. Within an elite-ruled society any partial reform would tend to comply with the elite norms. It will create a new elite, in those arguments technical elite, which will supplement the existing elite class and more likely serve it.

The second error relates to the application of the principle of equality of opportunity to the existing system of operation, which in itself is undemocratic. For example, in the area of education they think in the advancement of the current system of education, which consists of a continuous education—elementary, secondary, and college—toward achieving a professional status and then enter the work market, with periodical retraining and updating programs. An improper and undemocratic system creates improper and undemocratic consequences. Education in a technological democratic society, as has been explained, is in no way similar to the system of education practiced in the United States as well as in other industrialized countries. Based on requirements of technological society, this type of education has built-in incompetency and substantial deficiencies.

The third error refers to the narrow interpretations and application of the principle of equality of opportunity. No one considers that technological democracy is a system by itself that is essentially based on the thorough application of the concept of equality of opportunity. There is no such system as technological democracy today. This system is independent and pure. It cannot coexist within the same society with undemocratic systems such as capitalism, socialism, or communism. It cannot be mixed with any of these systems without losing its democratic character. So for the sake of democracy it has to stand alone and be distinguished in its application to any society.

There are other errors in their approaches as well, but instead of going through those, we try to explain the application of the principle of equality of opportunity in a technological democratic society and let the explanation of the concept shed light upon the errors.

First, we must try to understand that technological democracy is a system in itself substantially distinguished from the existing societal systems of capitalism, socialism, and communism.[3] Under the requirement of the system it encompasses economic, social, political and technological aspects of the society. It encompasses the society as a whole, all its interactions, values, and objectives.

This theory of democracy has never been described before, since it has technology as its integral part. Here we refer only to some of its important aspects in relation to the application of the principle of equality of opportunity in an attempt, at the same time, to demonstrate the importance and complexity of the application of the principle.

SOCIAL DEMOCRACY: HEALTH CARE AND EDUCATION

Health care and education are the two basic and most important requirements for a progressive and advancing society. No progress can be achieved without a healthy and educated population.

Technological society regardless of its form—capitalistic, socialistic, or other—has its stresses of many kinds resulting from the complexities it creates in the daily operation of life. Thus many diseases, particular of technological society, are mental. Furthermore, in such a society, because of excessive and widespread use of synthetic materials in foodstuff, and pollution of air and water, many physical diseases develop, varieties of cancer in particular.

These unhealthy conditions and phenomena make health measures in technological society ever more important. There can be no substantial progress in an advanced but unhealthy society. If no proper health care is provided, such a society is doomed to failure and decay. The negative effect of misuse or careless use of technology has an accelerating effect on this decay.

Consequently, a democratic health-care program is imperative to maintain and improve the dynamism of the population as a whole, the working class in particular.

The only way the equality of opportunity in health care can be achieved is that it be accessible to all the population, and the only way this can be materialized is when it is available free of charge to all. Thus the health-care services must be made available through a nationwide institution, not necessarily a governmental agency, to all population. It must be noted that by health care it is meant preventive care. This covers not only the individuals and their physical and mental conditions, but also the environment tending to provide for a healthy life. The environment includes not only the air, water, and toxic and atomic waste disposals but also food and hundreds of products used in daily life. It is obvious that if the causes harmful to health care are diminished or eliminated, need for individual health care will be substantially reduced and so will the costs.

The total annual cost of health services in the United States was about $450 billion in 1986, and predictions are that it will continue to increase and may likely reach $760 billion by the year 1990. To understand the incredibly enormous size of this cost, one may consider that the annual cost amounted to $1,700 per person in 1986 and will rise to $2,550 by 1990.[4]

In an expert's view, the United States is now in an indefinite stage of management and control, attempting first to determine the amount of money needed and then directing it to appropriate destination of health services' need and demand.[5]

In evaluating health-care costs and sources of financial contribution, one must note that the federal government plays a substantial role and has a major influence relating to costs. It pays for about 50 percent of the hospital costs and more likely about 30 percent of the physician costs through Medicare. Within the private sector, there are hundreds of insurance companies bearing the costs. However, about 10 percent of these companies account for 75 percent of all payments by insurance firms. At the same time, of the 27 percent of all expenditures paid by insurance firms, about 80 percent is contributed by employers through payroll deductions.[6] A major problem is the very pluralistic nature of the health services. The plurality of sources of funds makes proper administration of the services difficult. On the public side of contribution, there is bureaucratic inefficiency and waste; on the private sector, there is a striving toward maximization of profits. Both factors together lead toward the unjustified and increasingly high cost of health care. Looking realistically, as presented previously, insurance business has moved, like any other major business, toward monopolization. Today a few giant insurance firms control a substantial majority of services. As is well known, monopoly capitalism is one of the causes of increased prices.

Despite substantial governmental and employer contributions toward health-care services, still the great majority of Americans do not receive nearly adequate health care and a substantial number receive practically none.

The solution seems to be in the unification of all health-service funds under one system, eliminating both private and public sectors from interfering in the administration of this nationally vital service. Such a health institution can impose just prices for health services, including doctors' fees, hospital charges, and medicine prices. It may require minor contributions from employers as per head of employees as well as from those self-employed. All people then will benefit from such services, and society will move toward equality of opportunity in relation to health-care services.

Thus in the area of health care the application of the principle of equality of opportunity prescribes that it be available to everyone with no obstacles, including the financial one. The very application of the equality of opportunity gives the health-care agency authority to interfere in any production process that the agency experts find harmful to the affected public, such as coal mines or asbestos factories where the individual is directly exposed to harmful effects of the improperly kept work environment or the operation of industries that pollute the air, water, and other aspects of the environment and expose individuals living within that environment to its consequential hazards. In fact, those polluting institutions are infringing upon the equal opportunity rights of the population involved by subjecting them to an unhealthy environment. This intrusion in the equality of opportunity of the population involved invests authority upon the health agency to interfere, punish, and demand corrections. The structure, finance, and operation of this health agency is described elsewhere.

Education

Along with health care, the most important requirement for the advancement of a society is education. As demonstrated, the education system, as well as programs in a technological society, are substantially different from the current systems practiced in industrialized societies.

Currently formal education starts from age seven in noncommunist societies and from age three in communist societies. It is then continued through high school. Education of the overwhelming majority of the population ends at the end of this level. Beyond this level, some go to vocational schools and some enter the institutions of higher education and continue full-time toward receiving a B.S. or B.A.; a much smaller number continue for a year or two toward a master's degree. A very few continue further toward a doctoral degree, which is the ultimate level of formal education. Though some study toward advanced degrees while working, the overwhelming majority get engaged in full-time study to achieve the goal. A person graduating from high school is usually eighteen years old. He is twenty-two when he receives his first college degree and at least twenty-six when he receives his doctoral degree. A person seeks employment after he finishes any of these stages. This means the majority enter the labor market at the age of eighteen or sooner and a few continue studying until they are twenty-six or older before seeking employment.

This kind of education has at least four major defects. First, the continuous full-time education keeps students out of the labor market. Though some students work part-time, a great majority of them do not work. Thus education becomes all expenditures without returning to the society the benefits of skills learned each year. It becomes a heavy economic burden upon the community, parents, and society as a whole.

Second, in technological society, with the rapid pace of

change and advancement, the knowledge received yesterday more likely becomes obsolete or of diminished value today. The current system of education then has built-in obsolescence.

Third, it is a one-shot process; after it ends and the diploma is received, it is considered completed for the purpose of employment. Yet changing conditions of work require continuous education to keep up with the changes and to be able to perform properly and efficiently.

Fourth, a very important defect of the current educational system is in its content. It emphasizes technical training to the detriment of cultural education such as history, philosophy, foreign and domestic languages and literature, music, and arts. Cultural education is the kind of knowledge that creates a healthy society, intellectually speaking, where reason and wisdom prevail over force and brutality. Because of destructive potential of technological society, at no time in history was such cultural education needed more than the present. In fact, advancing cultural education along with technical training is a matter of urgency before it gets too late to save humanity from self-destruction.

Education in technological society must remedy all these defects while, at the same time, making every individual a lifetime participant. It is divided into three phases as follows.

The formal education is full-time and heavily cultural, involving social sciences and humanities, and goes from the age of three to fourteen. From age fifteen each individual starts to work while continuing his studies part-time. He keeps at least two-thirds of his educational program, equivalent to twelve credit hours per semester under current standards. From the age of twenty-two he works full-time, reducing his education to one-third of the full load or equivalent to six credit hours per semester. He then continues this required minimum educational program for the rest of his working years. It is more likely that a person so habituated to continual education will continue to do so also after his retirement at the age of fifty-two. The method, content, and process of his education have been discussed elsewhere in this study and are no matter of concern here.

The period of full-time education that extends to twelve years is the most important part and is rigidly structured for the purpose of conveying the most possible knowledge to the students during the daily time specified for education. It is during this period that the principle of equality of opportunity must be applied strictly. In order to give each child the type of education required to understand and comfortably live within the technological democratic society, it is imperative that each child has the same opportunity for quality education as any other child in society. This very essential aim can be achieved if education is available to everyone without any burden, a financial one in particular. Therefore, the educational cost during this period must be afforded from the specific allotment for this purpose coming from the Public Consumption Fund.

From the date a person starts employment, one-third of his educational cost will be paid for by the employer and the rest from the Public Consumption Fund. Therefore, from this time on the public treasury will have a diminishing contribution to education. When the individual reaches the stage of spending one-third of time on education, all his costs will be paid by his employer.

In actual process the money allocated for this purpose in each institution will be transferred to the Public Consumption Fund; the latter then will pay the employer's educational expenses. By the use of the Technodem for educational purposes the cost to the employer will be nominal in comparison to the cost of such education today.

Equality of opportunity is the most important constitutional right of every individual, and it must be provided for, preserved, and protected. Therefore, there can be no infringement against this right either by the institutions or other individuals, whether education be for personal benefits or for attaining a better opportunity.

Accordingly, each individual has a positive right to equality of opportunity; it must be provided for him. Each individual also has a negative right to it; it cannot be abridged, denied to him, or taken away from him.

The most important aspect of this system of education is its social and economic equalizing powers. First, everybody starts education from the same level and more or less with the same quality. Thus there is no classwise distinctive education. This is particularly effectuated by considering that under technological democracy, despite the fact that there is a total ownership of the means of production and distribution by the private sector and there is moderate accumulation of wealth, there is no ground for class stratification, as is evidenced under capitalism. Each individual's wealth goes to the public treasury upon his death, and each person starts from scratch. This creates a fluid and mobile dynamic society that can be subject to no elite rule—the technical elite or others. This is essentially an equalitarian and equitable society. The adherence to the application of the principle of equality of opportunity tends to keep this society essentially democratic and incredibly stable.

The other important aspect of this system of education is that it provides for highly qualified individuals to rule and guide the system in technopolitical positions. Candidates come from the retired class because, first, each person from the time of retirement will have at least fifteen to twenty years of active life left, which he can spend in scientific or artistic creativeness, serving in the community voluntary institutions, or entering the world of technopolitics. All positions in this latter area are temporary as well as limited in length of service for each individual. So a full-time working person would not like to risk his development and progress within the work force and run for political office when he knows that he can hold office only for a limited time period. Furthermore, technopolitical elective positions will require such high qualifications and years of experience in different aspects of the work force that only a few within the work force would be qualified. These would be individuals having high positions who certainly would not be willing to leave them to accept an uncertain future.

Accordingly, this system of continuous education will provide highly qualified personnel for elective offices by the time of retirement. Once elected, individuals will be responsible for proper operation of the system. Since the term of office will also be limited to one term, none of the elected officials can establish strong or lasting influence on the matters of the state, like those enjoyed by the elective officials under capitalism or other political systems. It must be noted that the one-term limitation applies only to the elective position held by the individual. He will be eligible to run for election in other political bodies. He cannot serve more than one term in each of these public bodies.

ECONOMIC DEMOCRACY AND EQUALITY OF OPPORTUNITY

After the two social requirements, namely health care and education, both essential for having a progressive and dynamic society, the most important application of the principle of equality of opportunity relates to the economic sphere of society. Economic democracy is the most important aspect of the technological democratic system.

This goal can be achieved only by proper application of the principle of equality of opportunity. There are several strong factors in capitalistic society that work against economic equality of opportunity. It is primarily in these areas that the principle must apply in order to lead society toward economic democracy.

Accumulation of Wealth through Exploitation

As we have seen before, in a capitalistic society wealth is created and accumulated through the exploitation of labor and consumers. This is what a businessman calls profit and Marx has labeled social surplus. Profit is what a producer earns by appropriating a part from the work of labor or charging extra, beyond the exploitation of labor, to consumers. In fact, in modern industrialized capitalistic society, profit is the result of double exploitation. The result has been a phenomenal concentration of wealth and ensuing power in the hands of a very small class. This class, as a result, has been able to dominate the socioeconomic and political spheres of activities and attain and sustain a highly privileged status. Thus an industrialized capitalistic society brings into existence a society with a very high class stratification, the power being concentrated in the hands of a small and enormously wealthy class. Consequently, there is no equality of opportunity in such capitalistic society and it can never exist. Those who have wealth have a much higher opportunity than those who are considered poor.

Accumulation of Wealth under Equality of Opportunity

Appropriation of profit has caused the accumulation of wealth which has provided opportunity for power and privilege. Thus one requirement for providing ground for establishment of equality of opportunity is to abolish profit and gradually return the ownership of the means of production to the workers and thus ultimately eliminate capitalism. Furthermore, the abolishing of profit would highly increase the moral values of the population, since profits are nothing but cheating both the workers and the consumers, they cause sanctioned justification of fraud and corruption, which will tend to disappear once profits are prohibited. As has been discussed, this prohibition will multiply workers' incentive to produce, which is not the subject of consideration here.

The elimination of profits entails the elimination of exploitation of workers as well as the consumers. But above all it eliminates the uncontrolled and free accumulation of wealth. This will be an essential step toward bringing about the economic equality of opportunity.

TRANSFER OF WEALTH

The elimination of profit alone will not solve the problem of inequalities of opportunities that exist under capitalism. Those who have accumulated wealth if allowed to transfer it to others can also transfer with it the accompanying power and privileges. Anyone receiving wealth through transfer without paying a comparable price for it is being moved up in the hierarchy of opportunities proportional to the size of transferred wealth. Such transfer, therefore, increases his opportunities to the detriment of the rest of the population. One of the most traditional and sanctioned transfers of wealth is through inheritance. If a person dies and leaves enormous wealth behind, it is transferred to his legal heirs, enhancing their status, power, and privilege compared to that of other citizens. Thus if a family is centimillionaire, that family, short of a catastrophe, will remain centimillionaire through inheritance, nearly perpetuating the power and privileges in the family members. It is in this way that the economic elite is created, with a dominating influence in society. The same is true not only of inheritance but of any transfer of wealth without comparable compensation.

If, upon death, an individual's wealth is transferred to the public treasury, the children of the deceased have to start from scratch like any other citizen. They would be deprived from transfer of power and privileges accompanying the wealth of the deceased.

The result in the long run would be gradual elimination of all wealthy families, tending to bring the wealth of society toward equitable distribution among its members. This is also an essential movement toward equalizing economic opportunities.

Since the size of official government in technological democratic society is very small, a substantial part of wealth received through such transfers by the public treasury will be spent on essential public services such as education and health care, which will further enhance the equality of opportunity among citizens.

EQUITABLE PRIVATE OWNERSHIP OF THE MEANS OF PRODUCTION

As stated before, in technological democratic society all means of production and distribution are privately owned and operated. This becomes gradually materialized by allocating to each worker, in addition to his wages, a proportional amount of share of ownership, primarily of the institution where he works. As a result, each worker from the very beginning of his work becomes, at the same time, a part-owner of his institution. As he continues his work, his ownership share increases. In a matter of time the capitalistic ownership is eliminated and the workers become full owners controlling the system of production. The term *worker* in this study applies to anyone who works in production of goods and services. This encompasses managerial-professional members down to skilled and unskilled ones. In fact, under capitalism all these individuals work for the capitalist and thus are workers in the real meaning of the term. This is a broad definition of the working class under monopolistic capitalism as well as technological democracy. Simply, a worker is anyone who works.

The application of this system of ownership will gradually

eliminate the influence of economic elite by transferring the power to the workers, enhancing the sense of responsibility and incentive among workers, and contributing substantially to the advancement of the equality of opportunity among the working class and stability and tranquillity in society.

TECHNOLOGICAL DECENTRALIZATION

As the share of the working class increases by the passage of time it reaches a point where the workers take control of the board of directors. From this point on the institutional policies are made by the representatives of the workers rather than those of the capitalists. This change on the leadership automatically tends to decentralize large institutions. Consider a larger food production corporation, which operates hundreds of supermarkets and scores of food processing and meat processing units. While the central management continues to remain in the hand of capitalists, these subsidiary institutions, one after another, fall under the direct control of the workers. After attaining this point, each institution tends to assume independence from the central office.

For example, once a supermarket unit operation is taken over by its workers, first it tends to make independent decisions that may be in conflict with those of the central office; second, the owners tend to operate independent from the mother corporation. The only thing the mother corporation can do is restrain from supplying goods. If this happens, the supermarket may decide to operate like any other independent supermarket and buy goods from the competitors. It is more likely that the mother corporation will not resort to this policy, since it will affect the marketing of its own products. Quite likely it will go along with the independent operation of the supermarket in order not to harm its size of the share in food marketing. The corporation may also think to stop relations with the supermarket and initiate a new one. Not likely, because of its cost and similar consequences a few years later. It also has to compete with its previous supermarket, which now operates independently and is quite familiar with the market and operation policies of the mother corporation. The same thing will happen also to other food processing institutions operating under the control of the mother corporation.

Consequently, this great movement toward equality of opportunity in the production process would tend to sharply decentralize the institutions of production and distribution. This decentralization will automatically cause decentralization or democratization of technology. The latter is a great step toward democratization of society as a whole by taking control of technology out of the hands of a few who controlled it for the benefit of the capitalist elite and to the detriment of society as a whole.

SHARED OPPORTUNITY

As mentioned before, equality of opportunity may be positive or negative. Positive processes refers to those that tend to enhance the opportunities of the masses of the working class to the detriment of the opportunities of a small privileged class. Negative equality of opportunity is when the opportunity of a small group of workers is increased to the detriment of the opportunities of the masses of the working class.

The latter concept, the negative equality of opportunity, is what we may justifiably call shared opportunity. The purpose is first, to tend to equalize opportunities among the working class, second, to guarantee employment to every able citizen, thus providing for full employment at all times.

In a technological democratic society, except for those totally disabled, there is no unemployment. As has been presented before, if there is a group of unemployed workers such as the class newly graduated and if there are no open positions to absorb them, the working employees within each class of employment let an hour or more of their work per week be reduced. They lose their pay for this hour. This one work-hour donation by the workers put together creates employment for those entering the labor market. For example, if 10,000 workers each give up one hour of the forty-hour-per-week work, that creates ten thousand hours of open position or full-time work for 250 new workers. Within a work force of 100 million, 2.5 million new jobs will be created.

By doing this, the opportunities of the mass of working labor force are reduced by 2.5 percent while the new workers who were jobless with zero opportunity increase their opportunities by 100 percent by getting employed in positions created through donation of one hour per week by each member of the working labor force.

It is very important to notice that new workers entering the market come nearly exclusively from those finishing their general education who are about fifteen years of age and are looking for part-time, low-skilled jobs. This actually does not disturb the employment opportunities at the other levels of the production system.

A very few may enter the work force at the higher levels of employment. These are specialists entering society from the outside or individuals within the work force who desire to change their line of work or profession. Since the number will be very small, its effect on the opportunities of other workers will be negligible. In any case, shared opportunity is a requirement in democratic society. Those who have a better opportunity share it with those looking for the same kind of opportunity while lacking it and at the same time being qualified to receive such opportunity. For example, mechanical engineers who are employed enjoy this opportunity. Now if there is a mechanical engineer looking for a job, those mechanical engineers all together should provide the unemployed one with the same opportunity as their own by partial donation from their weekly work hours. But if the unemployed person is an accountant, he is not qualified to take a position appropriate for a mechanical engineer. His shared opportunity comes from the working accountants. To accommodate this principle sometimes a minor structural revision to work may be required. But, as practice continues, its problems of application will gradually be resolved by innovating new processes and methods. These mostly will be helped by advanced technology and availability of electronic information in regard to the issue.

THE ESSENCE AND MEANING OF EQUALITY OF OPPORTUNITY

Generally speaking, equality of opportunity is absolute. This means that every person has the same opportunity as any other person. From this definition it is also implied that the exercise of equality of opportunity by a person cannot infringe upon equality of opportunity of another.

More precisely, equality of opportunity is of two kinds: vertical and horizontal. Vertical equality of opportunity is universal. It means that the same equality of opportunity is enjoyed by everyone in the society. It mainly applies to those aspects of life essential for personal development and well-being, such as education and health care. It also applies to relations between individuals, institutions, and institutions with individuals such as speech, press, assembly, travel, access to information, justice, property rights, et cetera.

In the area of production of goods and services, public as well as private, equality of opportunity is based on the level of education and years of experience. This means that every person has the same opportunity as any other person with comparable education and experience. The reason for these prerequisites is the requirement and absolute necessity for competence, which is essential for effective, efficient, and creative production of products and services.

In this respect, equality of opportunity exists horizontally within the hierarchical structure of the workplace as well as nationwide among the working class. If it is understood that in a democratic society every able person works between the age of fifteen and that of retirement, the full expansion of this horizontal equality of opportunity is visualized as follows: At the societal level, up to the age of fifteen equality of opportunity is applied in its universal sense, particularly in the area of education. This comprises some twelve years of formal full-time education, providing each person with a good liberal education background encompassing humanities, normative social sciences, natural and physical sciences, and mathematics.

At the age of fifteen each person enters the work force. From here on one's progress depends on one's advancement of knowledge and experience. So at the age of fifteen everyone starts work more or less from the same level, the lowest level of employment, and moves upward. From here on the application of equality of opportunity is horizontal. This means that all those having a comparable level of education and experience are entitled to the same level of employment as determined by the national position classification lists and receive the same pay and capital shares. As individuals educate themselves while working, their level of opportunity goes up, but not all at the same level or with the same speed. This depends on the programs of education that individuals choose for themselves, both at the technical-professional as well as the liberal arts levels. Consequently, each individual's advancement differs from another based on the individual's choice of courses offered through these two programs of compulsory education. It must be understood that while education is a continuous requirement for maintenance and improvement of competence, the selection of subject matters, area of specialization, and liberal art subjects are elective based on each individual's interest and desire. Though liberal arts education is very valuable to technical-professional knowledge toward becoming more efficient and creative, it is also a prerequisite for the realization, maintenance, and betterment of a democratic system. Therefore, it is an indispensable part of each individual's education. Therefore, based on individual choices, certain individuals increase their level of horizontal opportunity much faster than some others and progress upward with a more rapid pace.

The pay system is based on technical and cultural education and experience. Every worker increases his years of experience as he continues to work. From this viewpoint, all those who work accumulate the same years of experience by the time of retirement. This leaves the pay increases primarily dependent on the other two factors, namely technical and cultural education.

A person choosing a highly technical area as his line of work will need a good deal of related education to keep him up to date as the years go by. He must sustain his high level of competence. Such a person will be obliged to devote one-half of his required continued education program to technical subjects.

Another person may not have interest in highly technical or professional work, but desires to become an artist or a poet. He may choose to work as a garbage disposal man, which does not require much technical knowledge or upkeeping. He then may spend a major part of his required continued education in general and cultural areas and thus enhance his knowledge in the nontechnical areas he desires. As he increases his years of experience and pursues his required educational program, he climbs in the pay scale. However, since his job is not technical or professional during the early stages of his career, his pay increases may not be as high as those in technical or professional areas. Therefore, a small gap develops between the two levels of work. Figure 8–1 illustrates the situation. Every person starts with the same level of pay when he enters the market as a part-time worker. The pay schedule stays the same until the person assumes a full-time position at the age of twenty-two. From then on, those in highly technical areas receive a little more pay increase than the others during the early stages of work. As the years of experience accumulate and education continues, the annual increases level off and during the last stage of working years the pay increases become greater for those who had remained behind. At the time of retirement there are only negligible differences in income, if any, between the different sectors of the workforce.

The reason for this equalization process in the later stages of work is that the person in nontechnical work accumulates the same number of years of experience as the others and has the same amount of education. The difference is that others have more technical and professional education, useful for effective and efficient production in the early years, and those in nontechnical positions have more cultural education capable of enriching society as well as the work process more than the others. The same will be true in the case of a worker who wants to stay at a certain level of work and does not want to climb upward, yet he continues his required educational program.

This will be very much possible, even desirable, in a technological democratic society where cultural rewards of life are very high and often may override small material gains received by technical workers.

In figure 8–1, curve A represents the pay scale for highly technical positions and curve B shows the scale for positions with the least technical knowledge required. The rest of the positions fall between these two extremes. On the monetary scale shown here, the average annual pay increase during the thirty years of full-time work is around 6.5 percent. The high-tech positions receive little more than this, let us say 7 percent, while the

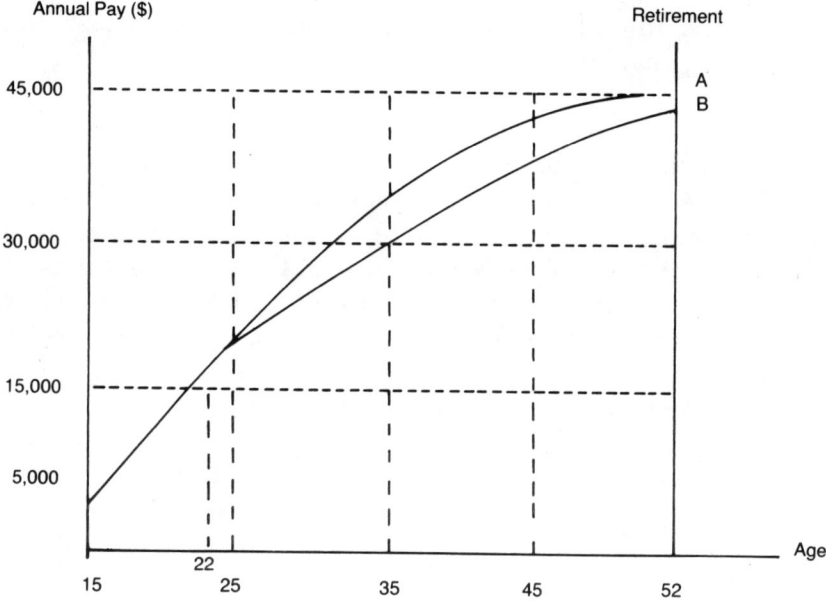

Figure 8-1. The Process of Pay Schedule in Technological Democratic Society

lowest level receives 6 percent. This may continue during the first few years where the acquiring of technical knowledge has a high productive return (let us say until the time a person receives his Ph.D.). After that the pay increases approach one another, and during the last years of the working period nontechnical workers receive little more of a pay raise than the technical. The higher pay increase becomes justified on two grounds. First, nontechnical workers have accomplished more in cultural education acquiring a higher quality as thinkers; second, the technical workers have approached the prescribed maximum level of wages and cannot get more substantial raises.

At the height of pay differentiation, the difference will be about 10 percent or three thousand dollars. At the end of a career, this will tend to be reduced to about 4 percent or two thousand dollars. For the whole period of a thirty-year career the difference will amount to about fifty thousand dollars or about one year's salary. Yet those who received lesser pay had had more resourceful and enjoyable years of life than those with high-tech or professional positions.

From one level to another, horizontal equality of opportunity moves upward in the hierarchical structure of production institutions until it reaches its highest level in each institution. This level of competence in one institution is comparable to the same class of competence in other institutions according to the requirements and responsibilities prescribed by the national position classification. Therefore, based on the national standards, not all top positions in every institution may be on the same level.

From both the social and economic standpoint, technological democratic society is a single class or classless society, where everyone starts from scratch and advance in education and work processes and retires at the same socioeconomic level.

The little economic advantages of some individuals are offset by a better societal education of others with lesser economic advantages. Where there are differences in economic advantages, they are so small that they are negligible within a single class structure.

For a better comprehension of the application of the principle of equality of opportunity as an indispensable component of democratic organism, one must not forget that the equality of opportunity is absolute in both its vertical and horizontal aspects. It can never be disturbed. It is disturbed when one encroaches on another's equality of opportunity, when there are secret agreements, when effective information is withheld from free access, when there is transfer of property without comparable compensation, when profits are made, when required competence is disregarded in the employment or electoral process, et cetera. Therefore, the essential principle to govern absolutely the dealings of society with individuals and those of individuals with society is equality of opportunity. The sole purpose for which men are permitted, individually or collectively, in interfering with liberty of action of any other individual or individuals, is protection of equality of opportunity warranted to him or them by the community. No man alone can be the judge of equality of his opportunity when such judgment is in conflict and adversely affects the equality of opportunity of others related to that of his. It is also implied that equality of opportunity of no person can be taken away from him either by force or consent, since this will lead to subjugation, servitude, or loss of opportunity affecting the present or future well-being of the individual.

Some important rights and liberties protected by equality of opportunity are as follows.

1. Socioeconomic

1. *Right to employment.* Since those who have employment will have necessarily a better opportunity to employment than the person who is not employed, the latter acquires the right for the same employment opportunity. Right to employment is one of the prime individual rights in the society, since unemployment adversely affects many other opportunities and liberties of the unemployed person, particularly in the long run. Consequently, when the right to employment is in conflict with other individual rights or opportunities, it supersedes the others and thus receives priority. The existence of democracy and its maintenance depends primarily on the economic operation of society toward the economic well-being of every

individual on the basis of knowledge, experience, and capability, the latter being heavily based on the other two. Thus the prime democratic aspects of a democratic system are economic. However, this should not be confused with materialism, since the economic purpose of the democratic system is essentially distinct from that of a capitalistic system. It is not for the purpose of accumulation of wealth and the establishment of economic classes, but quite to the contrary, it is for the economic well-being of all members of society without economic class distinction. It is for this very purpose that employment is considered the prime right of the individual and the prime responsibility of the institutions, communities, and society as a whole. Accordingly, in cases where there are unemployed persons, in order to guarantee appropriate employment to them, the principle of shared opportunities is used. This sharing is proportional to the level of unemployment and is shared equally by all those who are employed in positions corresponding to the qualifications of those seeking employment. This appears to be a complex process, but under a computerized information system, the Technodem, it is practical. Since some 95 percent of positions sought are at the lowest entry level, the application of the principle is of no problem. In the case of the rest, similar positions can easily be searched areawide or nationwide, if necessary, and shared opportunities ascertained, new vacant positions determined for employment purpose. Right to employment and its application by employing the concept of shared opportunities have certain very fundamental effects in providing for a sound, stable, and healthy economy for the society. First, it eliminates unemployment, which has been the source of many ill effects in a capitalistic society. Second, it provides for economic security of the individual and his family by guaranteeing employment until retirement. The positive psychological effect of this economic security on an individual's life and its effect on and stability of family should not be disregarded. Third, it eliminates the large welfare institutions established in a welfare state like the United States and other industrialized countries, thus releasing a vast amount of capital to be invested for productive purposes. Fourth, there are no individuals graduating from colleges or other higher educational institutions and then looking for appropriate employment. As explained elsewhere, based on the combined system of lifelong work and education, every person starts with general or less skilled work at the age of fifteen and proceeds to move upward, while continuing his education in an area of his choice. He thus moves upward and later on horizontally, if he decides to change his line of work, leaving behind his previous position open for those following him. Continuity of education while working makes possible this orderly work system never experienced before. Individuals looking for employment will be primarily those terminating their general education at the age of fifteen and entering the employment market.

2. *Right to ownership of means of production and distribution.* In a democratic system, there is capital but not capitalist in the traditional meaning of the term. The nature of capital in a democratic economy is sharply distinct from that of capital under a capitalistic economy. In the latter, capital formation is the result of accumulation of social surplus, namely profits through exploitation of labor and consumers. Capital, under democratic organism, is the result of accumulation by each worker of savings from his wages. It is not through exploitation of labor. Also, since no profits are allowed in a democratic economy, therefore capital accumulation cannot result from the exploitation of consumers. The process of ownership is accomplished by two ways. First, the standard way, according to which every person who works in any societal institution, whether it relates to production of goods and services in private or public sectors, receives, as part of his monthly pay, a number of shares of production firms. If the firm has no capital and its purpose is not production of income but certain social or public services, the worker still receives as part of his income a certain number of shares to which

he is entitled. These shares are acquired by the employer institution from the stock market. Example institutions include government agencies and educational institutions. Thus every worker, whether working for an income-producing firm or not, from the time he receives his first paycheck becomes part-owner of the production and distribution means. As he continues work, his ownership of capital grows. By the time of retirement he has accumulated enough capital, providing him with sufficient income for his retirement life. As discussed elsewhere, these shares are not transferrable; they constitute some kind of old age insurance. However, they are interchangeable with other nontransferrable shares in the stock market depending on the market value of the shares. Accordingly, for the first time in modern society there is no separation between labor and capital, and one of the basic tenets of Marxism, struggle between capitalist and labor classes, becomes nonexistent. Ownership becomes a right for the working class. For the first time, workers are in a position not only to produce whatever they desire to produce, but also to manage the production as well as its marketing. The second way of capital accumulation relates to purchase of stocks from the stock market by the money saved from wages. These shares of stock are transferrable and can be bought and sold at will. By relating capital and labor together, the industrial worker more likely for the first time, by finding himself the owner and worker at the same time, will sense a great incentive to produce. Under capitalistic production, he was nearly totally isolated from his production. The incentive was to survive, which was totally unrelated to the nature of his work. In a democratic economy, he suddenly and increasingly becomes the policymaker, he or his representative sits on the board of directors and what he is producing he is a part owner. These factual situations tend to multiply his incentive to produce. Not only does he become an efficient worker, but he also tends to become creative, which is a very important factor in the effectiveness of production. All together, a highly dynamic process of production takes place, expanding from one firm to another and ultimately encompassing the whole society.

3. *Right to education.* Without an appropriate education no society can progress. This is one essential individual right in democratic society. The process of education has been explained elsewhere. The National Education Council will provide for a model lifelong program on liberal arts that will include minimum requirements in different areas of liberal arts and recommended electives. The program also will provide for several levels of certification with special titles such as B.A., M.A., Ph.D., P.Ph.D. (postdoctoral). There will be no degrees such as B.S., since all educational programs will consist of at least 50 percent liberal arts education. Every normal individual will be able to receive his first advanced degree by the age of twenty-two.[7] Not only will he be professionally well educated, but more important, he will be a well-rounded intellectual. In technological society every individual needs to have a profound understanding of humanity, human history, and nature, along with high technology. It might come as a surprise to many scholars in humanity, but in a technological democratic society, study of high technology and its effect on human and humane values will be an important part of studies in the humanities. We will be concerned, intensively, with areas such as technological humanity, technological moral values and philosophy, technological sociology, and psychology expanding to technological literature and art.

4. *Right to health care.* For progress not only is there need for an educated society but also for a healthy one. Furthermore, good health and education provide opportunities for a much enjoyable and pleasurable life. Education and health care are two fundamental rights in a democratic system, and under the framework established through democratic organism, in order to provide equal opportunity of access to education and health care for each and every individual, they are made available free of charge and conveniently accessible to all.

5. *Freedom of speech and press,* which comprise freedom of conscience, thought, and feeling in its most comprehensive sense, and freedom of opinion and expression of sentiment relating to any and every area of life and corresponding issues. These can only be materialized in full by the application of equality of opportunity. For example, in relation to freedom of speech or press, the application of the principle implies that there could not be any secrecy in speech or press when such speech or press affects any individual in any way. Thus speech or press could not be classified or secret. It must be made public or freely accessible by the public. This is a very important aspect of freedom of speech or press in a democratic system. Benefits of access far exceed those of secrecy. The case is the same in international or foreign relations. There are no different standards for the same principle in democracy. In democracy people must have the opportunity to know exactly how their government policies are concerning all domestic as well as foreign issues and relations. The only limitation is that freedom of speech and press cannot negatively affect the liberties and opportunities of others properly guarded by the principle of equality of opportunity. The Technodem is the backbone of freedom of speech and press.
6. *Pursuit of happiness.* Every person is free to pursue his own good in his own way, so long as his action does not deprive others of theirs or impede their efforts to realize it. The test here again is that an individual's action in pursuit of his life does not infringe upon the equality of opportunity of others. Major factors in materializing happiness in a democratic society are good health, broad education, desirable employment, feeling of economic security, creativeness, and accessibility of and desire for recreation, sportive as well as artistic.

2. Political

The political system under technological democracy is the least important, but yet necessary, component of the democratic organism.

1. *Popular sovereignty through free and frequent elections.* Equality of opportunity requires freedom to elect and be elected, freedom from financial burdens, freedom of information, public as well as private, and freedom of expression and organization for electoral purposes.
2. *Majority rule with equal consideration of minority rights.* The principle requires that every member of a decision-making group be given exactly the same opportunity as any other in the decision-making process, including expression of views, participation in debate, access to information and all deliberations, voting, et cetera.
3. *Limited governmental powers.* First, in a democratic society the bulk of an individual's needs are taken care of through the institution where he works. The remainder is taken care of by the local government, which is very close to the people. Regional government has certain law enforcement as well as supervisory power to see that national standards relating to equality of opportunity are carried out properly by the individuals and institutions. Thus both the local and regional governments have a passive role and their general authority is extremely limited, based on the application of the principle of equality of opportunity to the extent that as the individuals move toward being accustomed to the principle of equality of opportunity and arrive to realize its importance for their pursuit of life, liberty, and happiness, the society automatically adheres to its application and need for a public institution to monitor its proper application tends to disappear. In the long run, the importance of government as a factor in equilibrium will tend toward zero and society will continue to function without need for governmental intervention. The government's function will tend to be limited to establishing standards necessary to materialize equality of opportunity and provide for coordination and harmony among different regions of society. Thus close to the mature stage of a democratic system government tends to become invisible and nearly, functionally speaking, will disappear from the scene of

an individual's daily life. Second, governmental powers are extremely limited regarding individual rights and liberties. These rights and liberties are materialized by the application of the principle of equality of opportunity, preservation of which is the prime task of government under a democratic system.

As has been stated before, individual rights are nearly absolute in a democratic society and are all governed by the principle of equality of opportunity. The government has no special powers in these regards and is only responsible for the realization of the equality of opportunity in determining the extension of freedom of individuals and institutions, including government itself.

DEMOCRACY AND THE MEANING OF LIFE

One must never forget that other civilizations of far greater significance than the United States from the standpoint of spiritual achievements—the only true measure of comparison possible—have appeared before, flowered forth reaching a magnificent spiritual expression, and disappeared again, engulfed in the shadows of oblivion and covered by a few layers of sand or by the triumphant vegetation in the wilderness. The civilization has plunged gradually into the dark ages until the flourishing of another one.

A new dark age is still possible, and it will dawn upon this civilization soon enough unless we discover a meaning for life, a different purpose than the drive for materialism and satisfaction of senses, and finally, a new goal for human efforts that currently is so implacably frustrated by the emptiness and the futility of the goal which we try so desperately and still so vainly to reach.

It is the possibility of such a dark age that democracy will try strenuously but successfully to stave off by teaching people anew the truth that is needed to visualize and to appreciate a deeper reality lying behind and beyond the immediate and closely bound world of the self toward a desire to find peace, achieve salvation, and restore dignity and purpose to life.

It may not be so obvious to common man, but this is an

extremely critical time in history, and the fate of a whole civilization is at stake. Democracy can take up the challenge, and to the perplexing age-old query it can answer emphatically that besides materialism, life has a meaning, a purpose and a goal, worth, dignity, and beauty.

When individuals become aware that their individuality is truly and fully realized, then they realize the great significance and the deep import of the democratic philosophy of life. Democracy prescribes in effect that the meaning of life is found only in the realization of a full spiritual life and that this realization in turn is achieved only when the individual's spiritual needs, aspirations, and longings are rooted, integrated, and nurtured within the organism of democracy. One should not confuse the meaning of spirituality as employed here with the spirituality related to different religions. The latter is external, artificially induced, based on certain dogma. *Spirituality* as employed here refers to the individual's self, a deep, commited inner feeling, independent of external factors. It is mainly the result of self-consciousness through self-education, through seeking the truth by studying self, others, the natural environment, and the meaning of life.

Within the context of its organic being, democracy is also a philosophy. It relates to the process of human life and institutions within the organic system of democracy. This is to say that democracy per se is not a philosophy or a theory but a living institution with its organic structure and norms. What happens to individuals and institutions that live and operate under this democratic system, their personality traits, tendencies, aspirations, outlook in life, attained socioeconomic cultures, all together, form the democratic philosophy of life.

Organism refers to the functional body or thing that is made up of parts that are quite distinct from one another, where removal of one part destroys or substantially alters the operation of the rest. It must be noted that democracy as an organism is timeless and absolute and thus its existence is not contingent upon the individual will or action. The system exists and the question is whether or not men discover it and subject themselves to its domain and to its benefits as a result.

Within a democratic organism, through the democratic

philosophy of life, individuals rise to the capacity of a true spiritual being. They find something that expresses the fundamental continuity of their human experience without determinate limits of space, and the fundamental way of life. In democracy, they find an organism that offers limitless scope to the expression of their spiritual life, to the full play of their activity, the full extent of their freedom and equality of opportunity, and the full recognition of the same to their fellow beings. In democracy one's life flowers forth in an expression of great spiritual achievement with visualization and admiration of a deeper reality than the immediate materialistically oriented and closely bound world of self.

DEMOCRACY AND THE CONDUCT OF LIFE

The conduct of life under democracy rests upon three great, unalterable principles: authority, duty, and productivity. The principle of authority refers not to any individual ruler or governmental institution but to the democratic organism. It refers to the authoritative state of democratic principles and their implementation within the society. The national supervisory councils establish the foundation and operation of society in strict accordance with these principles. The regional institutions supervise their implementation; individuals and producion organizations become responsible for the full implementation of those principles. Thus governments have very little to do with direct implementation of democratic principles. Implementation remains mainly the individual's task, along with the institution where he works. Any dispute regarding the principles is resolved by the appropriate high council and ultimately by a supreme judicial system.

Duty is the second principle affecting the conduct of life. Though democracy as a system cannot be destroyed, democratic philosophy of life can be infiltrated by nondemocratic norms and actions and can be abused. If such infiltration is allowed, the very existence of democratic life will face danger. Those who attempted to destroy the democratic nature of life by disobeying or twisting democratic principles must be distinguished and singled out by the individuals and subjected to authoritative investigation. Punishments must be harsh, relating to abuse of the basic principles. There is no death penalty in a democratic society, but there are strenuous educational and rehabilitation means. The individual faces hard labor and education to undo the wrong done and to understand the importance of the principles and the consequences of abusing them. An individual committed to the democratic way of life will automatically respond to duty to protect the system from destructive interference. This duty is concerned with action and by no means relates to speech or press, which are free. It is the outcome of adherence to the principle of equality of opportunity.

The third principle of democratic life is productivity. The principle of equality of opportunity prescribes that each individual must be productive in life to the best of his ability. He must contribute, through his activities and participation in the productive process, to the well-being of his society. The extent of a person's material benefits from democratic society depends on the scope and level of his participation in the production process. There is no place for laziness or inactivity in a democratic society. Society helps only those who, due to physical or mental deficiencies, are not able to produce and sustain themselves. A person who is productive below his individual capacity does not use his equality of opportunity to its full extent and thus remains behind compared to those with the same opportunity.

Equality of opportunity is the invisible tie that binds together the destinies of all people in a democratic society and is a ruling guide in the application of the above stated three principles relating to the conduct of life. It is the most important and most essential principle sustaining the democratic organism. It is one whose consequences are the most far-reaching in the life of a society. It is the foundation for durable and satisfying socioeconomic life in which the good of the whole is dependent upon the material and spiritual welfare and intellectual well-being of the individual. Each individual, group, private and societal institution, and society as a whole operates and prospers by adherence to the indisputable norms of the organism of democracy, whose entity is absolute, and thus its characteristics are absolute and not subject to alteration. The democratic system is a living organism, independent from people who live under it. the degree of adherence to the organism determines the extent of approach to a democratic system.

Never before had a socioeconomic system advanced such penetration to the inner world of man, and never before had men experienced a combination of knowledge and understanding leading not only to their individual happiness and joy in life, but also to those of the society as a whole. Life, as thus conceived by the democratic organism, is free, serious, austere, spiritual, and pleasant; its development takes place in a world sustained by the just and responsible principles of the organism. He who subscribes to the ensuing rules of conduct, with their exacting claims upon individual will, lives a satisfactory sensual life. He is ready, willingly and pleasantly, to sacrifice a fraction of his own well-being in order to enhance the well-being of others toward the level of his own. He volunteers to share his opportunities with those less fortunate. Thus, though he learns and works primarily for his personal benefit, he thinks of himself as a part from the whole, namely his other fellow human beings, related institutions, and the environment. He holds the unity of his community to be a sacred means for realization of the true good of life and his efforts to be just and true, the supreme test of high qualities required by the system that has provided him with opportunities for knowledge, comfort, and wisdom.

The individual in a democratic society does not use his freedom and opportunity solely for the satisfaction of his instincts and desires but also for the well-being of his community and society as a whole, of which his is an indispensable part, though individually independent.

In the democratic conception, the meaning of freedom expands beyond pursuing of one's own passion, ambitions, or desires. It extends to discovering and maintaining what is true, good, and just at all times, in all cases. This is the realization of the true mission of man. Personal liberty allows the individual to follow the call of one's own nature and one's own faith, to think, act, or speak according to the dictates of one's own mind, and to earn, spend, or save. It causes men to strive for wealth, health, happiness, and pleasure; it also provides that all be enjoyed within the framework of the principle of the equality of opportunity. No exercise of freedom is democratic if it hinders or encroaches on the quality of opportunity of others or is an impediment toward its realization. Here the individual is the center of whole society, but he must realize that every other individual is so, too. The relationship, therefore, is prescribed by the principle of equality of opportunity. Without application of this principle, the individual would not know the framework of his societal life and how to use his freedom in a just manner. It could be used for the satisfaction of one's personal instincts and desires not necessarily in a democratic manner. Under democratic organism, the individual is brought back to the vision of his true place in society and the universe. He must sincerely, tirelessly try to learn how to curb and master his self in realization of the democratic way of life.

A true and great spiritual life cannot take place unless democracy has risen to a position of preeminence in the society of men. Maximum liberty coincides with the maximum strength of democracy. A man's liberty is interrelated, interactive, and interrestrictive in relation to the liberty of others. It finds its maximum realization in the fullest expression of democracy.

The democratic organism is not a term denoting the authority underlying a complex system of relationships between individuals, classes, organizations, et cetera. It is an organism of far greater import and meaning. It is not a state; it is not a government; it is a societal entity, a well structured societal system. It is there to bring mankind back to the true vision of the relative worth of the individual and of the system, the organism of which each individual is an integral and essential part.

Gone forever is the time when it was possible to find a way to the heart of man by appealing to the mystic side of his nature through a religious commandment, through his devotion to his unalienable natural rights, or through so-called utilitarian, political, democracy masking grave economic injustices. It is time when it is possible to illuminate the reasoning powers of man's mind with the light of ideals whose existence and whose reason of being for his well-being can be proven through the powers of reason.

What is needed is a societal consciousness through learning, debating, and understanding the democratic system, its organism as well as its operation, in order to progress slowly but surely toward the comprehension of its worth, beauty, and significance.

Though democracy is an organism, its power and operation are conditioned to the will of the people as one of its integral components. However, democratic organism is unique and unalterable in its structure. There are no different kinds of democracy; there is one and only one kind. As such, democracy is above individuals, organizations, classes, interest groups, and ambitions. It is also above the state; the public sector is but a small component of the organism. There is no welfare of the state, but only that of the individual. The triumph of democracy means, in fact, that the role of the people is finally brought to its highest importance, which it assumes when considered in its proper relation to the other components of the system. The normative components of the organism determine the role and manner the individuals have to take for full realization of democratic norms. Thus the power to operate rests wholly on the people. The organism provides only the method and process by which people govern themselves best. Structurally speaking, under this system people are governed the least. The government is minimum in its initial state. It continues to diminish further in size, tending toward zero as the operation of society moves to a closer association with the organism and approaches to the closest adherence to its fundamental principles.

When it is claimed that the democratic organism as well as its three major components—individual, technology, and equality of opportunity—are permanent and absolute, it does not mean that their nature, value, and characteristics cannot be discussed, argued, or criticized. The very existence of the organism is based on freedom of information, striving for knowledge based on reason, seeking the true purpose and meaning of life and the extent of the manner of human participation in its conduct.

THE ESSENCE OF DEMOCRATIC ECONOMY

In a capitalistic system the betterment of life is understood to be in increased production and increased profits. In the case of the working class, advancement toward happiness is thought to be based on increased income and capability of the purchasing of more goods. Simply, under capitalism progress is based on the upward movement of material gains heavily based on production and sale.

The outcome is that those able to subjugate technology and workers accumulate immense wealth and those who do not have access to production means produce for those who have, for a meager return relative to the value of their work. The result of this materialistic concept is a highly stratified, power-concentrated, and unjust society.

In the democratic economy, materialism leaves its prime importance and becomes responsive only to the average needs of the individual for a comfortable living condition. Its essence from maximization of profits shifts to satisfaction of needs. Profit resulting from exploitation of workers and consumers becomes prohibited. Therefore, progress is not based on the economic upward movement but relates to improvements of the individual characteristics, value, and upward movement of humane values. The economic class stratification disappears, and social distinction becomes based on the individual's knowledge, experience, and humane concerns. Economic hardship does not present backwardness as long as there is an equitable distribution of income. So, based on the economic conditions, individual income may go up or down. It is considered an ordinary consequence of operation of the economy, yet there is no unemployment at any time, regardless of the state of the economy. There is lifetime security of a job and income for every individual, except those incapable of participating in production for physical or mental defects, whose life and security are guaranteed by the community. While under capitalism, concentration of wealth creates power through exercise of which individuals or groups tend to control, or at least influence, operation of the societal systems; in technological democratic society there is no concentrated source of power. This occurs because there is no sustained power structure in the first place. All production institutions are decentralized and dispersed; all information systems are mainly responsive to the people as a whole and are fed by the whole society—individuals and public and private institutions. It directly feeds the society without any individual or group influence or interference; all important governmental agencies or offices are ruled by elected people whose term of office is limited without offering an opportunity to anyone to build a political or economic power base. The only meaningful influence in technological democratic society will be that of intellectuals, whose effect and influence in the form of ideas may last for generations. Therefore, the technological democratic society, in its matured stage, is essentially a classless and nearly stateless society. This is a radically different concept of economy and society and must be studied carefully in order to be understood properly. It can occur only in a technological democratic system.

The establishment of a democratic system will produce one of the most painful—because of radical adjustments to be made—but the most promising characteristics of modern existence. Through a new form of consciousness, men will come to sense that their education is utterly inadequate. They will come to assert that they have a right to be properly educated, meaning that this education must be social as well as technical, general as well as special, free from indoctrination and based on reason, aimed to free men rather than to subjugate them, all geared toward consciously structured democratic norms, values, and processes. It will also be understood that in order to improve productivity as well as knoweldge, education must be continuous, a lifetime responsibility. It is under this kind and system of education that men will come to realize the irrational and utterly unjust aspect of capitalistic economy, disapprove it, and be determined to cause its eradication.

Any other prevailing economic system, whether communistic, socialistic, or mixed, will become subject to the same rationalization relating its unjust aspects. The Marxist economy, for example, though it provides for a more equitable distribution of income, is state-controlled where the individual worker, though he receives more equitable benefits, is subject to state authority. All his conditions of work and economic life are subject to state authority.

Education is a prerequisite for democracy; democracy is a stimulator and contributor to education. Under a democratic system, economy may achieve its own form of excellence, but the more important human excellences are achieved elsewhere. Economy, though still important, leaves the driver's seat, and the individuals are able to define the important ends of life in their own voluntary pursuits, free from economic pressures. Democracy brings different qualities to an individual's life. It nourishes his mind, imagination, and conscience, providing for a strong democratic attitude, a vast domain of freedom, variety, and self-consciousness.

Democracy, by requiring extensive and continuous education, makes individuals wiser and more virtuous. It invites man to think of alternatives consciously and rationally, to reduce the barrier of class, caste, and inherited economic and power privileges. It adds to the variety of individuals and occasions one meets. It places greater pleasure in one's capacity to adapt to the new and different norms and conditions.

Democracy stands as the nemesis of all economic doctrines and all economic practices of both the capitalistic and the communistic systems. In a democratic society:

1. The economic life of man, though independent, cannot be abstracted and separated from the societal life. The economic aspect of life is not the most important but remains in balance with the intellectual and spiritual aspects of life.
2. The economic life of man is structured upon and influenced by democratic principles as components of democratic organism.
3. Economic progress is the outcome of concerted efforts of individuals who, by acculturation to democratic norms, have come to know how to overcome their egotistic tendencies and ambitions for their own good and the good of society as a whole.
4. Economic initiatives are not based on profit motives or arbitrary decisions. They are based on efficiency, effectiveness, and fair return for the individual's efforts. They are based on the democratic collective decision-making process of production and distribution.
5. Open competition is the backbone of the democratic market, but it becomes free of fraudulent and propagandic advertisement. Exact specifications of the product are stated, and it is left to the consumer to make a choice.

6. The wealth of a society is the sum total of individual wealth plus all natural and other resources. The important part of the wealth of society is not economic but technological in the form of knowledge, expertise, and means.
7. More important than the production of wealth is its equitable distribution among the working class, subject only to the level of expertise and experience.
8. In a democratic system, there is no class structure or class distinction. The differentiation is only at the workplace, based only on the level of expertise and experience.
9. The proper function of the state is to establish, maintain, and periodically revise the standards required by the principle of equality of opportunity, particularly relating to division of labor and compensation. National government has no domestic line functions except some supervisory authority in the areas relating to the national consumption fund, such as education, health care, and corresponding standards.
10. Since there are no classes, there is no class struggle in democratic society.
11. Private wealth totally belongs to the individual. It is a wealth initiated, created, and accumulated through an individual's own labor.
12. Public wealth mainly constitutes the society's natural resources. It belongs to the society as a whole; thus proceeds from it go to the national consumption fund and are used for the society's benefit as a whole, such as education and health care.
13. A prime distinction of the economy under a democratic system with that of other systems, is that there is no separation between capital and labor; thus workers receive full return for their productive labor.
14. A worker's wage is paid in two parts, one part in cash and the other in captial (stocks and shares). Thus each laborer starts with no capital ownership and builds up capital through the time of his retirement. However, this capital is a public resource belonging to the society as a whole, except for the new capital produced by the worker through his personal savings. It remains his absolute property during his lifetime, and then it is added to the societal capital after his

death. The public capital is distributed among all workers through the pay process, and each worker has the full benefit of his share of it during his lifetime. Since it is a societal property, it reverts to the public treasury at the end of an individual's life.
15. Except for the disabled and handicapped, there are no public assistance programs of any kind. It is not needed. There is also no Social Security or retirement plan. When retiring, the individual has sufficient wealth accumulated to provide him with a comfortable life.

These fundamental tenets of a democratic system's economy drive essentially from the principle of equality of opportunity and its proper implementation. Equality of opportunity is the supreme principle and the supreme law of the land. The result is that under a democratic system there is not any single economic interest dominating others; there is no monopoly of any kind; there are also no conglomerates or giant economic institutions. The very application of the principle automatically and necessarily breaks down giant institutions into independent component parts.

16. Supervision of the operation of equality of opportunity within the framework of democratic organism is primarily the responsibility of local and then regional governments. Enforcement will be according to the standards established by responsible national organs.
17. The primary responsibility of the application and implementation of equality of opportunity within the framework established by the national organs rests upon each production institution, large and small, all the way down to the self-employed. No public agency interferes with this process. The outcome as a plan of operation is submitted to local and regional governments. If those comply with the standards, there will be no government intervention. Otherwise, the plans may be modified by the institutions, under the government's advice, in order to comply with the requirements.
18. Thus the total policy-making and operation of a production system is under the command of individuals

within such production institution. The individual is the master of his own destiny and responsible for that of society as a whole.

19. Equality of opportunity is an invisible but strong tie that binds together the destiny of the people of a society and ultimately the world. It causes joys and pains experienced by individuals to be shared, thus enhancing the joy and reducing the pain of society as a whole. The terms *wealthy* and *pauper, capitalist* and *worker,* and *employer* and *employee* will lose their antagonistic meaning and the distinction will actually disappear. The individual worker, through and within his institution, dictates the extent and manner of the relationship between capital and labor, employer and employee, landlord and tenant.

20. The production and distribution of goods and services become harmonized to the actual needs of the individual and society as a whole. The system tends toward coordination of all economic forces of the society under one principle, thus providing a material life for the people free of struggles, strikes, unemployment, too much wealth, or poverty.

21. Operation of the system makes unnecessary the unionization of labor, thus from an economic standpoint eliminating all kinds of labor unions, syndicates, and guilds. There are no class wars between capitalist and labor and no need for the protection of material welfare of the workers. Duties and compensation for every position are determined by the worker's firm, according to prescribed national standards, and the worker gets the same minimum pay for the same job, regardless of the place of his work. Simply, in place of the unions and capitalist employers who determined the duties and compensation for each position in their firm according to their own norms, now there is a national position classification norm that the firms must follow in assigning the duties and compensation for each position within the firm. Now all the working citizens of society are brought by an all-comprehensive national manifestation into the framework of one superior and far-reaching organization that has for its purpose the material welfare of the whole nation. This brings the egotistic tendencies of the

individual, particularly during the early years of democracy, under discipline of the nation toward realization of not only the guarantee of individual well-being but also that of the society as a whole.

22. Within each production firm the interests of producers and consumers, employers and employees, and individuals and groups are interlocked and integrated in a unique way by bringing all types of interests under the aegis of the firm. Necessarily, interests of the workers are protected and preserved, since each firm is governed by the workers themselves, who are also the owners.

23. The economy of a democratic system, unlike those under other ideologies, is heavily affected by ethical principles mainly generated through the application of the principle of equality of opportunity. It is a translation of ethics into economics. It is a totally new form of economics. It is an economy without exploitation of neither the labor nor the consumer.

24. Unlike capitalism, where an economic elite ruled the system of production and distribution, in technological democracy the individual is the ruler. To carry out this responsibility he is required to properly educate himself, not restricted to knowledge concerned with the production process alone, but also that of developing mental and intellectual capabilities. For proper participation in the decision-making process he must be able to develop an inner vision to the very heart of things, to discover the truth, and to translate his inner thoughts into deed and action. Each individual in democratic society is a hero on his own account. He must prepare for and make himself capable of acting like one. His heroism is an integral part of that of others and all together they create a heroically dynamic society.

SOME CHARACTERISTICS OF THE DEMOCRATIC SYSTEM

Toward technological democracy, the task is not just to reformulate the traditional ideals of "democratic capitalism" or "democratic socialism," but to establish a totally new system that will give life and society concrete content through norms and institutions that are democratic as well as practical in a highly industrialized and densely populated society with a rapidly changing environment. The economic and technological means of extraordinary dimensions must be directed by all men, each according to his capability, for the benefit of each and all.

The concrete needs of individuals in a democratic system are best met in the long run by close adherence to democratic norms and proper functioning within the framework of democratic organism. The social goal and common purpose for which society is to be organized concerns itself in providing equality of opportunity for everyone. In such an accomplished society:

1. Everyone starts life from scratch.
2. Everyone receives free and general education up to age fifteen.
3. Everyone starts to work at age fifteen, starting with part-time and proceeding to full-time by age twenty-two.
4. Everyone continues his education after the age of fifteen until retirement. Such education is a balanced combination of technical and cultural subjects. It is reduced to two courses on each subject per year after the age of twenty-two.
5. Everyone receives free health care from birth until death.
6. Everyone, starting from zero, gradually becomes a part-owner of the means of production and distribution. These ownership shares are destined for the old age support and thus are not transferrable.
7. Everyone works full-time for thirty to thirty-five years or the equivalent.
8. Equivalent to one-fourth of the working hours are allocated to education. So for forty-hour-a-week work, the person will work for thirty-two hours and study for eight hours.
9. Promotion is based on the level of education and years of experience, cultural education having the same importance as technical or professional education.
10. The age of retirement depends on the supply of young labor force for the purpose of allowing them equal

opportunity for employment. However, to guarantee a comfortable retirement life no capable person works for less than twenty-five years full-time before retirement. The general retirement occurs after thirty years of full-time work.

11. After retirement, which more likely will occur when an individual is in his early fifties, he has enough capital accumulated to give him returns sufficient for a comfortable life.
12. All elective public positions will: (a.) require very high qualifications relating to education as well as experience; (b.) be temporary; no one could be elected to the same office for more than one term; besides other benefits, this is also to allow opportunities to a greater number of well-qualified citizens to hold public office; (c.) these two requirements would allow a better chance of being elected to retired individuals, since they are better educated and also are not looking for a permanent position. They are still young but matured and thus capable of fruitful participation in the public policy-making process.
13. As a result of the democratic norms and technological developments, family life is transformed from its traditional form into a democratic unit, parents being responsible, though in different manner, for upbringing of the children up to age fifteen, after which the person, who is considered an adult, will enter the labor force and will become independent.
14. By the time of retirement, the family, more likely because of voluntary birth and population control, will have no children to take care of and the couple, if they desire to remain together, will have a very fruitful, still productive, and enjoyable life.
15. After death, individual's wealth will return to society, to the public consumption fund, to sustain free services, including health care and education for the newcomers, who will also start from scratch.
16. Though some individuals will accumulate more wealth than others, the difference will not be so great as to cause class distinction. Such difference is only for the life of the person and will disappear after his death. In reality, this will be a classless society.

17. An individual's obligatory relationship is in his family and workplace. Outside these, he remains free to enjoy life with a great many things accessible in an infinite variety of combinations.

The moral boundaries of democracy are very broad and center around the principle of equality of opportunity. No common ethical code can be compehensive enough to cover the nearly boundless domain of these moral possibilities. It will be impossible for any mind to comprehend the infinite variety of individual freedoms and good deeds ensuing from this concept of democratic morality. It is impossible to even vaguely determine the boundaries. Whether one's interests center around his own well-being or the welfare of others, regardless how broad and expanded these interests may be, the ends that he may concern himself with will always be only an infinitesimal fraction of what could be possible under a democratic system. It is within these nearly limitless confines that the individual pursues his life, liberty, and happiness within a democratic system.

INDIVIDUALISM

Democratic organism is the kingdom of the individual. The whole operation of society is geared toward well-being, freedom, and happiness of an individual. The individual is the center of attention in all societal interactions. His integrity, honor, individuality, independence, opportunities, and liberties all are flourished, sustained, and protected under a democratic system. The organism provides only the tools and means to achieve these. The individual is the operator, initiator, sustainer, and protector of all these conditions and values. The operation of society and its regulation start from the bottom, namely the individual and his immediate production institution; it then extends to local, regional, and national levels. However, as the organization moves upward from the individual to the national level, the concern with and involvement in operation of the system diminishes, the national level having the least, or the minimal, involvement in the operation of the system. This situation becomes very clear when the detailed structure and operation of the system is studied and understood.

RELIGION

None of the current world religions will survive under a democratic system because, first, none is democratic; second, all are superficial; third, they are the glorification of personalities rather than rationalization of creed.

Any religion that intends to subjugate individuals through a set of commands, e.g., the Ten Commandments, and a set of rituals cannot be considered democratic. Christianity, Islam, and Judaism, as well as other major religions, fall under this characteristic. Their undemocratic nature therefore makes them unfeasible to come under or to survive within a democratic system.

These major religions are artificial in existence and in practice. For example, both Christianity and Judaism prescribe that thou shalt not kill. Yet Christian as well as Jewish societies have been the cause and initiator of bloody wars during this century, let alone past history. Capitalism, in reference to teachings of Christ, is the most un-Christian act, yet, it has developed, flourished, and advanced in Christian and Jewish societies and been sustained by them. Capitalism is identified by exploitation of workers and consumers, cheating, dishonesty, bribery, brutality, and lack of concern for human life. All of these qualities are utterly un-Christian as well as anti-Islamic. These are good examples of the artificiality of all major religions of today.

Major religions are associated with glorification, agrandizement of specific persons in order to force subservience and compliance with the rules and obedience to religious authorities who have been able to place themselves as representatives of so-called Holy Spirit. Religion, in its essence, is not and cannot be external to human. True religion relates to the individual's inner feeling; it is his faith. If it is induced, by conditioning or indoctrinating the individual's mind, it is not then real but artificial. A true religion that conquers the inner self of the individual has to be rational, subject to inquiry, analysis, and verification. In a democratic system, there can be room only for this kind of faith developed by individual deliberation, resulting in adherence to certain norms. Even if they relate to the supernatural, they are within the reach of reason. It must be remembered that in every aspect of life, material or spiritual, individual is the king, a conscious, curious, knowledgeable, and humane ruler of his life and considerate the same to the life of his other fellow beings. Democratic society is the union of many kings, conscious of well-being of others as that of their own.

In a democratic society, man is the seeker of his own religion. In his continuous analysis of self and search for the truth, he is the person to succeed or not to succeed in establishing relations with his Creator. Once he reaches this stage of accomplishment, he believes deeply in what he has discovered. Religion relates to his relation with his Creator within the realm of self and through his own self-consciousness. To him it is a discovery based on reason, a belief resting on a solid foundation. In this regard, he has no external relationship; his religious privacy is complete and is sacred to him. Of course, his acculturation to human and humane values through his democratic life will be an important factor and guidance in his efforts to discover the secret of the universe and the truth about it and life.

This kind of individualized religion, apart from outside interference, suggests that in a democratic society there will be neither a place nor use for traditional or new religious institutions. The society will rid itself from these kind of reactionary and wasteful institutions, and each individual, based on the extent of his personal efforts and convictions, will establish his relations with the spiritual world and his Creator. Since everyone will be seeking the truth based on reason, the outcome will be a faith through consensus and unanimity of those who reach the same conclusion. However, religion will remain individualized without institutionalization. This will show one true aspect of individual freedom.

CONCLUSION

Becoming acculturated to all democratic norms, man will enter into the realm of timeless and true reality and will become able to translate his vision of good into deeds and to act automatically according to the dictates of his conscience, which demands from him nothing but good. There will gradually develop a sincere and deep belief that man lives a true human life only when his life is devoted to and, if necessary, sacrificed for the triumph of the ideals of democracy and that only by living such a life can he ever find true happiness in the world. Through enlightenment, by continually studying society and humanity, in seeking the true meaning of life he will come to realize that by his democratic deeds he is answering the call of history in delivering a message of hope, trust, and faith by devotion to materialize a new way of life, a life capable of leading man out of his current miserable and unhappy state. As an example, through his words, actions, influence, and whole being he will demonstrate a true and sincere being who lives according to the very democratic messages he is delivering to his fellow citizens and his children.

Nothing good and great, nothing of any value or of any meaning to humanity can ever be accomplished in the world if all fear of, and temptation toward, the known and unknown hostile, belittling, or derisive forces is not banished from the heart and mind of man. To achieve this, man needs sincerity, courage, and belief. In order for society to be actually and effectively changed through an individual's own efforts, he must believe in democratic norms, in his own destiny, in the role that he is destined to play on the stage of life, and in his own individual capacity, capability, and power.

Man, burning with the great flame of goodness that he has carried and still carries deep within, strives to bring forth that inner flame, to follow the call of destiny without being aware of exactly what that destiny expects from him. He only dimly, in a blurred vision, perceives the image of some great and good thing shaping itself in the mist, calling, leading, and drawing him toward a yet unknown but delightful end. As he proceeds, the mist enveloping the vision, haunting his dreams since the early days, is finally lifting; the contours of his vision tend to become sharp, distinct and clear. Ultimately, the image of the great, democratic, and equalitarian society is revealed.

It will not be easy for him to reach this ultimate stage of life. It will need consciousness leading toward a complete revolution of all thoughts, all feeling, all sensations, taking his soul by storm and forcing him to examine critically his whole past, revise all his beliefs, and fashion for himself a new creed, the democratic creed, a creed that a whole society, a whole continent, a whole civilization is in need of, is waiting to see, and desires to embrace. At this stage of enlightenment, he will then have true vision of the current society, sunk in the mire, seeking light, pleading for help.

On the one side, there stands decaying capitalistic-materialistic organization of society, on the other authoritarian socialism and abjection. It will become imperative for him to choose another way of life in tune with his soul's aspirations, in accord with his conscious enlightenment, and away from his animal nature's desires. It will be then that the dumb, inchoate historical forces that shape the destinies of man will find suddenly a true purpose; it is then that centuries of thought and action will be brought suddenly to a climax by such a purpose; it is then that the people themselves will suddenly acquire the purpose so earnestly, and yet so vainly, they had sought.

Technological democracy actually expresses and explains in words what remained unexpressed in the innermost heart of the people; it translates into action what lay dormant in a potential state within the very nature of the people.

NOTES

1. For example, see Zbigniew Brzezinski's concept of technetronic society and his application of the concept of equality of opportunity, in his article in the *New Republic,* December 1967.

2. See, for example, John McDermott, "Technology: The Opiate of the Intellectuals," in Albert H. Teich, ed., *Technology and Man's Future,* 3rd ed. (New York: St. Martin's Press, 1981). For a more detailed account, see Theodore J. Gordon and Robert H. Ament, *Institute for the Future, Report R-6* (Middletown, Connecticut: IFF, September 1969).

3. The term *communism* in this essay, unless otherwise distinguished, refers to the existing socialistic systems with communism as the objective.

4. Odin W. Anderson, "Wisconsin: 2000 A.D.," *On Wisconsin* 9, no. 1 (April 1987), p. 4.

5. Ibid.

6. Ibid.

7. By age twenty-two each person will accumulate at least 144 credit hours, entitling him to a B.A. degree. When he accumulates seventy-two more credits,

he will be entitled to an M.A. degree. This will take about six years. A Ph.D. is received when eighty-four additional credits are acquired beyond an M.A. This will take about seven years to achieve, including a creative work or writing in technology or liberal arts. P.Ph.D. is a postdoctoral degree that will be granted after an additional seventy-two credit hours of study and a creative work in any area of knowledge is completed (in about six years). The credit hours gained after each degree will be indicated after the degree symbol. For example, P.Ph.D. 48 means that the person had forty-eight credit hours of education beyond his terminal degree. The same presentation applies to other degrees. If a person has fifty-four credits achieved beyond his B.A. degree, his educational designation will be BA54. An MA100 means that a person has completed course requirements far beyond a Ph.D. but has not yet been able to receive his degree because he has not completed the additional required creative performance or writing.

Glossary of Terms and Abbreviations

ADONIS. Article Delivery Over Network Information Service.
AI. Artificial Intelligence.
ANALOG SIGNAL. A signal that is formed by a continuous range of amplitudes or frequencies; for instance, a continuously varying current or the human voice.
APOLLO. Article procurement with on-line ordering, used by European space agency.
ARIANE. A European-produced powerful rocket.
ARTEMIS. Automatic Retrieval of Text from Europe's Multinational Information Service.
ARTIFICIAL INTELLIGENCE. The concept that machines can be improved to assume some capabilities normally thought to be like human intelligence, such as learning, adapting, self-correction, et cetera.
BATCH PROCESSING. A technique by which similar data to be processed are accumulated into groups or batches in advance and processed during one computer run.
BIBLIOGRAPHIC DATA BASE. Refers the user to the document sought.
BIT (BINARY DIGIT). May be a 0 or a 1, the digits used in the binary numbering system.
BRS. Bibliographic Retrieval Services.
BYTE. A sequence of adjacent bits that are treated as a unit. Ordinarily, a character is represented by one or two bytes.
CAD/CAM. Programs that make up computer-aided design and computer-aided manufacturing systems.
CAI. Computer Assisted Instruction. A concept that applies computers and specialized input/output display devices directly to individualized student instruction.
CAN-OLE. Canadian On-Line Enquiry.
CATV. Cable or community TV. A system with two-way capacity to conduct signals to the lead end as well as away from it, providing entertainment and educational programs to customers on a coaxial cable system for a fee.
CBE. Computer Based Education.
CD. Compact Disc. Uses digital technology to create sound far superior to that created by traditional methods.
CENTRAL PROCESSING UNIT (CPU). Part of a computing system that contains circuits to execute instructions in order to intelligently accomplish a desired objective.
CGI. Computer-Generated Image.
CHEMLINE. A data base produced by the U.S. National Library of Medicine. It is an on-line chemical dictionary file containing various nomenclatures.
CHIP. A tiny piece of silicon on which an integrated circuit is built, the circuits being mass-produced on circular sheets of silicon, called wafers, that are

then cut into dozens of individual chips, often square or rectangular.

CNET. French national communications research center.

COBOL. A computer language.

COM. Computer Output Microfilm.

COMMUNICATIONS. A term used to denote integrated data processing and transfer systems using computers and data communications or telecommunications.

COMSAT. Communications Satellite Corporation. Represented by more than eighty-five members of the INTELSAT organization to provide technical and operational services for the global satellite communications system under a management contract with INTELSAT, headquartered in Washington, D.C.

CONNECT TIME. Time period during which a user is accessing a computer system.

CRT. Cathode Ray Tube. A televisionlike display device attached to a computer or used as a remote terminal.

CSO. Central Statistics Office.

CYBERNETICS. A field of science relating the operation of automatic equipment to functions of the human nervous system.

DATA BANK. A collection of data that relate to a given set of subjects.

DATA BASE. A collection of files that are interrelated to reduce redundancy and provide for data independence, security, integrity, and reliability.

DATA COMMUNICATIONS. Electronic transmission of encoded data from one location to another.

DBMS. Data Base Management Systems.

DBS. Direct Broadcasting Satellites.

DDS. Document Delivery Service.

DIALOG. A dial-up information retrieval service offered by Lockheed Information Retrieval System.

DIANE. Direct Information Access Network for Europe available through EURONET.

DIGITAL SIGNAL. A signal formed by discrete electrical impulses using a two-state or binary system.

DIMDI. The German institute for medical documentation and information.

DIRECT ACCESS. Any method of accessing data in which the time required for such access is independent of the storage location. It is also known as random access.

DISK DRIVE. A direct access device used to read from and record data on a magnetic disk.

DOS (DISK OPERATING SYSTEM). A versatile operating system for IBM 360 computer system having disk capability.

DOWNLOADING. Receiving information from outside data bases, storing and indexing them, building a new data base.

D-RAM. Dynamic Random Access Memory, a volatile memory system.

DUMB TERMINAL. A terminal that can perform input or output to a computer system but has no data processing capabilities.

EDP. Electronic Data Processing.

EDSAC. Electronic Delay Storage Automatic Calculator.

ELECTRONIC INFORMATION. Information through computerized systems.

ENIAC. Electronic Numerical Integration and Calculator.

ERGONOMICS. The study of human capability and psychology in relation to

the working environment and the equipment operated by the worker.
ESA. European Space Agency.
EURONET. A computer-based European network. It was established by the European Economic Community to access scientific and other data banks running on host computers connected to the network in different countries.
FA. Financial Advisor, a thinking computer.
FACSIMILE. A method of transmitting paper documents, pictures, et cetera by communications channels (e.g., telephone). The document is scanned at the transmitter land reconstructed at the receiver.
FAILSAFE. A procedure that allows the computer to store certain data from its own memory when it detects that it is failing, e.g., through loss of power. It facilitates easy recovery of data in case of accidental malfunction.
FIBER OPTICS. Cables composed of glass fibers that carry data through pulses of a laser beam.
FLIP-FLOP. A circuit capable of assuming either of two stable states.
FLOPPY DISK. Flexible disk of magnetic coated mylar. It provides low-cost storage and is used in minicomputer and microcomputer systems.
FOIA. Freedom Of Information Act.
FORTRAN. A computer language.
FULL-TEXT DATA BASE. Contains records of the complete text of the item sought.
GATT. General Agreement on Tariffs and Trade.
HARDWARE. Computer and data processing equipment, the electronic and mechanical devices, and the equipment itself, as contrasted with software and firmware.
HERMES. European space aircraft designed to carry up to six astronauts with a 4.5 ton payload.
HMH. Home Management Helper, a computer that flashes reminder and dates programmed by the user and performs some other functions.
IBM. Inernational Business Machines, a corporation.
IC. Integrated Circuit.
IDS. Information Delivery System.
INA. French national communications institute.
INFORMATICS. Studies related to information systems design analysis and evaluation.
INFORMATION. An aggregation of data with assignable meaning.
INFRASPHERE. A multitude of nationwide or global systems network.
INPUT/OUTPUT. Refers to the insertion of data or instructions into a computer or transfer of processed data from the computer to the user. Examples of input/output media are: cathode ray tubes, punched cards, disks, and printers.
INSEE. The French central statistics office.
INTEGRATED CIRCUIT. The entire circuit, including active and passive components built on a chip. Integrated circuits result in small size, high reliability, low cost, and high speed.
INTELLIGENT TERMINAL. A terminal with internal logic circuitry, which allows some functions to be done at the terminal, such as syntax error editing.
INTERACTIVE COMPUTER GRAPHICS. The use of terminals for drawing lines and images.
ITU. International Telecommunication Union.

K. When referring to storage capacity of computer systems or components, 2^{10}, in decimal notation 1024.

LARGE SCALE INTEGRATION (LSI). Fabrication of circuits with a large number of transistors on a single chip.

LEXIS. Data bank on law literature developed by Mead Corporation.

LIGHT PEN. A stylus used with CRT display devices to edit information on the CRT screen.

LISP. List processing, a language of advanced computers symbols rather than numbers and letters.

LSI. Large Scale Integrated circuit.

MAGIC MIRROR. A computer screen that produces a full body image of the person standing in front of it and projects any number of outfits the store customer desires to see on her without actually putting on the outfit.

MAGNETIC BUBBLE MEMORY. Very high-capacity chips that use small cylindrical magnetic domains ("bubbles"), which move over the surface of a magnetic film. The presence of a bubble corresponds to a "1" bit, and the absence of a bubble to a "0" bit.

MAGNETIC CORE MEMORY. Main memories made of iron cores, which can be magnetized in either of two directions. Such memories have been replaced gradually by memories using semiconductors.

MAGNETIC DISK. A storage device consisting of a magnetized recording surface on a metal disk.

MAGNETIC TAPE. A plastic tape coated with magnetic material upon which data may be recorded.

MAINFRAME. The CPU (Central Processing Unit) of a computer (doesn't include any of the other devices, such as input/output, et cetera). The term has been extended to mean the large types of computer systems.

MAIN MEMORY. The internal storage in a computer, used to store data being processed.

MEDLARS. Medical Literature Analysis and Retrieval System, developed by the U.S. National Library of Medicine.

MEDLINE MEDLARS ON LINE. A computer-based data bank developed by the U.S. National Library of Medicine. It contains literature on medical sciences, and biological sciences.

MEGABYTE. One million bytes.

MICROCOMPUTER. A general term referring to a complete tiny computer system consisting of hardware and software whose main processing blocks are made of semiconductor integrated circuits and that is similar in function and structure to a minicomputer but is at least several orders cheaper due to mass production; components are: ALU (Arithmetic-Logic Unit), memory, peripheral circuits, such as input/output, clock, control devices.

MICROFICHE. The most popular COM or Computer Output Microfilm format; a fiche is approximately four inches by six and can include an eye-readable title row, often up to 269 data frames at the 48X reduction ratio, and an index frame.

MICROPROCESSOR. A central processing unit constructed on a single chip. Microprocessors are used in microcomputers and intelligent terminals.

MICROSECOND. One-millionth of a second.

MINITEL. A French electronic system consisting of a keyboard, screen, and modem.

MIPS. Million Instructions Per Second.

MODEM. An instrument that translates telephone signals into computer-readable graphics.

MULTIPROCESSING. The use of two or more computer processing units in the same system at the same time.

MULTIPROGRAMMING. Using paging (partial processing) and entering a variety of functions or program executions into a specified time limit.

NANOSECOND. One-billionth of a second.

CNLIS. National Commission on Liberties and Information Science.

NETWORK. A set of locations (nodes) connected by communication channels.

NIS. Network Information Services.

NLM. National Library of Medicine.

OATS. Original Article Text Service, a commercial document-delivery system of the Institute for Scientific Information.

OCLC. On-line Computer Library Center.

OCR. (OPTICAL CHARACTER RECOGNITION). A process by which a variety of devices are employed to read in data without typing.

OECD. Organization for Economic and Community Development of the European Community.

OFFLINE. A term used to describe equipment, devices, or persons not in direct communication with the central processing unit of a computer system. Equipment is not connected to the computer system; contrast with on-line.

ON-LINE. An on-line system is one in which the input data enter the computer directly from their point of origin and/or output data are transmitted directly to where they are used. The intermediate stages, such as punching data, writing tape, loading disks, or offline printing, are avoided.

OPERATING SYSTEM. Programs that manage the hardware resources and the data for a computer system.

OPERATIONS RESEARCH. The application of objective and quantitative criteria to decision making previously undertaken by empirical methods.

ORBIT. A dial-up information retrieval service offered by Systems Development Corporation.

PAGING. In virtual storage systems, the technique of making memory appear larger than it is by transferring blocks (pages) of data or programs into that memory from external storage when they are needed.

PICOSECOND. One-trillionth of a second. Sometimes spelled *pecosecond*.

POP. Print On Paper.

PROTOCOL. A set of conventions between communicating processes on the format and content.

PTT. French Postes, Telephones, Telecommunications. The same symbol is used in other European countries.

RA. Random-Access, indicating the ability to reach each memory cell at will.

REAL TIME. Time during which a physical process actually takes place. A real-time data processing system performs computations rapidly enough for the results to influence the event.

REFERENCE DATA BASE. Refers the user to the source of information sought.

REMOTE TERMINAL. An input/output device that is located at a remote distance from a computer system. It is used to input programs and data to a computer and to accept computed data from a computer.

RESPONSE TIME. The amount of time that elapses between the presentation of a transaction to a system and the completion of processing that transaction.

RLIN. Research Libraries Information Network.

ROBOT. A completely self-controlled electronic, electric, or mechanical device. Most information age robots will be computer-controlled.

ROBOTICS. Study, analysis, design, and operation of robots.

SCP. System Control Program.

SDC. Systems Development Corporation.

SDI. Selective Dissemination of Information.

SEMIOTICS. The study of relationships between signs or symbols and what signify or denote.

SEQUENTIAL. Refers to occurrence of events in time sequence with little or no overlap of events.

SOFTWARE. All the programming systems and programs used to support a computer. The computer or equipment itself is called hardware.

SOLID STATE. The electronic components that convey or control electrons within solid materials—for example, transistors, germanium diodes, and magnetic cores.

SPOT. French remote sensing and highly sensitive satellite capable of providing more precise data than the U.S. Landsat.

TAPE DRIVE. A sequential access device used to read from and record data on a magnetic tape.

TBDF. Transborder Data Flow.

TECHNODEM. A futuristic centralized but dispersed information-communication system connected to every home and business terminal.

TECHNOLOGICAL DEMOCRACY. An independent democratic system encompassing all aspects of society, including social, economic, political, and technological.

TECHNOPHOBIA. Fear of technological machines and using them

TELECOMMUNICATION. To transmit or receive signals, sounds, or intelligence of any nature by wire, light beam, or any other means.

TELECONFERENCING. A conference between people who are linked by a telecommunications system. The link, increasing order of complication and cost, can be telephone, group audio, or video.

TELEMATIC. Anglicized term from French term *telematique*. It means information processing using computers and communications networks in an information processing system.

TELENET. A U.S.-based commercial international data communications network.

TELEPROCESSING. The combination of computers and communications networks in an information processing system.

TELETEL. French national videotex system.

TELETYPE. A device with a keyboard and printing capabilities, used to enter information into a computer and to accept output.

TIME-SHARING. A technique by which available computer time is shared among several users. This is done by timewise interweaving of processor requests by different users. It occurs so fast that users are not aware of it.

TOS (TAPE OPERATING SYSTEM). An operating system of System 360 computers used in magnetic tape, no random access system.

TRANSISTOR. A device made by attaching three or more wires to a small wafer of seminconductor material (a single crystal that has been specially treated so that its properties are different at the point where each wire is attached). The three wires are usually called the emitter, base, and collector. They perform functions somewhat similar to those of the cathode, grid, and plate of a vacuum tube, respectively.

UNESCO. United Nations Educational, Scientific and Cultural Organization.

UNIVAC. First computer designed for commercial purposes, 1951.

UPC. Universal Product Code. The symbols in the form of vertical bars of varying widths reflect light emitted by an optical scanner, the code numbers going to computers for transmission to other sources and to control printing devices to provide customer receipts after the computer responds with the identification of the product and the price.

UTILITY PROGRAMS. Programs often supplied by the hardware manufacturer, for executing standard operations such as sorting, merging, reformation of data, renaming files, and comparing files.

VDT. Video Display Terminal.

VERY LARGE SCALE INTEGRATION (VLSI). Fabrication of circuits with a very large number of transistors on a single chip.

VIDEODISK. A disk on which optical images may be stored. Videodisks are often written and read using laser beams.

VIDEOTEX. A two-way television system utilizing the process of sending and receiving texts and graphics primarily over telephone lines between a central computer and a terminal or personal computer.

VIRTUAL MEMORY. Manipulation of primary and secondary memories to show the apparent capacity of the computer as enhanced.

VLSI. Very Large Scale Integrated circuit.

VOLATILE MEMORY. An electronic memory that loses its data unless constantly refreshed by electric inputs. Dynamic RAMs are of this kind.

WAND. A device for reading labels on retail goods in a point-of-sale automation system.

WLN. Washington Library Network.

WORD. A set of characters that occupies one storage location and is treated by the control unit as a quantity. Word lengths may be fixed or variable, depending on the particular computer.

WP (WORD PROCESSING). Interactive information-retrieval, management-information, text-editing, translation, and typesetting systems are controlled by WP.

Bibliography

BOOKS

Adams, Henry. *Democracy*. New York: NAL Penguin, Inc., 1983.
Adams, Richard M. *Energy and Structure: A Theory of Social Power*. Austin: University of Texas Press, 1975.
Akin, William E. *Technocracy and the American Dream: The Technocrat Movement, 1900–1941*. Berkeley: University of California Press, 1977.
American Academy of Arts and Sciences. *Appropriate Technology and Social Values*. Ballingers: AAA and S, 1980.
Amin, Samir. *Accumulation on a World Scale*. New York: Monthly Review Press, 1972.
———. *Imperialism and Unequal Development*. New York: Monthly Review Press, 1977.
Anderson, Walt. *A Place of Power: The American Episode in Human Evolution*. Santa Monica, California: Goodyear, 1976.
Arendt, Hannah. *The Human Condition*. Chicago: University of Chicago Press, 1970.
Atkinson, A. B. *The Economics of Inequality*. New York: Oxford University Press, 1975.
Bachrach, Peter. *The Theory of Democratic Elitism*. Boston: Little, Brown, 1967.
Baran, Paul A., and Paul M. Sweezy. *Monopoly Capital: An Essay on the American Economic and Social Order*. New York: Monthly Review Press, 1966.
Barker, Sir Ernest, ed. *Social Contract: Essays by Locke, Hume, and Rousseau*. London: Oxford University Press, 1947.
Bauer, P. T. *Equality, the Third World, and Economic Delusion*. Cambridge, Massachusetts: Harvard University Press, 1981.
Bell, Daniel. *The Coming of Post-Industrial Society*. New York: Basic Books, 1973.
———. *The Cultural Contradictions of Capitalism*. 2d ed. Eexeter, New Hampshire: Heinemann Educational Books, 1979.
Bellamy, Edward. *Looking Backward 2000-1887*. New York: Modern Library, 1951.
Bentham, Jeremy B. *Principles of Legislation*. 1802.
Bereano, Phillip L. *Technology as a Social and Political Phenomenon*. New York: Wiley, 1976.
Bernard, H. Russell. *Technology and Social Change*. New York: Macmillan, 1972.
Bernstein, Eduard. *Evolutionary Socialism*. Translated by E. C. Harvey-B. W. Huebsch, New York: 1909.

Berry, Brian. *The Human Consequences of Urbanization.* New York: St. Martin, 1974.
Bettelheim, Charles. *Economic Calculation and Forms of Property: An Essay on the Transition Between Capitalism and Socialism.* New York: Monthly Review Press, 1974.
Biddle, Derek. *Human Aspects of Management.* Brookfield, Vermont: Renouf, 1981.
Blumberg, Paul. *Inequality in an Age of Decline.* New York: Oxford University Press, 1980.
Bock, Kenneth. *Human Nature and History: A Response to Sociobiology.* New York: Columbia University Press, 1980.
Bookchin, M. *The Ecology of Freedom.* Palo Alto, California: Cheshire Books, 1982.
———. *Post-Scarcity Anarchism.* Berkley: Ramparts, 1980.
Borchert, Donald M., and David Stewart (eds.). *Being Human in a Technological Age.* Athens: Ohio University Press, 1979.
Braverman, Harry. *Labor and Monopoly Capital: The Degradation of Work in the Twentieth Century.* New York: Monthly Review Press, 1976.
Bork, Alfred. *Learning with Computers.* Bedford, Massachusetts: Digital Press, Educational Services, Digital Equipment Corporation, 1981.
Bretton, H. L. *The Power of Money.* New York: State University of New York Press, 1980.
Brown, Bruce. *Marx, Freud, and the Critique of Everyday Life: Toward a Permanent Cultural Revolution.* New York: Monthly Review Press, 1972.
Bruce-Briggs, B. *The New Class.* New Brunswick, New Jersey: Transaction Books, 1979.
Buchanan, James M. *Democracy in Deficit.* San Diego, California: Academic Press, 1977.
Burke, John G. *The New Technology and Human Values.* Belmont, California: Wadsworth Pub., 1967.
Burke, John G., and Marshall C. Eakin. *Technology and Change.* San Francisco: Boyd and Fraser, 1979.
Burnham, James. *The Managerial Revolution.* Bloomington: Indiana University Press, 1960.
Calhoun, John C. *A Disquisition on Government.* Columbia, South Carolina: State Printing, 1851.
Callenbach, Ernest. *Ecotopia.* New York: Bantam, 1977.
Carellil, M. Dino, and John G. Morris (eds.). European Cooloquy for Directors of National Research Institute in Education. *Equality of Opportunity Reconsidered: Values in Education for Tomorrow.* Netherlands: Swets and Zeitinger, 1979.
Carnoy, Martin, and Derek Sheafer. *Economic Democracy: The Challenge of the 1980s.* White Plains, New York: Middle East Sharpe, 1980.
Chapman, G. P. *Human and Environmental Systems: A Geographer's Appraisal.* New York: Academic Press, 1978.
Chester, Robert. *Equalities and Inequalities in Family Life.* San Diego: Academic Press, 1978.
Clecak, Peter. *Crooked Paths: Reflections on Socialism, Conservatism, and the Welfare State.* New York: Harper and Row, 1977.
———. *Radical Paradoxes: Dilemmas of the American Left, 1945–1970.* New York: Harper and Row, 1974.

Clontz, R. C., and E. K. Tarlow. *Equal Credit Opportunity Manual*. 3d ed. New York: Warren, Graham and Lamont, 1980.
Cnudde, Charles F., and Deane E. Neubauer. *Empirical Democratic Theory*. Chicago: Markham, 1969.
Cochran, Thomas C. *Social Change in Industrial Society: Twentieth Century America*. London: St. Anthony's Press, 1972.
Coggin, P. A. *Technology and Man*. Oxford: Pergamon Press, 1978.
Cohen, Carl. *Communism, Fascism, and Democracy*. 2d ed. New York: Random House, 1972.
Cohen, Marshall. *Equality and Preferential Treatment*. Princeton, New Jersey: Princeton University Press, 1976.
Coleman, James S. *Equality of Educational Opportunity*. Totowa, New Jersey: Littlefield, 1973.
Commoner, Barry. *Poverty of Power*. New York: Knopf, 1976.
Conley, Patrick T. *Democracy in Decline*. Providence: Rhode Island Publications in Society, 1977.
Coser, Lewis A., and Irving Howe, eds. *The New Conservatives: A Critique from the Left*. New York: New American Library, 1977.
Curti, Merle. *Human Nature in American Thought: A History*. Madison: University of Wisconsin Press, 1980.
Coulter, P. *Social Mobilization and Liberal Democracy*. Lexington: Lexington Books, 1975.
Croly, Herbert. *The Promise of American Life*. Hamden, Connecticut: Anchor Books, 1914.
Daniels, Norman, ed. *Reading Rawls*. New York: Basic, 1975.
Davis, Gregory H. *Technology: Humanism or Nihilism: A Critical Analysis of the Philosophical Basis and Practice of Modern Technology*. Lanham, Missouri: University Press of America, 1981.
Davis, William, and Allison McCormack. *The Information Age*. Reading, Massachusetts: Addison Wesley Publishing Company, 1979.
DeNevers, Noel, ed. *Technology and Society*. Reading, Massachusetts: Addison-Wesley Publishing Company, 1972.
Denitch, Bogdan, ed. *Democratic Socialism: The Mass Left in Advanced Industrial Societies*. Allanheld: Osmun and Company, 1981.
DeVore, Paul W. *Technology: An Introduction*. Worcester, Massachusetts: Davis Publications, Inc., 1980.
Diggins, John P. *The Bard of Savagery: Thorstein Veblen and Modern Social Theory*. New York: Continuum, 1978.
Dizard, Wilson T., Jr. *The Coming Information Age*. 2e ed. New York: Longman, 1985.
Doel, Hans Van Den. *Democracy and Welfare Economics*. Cambridge, Massachusetts: Cambridge University Press, 1979.
Dolbeare, Patricia, and Jane Hadley. *American Ideologies: The Competing Political Beliefs of the 1970s*. wd ed. Chicago: Rand, 1973.
Dolota, T. A. *Data Processing in 1980–1985*. New York: Wiley, 1986.
Dorsey, Gray. *Equality & Freedom, International and Comparative Jurisprudence: Papers of the World Congress on Philosophy of Law and Social Philosophy*. Dobbs Ferry, New York: Oceana Publications, 1977.
Douglas, Jack D., ed. *The Technological Threat*. Englewood Cliffs, New Jersey: Prentice-Hall, 1971.
Drucker, Peter. *Technology, Management and Society*. New York: Harper and Row, 1977.

Drucker, P. F., and others. *Power and Democracy in America*. Westport, Connecticut: Greenwood Press, 1980.
Dudek, Louis. *Technology and Culture*. New York: New American Library, 1975.
Dumbauld, Edward, ed. *The Political Writings of Thomas Jefferson*. New York: Liberal Arts Press, 1955.
Dunn, Peter D. *Appropriate Technology: Technology with a Human Face*. New York: Schocken Books, 1978.
Durbin, E. F. M. *The Politics of Democratic Socialism*. London: Routledge and Kegan Paul, 1940.
Edison Centennial Symposium, 1979. *Science, Technology, and the Human Prospect*. Elmsford, New York: Pergamon Press, 1980.
Edmunds, Stahrl W. *Alternate U.S. Futures*. Santa Monica, California: Goodyear, 1978.
Ellul, Jacques. *The Technological Foundation of Law*. New York: Seabury Press, 1969.
———. *The Technological Society*. Translated by John Wilkinson. New York: Knopf, 1964.
———. *The Technological System*. Translated by Joachim Neugroschel. New York: Seabury Press, 1980.
Elsner, Henry, Jr. *The Technocrats: Prophets of Automation*. Syracuse, New York: Syracuse University Press, 1967.
Encel, Solomon. *Equality and Authority*. London: Tavistock Publications, 1970.
Etzioni, Amitai. *Technological Shortcuts to Social Change*. New York: Russell Sage, 1973.
Eulan, Heinz. *Technology and Civilization*. Stanford, California: Hoover Institute Press, 1977.
Feinberg, Walter. *Equality and Social Policy*. Champaign: University of Illinois Press, 1978.
Feldman, Anthony. *Technology at Work*. New York: Facts on File, 1980.
Ferkiss, Victor. *The Future of Technological Civilization*. New York: Brasiller, 1974.
———. *Technological Man: The Myth and the Reality*. New York: Braziller, 1969.
Fields, G. S. *Poverty, Inequality, and Development*. Cambridge, Massachusetts: Cambridge University Press, 1980.
Forbes, F. W. *Technology and Utilization Ideas for the 70's and Beyond*. San Diego, California: American Astronautical Society, 1970.
Forcey, Charles. *The Crossroad of Liberalism: Croly, Weyl, Lippmann and the Progressive Era 1900–1925*. New York: Oxford University Press, 1961.
Fried, Jacob. *Technological and Social Change*. Princeton, New Jersey: Petrocelli, 1979.
Friedman, Milton. *Capitalism and Freedom*. Chicago: University of Chicago Press, 1962.
Fromm, Erich. *Revolution of Hope: Toward a Humanized Technology*. New York: Harper and Row, 1974.
Fromm, E., ed. *Socialist Humanism*. Garden City, New York: Doubleday, 1966.
Fuller, R. Buckminster. *Utopia or Oblivion*. New York: Overlook Press, 1969.
Galbraith, John K. *The New Industrial State*. 3d ed. Boston: Houghton-Mifflin, 1978.
Garvin, A. P. *How to Win with Information or Lose Without it*. Washington, D.C.: Bermont Books, 1980.

Gehlin, Arnold. *Man in the Age of Technology.* Translated by Patricia Lipscomb. Irvington, New York: Columbia University Press, 1980.
Gendron, Bernard. *Technology and the Human Condition.* New York: St. Martin, 1977.
Gibbs, Jack P. *Sociological Theory Construction.* Hinsdale, Illinois: Dryden, 1972.
Goddard, J. B., and A. T. Thwaites. *Technological Change and the Inner City.* London: Social Science Research Council, 1980.
Gold, Bela. *Technological Change: Economics, Management & Environment.* Elmsford, New York: Pergamon Press, Inc., 1975.
Goodman, Paul. *The New Reformation and Notes of a Neolithic Conservative.* New York: Random House, 1970.
Goodpaster, K. E., and K. M. Sayre, eds. *Ethics and Problems of the 21st Century.* Notre Dame, Indiana: University of Notre Dame Press, 1979.
Graham, Otis L. *Toward a Planned Society: From Roosevelt to Nixon.* New York: Oxford University Press, 1977.
Gray, Francine du Plessix. *Divine Disobedience: Profiles in Catholic Radicalism.* New York: Random House, 1971.
Green, Thomas H. *Liberal Legislation and Freedom of Contract.* 1880.
Guerin, Daniel. *Anarchism: From Theory to Practice.* New York: Monthly Review Press, 1971.
Gurwitch, Aron. *Human Encounters in the Social World.* Pittsburgh: Duquesne University Press, 1979.
Gutmann, Amy. *Liberal Equality.* Cambridge, Massachusetts: Cambridge University Press, 1980.
Gutman, Herbert. *Work, Culture and Society in Industrializing America.* New York: Random House, 1977.
Haksar, Vinit. *Equality, Liberty and Perfectionism.* Oxford: Oxford University Press, 1979.
Hale, Matthew, Jr. *Human Science and Social Order.* Philadelphia, Pennsylvania: Temple University Press, 1980.
Hamilton, David. *Technology, Man and the Environment.* London: Faber, 1973.
Hammond, Kenneth R. *Human Judgment and Decision Making.* New York: Praeger, 1980.
Hansot, Elizabeth. *Perfection and Progress: Two Modes of Utopian Thought.* Cambridge, Massachusetts: MIT Press, 1974.
Harrington, Michael. *Socialism.* New York: Dutton, 1972.
──────. *The Twilight of Capitalism.* New York: Simon and Schuster, 1977.
Harris, Anthony B. *Human Measurement.* New York: Heinemann Ed., 1978.
Hartz, Louis. *The Liberal Tradition in America.* New York: Harcourt Brace Jovanovich, 1962.
Hayek, Freidrich A. *Constitution of Liberty.* Chicago: University of Chicago Press, 1960.
──────. *Road to Serfdom.* Chicago: University of Chicago Press, 1949.
──────. *Social Justice Socialism and Democracy.* Terramurse, Australia: Center for Independent Studies, 1979.
Heilbroner, Robert L. *An Inquiry into the Human Prospect.* New York: W. W. Norton, 1974.
Henkin, Alice H. *Human Dignity.* New York: Aspen Institute for Humanistic Studies, 1978.
Herrington, Michael. *Socialism.* New York: Dutton, 1972.
──────. *The Twilight of Capitalism* New York: Simon and Schuster, 1977.

Hess, Karl. *Community Technology.* New York: Harper and Row, 1979.
Hetzler, Stanley A. *Technological Growth and Social Change.* New York: Praeger, 1969.
Hickman, Larry, and Azizah Al-Hibri, eds. *Technology and Human Affairs.* St Louis: Mosby, 1981.
Hobhouse, Leonard T. *Liberalism.* London: Oxford University Press, 1911.
Hodges, Wayne. *Technological Changes and Human Development.* Ithaca, New York: ILR Publications, 1970.
Holoein, Martin O. *Computers and Their Societal Impact.* New York: Wiley, 1977.
Howard University. Institute for the Study of Educational Policy. *Equal Education Opportunity.* Washington, D.C.: Howard University Press, 1978.
Hughes, John F. *Equal Education.* Bloomington: Indiana University Press, 1973.
Hunt, G., ed. *Writings of James Madison.* New York: G. P. Putman, 1910.
Hurst, Charles E. *The Anatomy of Social Inequality.* St. Louis: Mosby, 1979.
Information Industry Association. *The Business of Information Report.* Washington, D.C.: Information Industry Association, 1981.
Jackman, Robert W. *Political and Social Equality: A Comparative Analysis.* New York: Wiley, 1975.
Jantsch, Reich. *Technological Planning and Social Futures.* London: Associated Business Programmers, 1974.
Joseph, Keith and Jonathan Sumpton. *Equality.* London: John Murray, 1979.
Judson, H. F. *The Search for Solutions.* New York: Holt, Rinehart and Winston, 1980.
Kanowitz, Leo. *Equal Rights: The Male Stake.* Albuquerque: University of New Mexico Press, 1981.
Kaplan, Max, and Phillip Bosserman, eds. *Technology, Human Value and Leisure.* Nashville: Abingdon Press, 1971.
Kariel, Henry. *The Decline of American Pluralism.* Stanford, California: Stanford University Press, 1961.
Kaufman, Arnold. *The Radical Liberal.* New York: Simon and Schuster, 1970.
Keating, W. T. *Politics, Technology, and the Environment.* New York: Arno Press, 1979.
Kheel, Theodore W. *Technological Change and Human Development: An International Conference.* Ithaca, New York: Cornell University, ILR Publications Division, 1970.
Knight, T. J. *Technology's Future: The Hague Congress Technology Assessment.* Melbourne, Florida: Robert E. Krieger Publishing Company, Inc., 1976.
Kolko, Gabriel. *Wealth and Power in America.* New York: Praeger, 1962.
Kozol, Jonathan. *Illiterate America.* Garden City, New York: Anchor Press/Doubleday, 1985.
Kranzberg, Melvin. *Technology and Culture.* New York: New American Library, 1975.
Kuhns, William. *The Post-Industrial Prophets: Interpretations of Technology.* New York: Weybright and Talley, 1971.
Kumar, Krishan. *Prophecy and Progress: The Sociology of Industrial and Post-Industrial Society.* New York: Penguin, 1978.
Laing, Neil F. *Technological Uncertainty and the Pure Theory of Allocation.* Bedford Park, Australia: Flinders University of South Australia, 1978.
Langone, John. *Human Engineering: Marvel or Menace?* Boston, Massachusetts: Little, 1978.

Lawless, Edward W. *Technology and Social Shock*. New Brunswick, New Jersey: Rutgers University Press, 1977.
Lecky, William E. H. *Democracy and Liberty*. Indianapolis, Indiana: Liberty Fund, 1896. Reprint, 1981.
Leiss, William. *The Domination of Nature*. New York: Braziller, George, Inc., 1972.
―――. *The Limits of Satisfaction*. Toronto: University of Toronto Press, 1976.
Lenski, Gerhard. *Human Societies*. New York: McGraw-Hill, 1974.
Lerner, Daniel. *The Human Meaning of the Social Sciences*. Magnolia, Massachusetts: Peter Smith, n.d.
Lindsay, A. D. *The Essentials of Democracy*. Oxford: Clarendon Press, 1929.
Locke, John. *Second Treatise of Government*. London: Thomas Tegg, 1823.
Loscerbo, J. *Being and Technology: A Study in the Philosophy of Martin Heidegger*. Boston: Klurver, 1982.
Lothstein, Arthur, ed. *The Philosophy of the New Left*. New York: Putnam, 1975.
Lovings, Amory. *Soft Energy Paths: Toward a Durable Peace*. Cambridge, Massachusetts: Ballinger Publications, 1977.
McDonald, J. Ramsay. *Parliament and Democracy*. Manchester, England: National Labour Press, 1920.
Machlup, Fritz. *The Production and Distribution of Knowledge*. Princeton, New Jersey: Princeton University Press, 1962.
MacPherson, C. B. *The Political Theory of Possessive Individualism: Hobbs to Locke*. New York: Oxford University Press, 1962.
McKinlay, John B. *Technology and the Future of Health Care*. Cambridge, Massachusetts: MIT Press, 1981.
McNeill, William H. *The Human Condition: An Ecological and Historical View*. Princeton, New Jersey: Princeton University Press, 1980.
Mae Kay, Donald. *Human Science and Human Dignity*. Downers Grove, Illinois: Inter-Varsity, 1979.
Magdoff, Harry, and Paul M. Sweezy. *The Deepening Crisis of U.S. Capitalism*. New York: Monthly Review Press, 1981.
Marcuse, Hubert. *One Dimensional Man*. Boston: Beacon Press, 1964.
Martin, James. *Design of Man-Computer Dialogues*. Englewood Cliffs, New Jersey: Prentice-Hall, 1970.
Marx, Leo. *The Machine in the Garden: Technology and the Pastoral Ideal in America*. New York: Oxford University Press, 1967.
Masi, Dale A. *Human Services in Industry*. Lexington, Massachusetts: Lexington Books, 1981.
Mayo, Henry B. *An Introduction to Democratic Theory*. New York: Oxford University Press, 1960.
Mead, Carver, and Lynn Conway. *Introduction to VLSI Systems*. Reading, Massachusetts: Addison-Wesley, 1980.
Meissner, Martin. *Technology and the Worker*. San Francisco: Chandler Publishing Company, 1969.
Miles, Rufus E., Jr. *Awakening from the American Dream: The Social and Political Limits to Growth*. New York: Universe Books, 1977.
Miliband, Ralph. *The State in Capitalist Society*. New York: Basic, 1978.
Mill, John Stuart. *Considerations on Representative Government*. New York: Harper, 1862.
Miller, A. R. *The Assault on Privacy*. Ann Arbor: University of Michigan Press, 1971.
―――. *Democratic Dictatorship*. Greenwood Press, 1980.

Montgomery, John D. *Technology and Civic Life.* Cambridge, Massachusetts: MIT Press, 1974.
Moor, Wilbert E. *Technology and Social Change.* Chicago: Quadrangle Books, 1972.
Muedler, Eva. *Technological Advance in an Expanding Economy: Its Impact on a Cross-Section of the Labor Force.* Ann Arbor: University of Michigan, Institute for Social Research, 1969.
Mulford, Sibley. *Nature and Civilization: Some Implications for Politics.* Itasca, Illinois: University of Notre Dame Press, 1977.
Naidbitt, John. *Megatrends: Ten New Directions Transforming Our Lives.* New York: Basic Books, Inc., 1979.
Nash, George T. *The Conservative Intellectual Movement in America Since 1945.* New York: Basic Books, Inc., 1979.
NATO. *Advanced Study Institute on Perspectives in Information Science.* Leyden: Noordhoff, 1975.
Noble, David. *America by Design: Science, Technology and the Industrial Revolution.* New York: Knopf, 1977.
Nordliner, E. H. *On the Autonomy of the Democratic State.* Cambridge, Massachusetts: Harvard University Press, 1981.
Norman, C. *The God That Limps.* New York: W. W. Norton, 1981.
Nozick, Robert. *Anarchy, State and Utopia.* New York: Basic Books, Inc., 1974.
Odum, Howard D. *Environment, Power, and Society.* New York: Wiley, 1971.
Ogburn, William F. *Technology and the Changing Family.* Westport, Connecticut: Greenwood, 1976.
Ophuls, William. *Ecology and the Politics of Scarcity: Prologue to a Political Theory of the Steady State.* San Francisco: W. H. Freeman, 1977.
Parat, Marc Uri. *The Information Economy.* Washington, D.C.: Government Printing Office, 1977.
Parenti, Michael. *Democracy for the Few.* 4th ed. New York: St. Martin's Press, 1983.
Parsons, Harold L., ed. *Marx and Engels on Ecology.* Westport, Connecticut: Greenwood Press, 1977.
Pascarella, Perry. *Technology—Fire in a Dark World.* New York: Nostrand Reinhold, 1979.
Pavitt, Keith. *Technical Innovation and British Economic Performance.* New York: Macmillan, 1981.
Phillips, Derek L. *Equality, Justice and Rectification: An Exploration In Normative Sociology.* London: Academic Press, 1979.
Pillans, T. Dundas, ed. *Forgo These Truths: Selections from the Speeches and Writings of the Right Hon. Edmund Burke.* London: Liberty Review Publishing Company, 1898.
Plamenatz, John. *Democracy and Illusion.* New York: Longman, 1977.
Preston, Ronald H., ed. *Technology and Social Justice.* 1st American ed. Valley Forge: Judson Press, 1971.
Pyke, Magnus. *Our Future.* New York: Hamlin/America, 1980.
Quarles, John. *Cleaning Up America.* Boston: Houghton-Mifflin, 1976.
Rae, D. W. *Equalities.* Cambridge, Massachusetts: Harvard University Press, 1981.
Rand, Ayn. *The New Left: The Anti-Industrial Revolution.* New York: New American Library, 1971.
Rescher, N. *Unpopular Essays on Technological Progress.* Pittsburgh, Pennsyl-

vania: University of Pittsburgh Press, 1980.
Rhodes, Harold V. *Utopia in American Political Thought*. Tucson: University of Arizona Press, 1967.
Rink, Evald. *Technical Americana*. Millwood, New York: Kraus International, n.d.
Ritterbush, Phillip C. *Technology As Institutionally Related to Human Values*. Washington, D.C.: Acropolis, 1974.
Rosenblatt, Samuel M. *Technology and Economic Development*. Boulder, Colorado: Westview, 1979.
Ryan, W. *Equality*. New York: Random House, 1982.
Sanford, Charles L. *The Quest for Paradise: Europe and the American Moral Imagination*. Urbana: University of Illinois Press, 1961.
Schumacher, E. F. *A Guide for the Perplexed*. New York: Harper and Row, 1977.
_____. *Small Is Beautiful*. New York: Harper and Row, 1973.
Schumpeter, Joseph A. *Capitalism, Socialism, and Democracy*. New York: Harper and Row, 1950.
Schuster, Edward. *Human Rights Today: Evolution or Revolution*. New York: Philosophical Library, 1980.
Silver, Harold. *Equal Opportunity in Education*. New York: Methuen, Inc., 1979.
Sinai, I. Robert. *The Decadence of the Modern World*. Cambridge, Massachusetts: Schenkman, 1977.
Slusser, Dorothy M., and Gerald H. Slusser. *Technology—the God That Failed*. Philadelphia: Westminster Press, 1971.
Skinner, B. F. *Beyond Freedom and Dignity*. New York: Bantam, 1972.
Smith, D. M. *Where the Grass Is Greener*. Baltimore, Maryland: Johns Hopkins University Press, 1982.
Smith, Sharon P. *Equal Pay in the Public Sector: Fact or Fantasy*. Princeton, New Jersey: Princeton University, Industrial Relations Section, Department of Economics, 1977.
Snyder, Gary. *The Old Ways*. San Francisco, California: City Lights, 1977.
Stafford, Beer. *Designing Freedom*. New York: John Wiley and Sons, 1974.
Stanley, Manfred. *The Technological Conscience*. Chicago: University of Chicago Press, 1981.
Steinfels, Peter. *The Neo-Conservatives: The Men Who Are Changing America's Politics*. New York: Simon and Schuster, 1979.
Stover, Carl F., ed. *The Technological Order*. Detroit: Wayne State University Press, 1963.
Teich, Albert H. *Technology and Man's Future*. 4th ed. New York: St. Martin, 1986.
Thomas, Norman. *Democratic Socialism: A New Appraisal*. New York: League for Industrial Democracy, 1953.
Thrall, Charles A., and Jerold M. Starr, eds. *Technology, Power and Social Change*. Carbondale: Southern Illinois University Press, 1974.
Toynbee, Arnold. *Mankind and Mother Earth*. New York: Oxford University Press, 1976.
Usher, D. *The Economic Prerequisite to Democracy*. Boston: Columbia University Press, 1981.
Van Den Berghe, Pierre L. *Human Family Systems: An Evolutionary View*. Westport, Connecticut: Greenwood, n.d.
Van Den Doel, Hans. *Democracy and Welfare Economics*. Cambridge, Mas-

sachusetts: Cambridge University Press, 1979.
Veblen, Thorstein. *The Engineers and the Price System*. New York: Kelley, 1944.
Walters, V. *Class Inequality and Health Care*. London: Croom Helm, 1980.
Watkins, Bruce O. *Technology and Human Values*. Woburn, Massachusetts: Ann Arbor Science, 1979.
Weale, Albert. *Equality and Social Policy*. Boston: Rougledge and Kegan, 1978.
Welhoit, F. M. *The Quest for Equality in Freedom*. New Brunswick, New Jersey: Transaction Books, 1979.
Westley, William A. *The Emerging Worker: Equality and Conflict in a Mass Consumption Society*. Downsview, Ontario: McGill-Queens University Press, 1971.
Weston, A. F. *Privacy and Freedom*. Bodley Head, 1967.
White House Conference on Library and Information Services, Washington D.C., 1979. *Information for the 1980's*. Washington, D.C.: Government Printing Office, 1980.
Wilensky, Harold I. *The Welfare State and Equality: Structural and Ideological Roots of Public Expenditures*. Berkeley: University of California Press, 1975.
Wilson, H. B. *Democracy and the Workplace*. Montreal: Black Rose Books, 1974.
Winner, Langdon. *Autonomous Technology: Technics-Out-of-Control As a Theme in Political Thought*. Cambridge, Massachusetts: MIT Press, 1977.
Witte, J. F. *Democracy, Authority and Alienation in Work*. Chicago: University of Chicago Press, 1980.
Wolf, Don C. *The Image of Man in America*. 2d ed. New York: Apollo Editions, 1970.
Wolfe, Alan. *The Limits of Legitimacy*. New York: Free Press, 1977.
Wolgast, E. H. *Equality and the Rights of Women*. Ithaca: Cornell University Press, 1980.
Wood, Clive. *Human Health and Environmental Toxicants*. New York: Grune, n.d.

ARTICLES AND DOCUMENTS

Ackoff, R. K. "Management Information Systems." *Management Science* 14, (1967), B147–B156.
Allen, William R. "Scarcity and Order: The Hobbesian Problem and the Human Resolution." *Social Science Quarterly* 57 (1976) 263–75.
Anderson, Odin W. "Wisconsin: 2000 A.D." *On Wisconsin* (April 1987), 1.
Arato, A. C. Castoriadis. "From Marx to Aristotle, from Aristotle to Us." *Social Science Research* 45 (Winter 1978), 667–738.
Archibald, W. P. "Face to Face: The Alienating Effects of Class, Status and Power Divisions." *American Sociological Review* 41 (October 1976), 819–37.
Artandi, Susan. "Man, Information and Society: New Patterns of Interaction." *Journal of American Society for Information Science* 30 (January 1979), 16.
Barry, B. "Political Accomodation and Consociational Democracy: Review Article." *British Journal of Political Science* 5 (October 1975), 477—505.
Basche, James. "Information Protectionism, Across the Border." *Conference Board* 20 (September 1983), 38–44.

Bell, Daniel. "The Social Framework of the Information Society." in *The Computer Age: A Twenty-Year View,* eds. Michael L. Dertouzos and Joel Moses. Cambridge, Massachusetts: MIT Press, 1979, pp. 163–211.

Benn, A. W. "Democracy in the Age of Science." *Political Quarterly* 50 (January 1979), 7–23.

Bentham, Jeremy. "Of the Principle of Utility." In *Communism, Fascism, and Democracy* ed. Carl Cohen. 2d ed. (New York: Random House, 1972), 443–45.

Berkeley, Alfred R. "Millionaire Machine." *Datamation* 27 (August, 1981), 21–22.

Beum, Robert. "The Old Regimes and the Technological Society." *Journal of Politics* 37 (November 1975), 937–54.

Bhatta, Charya, D. "Development and Technology in the Third World." *Journal of Contemporary Asia* 6, no. 3 (1976), 314–22.

Bilson, J. F. D. "Civil Liberty—an Econometric Investigation." *Kylos* 1, no. 35 (1982), 94–114.

Birch, A. H. "Some Reflections on American Democratic Theory." *Political Studies* 23 (June/September 1975), 225–31.

Blake, F. M., and E. Perlmutter. "The Rush to Use Fees: Alternative Proposals." *Library Journal* 102, No. 7 (1977) 2005–10.

Bollen, Kenneth A. "Issues in the Comparative Measurement of Political Democracy." *American Sociological Review* 45 (June 1980), 370–90.

———. "Political Democracy and the Timing of Development." *American Sociological Review* 44 (August 1979), 572–87.

Boulding, Kenneth E. "The Stability of Inequality." *Review of Social Economy* 33, no. 1 (April 1975), p. 1–14.

Bowles, Samuel, and Herbert Gintis. "The Crisis of Liberal Democratic Capitalism: The Case of the United States." *Politics and Society* 1 (1982), 51–93.

Brosnan, Peter. "Who Owns the Networks?" *Nation,* November 25, 1978, 561, 577–79.

Brown, Lynn E. "High Technology and Business Services." *New England Economic Review,* July–August, 1983, 5–17.

Brown, S. R. "Foreign Technology and Economic Growth." *Problems of Communism* 26 (July 1977), 30–40.

Budd, Edward C. "Postwar Changes in the Size of Distribution of Income in the United States." *American Economic Review* 60 (May 1970), 247–60.

Bylinsky, Gene. "Semiconductors: The Next Battle in Memory Chips." *Fortune,* May 16, 1983, 152–55.

Camiller, p., and H. Weber. "Euro-Communism, Socialism, and Democracy." *New Left Review,* no. 110 (July 1978), 3–14.

Campine, Benjamin. "The Evolution of the 'New Literacy.'" *National Forum,* no. 3 (Summer 1983), 10–12.

Chapman, John W., John C. Harsanyi, Vernon Van Dyke, James Fishkin, Doublas Rae, Allan Bloom, and Benjamin R. Barker. "Justice: A Spectrum of Responses to John Rawls's Theory." *American Political Science Review* 69 (1975) 588–674.

Coleman, J. S. "Inequality, Sociology, and Moral Philosophy." *American Journal of Sociology* 80 (November 1974), 739–64.

Council of American Library Association, San Francisco, California. *Council*

Document No. 71.2, July 1, 1981.
Cuadra, Carlos A. "The Microcomputer Link: Online Database Services and Local Electronic Libraries." *National Forum* 63, no. 36 (Summer 1983) 23–24, 32.
Cummings, Martin M. "Medical Information Services: For Public Good or Private Profit?" *Information Society Journal* 1, no. 3 (1982), 249–60.
Cutright, Phillips. "Income Redistribution: A Cross-National Analysis." *Social Forces* 46 (December 1967), 180–90.
———. "Inequality: A Cross-National Analysis." *American Sociological Review* 32 (August 1967), 562–78.
Dahl, R. A., "On Removing Certain Impediments to Democracy in the United States." *Dissent* 25 (Summer 1978), 310–24. P. Green, "Reply with Rejoinder," 26 (Summer 1979), 351–68.
Daina, Luciano. "Public Data Banks in Europe." *European Research* 12 (April 1984), 84–87.
David, E. E., Jr. "On the Dimensions of the Technology Controversy." *Daedalus* 109 (Winter 1980), 169–77.
Devall, William B. "Reformist Environmentalism." *Humboldt Journal of Social Science* 6 (1979), 129–58.
Devine, F. E., "Absolute Democracy or Indefeasible Right: Hobbes Versus Locke." *Journal of Politics* 37 (August 1975), 736–68.
Dervin, Brenda. "Communication Gaps and Inequities." in Brenda Darvin and Mel Voigt, eds., *Progress in Communication Sciences,* vol. 2. Norwood, New Jersey: Ablex, 1980), 73–112.
———. "Mass Communicating: Changing Conceptions of the Audience." In William Paisley and Ronald Rice, eds., *Public Communications Campaigns.* Beverly Hills: Sage Publications, 1981, 71–88.
———. "More Will Be Less Unless: The Scientific Humanization of Information Systems." *National Forum* 63, no. 3 (1983), 25–26.
Dewey, John. "The Future of Liberalism." *Journal of Philosophy* 32. no. 9 (April 25, 1935).
Diamond, Martin. "The American Idea of Equality: The View from the Founding." *Review of Politics* 38 (July 1976), 313–31.
Dworkin, Ronald. "What is Equality? Part 1: Equality of Welfare." *Philosophy and Public Affairs* 10, no. 3 (Summer 1981), 185–246.
Economist. "How Much Technology?" *Economist* 261 (November 6, 1976), 102.
Egan, Jacques. "Publishing for the Future." *New York Times,* August 16, 1982, 10.
Ellul, Jacques. "The Technological Society." In Albert H. Teich, ed., *Technology and Man's Future.* 3rd ed. New York: St. Martin's Press, 1981, 40–62.
Encel, Sol, and Jarlath Ronayne, eds. "Conference on Science, Technology, and Public Policy." *Science, Technology and Public Policy: An International Perspective.* Elmsford, New York: Pergamon Books, 1979.
Enzenberger, Hans Magnus. "Constituents of a Theory of the Media." *New Left Review* 64 (November–December 1970), 13–36.
Epstein, Nadine. "Et Voila! Le Minitel." *France Magazine,* nos. 4–5 (Summer 1986), 71 and 75.
Fave Della, L. R. "In the Structure of Egalitarianism." *Social Problems* 22 (December 1974), 199–213.
Ferkiss, Victor. "Christianity and the Fear of the Future." *Zygon* 10 (1975) 250–62.

―――――. "Man's Tools and Man's Choices: The Confrontation Between Political Science and Technology." *American Political Science Review* 67 (1973) 973–80.

―――――. "The Pessimistic View of the Future." In Jib Fowles, ed. *Handbook of Futures Research*. Westport, Connecticut: Greenwood Press, 1978.

―――――. "Post Industrial Society: Theory, Myth, Ideology." *Political Science Review*, 1981.

―――――. "Technology and Culture: Gnosticism, Naturalism and Incarnational Integration." *Cross Currents* 30 (September 1980), 13–26.

―――――. "Technology Assessment and Appropriate Technology." *National Forum* 58 (1978) 3–7.

―――――. "Technology and American Political Thought: The Hidden Variable and the Coming Crisis." *Review of Politics* 42 (July 1980), 349–87.

Fliegel, F. C. "Comparative Analysis of the Impact of Industrialization on Traditional Values." Bibliography, *Rural Sociology* 41 (Winter 1976), 431–51.

Fortune. "A Cheap-Memory Chaser Pursues the 4,000 K Chip." *Fortune*, May 16, 1983, p. 155.

Frisbie, W. P., "Measuring the Degree of Bureaucratization at the Societal Level." *Social Forces* 53 (June 1975), 536–73.

―――――. "Technology in Evolutionary and Ecological Perspective: Theory and Measurement at the Societal Level." *Social Forces* 58 (December 1979), 591–613.

Garrfield, Eugene. "Document-Delivery Systems in the Information Age." *National Forum* 63, no.3 (Summer 1983), 8–10.

Gates, R. D., and A. St. Germain. "Interface '80—Humanities and Technology: Southern Technical Institute, Marietta, Georgia, October 23–24, 1980." *Technology and Culture* 22 (October 1981), 763–70.

Gilkey, Langdon. "Robert L. Heilbroner's View of History." *Zygon* 10 (1975), 215–33.

Goodwin, J. "Current Bibliography in the History of Technology." *Technology and Culture* 20 (April 1979), 403–514.

Gordon, Theodore J., and Robert H. Ament. *Institute for the Future, Report R-G*. Middletown, Connecticut: JFF, September 1969.

Green, Philip, and Robert A. Dahl. "What Is Political Equality?" *Dissent* 26 (Summer 1979), 351–68.

Grove, D. J. "Ethnic Socio-economic Redistribution: A Cross-cultural Study." *Comparative Politics* 12 (October 1979), 87–98.

Gruber, M. L. "Inequality in the Social Services." *Social Services Review*, 54 (March 1980), 59–75.

Haas, E. B. "On Systems and International Regimes." *World Politics* 27 (January 1975), 147–79.

Hanes, D. "Democracy in the Service of Peace and Man." *World Marx Review* 19 (April 1976), 56–66.

Hanft, R. S., and J. Eechenholtz. "Regulating of Health Technology." *Academy of Political Science Proceedings* 4, (1980), 148–57.

Harton, Forest W. "The Paperwork Reduction Act of 1980—Reality at Last." *Information and Records Management* 15 (April 1981).

Heilbroner, Robert. "The Human Prospect: Second thoughts." *Futures* 7 (1975), 31–40.

Heise, D., G. Lenski, and J. Wardell. "Further Notes on Technology and the

Moral Order." *Social Forces* 55 (December 1976), 316–37.
Heise, D. R., and G. W. Bohrnstedt. "Validity, Invalidity, and Reliability." In Edgar F. Borgatta and George W. Bohrnstedt, eds., *Sociological Methodology*. San Francisco, California: Jossey-Bass, 1970.
Heller, Agnes. "Past, Present, and Future of Democracy." *Social Research* 45 (Winter 1978), 866–86.
Herz, J. H. "Technology, Ethics, and International Relations." *Social Research* 43 (Spring 1976), 98–113.
Hewitt, C. "Effect of Political Democracy on Equality in Industrial Societies: A Cross-national Comparison." *American Social Review,* 42 (June 1977), 450–64. "Discussion," 44, 168–72; 45, 344–49 (February 1979, April 1980).
Hoivik, Tord. "Social Inequality—the Main Issues." *Journal of Peace Research* 7, no. 2 (1971), 119–41.
Horowitz, Irving Louis. "Printed Words, Computers, and Democratic Societies." *Virginia Quarterly Review,* Autumn 1983, 620–36.
Howe, I. "Seasons for Democracy." *Dissent* 21 (Fall 1974), 469–70.
Huskey, Harry D. "Computer Technology." *Annual Review of Information Science and Technology,* no. 5 (1970).
Hutchins, R. M. "Is Democracy Possible?" *Center Magazine* 9 (January 1976), 2–6.
Hyneman, Charles S. "Equality: Elusive Ideal, or Beguiling Delusion?" *Modern Age* 24, no. 3 (Summer 1980), 226–37.
Inose, Hiroshi. "Social Benefits of Information Technology." *Economic Eye,* March 1985.
Iueller, D. C. "Constitutional Democracy and Social Welfare." *Quarterly Journal of Economics* 87 (February 1973), 60–80.
Jackman, R. W. "Political Democracy and Social Equality: A Comparative Analysis." *American Sociological Review* 39 (February 1974), 29–45.
Jacobs, D. "Dimensions of Inequality and Public Policy in the States." *Journal of Politics* 42 (February 1980), 291–306.
Jacqz, Jane W. *Report on a Workshop on Technology Choices, Work, and Society's Future*. New York: Aspen Institute for Humanistic Studies, 1979.
Joannidis, Marie, and Jan Kristiansen. "Telecommunications: Its Irreversible Impact." *France Magazine,* nos. 4–5 (Summer 1986), 69–72.
Kellner, M. M. "Democracy and Civil Disobedience." *Journal of Politics* 37 (November 1975), 899–916.
Kelly, J., and H. S. Klein. "Revolution and the Rebirth of Inequality: A Theory of Stratification in Post-Revolutionary Society." *American Journal of Sociology* 83 (July 1977), 78–98.
Kent, A. K. "Scientific and Technical Publishing in the 1980s." In Phillip Hills, ed., *The Future of the Printed Word: The Impact and the Implications of the New Communications Technology*. Westport, Connecticut: Greenwood Press, 1980, 163–69.
Kishida, Junnosuke. "Civilized Society: In Search of New Forms." *Impact of Science on Society* 30, no.2 (1980), 101–109.
Korek, Michael, and Ray Olszewski. "Telecom: The Winds of Change." *Datamation* 27 (May 1981).
Krolikouski, W. "Socialism and the Technological Revolution." *World Marx Review* 18 (September 1975), 44–51.
Laird, R. "Post-Industrial Society: East and West." *Survey* 21 (Autumn 1975), 1–17.

Lancaster, F. Wilfrid. "Electronic Publishing: Its Impact on the Distribution of Information." *National Forum* 63, no. 3 (Summer 1983), 3–5.

Lanson, Gerald. "Databases." *National Forum* 63, no. 3 (Summer 1983), 18–20.

Lemos, R. M. "Moral Arguement for Democracy." *Social Theory and Practice* 4 (Fall 1976), 57–74.

Levin, M. F. "Equality of Opportunity." *Philosophical Quarterly* 31 (April 1981), 110–25, 25–26.

Livingston, David, and Richard Masson. "Ecological Crisis and the Autonomy of Science in Capitalist Society: The Canadian Case Study." *Alternatives* 8 (1977), 3–19.

Lombardo, Rita. "AIM Looks at NICE V." *Information and Records Management,* no. 15 (June 1981).

Long, F. "Role of Social Scientific Inquiry in Technology Transfer." *American Journal of Economics and Sociology,* 38 (July 1979), 261–74.

Lovins, Amory. "Energy Stragegy: The Road Not Taken." *Foreign Affairs* 55 (1976), 65–96.

Lowenthal, R. "Social Transformation and Democratic Legitimacy." *Social Research* 43 (Summer 1976), 241–75.

Luhmann, N. "Future Cannot Begin: Temporal Structures in Modern Society." *Social Research* 43 (Spring 1976), 130–52.

Lukes, S. "Socialism and Equality." *Dissent* 22 (Spring 1975), 154–68.

Lustick, I. "Stability in Deeply Divided Societies: Consociationism Versus Control." *World Politics* 31 (April 1979), 325–44.

Maaranen, S. A. "Leo Strauss: Classical Political Philosophy and Modern Democracy." *Modern Age* 22 (Winter 1978), 47–53.

McBride, W. L. "Concept of Justice in Marx, Engels, and Others." *Ethics* 85 (April 1975), 204–18.

McDermott, John. "Technology: The Opiate of the Intellectuals." In Albert H. Teich, ed., *Technology and Man's Future*. 4th ed., New York: St. Martin's Press, 1981, 95–121.

Machlup, Fritz. "Science of Information: Looking Over the Fences." In *The Information Community: An Alliance for Progress: Proceedings of the 44th Annual conference of the American Society for Information Science.* Washington, D.C.: American Society for Information Science, 1981.

Madsen, D. "Structural Approach to the Explanation of Political Efficacy Levels Under Democratic Regimes." Bibliography, *American Journal of Political Science* 22 (November 1978), 867–83.

Malita, M. "Learning Processes in Man, Machine and Society." *Impact of Science on Society* 27 (January 1977), 93–103.

Mankoff, Milton. "Toward Socialism: Reassessing Inequality." *Social Policy* 4 (March 1974), 20–31.

Margolis, J. "Political Equality and Political Justice." *Social Research (Summer 1977), 308–29.*

Meadows, Donald H., et al. "Technology and the Limits to Growth." In Donald H. Meadows and Others *The Limits to Growth: A Report for the Club of Rome's Project on the Predicament of Mankind* New York: Universe Books, 1972.

Meadows, P. "Technology Assessment and Impact Analysis: A Sociological Analysis." *International Journal of Comparative Sociology* 20 (S/D 1979), 199–212.

Mellors, Colin, and David Pollitt. "Legislation for Privacy: Data Protection in

Western Europe." *Parliamentary Affairs* 37 (Spring 1984), 199–215.

Menninger, D. C. "Political Dislocation in a Technical Universe." *Review of Politics* 42 (January 1980), 73–91.

Meserve, Everett T. "A History of Rabbits." *Datamation* 29 (September 1981).

Miller, D. "Democracy and Social Justice." *British Journal of Sociology* 8 (January 1978), 1–19.

Miller, Frederick, and W. Miller. "CRT Terminals Get Smarter, Cheaper." *Infosystems* no. 28 (September 1981), 101–106.

Miller, Herman P. "Inequality, Poverty, and Taxes." *Dissent* 22 (Winter 1975), 40–49.

Misra, Ramesh. "Welfare and Industrial Man: A Study of Welfare in Western Industrial Societies in Relation to a Hypothesis of Convergence." *Sociological Review* 21 (1973), 535–60.

Morison, Robert S. "Visions." In Albert H. Teich, ed. *Technology and Man's Future*. New York: St. Martin's Press, 1981, 7–22.

Mushra, R. "Technology and Social Structure in Marx's Theory: An Explanatory Analysis." *Science and Society* 43 (Summer 1979), 132–57.

Namus, Burt. "Restructuring the Information Ecology." *National Forum* 63, no.3 (Summer 1983), 11–17.

National Commission on Libraries and Information Science. *Public Sector—Private Sector Interaction in Providing Information Services*. Washington, D.C.: Government Pringing Office, 1982.

Neubauer, Deane E. "Some Conditions of Democracy." *American Political Science Review* 61 (December 1967), 1007–1009.

Nielson, K. "Impediments to Radical Egalitarianism." *American Philosophical Quarterly* 18 (April 1980), 121–29.

Nilles, J. M. "Opportunities and Threats from the Personal Computer." *Futures* 11 (April 1979), 172–76.

Nixon, C. R. "Equity, Identity, and Social Cleavage: Cross-Cultural Perspectives." *American Behavioral Scientists* 18 (Summer 1974), 4–14.

Noel, Mathilde. "The Phenomenon of Technology: Liberation or Alienation of Man." In E. Fromm, ed., *Socialist Humanism,* Garden City, New York: Doubleday, 1966, 334–46.

North, J. "Landscape of Equality." *Times Literary Supplement* 4088 (August 7, 1981), 903–904.

Orr, J. "German Social Theory and the Hidden Face of Technology." *European Journal of Sociology* 2 (1974), 312–36.

Owen, D. "Communism, Socialism and Democracy." *Atlantic Community Quarterly* 16 (Summer 1978), 154–66.

Painter, John H. "Approaching Computer Based Education: How Will the University Respond?" *National Forum* no. 3 (Summer 1983), 20–22.

Pauly, David, and Carolyn Friday. "Computers Make the Sale." *Newsweek,* September 23, 1985, 46–47.

Peters, B. G. (and others). "Types of Democratic Systems and Types of Public Policy: An Empirical Examination." *Comparative Politics* 9 (April 1977), 327–55.

Pion, G. M., and M. W. Lipseg. "Public Attitudes Toward Science and Technology: What Have the Surveys Told Us?" *Public Opinion Quarterly* 45 (Fall 1981), 303–16.

Piskinov, A. I. "The Soviet School and Soviet Pedagogy in the Period of the

Competition of Socialist Construction and Gradual Transition to Communism." *Soviet Education,* February–March 1978, 106–94.

"Public Services Plan for Public Libraries in Montgomery County, MD." *FY 83–88,* May 1982, 10.

Pyatt, G. "On International Comparisons of Inequality." *American Economic Review; Papers and Proceedings* 67 (February 1977), 71–75.

Raman, N. P. "Devising and Introducing Technology to Aid the Poorest." *Internal Development Review* 18, no. 3 (1976), 8–11.

Ramawamy, G. S. "Transfer of Technology Among Developing Countries." *International Development Review* 18, no. 2 (1976), 7–10.

Ranetz, J. R. "Science and Technology as Promise and Threat: The Scale and Complexity of the Problem." *Ecumenical Review* 31 (October 1979), 364–71.

Rick, R. F. "Systems of Analysis, Technology Assessment and Bureaucratic Power." *American Behavioral Scientist* 22 (January 1979), 393–416.

Rickson, R. E. "Knowledge Management in Industrial Society and Environmental Quality." *Human Organization* 35 (Fall 1976), 239–51.

Robertson, Lawrence S. and Robert F. Aldrich. "Dissemination of Information." In Helen A. Shaw, ed. *Issues in Information Policy,* Special Publication, National Telecommunication and Information Administration, U.S. Department of Commerce, 1981, 5–18.

Robinson, R. V., and W. Bell. "Equality, Success, and Social Justice in England and the United States." *American Sociological Review,* 43 (April 1978), 328–39. A. C. Kerckhoff and R. N. Parker, "Reply with Rejoinder," 44 (April 1979), 328–39.

Rubinson, R., and D. Quinlan. "Democracy and Social Inequality: A Reanalysis." *American Sociological Review* 42 (August 1977), 611–23.

Rodman, John. "The Liberation of Nature?" *Inquiry* 20 (1977), 83–131.

Rohman, A. "Interaction Between Science, Technology, and Society: Historical and Comparative Perspectives." *Social Science Journal* 3, no. 33, (1981), 508–21.

Rosen, Saul. "Electronic Computers: A Historical Survey." *Computing Surveys* no.1 (March 1969), 7–36.

Routley, Richard and Val. "Nuclear Energy and Obligations to the Future." *Inquiry* 21 (Summer 1978), 133–79.

Rubin, S. J. "International Code of Conduct on the Transfer of Technology." *American Journal of International Law* 73 (July 1979), 519–20.

Rubinson, R., and D. Quinlan. "Democracy and Social Inequality: A Reanalysis." *American Sociological Review* 42 (1977), 611–23.

Sartori, G. "Will Democracy Kill Democracy? Decision-Making by Majorities and Committees." *Government and Opposition* 10 (Spring 1975), 131–58.

Schonfield, W. R. "Meaning of Democratic Participation." *World Politics* 28 (October 1975), 134–58.

Scheffres, Manuel. "Compact Discs Now the Hottest Sound in Town." *U.S. News and World Report,* June 17, 1985, 62–63.

Simpson, E. "Socialist Justice."*Ethics* 87 (October 1976), 1–17.

Sinal, I. R. "What Ails Us and Why?" *Encounter* 52 (April 1979), 8–17. "Discussion," 54 (February 1980), 87–93.

Smith, Kent A. "Information as a Commodity or Public Good." *National Forum* (Summer 1983), 27–29.

Spitz, P. "Silent Violence: Famine and Inequality." *International Social Science Journal* 4, no. 30 (1978), 867–92.

Stack, S. "Political Economy of Income Inequality: A Comparative Analysis." *Canadian Journal of Political Science* 13 (June 1980), 273–86.
Stillman, Peter J. "The Limits of Behaviorism: A Review Essay on B. F. Skinner's Social and Political Thought." *American Political Science Review* 69 (1975), 212–13.
Strassman, W. P. "Can Technology Save the Cities of Developing Countries?" *Journal of Economic Issues* 12 (June 1978), 457–65, 497–500.
Thompson, K. W. "American Democracy and the Third World: Convergence and Contradictions." *Review of Politics* 41 (April 1979), 256–72.
Thurow, L. "Pursuit of Equity." *Dissent* 23 (Summer 1976), 253–59.
Tonsor, S. J. "Liberty and Equality as Absolutes." *Modern Age* 23 (Winter 1979), 2–9.
Tonsor, S. J. "New Natural Law and the Problem of Equality." *Modern Age* 24 (Summer 1980), 238–47.
Tyree, A. "Gapo and Glissandos: Inequality, Economic Development, and Social Mobility in 24 Countries." *American Sociological Review* 44 (June 1979), 410–24.
UNESCO. "Information and Society." *UNESCO Journal of Information Science, Librarianship and Archive Administration*, no. 2 (January–February 1980).
U.S. News and World Report. "Quantum Leaps: The Video Revolution." *U.S. News and World Report,* June 17, 1985, 63.
Van Es, J. D., and D. J. Koenig. "Social Participation, Social Status and Extremist Political Attitudes." *Sociological Quarterly* 17 (Winter 1976), 16–26.
Wagner, J. "Defining Technology: Political Implications of Hardware, Software, Power, and Information." *Human Relations* 32 (August 1979), 719–36.
Watts, Meredith W. "B.F. Skinner and the Technological Control of Social Behavior." *American Political Science Review* 69 (1975), 214–27.
Wetlanfer, Suzanne. "Thinking Computers No Longer Science Fiction." *Wisconsin State Journal,* January 19, 1986, sec. 5, p. 1.
Wiarda, H. J. "Democracy and Human Rights in Latin America: Toward a New conceptualization." *Orbis* 22 (Spring 1978), 137–60.
Wicklein, John. "How to Guarantee Diversity in the New Communications." *National Forum* 63, no. 3 (Summer 1983), 14–16.
Winner, Langdon. "The Political Philosophy of Alternative Technology." *Technology in Society* 1, no. 1 (1979), 75–86.
Wright, W. D. "Du Bois Theory of Political Democracy." *Crisis* 85 (March 1978), 85–89.
Wrong, D. H. "Development and Democracy." *Dissent* 21 (Spring 1974), 277–89.
———. "Rhythm of Democratic Politics." *Dissent* 21 (Winter 1974), 46–55.
Zetterbaum, M. "Equality and Human Need." *American Political Science Review* 71 (September 1977), 983–98.

Index

Artificial inteligence, 39
Atoms, 245
Authority, 317
Automation, 244, 245

Banking, 242
Beneficial capital, 193
Bibliographic data base, 52

Cable system, 46
Capital, 229
Capital accumulation, 192, 193
Capitalism, 162, 211, 212, 289, 290
Capitalist, 288
Child care, 243
Communism, 289, 290
Compact disks, 40
Compensation, 207
Computer generated image, 73
Computer ID card, 242
Computerized indexing, 42
Conduct of life, 317
Corporate decentralization, 243
Cultural, 241, 242

Data base, 51, 54, 55
Decentralization, 244
Democracy, 187, 317
Democratic capitalism, 219
Democratic goals, 220
Democratic organism, 229, 312, 313, 318, 321, 326, 331
Democratic person, 205, 206
Democratic processes, 220
Democratic socialism, 219
Democratization, 98, 99, 100
Direct broadcasting satellite, 73

Direct view TV, 41
Downloading, 52
Duty, 317
Dynamic RAM, 52

Economic and production council, 249
Economic elite, 161, 162, 300
Education, 241, 251, 252, 293
Education, right to, 312
Education services, 146
Educational standards, 243
Electoral process, 159
Electronic ID card, 119, 122, 165, 166
Electronic publication, 57, 58, 61
Elite control, 133, 134
Employment, 301, 308
Entertainment, 153
Equality of opportunity, 179, 180, 181, 187, 188, 220, 243, 244, 245, 285, 286, 318, 326, 327, 328
Equality of opportunity—horizontal—303, 308
Equality of opportunity—vertical—, 303, 308

Fair accumulation, 193
Fiber optic, 73
Financial adviser, 39
Financial burden, 225
Fine arts, 170
Food preparation, 243
Free elections, 222
Freedom, 220, 315
Freedom of expression, 224
Freedom of information, 224
Freedom of organization, 224
Freedom of press, 313
Freedom of speech, 313

363

Freedom to be elected, 222
Freedom to elect, 222
Frequent elections, 222
Full employment, 234, 235, 251
Full-text data base, 52

Gained opportunity, 195
Galaxies, 245
Gardening, 243
Geostationary orbit, 114

Health & Education council, 236
Health care, 249
Health care, right to, 241, 243, 252
Home-management helper, 312
Human mind, 41

Individual rights, 244
Individualism, 315
Inflationary process, 220
Information downflow, 236
Information protection control, 144
Information upflow, 106
Inheritance, 143
Initial opportunity, 229, 298
Interest rate, 195
Interlibrary loan, 243
Interactive videotax, 42
International affairs, 45
International Affairs Council, 243
International Corporation, 247, 249, 252

Job market, 236

K, 153
Kiosque, 53

Laissez-faire, 72
Laissez-innover, 286
Landsat satellite, 98, 286, 288
Laser pulsars, 73
Legal, 73
Legal persons, 241
Legal services, 113
Legislative Assembly, 148
Librarians, 247

Libraries, 44
Library services, 43, 44
List processing, 151
Live program, 40
Living universe, 245
Lost opportunity, 197

Machine, 244
Magic mirror, 70
Magnetic tape, 56
Majority dictatorship, 226
Majority rule, 226, 314
Malignant capital, 193
Marketing, 149
Medical services, 147
Microchip, 57
Microcomputers, 52
Minitel, 71, 74
Minority rights, 226, 314
Mixed capitalism, 184
Mobility, 207
Monolithic control, 45
Music, 170

National Executive Council, 247
National Government, 246
Natural rights theory, 218
Nibble, 53
Nontransferrable share, 311
Nontransferrable stock, 204, 205, 237

Old age benefits, 236, 237
On-line database, 51
Opportunity classes, 195
Opportunity levels, 195
Optical disk, 57

Part-time education, 251
Part-time employment, 235, 236, 251
Pay system, 170, 202, 203, 204
Photocomposition, 57
Placement service, 153
Planets, 245
Planting, 243
Political education, 161
Political process, 243
Popular sovereignty, 159

Position classification, 222, 314
Postal communication, 200, 201, 202, 232, 243
Privacy, 155
Production technology, 102, 105, 112
Productivity, 245
Profit, 243, 244, 245
Proletariat, 317, 318
Public Consumption Fund, 229, 298
Pursuit of happiness, 288

Random access, 251, 252
Random access memory, 313
Recession, 52
Recreational, 52
Reference data base, 235
Representative democracy, 241, 242
Retirement, 52
Ripple, 203, 209, 210
Robotic technology, 245

Salary range, 207, 208
Satellite, 72
Scientific research, 245
Shared opportunity, 198, 234, 235, 301
Shopping, 150
Smart card, 73, 74
Social Revolution, 288
Socialism, 211, 212, 289, 290
Socialist system, 184, 185, 191
Spacenet I, 73
Spirituality, 234, 235, 301, 316
Sports, 170
Spot satellite, 73
State capitalism, 183
Super communication, 154, 155

Technical impulse, 286
Technical rationality, 287

Technodem, 101, 118, 135, 240, 241, 242, 243, 245, 309, 313
Technological capitalism, 186
Technological decentralization, 137
Technological democracy, 187, 190, 191, 192, 289, 290
Technological housekeeping, 242
Technological humanity, 312
Technological literacy, 59
Technological literature, 312
Technological person, 244
Technological philosophy, 312
Teletel, 71, 72, 74
Teletext, 59
Televerket, 45
Thinking computers, 39
Transboder data flow, 102, 107, 108, 111, 114, 120, 138
256K, 53

Unemployment, 237
Unfair accumulation, 44
Universe, 235
Unjust enrichment, 193
Utilitarian democracy, 189
Utility, 245
Two-way CTV, 311

Videocassette, 218, 219
Videodisk, 58
Videotax, 41
Videotechnology, 58
Viewdata, 43, 45, 71, 72

Wage system, 59
Welfare program, 243
Work system, 236
Worker, 299, 300
Working class, 194, 287

365